SNAPSHOTS

A Reporter's Life

SNAPSHOTS

A Reporter's Life

John Chadwick

ATHENA PRESS
LONDON

SNAPSHOTS
A Reporter's Life
Copyright © John Chadwick 2009

ISBN 978 1 84748 613 4

First published 2009 by
ATHENA PRESS
Queen's House, 2 Holly Road
Twickenham TW1 4EG
United Kingdom

Printed for Athena Press

With best wishes to fellow scribes –
who, amid budget cuts, takeovers and technological change,
may be something of an endangered species.

Contents

Prologue   11

Chapter 1

AMONG THE MILL CHIMNEYS,

WE WAVE FLAGS FOR THE KING AND QUEEN   13

Chapter 2

AFTER NIGHTS IN THE AIR-RAID SHELTER,

WE DODGE MISSILES AT SCHOOL   35

Chapter 3

I MEET BEOWULF AND SIR GAWAIN

AND TAKE A DISLIKE TO FRANK LEAVIS   56

Chapter 4

CRIME AND CRICKET, MUSIC AND DRAMA –

IT'S A HEADY MIXTURE   65

Chapter 5

THE ICELANDERS GET STROPPY:

WHAT ABOUT OUR COD AND CHIPS?   86

Chapter 6

GRILLED SAUSAGES AND CARLSBERG –

AND I TALK WITH THE KING   104

Chapter 7

WORLD WAR LOOMS, KENNEDY'S SHOT,

BRITAIN BATTLES THE COLONIES   119

Chapter 8

INDIANS AND PAKISTANIS GO TO WAR,

BUT VIGILANTES ARE THE DANGER   137

Chapter 9

'KEEP YOUR HEAD DOWN,' THEY SAID,

'AND WALK IN THE TANK TRACKS'   146

Chapter 10

'NO COMMENT,' SAID THE EGYPTIAN SPOKESMAN,

'BUT DON'T QUOTE ME'   162

Chapter 11

'SURE, IT'D BE A NICE DAY IF IT WASN'T RAININ' ' –

A MAN I MET IN TIPPERARY   188

Chapter 12

UP THE NILE AND IN NEXT-DOOR LIBYA,

TWO MORE SOLDIERS GRAB POWER   200

Chapter 13

HOW GERMAN ORGANISATION FAILED TO

STOP THE MUNICH TERRORISTS   211

Chapter 14

IN OLOF PALME'S SWEDEN,

THE BIGGEST SIN SEEMED TO BE TAX EVASION   219

Chapter 15

GUN BATTLE ON A TEL AVIV BEACH,

CHRISTMAS IN OCCUPIED BETHLEHEM   239

Chapter 16

WAR CRIMES TRIALS AND BAADER-MEINHOF KILLINGS

SHOCK GERMANY   260

Chapter 17

IN THE COUNTRY OF WILLIAM TELL,

SOME WOMEN STILL DIDN'T HAVE THE VOTE   285

Chapter 18

A CHINESE SCHOLAR IN A PAPER HAT

AND MEN IN WHITE COATS   302

Chapter 19

IN THE FORMER COMMUNIST BLOC,

CENSOR-FREE JOURNALISM IS BACK   314

Chapter 20

POLAR BEARS AND AN ANGRY WALRUS

IN FRANZ-JOSEF LAND   325

Chapter 21

I WASN'T GOING TO SIT BY THE WINDOW,

WATCHING THE WORLD GO BY   337

Chapter 22

'IF YOU HAS TO ASK WHAT IT IS,

YOU AIN'T GOT IT' – LOUIS ON SWING   346

Chapter 23

    DOWN THE SEWERS, FIFTY YEARS ON,

    IN THE FOOTSTEPS OF HARRY LIME   354

Chapter 24

    ABOARD THE *CALIFORNIA ZEPHYR*,

    I TAKE A SENTIMENTAL JOURNEY   360

Chapter 25

    A BELATED RETURN TO ENG. LIT. –

    THE SOMBRE WORLD OF OLIVER ONIONS   364

Chapter 26

    PALM TREES, MINARETS AND A BLUE SEA –

    I'M BACK IN THE MIDDLE EAST   370

Chapter 27

    'WELL, IT'S BETTER THAN WORKING, ISN'T IT?'   390

Prologue

Suspended over the ocean west of Iceland, my hands were clenched around a thick rope. Below me, the North Atlantic surged and foamed between two Royal Navy frigates steaming along in parallel as I was hauled from one ship to the other. I was riding something called a jackstay, my feet tightly crossed at the ankles and jammed into a sort of stirrup, buttocks supported – but not held – by a wide canvas strap. On the foredeck of the other ship, a line of ratings, looking a bit like a tug of war team, were pulling me slowly but firmly across the watery divide. Halfway across, there was an unnerving dip in the line and I wondered what would happen if I lost my grip… Maybe I'd freeze to death before they could fish me out of the sea. So why am I doing this? I asked myself. There's not even a story in it!

Chapter 1
AMONG THE MILL CHIMNEYS,
WE WAVE FLAGS FOR THE KING AND QUEEN

When he was old enough to know what I did for a living, my son started calling me a 'newsfreak'. Fair comment, and I seem to have started at an early age. After a shopping trip with my mother, I recorded for posterity, in a poem replete with rhymes, all our purchases, however unglamorous. They included 'a mutton chop at the butcher's shop'. (You don't hear either of those mentioned much these days, do you?)

'Then we went to another shop / And bought a 1s 3d mop.'

If you read the price as 'one-and-threp'ny', as we would have said then, the line scans perfectly. At seven, I dedicated a song with words to my small sister. The simple tune, which I can still knock out on a keyboard, is characterised by what I now know as a 2–5–1 chord sequence. A collection including this and other juvenile poems was recently unearthed in a tattered purple-backed notebook which my mother had kept all her life. I venture to suggest it reveals a reporter's documentary instincts – as well as an early grasp of the rules of metrics and rhyme.

We lived down Wash Lane. Traditionally, the Chadwicks of Bury, Lancashire, always had done. The origin of the street name remains a mystery to me (perhaps some local historian knows). The address would certainly come to haunt my brother and me later, once our fellow grammar school boys at Thornleigh College, Bolton, got wind of it. 'Does your mother take in washin', then?' was a typical jibe. Nobody could be as snobbish as the working classes at their worst, and there are none so vindictive as schoolboys. No problem among our Bury pals, of course, for whom it was just another place to live. Note the 'down' by the way. We didn't live '*up* Brick Street' or '*along* Wellington Road', for instance, two other well-known local addresses. The prepositions simply indicated in a practical Lancashire way whether – according to where you were at the moment – a street went up, or down, or remained on the flat. Nice touch, lost on present generations, I imagine.

The name of the town, originally *Byri* or *Buri*, is of Saxon origin, meaning a 'stronghold'. One old road, Watling Street, leading over hills and dales from Mancunium (now Manchester) to Ribchester, dates back to Roman days. In mediaeval times, a French lord of the manor held sway. By the time I arrived on the scene, my home town was better known for cotton and paper mills and engineering works – and for black puddings, a concoction made from pigs' blood which have never been to everyone's taste. Also a football team which in its glory days twice won England's prestigious Football Association Cup. Recently, the cash-strapped club has struggled at the end of most seasons not to be ousted from the Football League.

My father, proud of his Lancastrian origins – the first Chadwicks are recorded in the fourteenth century in nearby Rochdale – had a building business going back two centuries. It had come down through the generations to two brothers, my father and my uncle, who for some reason never completely understood by us kids were not on speaking terms and, we gathered, hadn't been for years. To me, fed on the novels of Charles Dickens, such family mysteries seemed reasonable enough; rather exciting, in fact. As the two brothers lived in adjacent two-up and two-down houses, however, it did cause difficulties. Although the two dwellings shared a small backyard, it was made clear to us by our parents from an early age that we shouldn't fraternise with those next door.

So if one of the battered old tennis balls we used for football or cricket practice was accidentally punted or hooked into the other half of the back yard, we chased after it quickly, without glancing at the kitchen window of the adjoining house, and dashed back into our 'half' as swiftly as possible.

My father was the latest generation to run the firm, if that doesn't make it sound rather grander than it was. GHQ, a few yards down York Street, mostly lined with mills on either side, was a small builders' yard, known to us and our sister as 'Dad's

Yard', and a source of adventure. My brother and I, separated by just over a year, and good playmates, weren't allowed into the yard officially. But we easily clambered over the black-tarred wooden gates through which generations of Chadwicks builders had trundled handcarts in and out, as they left for or returned from jobs around Bury and adjacent villages. For us, the yard was a fascinating place, stacked with clutters of bricks, planks, troughs, chimney pots, picks, spades, wheelbarrows and the like. A gloomy storeroom, whose dusty windows let in little light, contained boxes of rusting nails, screws, washers and other necessaries of the building trade. Most fascinating for us boys was the old well we discovered in a back shed, roughly covered over by rather dangerously crumbling planks. We would lift these up and drop small stones down into the darkness, to be rewarded by a faint splash from far below. Another Dickensian touch was the old Victorian 'office', with ancient desk and high stool, clearly unused for decades, and dully stained windows half-shrouded with cobwebs.

Here, we gathered, our late uncle had sat and 'managed' the firm in earlier, perhaps more glorious, days, while my father trudged out behind the shafts of the handcart in wind and rain or summer heat (and his well-muscled forearms were the proof of it) to do the physical work as long as his ailing brother lived. Thereafter, my father took on a series of labourers. The latest of them was a jovial Irishman called Paddy O'Rourke, who also opened the batting for our church cricket team in the Sunday Schools League. On weekdays he helped push the traditional handcart over stone setts or tarmacked roads alike, until in the fifties my father finally bought a small lorry, or 'wagon', as he called it.

With the Irishman at the wheel, the wagon somehow left the road and came to an inglorious end against a wall in the village of Breightmet when they were returning from a job in Bolton. Thus ended my father's brief and inglorious flirtation with modern transport. I don't think his heart was ever really in it. I wasn't around at the time of the crash – working somewhere abroad, I imagine, But remembering one of Dad's favourite utterances, he probably said, 'I knew all along summat like this'd 'appen.'

Such were my English roots. My mother was an Irish immigrant, one of the Ryans of Clonmel, County Tipperary, forced to split up and emigrate in a pattern already well established by the early twentieth century. My grandparents on the Irish side I never met. At a small house in Irishtown – the street name reflected the historical situation of the time – they raised a family of a dozen (no mean feat) before deciding that the future, if there was to be one, lay across the Atlantic rather than the Irish Sea. The Ryans seem to have been a tough lot, though, and the last of those children, a nun named Sister St Peter, died well into the twenty-first century just a few years ago in a convent in North Wales, a few weeks short of her hundredth birthday.

My grandparents took the youngest children with them to America, travelling steerage no doubt, shortly after World War One. The older girls were despatched to relatives already living in the textile and mill towns of Lancashire, mainly Bolton; my mother went to an aunt in Bury, where she and my father met. She never saw her parents again, for when she and one of her sisters finally sailed the Atlantic in the aftermath of World War Two, my Irish grandparents were already dead in Queens, New York. I never realised at the time, as kids don't, how tragic this all was. I only began to get the immensity of it when I started reading Irish history, of which my mother had always been curiously reluctant to talk (maybe this is a characteristic of foreign incomers to this day). Then, some years ago, I visited Ellis Island, New York, first destination over many decades for immigrants from Europe, and got a much more graphic sense of it all from the fascinating films and archives there.

Big things, and not always pleasant, were happening around the world about the time I was born (maybe they subliminally influenced my later choice of career!). The Great Depression had started with the Wall Street Crash, and two million people in Britain were out of work. At the other end of the social spectrum, the *Daily Telegraph* reported the latest world wanderings of the man it called 'Our Traveller Prince', who it said had 'a flair for enjoyment'. He was later destined to become King briefly and then abdicate. In other parts of the world that year, Josif Stalin expelled his fellow communist Leon Trotsky, from Texas came the report of another black lynching, Britain's fascist sympathiser Oswald Mosley issued a right-wing manifesto, and another headline was 'Colour Problem In Britain' over what was called the menace of mixed trade unions. On the cultural side of things, Erich Remarque's *All Quiet on the Western Front* won tremendous acclaim, Evelyn Waugh's social satire *Vile Bodies* had mixed notices, while orgy scenes, marital infidelity, coarse speech and suggestive titles were all reported to have been deleted by our film censors. In the air, Amy Johnson had become the first woman to fly to Australia, and the Germans had completed the first round-the-world flight in the *Graf Zeppelin*. Aircraft would become almost a fixation with me.

My own slightly more mundane first memory (though some people understandably dispute this) is of sitting in a pram wheeled by my mother down a cobblestoned street in Lancashire towards the house of Irish relatives with names like Connell and Heenighan. I'd discovered that if I made a steady wailing sound it would be broken up interestingly into a series of staccato phrases as the pram wheels bumped over the uneven stones. The only other fleeting recollection from very early days in Bury is of seeing my English grandmother sitting in a high-backed chair next door. Of my first visit to Ireland I remember little, though my brother, thirteen months older, recalls dockside lights at Liverpool as we boarded an overnight ferry to Dublin, and playing in the back garden of the house in Irishtown where my mother was born. My only recollection from that time, for some reason, is of the smell of cooked potatoes at the house in Clonmel. Well, it's possible, I suppose. We were in Ireland.

Fast-forwarding a few years, blurred memories of life in Lancashire begin, radiating from the house at the corner of Wash Lane. There, in simpler days, the milkman parked his horse-drawn cart, dipped a ladle into a big milk churn and poured the fresh bubbling liquid into a large jug held out by my mother. Then he clip-clopped on to other customers at the top of York Street. The coal man arrived periodically too, his cap worn back to front, his face sweaty and streaked with coal dust, and hoisted a heavy bag off the back of a flat-backed lorry into our backyard. Further down York Street there were only mills, whose tall brick chimneys encircled the area like candles on a birthday cake. Not an attractive area in daylight, but the massive three-storey Ring Mill in York Street did fascinate me at night. With its throbbing machinery and long rows of lighted windows, it became for me a great ocean liner with illuminated portholes, racing across the Atlantic.

I got to know the shops. Passing by a short row of houses with front gardens – I thought this was rather grand at the time – you reached Lund's, the bread shop. I liked the warm smell of baking there and the taste of their 'lunch buns'. Then came a newspaper shop and, at the end of the row, that happily forgotten (I hope) symbol of between-the-wars Lancashire, the tripe shop. I can't say I ever got to like the stuff, though it was cheap. My father seemed to enjoy it occasionally, cut into small slices, with a touch of salt and vinegar. It was, I suppose, a matter of what you could afford.

Two pubs faced each other, the Blue Bell and the Cotton Tree, the latter presumably named after the raw material shipped in from America's Deep South, which had kept Lancashire families in work for decades. Further along the street were Fearnleys, the greengrocers (a couple I never liked, sensing anti-Catholicism). Mr Chatterley, the butcher, in contrast, was quite a jovial chap. Some of the grown-ups patronised a herbalists shop across the road, where drinks like sarsaparilla and dandelion and burdock were available. Have these drinks survived? I wonder. More interesting to small boys was the place next door, Ma James's toffee shop, where with our Saturday pennies we could buy a bag of Liquorice Allsorts or Mint Imperials.

Small boys' pleasures were simple. The crevices between cobblestones on the road (more correctly called setts) were filled with ribbons of black tar. On hot summer days, the tar would rise in bubbles, which my brother and I, sitting on the kerb, would happily pop with our forefingers. Today, commuters' cars roar past the spot where the old house stood, now a cindery patch of wasteland. And no one would dare to sit on the kerbstone any more.

In industrial Lancashire there always seemed to be a fair amount of 'slutch' about – sludge, in the modern vernacular. It's defined in my *Oxford Dictionary* as 'a viscous mixture of solid and liquid components'. That seems about right. There was lots of rain, and lots of other stuff floated down from the chimneys. Nestling in the 'slutch' could often be seen empty cigarette packets – the English have always been an untidy lot – which we'd pick up, to see if a picture card had been left inside. These 'cigarette cards' carried interesting shots of cars, ships or planes, and we'd keep them, or maybe swap them with friends. They've now become highly collectible, I gather. As for cigarettes themselves, I was eventually tempted, as I got a bit older, to have a go myself. Packets of 'five Woodies' (Woodbines) were highly popular with smokers who didn't have the money to shell out for a packet of twenty. But Woodies didn't have cards inside. When my schoolmate Brian Walker and I decided to try smoking ourselves, we went for the slightly more upmarket 'Park Drive', and lit up in a backstreet off Moorside. I dragged, puffed, spluttered and nearly threw up. I hastily abandoned the weed.

Directly across the street from Number 12 was the Church of England's Bell School. We Catholics had pals there, with whom we congregated around a lamp post at the school entrance on winter evenings – the 'BOYS' entrance, mind you. 'GIRLS' had to enter through another door. The last time I was in Bury, the separate 'Boys' and 'Girls' signs had survived, etched in stone, though the building had long been put to other uses. In the thirties it was attended by most of the neighbouring kids, known to us Catholics as 'Proddy dogs'. That was in retaliation for being called 'Cat-licks'. We Catholics understood, somehow or other, that we should treat Protestants with some caution. Next to Bell School was, we gathered, a potential source of sin, a billiard hall, and beyond that yet another moral hazard, the Star Picture House. And never, ever, as Catholics, were we to cross the porch of St Paul's Protestant Church, an imposing stone edifice half a mile down Wash Lane.

For years I thought I'd be struck down by a bolt from Heaven if I did; or if I escaped God's wrath, I would certainly have to tell the priest what I'd done at confession. There were other religions about too. At the top end of York Street lived the Garsides, a mother and two daughters who regularly marched in their striking navy blue uniforms and bonnets, singing and playing castanets with the Salvation Army Band. My Protestant friend Eric Jennings (Baptist), from next door, disclosed one day, 'T' Sally Army's showin' pictures for kids at t' Citadel, and it's all free.' The Citadel was the Army's red-brick headquarters in nearby Moorgate. We went along to find out. I haven't the least recollection of what we saw, but if this was religious propaganda, it seemed enjoyable and harmless enough to me. I didn't tell Mother.

Though I drank plenty of milk, I didn't know what a cow looked like until I was about six years old. I'd been quarantined in the front room of Number 12 with scarlet fever. Only mother was allowed in there with meals. I always asked for rice pudding. I liked the nice golden-brown skin on the top. When I was in recovery mode, my Irish Auntie Mag arrived to take me for a bus ride – also a first. We sat on the top deck of one of Bury Corporation's new red buses. They had big double wheels at the back, thought necessary, we were told, for climbing hills. Our destination was Jericho, an oddly named village on the fringe of town. I didn't think the name curious at the time, of course, and even much later I thought Bury simply got in first, ahead of those people in the Bible.

At the terminus, we walked up a quiet country lane between grey stone walls as far as a farmhouse, where I was given a large glass of milk. I drank it down, gazing across apparently endless fields, and for the first time heard the mooing of real life cows. I'd never been in the countryside before. I thought the world consisted of houses, schools and mills.

And churches, of course. There were plenty of those. The Parish Church stood in the town centre, or at t' top o' t' Street, as the place was called for generations – 'Fleet Street', to give it its full name – and I'd work in the more famous one years later. One year – he only got away with it once – my father announced to my brother and me with mock seriousness, 'I've just seen a man at top o' t' Street with as many noses as there are days in the year!' Aghast, we tried to think what 365 noses must look like – and then we got the New Year's Eve joke and laughed. Innocent fun, as there was in those days.

A good job we never peeped into our father's *Daily Mail*,

perused religiously by the fire in the evening, evoking the occasional cry of disgust. There didn't seem to be much fun in there.

Well, by the mid-thirties, Hitler's thugs were well into their stride and the news from Europe couldn't have been encouraging. But as these were pre-television days, the worst of the world's cruelties – death camps in Europe, lynchings in America – never impinged on our consciousness. The worst thing we knew in Lancashire was relative poverty and, as all our pals were in much the same boat, that didn't bother us much either.

The Empire still seemed to be going strong, and it was an age of adventure. As my interest in flying grew, I became aware of exciting developments which made the world seem just a bit smaller – Jim Mollison's eight-and-a-half-day flight to England from Australia, Amy Johnson's hazardous flight in the other direction – while British airmen flew over Mount Everest for the first time.

In the fictional world, there were scary enough things on the big screen, where Boris Karloff made his debut as Frankenstein's monster; I still remember it.

The Catholic school, St Joseph's, stood on the other side of busy Moorgate – aptly named, I realised later, as it was the approach road to the Bury-Rochdale moors. A single-storey brick building housed the 'baby classes', as they were called. That's where I started school, at four. Two years on from that, my first school memory is of a history lesson when we were dressed up in two groups, as Romans or Britons. I insisted on being one of the Romans, who had nice shiny helmets and seemed to be the top dogs. The Brits, with blue woad daubed all over their faces, looked like losers to me.

After two years you moved across a stone-flagged schoolyard into a bigger two-storey building, its upper floor divided by sliding wooden partitions, with two adjacent classes on either side. These were known in the terminology of the time as 'Standards' One, Two, Three and Four. After Standard Four, as a fourteen-year-old, you usually left school and started work – if you hadn't passed the eleven-plus exam to get to a high school (luckily my brother and I both did). Not many of our friends' parents let them take the exam; as likely as not, they couldn't afford not to have the kids working. For Lancashire youth at our social level, it was mainly mills or foundries for the boys, and shops, offices or home service for the girls.

Teachers in the top classes at Josephs were mainly women, of whom I vaguely remember Miss Cruse, who seemed to like my art work; Miss Crossley, who wore sensible clothes and shoes; and the more elegantly dressed Miss Baron. You knew you'd offended Miss Baron if she pointed the way out of the classroom and uttered the dread words, 'Go to see Mr Murphy!' (or 'Bister Burphy' as it came out in her much-mimicked nasal tones). However, that pipe-smoking headmaster of Irish descent, fumes befogging his study, was a kindly man, and apart from a mild rebuke, such misdemeanours rarely went any further. I won a prize for writing, awarded by Bury and District branch of the RSPCA, of all people, my entries recounting real or imagined adventures with animals, with which I seem to have had a fixation. 'We have a cat, its name is Pat,' I wrote in that recently unearthed notebook. (Pat was my sister's name.) And, 'l saw a little rabbit once; I called it Fluffy Tail.' The story of Farmer Brown's cow was also recorded in twelve tedious lines. I won't go on.

The somewhat unnerving prize for these verses, presumably because I attended a Catholic school, was a biography of David Rizzio, an Italian musician and private secretary of Mary Queen of Scots. The account of his murder by jealous courtiers who inflicted fifty-seven dagger blows before hurtling him down the staircase at Holyrood Palace, Edinburgh, seems less than appropriate for a small animal-loving schoolboy. I'd rather have had a book about planes. Good job I found the opening pages too boring to continue. Maybe they we're just getting rid of a job lot of books nobody wanted to buy. Another competition, however, I didn't win – and rather resented it. Ten-year-olds at schools around town were invited (as part of a commercial campaign, I imagine) to dream up a slogan for Turog, a well-known bread manufacturer of the day. I came up with 'T for Turog, Turog for Tea' – which I thought was pretty smart and snappy, and had to be a winner. I was more than a little miffed when it wasn't. The episode seems to indicate an early interest in (a) words, and (b) their commercial power.

12 May 1937 was the date of the Coronation of King George the Sixth. Every school child in Bury received a blue-and-gold-covered book entitled *George VI, King and Emperor*. Still on my shelves, it contains black-and-white pictures of an always smiling Princess Elizabeth in Windsor Great Park, standing among flowers at the Royal Lodge in Windsor, and along with her more camera-shy young sister at Glamis Castle.

It was all remote fairy-tale stuff for kids in grim and grimy Lancashire. I couldn't have guessed that a quarter-century later, as a young Reuters correspondent, I'd be following Margaret's romantic meetings in London and Belgium with the dashing RAF Group-Captain Peter Townsend, and a few years later would be presented to her elder sister, now Queen, on the Royal Yacht.

In a rather sententious foreword to the Coronation gift book, Mayor John Whitehead reminded us kids of the meaning of the letters found on every penny – BRITT; OMN; REX; IND; IMP. The slogan referred, he wrote, to all the British dominions beyond the seas; stretching round the globe circle-wise, like the Imperial crown itself, set with great jewels like Canada, Australia, India, New Zealand, South Africa, and with lesser gems, though no less bright, like Ceylon, the West Indies, Rhodesia, Newfoundland, Malta and Gibraltar. How much meaning, declared the Mayor, could be packed into those seventeen letters on a copper coin. Waxing ever more lyrical, he said how wonderful would be a huge assembly of children from all those places: Indian children would speak of palms and palaces, Australian boys and girls could describe the sheep farms, South Africans the veldt, with its wonderful flowers and sunsets, while Canadian children would speak of great lakes, pine forests and snow in the Rockies. Well, out of that long list (I haven't mentioned them all) we still have Gibraltar, I suppose. Things have certainly changed. I think most of us at the time would have settled for one of those copper coins. For a penny we could at least have bought a bag of Mint Imperials at Ma James's toffee shop.

At eight I had my first real glimpse of royalty. When the King and Queen toured industrial Lancashire, I was one of 8,000 local children lining the route. As instructed, I waved my blue-and-white paper handkerchief and no doubt cheered shrilly with the rest of the kids when the open limousine, preceded by police cars, drove briefly past. A police aircraft circled above, which I liked.

'Flags and bunting enlivened drab-fronted houses' as the local paper quite objectively described the scene. A hundred men, it was recorded, climbed on the roof of the town centre Two Tubs pub for a grandstand view of the monarch. Disabled soldiers from the 1914 and Boer wars were presented by the Lord of the Manor, Lord Derby, quaintly described by the *Bury Times* in terms reminiscent of the Victorian age as 'the embodiment of graciousness, tact and good fellowship'. The Queen, it was reported, 'had a cheery word, for Bury's maimed soldiers', most of them on crutches or sitting in wheelchairs. Coverage of the event filled two pages of text with lots of pictures. An hour later, Their Majesties were on their way to the next shabby town along the route – Rochdale, I imagine. I wonder what they thought of our mean streets and those 'satanic mills'.

A decade and a half after the First World War and a year before the outbreak of the Second, Lancashire was still suffering from the recession. There were many jobless, lots of men were on the dole or living on measly compensation for war injuries. Like many others, my father had to graft for a living, often traipsing round the houses at weekends to get paid in instalments for building jobs he'd already finished. The St Joseph's families were all in much the same boat, hard up but respectable. I remember one poor lad who sometimes arrived at school with shoes but no socks on.

There wasn't a great deal to celebrate, one might think, but the main headline in the *Bury Times* – for which I was later to work – read: 'Cheering Bury Welcomes King and Queen'. Their Majesties had passed within a few hundred yards of the Chadwicks' ancestral home. I doubt if royal heads would have turned! The principal image that sticks in my mind is of the Queen, as the procession passed close to the kerb where I stood. Her face looked painted, I told my mother afterwards. Either she was elaborately made-up, or considerably more tanned than we sun-starved urchins were ever likely to get. As the royal limousine passed, she gave us what I came to know later as the royal wave. Then we went back to our classrooms. The souvenir books arrived later.

Though money was scarce, our parents always tried to give us a nice Christmas. My brother and I would hang up long woollen stockings on the posts of the big bed we shared and, sure enough, when we woke up on Christmas morning they looked satisfyingly bulky. It was mainly glossy apples and oranges (tangerines if they could get them), and model cars wrapped in silver paper, which were really made of chocolate when you took the paper off. The best present I ever got was a miniature red car with a wire and steering wheel attached to the top. Having wound it up and set it going, you could steer it between the legs of table and chairs on the living-room carpet. Interestingly enough, with war obviously on the horizon, it was a German-made Schuko, and one of the best Christmas presents I ever got. The apples and oranges were soon eaten, but the Schuko car kept me happy for months.

As for real life cars, I had my first ride in one of them in the late thirties. A couple of times a year we'd get a visit from distant relatives, also of Irish origin, whom we called Auntie Nellie and Uncle Jim. These were exotic folk to us, apart from the big car they parked in York Street. They lived in far-off Bradford, across the Pennines, and were described as 'being in the wool trade'. This meant they sold good Yorkshire wool in the market towns of Northern England – where they were also familiar with all the racetracks, like York and Pontefract, and knew some of the trainers and jockeys well. They injected a welcome cheery note into our often rather silent household, and it was always nice when Nellie invited us lads over for a week during the holidays. They'd lived in the United States for some years, and the story went that in the late twenties and early thirties, until Prohibition ended, Jim had been involved in liquor-running across the Canadian border. This gave him a big extra touch of glamour. He said little himself. Bald-headed and ever smiling, he was content to sit back in a chair beside the fire while Nellie chattered on. They seemed to know all the Catholics and others who mattered in Bradford, including the clergy. Their friends' children, who always seemed to be training as doctors or lawyers, were invariably described as 'brilliant', which made us boys feel rather inferior. We wondered how we could ever become as 'brilliant' as these Bradford lads. (But I'm sure she told the Bradford friends just the same thing about us.)

After quitting the wool trade, Jim set up as a bookie in their semi-detached house in Eccleshill Road. Unhappily, a few years later, he was virtually cleaned out after the young man from a horse racing family, whom they'd adopted and unwisely one day left in charge of the operation, omitted to lay off the bets on a big race at Doncaster, which cost Jim thousands. Well, they'd certainly led an eventful life. As they drove off in the big car towards the road over the moors, I envied them their colourful world. The house seemed silent when they left. They'd have fitted perfectly in the world of J B Priestley.

A couple of years after the Royal Visit, we gathered that there was now 'a war on', and German air raids might be expected. For this eventuality, we kids were all given gas masks with shoulder strap and case, to be hung over our shoulders and carried at all times. The masks were a weird sight when worn, with their broad plastic eye screens, behind which we made funny faces at each other, and a strange circular nozzle vaguely resembling a pig's snout. The nozzle, we were told, contained special chemicals which would protect us from being gassed, like our unfortunate soldiers in the First World War trenches. I remember well the rubbery smell of the masks. Another smell lingers. Suddenly, it seemed, a piece of waste ground beside the school had been excavated into tunnels, into which we filed regularly for 'air-raid shelter practice'. The special smell down there came from the prefabricated asbestos walls – which would hardly be considered a good idea today.

As with most elementary school pupils, we didn't have much in the way of books at home. Reading was largely confined to my father's *Daily Mail* and church magazines, one of which printed a poem of mine, suitably dedicated to St Joseph. To supplement this meagre intellectual fare, we boys joined Bury's public library as soon as we were old enough and took out books regularly from the children's section.

With our noses buried in these pages, we weren't always popular at home. 'Aren't you doin' a bit too much of this blinkin' readin'!' remonstrated the father of the household occasionally. ' 'Aven't a word to say to anybody these days.' However, we went on using the public library and art gallery, a handsome stone building which, gratifyingly, still stands in the centre of Bury, though now robbed of its Lowry picture, stupidly sold off to fill a hole in the town budget.

The Star Picture House, the smallest cinema in Bury, charged twopence at the kids' Saturday matinee. An old friend tells me his mother would give him twopence-halfpenny (the odd halfpenny for a chocolate bar). We at Number 12 seldom had money for the pictures and I queued for one Saturday afternoon matinee (usually cowboy films with Tom Mix or Buck Rogers) in battered football boots. My school shoes were in for repair. 'Nobody's going to notice,' my mother assured me. They did, and jeered. My next-door pal from York Street, Protestant Eric Jennings, whose father and elder brothers, unlike Catholics, all had well-paid engineering jobs at Bury Felt Works, was treated much more indulgently and frequently got to visit the Star. I think he tried not to gloat.

The hinterland beyond the Star was dangerous territory. A small but tough and wiry boy called Mick Hargreaves ran a gang in those parts. It was better to move at least in pairs in the Brick Street area. You might well be kidnapped and frogmarched a few blocks before being released. We had our own gang, led by Ted Eastwood, an older boy from York Street. It was usual practice in the run-up to the Fifth of November to raid other gangs' back yards and steal their 'bommy-wood' (bonfire wood) – assorted collections of battered old wooden fences, planks and trees. Not furniture; that people kept.

As the youngest and smallest of our gang, I'd be hoisted up on to the coping stone above the back gate and ordered to lean down and draw back the bolt, letting the others into the enemy stronghold. We'd take as much as we thought we could carry. We'd have checked the front of the house first, of course, to make sure the occupants of the house were 'out' – we hoped. Bonfire Night itself was celebrated, usually with parents in attendance, on a small patch of cindery waste ground between the houses in York Street. The sputtering sparks, fireworks and rockets temporarily lit up a damp Lancashire winter evening. I was never crazy about fireworks, though. I hated the Little Demons, bangers which might be suddenly thrown at your feet and explode. I preferred rockets and cascades of stars.

In summer, the thing to have was a 'bogey'. This was a home-made 'car', the body consisting of a short plank fixed lengthways across the axles from two discarded prams. For some reason (they had bigger families then) there seemed to be a regular supply of these. You attached the back axle, using two bolts, squarely under the rear of the plank. The front axle had just one bolt in the middle, so you could swivel to left or right with the help of a rope. On level streets, one of you would push the other along. The best place to race was a steep cross-street from Wash Lane to York Street. Here you could reach a good speed. The main thrill came when you had to swerve quickly to get round the right-hand corner at the end. If you didn't get the balance right, you fell off. And you just hoped nobody would be coming the other way, otherwise there could be angry words.

I was recently sent a black-and-white aerial photograph of Bury in 1933. Over an area of about two miles square, a ring of eleven mill chimneys, rather like candles on a birthday cake, more or less encircles the house in Wash Lane. The pilot must have chosen a fine Sunday afternoon for the filming, for not one of the chimneys is smoking. You can see St Paul's Church and graveyard, the Star Picture House, Bell School, the end-of-row house where I was born, and the nearby builder's yard. You'd need a microscope to get a closer look at the house. Maybe we were in there at the time – or more likely at church! The chimneys are all gone today, thank the Lord.

As we got older, my brother and I got as far as we could from the mills. We'd take a bus or tram to an end-of-town terminus, then strike off along old tracks and drovers' roads crossing the moors. Bleak Knowl Hill rose like a truncated pyramid to the north, and in summer the ridge of the Pennines smudged the horizon. The valleys housed the last relics of Lancashire's first industrial age. Tottering old stone chimneys pointed the way to long-abandoned industrial settlements. Along a winding stream once used to power mill machinery were the tracks of long defunct tramways and the weed-covered remains of waterwheels and workers' cottages. A now shuttered-up village school once educated over 200 children in the first phase of Lancashire's industrial age. In the nearby valley of Birtle Dene, cloth was woven, hauled by windlass up a steep hillside, then loaded on to horse-drawn wagons for delivery to Manchester merchants.

Lancashire's first immigrant workers worked here, mainly jobless farm labourers from Suffolk. Old church records tell of the baptisms, funerals and Christmas parties of a thriving community in the mid-nineteenth century. It was soon to be part of history. These remote valleys didn't link up with main roads, which wasn't good for business. One by one, the mills sold up and year by year the tall chimneys ceased smoking. Industry was concentrated in the towns. A few years later, I'd write all this up in the *Bolton Evening News*. After getting the story together, photographer Jack Deighton and I would take a swim in one of the old mill lodges, the water now crystal clear. The few remaining factory walls with their gaping windows are now used for background shots in historical TV dramas. The pub at the top of the lane I walked with my aunt as a six-year-old has now become an upmarket country restaurant. Along the 'Forgotten Valley', as local historians have dubbed it, the mill ruins get greener every summer. Soon you'll hardly know there'd ever been an industry there at all.

Like many of our pals, we avidly collected birds' eggs. We'd learned how to push a pin through one end of the egg and blow out the contents. Every schoolboy knew that. We already had song thrushes' and blackbirds' eggs, their nests frequently spotted as a dark patch in a hedgerow.

Suddenly one day, in a wooded valley near the village of Birtle, came the chance of getting an egg that none of our pals had. There was the bright blue-and-orange flash of a kingfisher as it flew off startled from a log bridging a stream. We knew kingfishers tunnelled into the sandy banks of streams, nesting in a cavity at the end. 'Have a look down there,' ordered my brother, asserting his thirteen-month seniority. I let myself down on to the gravelly edge of the stream and spotted the nesting hole. Quickly I thrust my arm into the tunnel, and out came a cluster of beautiful little white, almost round eggs. It was a triumphant moment. We were elated as we made our way home, and our friends were envious. Eventually, of course, other interests superseded the birdwatching, and those eggs went with the rest of the collection into the dustbin. I've always loved kingfishers, but I've never seen one since. If I did, I'd apologise. We tried to make amends by joining the junior section of the Royal Society for the Protection of Birds (RSPB), but then committed new misdemeanours by claiming, in our reports, sightings of exotic birds we'd certainly never spotted. Well, we were only trying to help...

Apart from reading and model-making, home entertainment on cold winter evenings, with the gas lamp glowing and a fire flickering in the grate, largely consisted of the wireless. And when I think back, we didn't get any less enjoyment from that simple radio set standing on a side table near the rear window than from the ever larger TV screens I see today, which seem to substitute size for content. With the radio, you used your imagination a bit more, and the result was maybe just as colourful. As kids, our first regular pre-war listening was *Toytown*, a delightful serial recounting the adventures of Larry the Lamb, his friend Denis the Dachshund, the stalwart Ernest the Policeman ('What's goin' on 'ere?') and grumpy old Mr Groucher. Over the years, we graduated to the exploits of Paul Temple, Detective, and his poshly accented wife, Steve, who clearly inhabited a sophisticated London milieu far removed from our own. We never missed an instalment, as Temple grappled with the urban underworld or German spies in disguise – except, of course, when the battery of the radio ran out, which always seemed to happen in the middle of a crisis.

' 'As that blinkin' battery gone again?' cried father – as much of a Paul Temple addict as ourselves. Nothing to do about it. There were two batteries in the old radio sets, wet and dry. The dry one could be inserted fairly straightforwardly in the back of the wireless. The wet battery was a square glass phial, rather larger than a jam jar, which had to be professionally charged. My brother and I lugged it in turns by the handle of its metal holder half a mile down York Street and Rochdale Road to 'Mr Monks' wireless shop'. There we'd hand it in for recharging, and take its already topped-up twin back home again. Too late for *Paul Temple* by then. To find out whether Temple and Steve had got out of that particular scrape, we'd have to wait a week for that ominous staccato signature tune – extracted as I found years later from Rimsky-Korsakov's *Scheherazade*. I thought the music frightening, hinting at evil events just around the corner. Things were never the same in later years when the highly evocative music by Rimsky-Korsakov and Arnold Bax was unaccountably dropped in favour of Vivian Ellis's anodyne 'Coronation Scot', which we didn't think sounded menacing at all.

Our post-war diet of radio thrills was supplied by *Dick Barton*, Special Agent, whose fifteen-minute adventures alongside Snowy the Cockney and Jock the Scot were heralded by the equally atmospheric 'Devil's Gallop'. How effective those signature tunes were. They introduced me to all sorts of music which, whenever I hear it half a century later, takes me back into other worlds. The extracts from Bizet's *L'Arlésienne*, only identified by me much later, I thought equally appropriate in a BBC serialisation of Louise Alcott's *Little Women*, especially the haunting passage allocated to the death of one of the participants. Another wartime 'must' – and my first insight into radio journalism – was *In Town Tonight*, which every Saturday 'stopped the mighty roar of London's traffic' for interviews with famous names of the day. Atmosphere was also expertly conjured up in pre-TV days by the eerie introduction to that first interplanetary serial, *Journey Into Space*, and by actor Valentine Dyall's menacing voice as 'The Man In Black'.

Throughout the years there were also the comics, not always bought but swapped with friends down the street – the *Dandy* and *Beano*, from which we graduated to the more literate *Hotspur*, *Wizard* and *Rover*, with fewer pictures and more text. During the war, we followed the exploits of Rockfist Rogan, the RAF fighter ace, and a mysterious man called 'Wilson', who lived for some reason in a cave on the moors, from where he came down occasionally to sort out problems in more comfortable surroundings. And of course the inimitable Biggles and his mates, Algy and Ginger, as they grappled with sneering Nazi henchmen in the Baltic, or international crooks like the 'King of the Forest' in the jungles of Latin America, but whose strongest expletives were 'Gosh!', 'By Jove!', or, in the direst of circumstances, 'Jumping Rattlesnakes!'. In these books were the forerunners of the James Bond villains.

The library books I borrowed were often about aeroplanes and the North, both of which topics strongly appealed to me (and still do). One adventure story had illustrations of a strangely modernistic vehicle looking rather like a railway carriage on skis. From this, white-coated Finnish soldiers would tumble, to swish like ghosts through snow-covered conifer forests as they fought the Russian invaders. I was captivated.

Then suddenly, from what one picked up from the adults or heard on the 'wireless', the Russians had become our allies… So now it was just the Germans we had to hate. I'd been similarly perplexed as an even smaller boy, during the Spanish Civil War, by catching snippets of adult conversation and odd news fragments that my father threw out from behind his *Daily Mail*. This man Franco didn't seem to us like a very nice guy – but we were Catholics and he was supposed to be fighting for Catholicism against the communists, and must therefore be supported, like the Germans who were helping him out. Then, a few years later, we suddenly had to hate the Germans and like the Russians! It was all very confusing. When Prime Minister Neville Chamberlain announced on 3 September 1939, in that effete and quavering upper-class voice, that Adolf Hitler hadn't played the game and we were at war with Germany, I asked my mother apprehensively as a nine-year-old what was going to happen now. 'Oh, it's nothing to worry about,' she said, and that was that. So I didn't.

But I was well aware of the air battles. As well as poems, my old notebook contains crude drawings of a Hawker Hurricane fighter, bullets spraying from the wings. As a grammar school boy later, I used some of my pocket money to buy the *Aeroplane Spotter* magazine regularly from a little shop in Bolton, and knew the silhouettes and front views of everything from a Supermarine

Spitfire to a Heinkel 111. On our kitchen table, I carved out a solid balsa-wood model of the Hurricane. Thus encouraged, I assembled a trickier balsa-wood-and-paper model plane with rubber-band motor which you wound up with the propeller. I had the enormous satisfaction of seeing it take off in a nearby park and land without crashing. I was among the first at a 'War Effort' exhibition in the town centre Co-op building to see a real Messerschmitt 109 fighter which had made a forced landing on the Pennine moors. Like other plane-crazy kids, I got to sit for a few moments in the cockpit. I reflected that there wasn't much room for a grown man in there.

Most of the visiting German aircraft, of course, didn't finish up on the moors. The air raids started in 1942, and Manchester was the worst hit north-west town. You could see the red fire glows in the sky at night. Ten miles north, we ourselves remained comparatively immune, but still had to go down to the shelters at night when the sirens sounded. The puny underground trenches dug out in our school playground were never used in earnest. In industrial areas such as ours, mill and factory basements became shelters, and sometimes we'd be woken up during the night to walk down York Street in darkness to the musty-smelling cellar of one of those mills. Half asleep most of the time as we huddled down there in blankets, we'd trudge back home after the all-clear, then get up again for school.

Manchester residents fared much worse, but courageously work went on. About this time, my little sister Pat had been chosen as May Queen. Splendid in her white dress and long train, she stood in the pulpit of St Joseph's Church and performed the traditional ceremony of placing a floral crown on the head of Our Lady's statue. Afterwards, my mother had arranged for this fine dress material to be made up into altar vestments for the church by a specialist firm in Manchester. In a letter preserved in the family files from the firm of Thos Brown and Co., Church Furnishers, of Brazenose Street, Manchester, I find them writing:

'What with air raids and sickness in our workroom, we don't know where we've been up to. Yes, it is awful getting up in the night and going to the shelter. I don't know what it will be like in winter.

But, like Brits everywhere, they carried on with the job – and apologised for any inconvenience.

For five years from 1940, despite the war, my brother and I travelled back and forth to school in Bolton. Kitted out in smart brown blazers with the school crest in gold thread on the breast pocket, we felt almost like traitors among friends who'd stayed on at St Joseph's – but I hardly think anyone got paranoid. Our main aim was not to look 'soft'. We had to tramp a mile to the railway station on the other side of town and we didn't think walking together would be a good idea. That would be 'soft'. And once I had acquired a smart brown canvas violin case after being enrolled in the school orchestra, my brother refused to be associated with me at all. Violins were for softies. We walked to the station on opposite sides of the street, preferably a hundred yards apart.

Pulled by one of those charming old 2-4-2 engines, the train left Knowsley Street Station at 0823 as scheduled, and continued to do so throughout the war, arriving in Bolton twenty minutes later after passing Burnden Park football ground. At Trinity Street Station, we transferred to a bus for a couple of miles, and then there was a final half-mile walk to school. Did someone say that kids today are mollycoddled?

Chapter 2
AFTER NIGHTS IN THE AIR-RAID SHELTER, WE DODGE MISSILES AT SCHOOL

I hardly think they'd allow it today. A French teacher (aptly named Father Power) hurling a wooden-backed duster like a German missile at someone lounging in the back row? Or rapping you on the head with his knuckles if you hadn't studied your verbs? But this was the early forties, and it was wartime. Maybe he thought it would prepare us for military service, if hostilities lasted that long.

Of course there were more engaging teachers. Brother Stephen, for instance, who taught Latin. He joined us boys at impromptu football games on the tarmacked tennis courts in the lunch hour, playing alternately for one side or the other, deftly threading the ball through the bottom folds of his black cassock as he moved swiftly goalwards. On the whole, Thornleigh College was good fun, a far cry from anything we'd been used to.

It was on the fringe of wooded countryside in one of the more exclusive residential areas of Bolton. There were only big houses out there, and the Salesian Fathers who established the school had shown fine perception in acquiring a group of these, around which newer classrooms were built.

The main house, where lived the priest and brothers of the community – and a few schoolboy boarders – was (and remains) a fine example of a distinguished country house, built largely of brick, set off with sculpted stone balustrades and wide steps leading down to the gardens and playing fields.

An archway led to new red-brick classrooms and open cloisters, on the pillars of which were posted school news and the line-ups for Saturday's soccer matches. I was, rather appropriately, allocated to St Chad's House, my brother to St Albans.

The school was established in the late 1920s, specifically to further the education of Catholic boys, and teachers were naturally of the same faith. The Rector was a Father Walsh (Irish origin again), but the presiding genius was the headmaster. The appropriately named Father Wiseman was very English. An Oxford man, he spoke in an upmarket accent, exotic to most of us Lancastrians, and ran the school with quiet authority. Most of our teachers were priests, the others Catholic laymen, some of them from neutral Ireland and thus not subject to wartime National Service.

We were not a 'rugger' school, though some of our schoolmates came from rugby league towns like nearby Wigan and Leigh. Soccer was the main game, top matches played on a pitch in the nearby countryside, for some reason dubbed 'Hill 60' – the name of a famous First World War battlefield in the Dardanelles.

French and Latin were taught from the very first year, for which I remain grateful. Though I see in an old prize day programme which my mother must have kept that I won special prizes at fifteen – the year of the old School Certificate – for Latin, as well as English and French, I never became a Latin enthusiast. The language remains a bit too dry and compact for my taste. I like a few prepositions and link words here and there. Its great value later was to help in learning modern Mediterranean tongues.

I never took to mathematics and science with much enthusiasm, though enjoying the Bunsen burners and bubbling experiments in the lab. I'd somehow manage to come out top of the class every year, though I don't remember ever being a 'swot'. Nor was I later at university, where my Top Second degree might have been upgraded to a First if I'd done more work, undiverted by such competing attractions as the English Society football team.

My father was now an air-raid warden, being too old for the call-up. With building jobs hard to find in wartime, he did some day work as a clerical assistant in, I think, the ration books department at Bury Town Hall. He could probably have competed with many of those permanently located in that building – who did not, I imagine, include any Catholics. He'd a sharp mind and, for someone who'd left school at fourteen and educated himself thereafter at technical school evening classes, had a remarkable facility in written English to match his idiomatic use of northern speech. His ARP (Air-Raid Precautions) post was at the Gladstone Club, one of several ostensibly political but mainly social clubs named after former political leaders; others included the Cobden, Salisbury and Trevelyan. So, to the Gladstone, as it was known, my brother and I would be despatched with meal baskets when he was on evening or night duty. This routine went on until the danger of air raids subsided.

Our nearest bomb scare would come, though, not during the days of the big Blitz but towards the end of the war, when my brother and I, sharing a big double bed in the cramped quarters of 12 Wash Lane on Christmas Eve, 1944, suddenly heard a deep rattling sound in the night sky. Like an oversized motorbike, and familiar to us from radio and press descriptions as the sound of a German V-1 flying bomb, or 'doodlebug' as they were nicknamed, maybe aimed at Manchester. We lay in trepidation as the menacing noise came ever nearer, and were half petrified when the motor stopped. We knew the rocket would now plunge to earth and hit some indiscriminate target. We were still counting the seconds when a minute later came the loud explosion. It had found a target three miles away in the nearby village of Tottington, wrecking a row of houses and the Red Lion pub and killing seven people who were not as lucky as us.

We had no relatives in England in the armed forces, but one of our Irish relatives did contribute, a handsome youngish man we knew as 'Brother Edmund Ryan'. He'd studied for the priesthood, as so many youngsters in Ireland then seemed to do, but, like them, quit the seminary. The first we kids knew of his existence was when he suddenly arrived in British Army uniform from the Far East, where he'd fought with the forces in the Burma campaign. He seemed a nice, sensitive man, and it was strange that after the war he just disappeared in the United States, though his parents (our Irish grandparents) and three sisters were living there. Apart from that, we saw few uniforms, though there was an occasional visit in Wash Lane or York Street from one of the young men on leave. And we heard, of course, whenever Catholic families in the parish lost a son.

Ironically, we probably saw more German soldiers (as

prisoners) than our own. Travelling home from school, we'd occasionally see them step off the train, where they'd presumably been kept in the guard's van under escort, and driven off in a truck. We knew where it was going: a POW camp a few miles away. Sometimes we'd trek down the still cobbled Manchester Old Road to the village of Warth, not to gloat at the men behind the barbed wire – who didn't look particularly unhappy – but to watch them play football. Some of them looked pretty good at the game.

One German POW at a nearby camp stayed on after the war, married a local girl and re-emerged as Bert Trautmann, a star goalkeeper at Manchester City. Though thousands protested at the time, he became highly popular, and was much later honoured with the Order of the British Empire. What I noticed particularly was that all these young Germans looked so brown and fit, in contrast to at least some of our pale and weedy countrymen. It was perhaps my first image of continental Europeans. Whatever these men may have done, they looked in pretty good shape. It was one positive image of Europe that would stay with me for a long time.

Despite the war, the train rides to school went routinely. The station names were as reassuringly English – Black Lane, Bradley Fold and Darcy Lever – as in that delightful Flanders and Swann song nostalgically recalling pre-Beeching days. And just before arriving in Bolton, we had a grandstand view from above the terrace of Burnden Park football ground, home of the Wanderers, whose regular post-war team one of my schoolmates in Bolton could recite by heart – 'Hanson, Threlfall, Hubbick etc. etc.' A couple of years after the war, in a cup match against Stoke City, the same standing-only terrace below the old railway line became a disaster scene, when thirty-three spectators were trampled to death after crowd barriers collapsed. The old railway line no longer exists.

The separate train compartments of the time were made for mischief. When we were passing over a high viaduct outside Bolton, older lads – whom we all thought extremely tough – would wrench light bulbs from the ceiling and hurl them down through the open window over the slate rooftops below. Maybe this was the effect of the bomb raids. Schoolboy vandalism is ever present, I fear. It was perhaps as well that, once my brother and I had bikes, we stopped using the train and pedalled seven hilly miles to school and back, which meant aching muscles, but kept us out of mischief.

The Thornleigh years were golden days. Compared with the drab streets back home, the green fields, country tracks and overgrown woods surrounding the school were paradise. Gang culture never seems to lose its attraction for boys, and during the extended lunch break, after eating sandwiches brought from home, we would roam through nearby woods, known as 'The Preserves' but easily entered through breaks in the surrounding stone walls, then team up into two groups and pursue each other through the trees, using small stones as ammunition. I can't remember anyone ever getting hurt. The stones seemed to mainly ricochet off tree trunks. The place was a small wonderland for mill town boys, with conveniently branched birch trees to climb, half-overgrown paths to explore and a gloomy stone-arched tunnel in which a tinkling stream ran from one glade to another. You could just about walk through it with your head down.

Being a schoolboy wasn't all sweetness and light. Forgetting (or maybe ignoring) what we in Form Two had been told, I made the big mistake during an end-of-term exam, as all our heads were bent over the papers, of chatting with a neighbour. Father Tyson, the teacher, decided I'd been cheating, and told me to report the incident to the headmaster. At the lunchtime break, a small queue of us lined up before the door of Father Wiseman's study. Whenever we saw the blind drawn swiftly down across the glass, we knew what was going to happen inside. The number of thwacks we heard gave us some idea of the extent of the crime. When I got to the head of the queue myself and entered the headmaster's room, he didn't have to tell me the punishment for cheating was six of the best.

They were administered with a wide wooden stick like a butter bat, and when I duly bent over the leather arm of the chair I knew what was coming. Morale demanded that you should take it like a man – and Father Wiseman was kind enough to let miscreants exit by another door, so they didn't have to run a mocking gauntlet with tears in their eyes. I never made the same mistake again.

I found myself in the school orchestra among the first violins. Unlike my exploratory fumblings on piano, I learnt from the start the correct things to do with my fingers on the strings, and could soon read at least single-note scores, and also know the sound of the four strings, E, A, D and G, which I can still hum correctly. Our music teacher, Mr Woods from Blackburn, shepherded us through items like the Minuet from Handel's *Berenice*, the Barcarole from Offenbach's *Tales of Hoffmann*, Elgar's 'Pomp and Circumstance' March No. 2 and the slower movements of Mozart's *Eine Kleine Nachtmusik*, whose breakneck final section we, perhaps wisely, never attempted. We performed at occasions like the annual prize-giving at Bolton's Victoria Hall, programmed among the prayers, speeches and solo items. Our musical contributions, I'm inclined to think, were better appreciated by those present than the hectoring tones of the Bishop of Salford, the very Irish Dr Henry Vincent Marshall, who seemed to like haranguing the faithful and running down the infidels. He'd be rather out of place today. Paradoxically, the chief benefit of such colleges as ours was to foster lively minds unwilling to bow and scrape to anyone – including the clergy (who are themselves, of course, rather different today).

I have a pretty good musical memory, and the Mozart work stuck in my head, with an amusing sequel. In the immediate post-war years, to make a bit of cash, I spent one summer with other undergraduates picking fruit in East Anglia. One fine day, standing up on a long ladder among the branches, I must have been absent-mindedly whistling the Mozart. Suddenly, from among the shaded leaves in a parallel row of trees, I was addressed by a German girl student standing on another ladder; she and compatriots were invited over by student bodies in reconciliation moves after the war. She asked in puzzled tones in heavily accented English, 'How comes it that you are knowing the "Little Night-Music" all the way through?' and I duly explained.

Rehearsals took place after normal school hours in the library of a lovely old country house called The Leas, bought by the

Salesian Fathers as an annexe. After we had sawn our way, with a few glitches, through the next classical work on our repertoire, Mr Woods would let us relax, take up his own violin, close his eyes and play for us his own favourite piece, the famous 'Meditation' from Massenet's *Thaïs*. To this day, when I hear the piece, I see a silver-haired old man, eyes closed, playing the poignant melody, as a setting sun streams through the windows, lighting up old oak-panelled walls.

It wasn't all classics. The quietly smiling and bespectacled Brother Anthony, who played cello in the school orchestra, astonished and impressed us all when he broke out one day into a very rhythmic pizzicato version of the swing number, 'I'm Beginning to See the Light'. So was I too. Jazz was not something we ever heard at home. There was the odd bit of dance music on the wireless, like *Henry Hall and his Orchestra*, but the big revelation for me came as we gathered round a wind-up gramophone at school camp and a classmate produced a 78 rpm black shellac record he'd brought from home. For the first time I heard the intoxicating rhythm of a black American pianist with the exotic name of Meade Lux Lewis playing his own 'Honky Tonk Train Blues'. I was hooked for life.

My musical career, such as it ever was, began when it was apparently discovered as a child that I had a good memory for a song and, presumably, quite a pleasant voice. I became familiar through the wireless with the light tenor voice and immaculate articulation of John McCormack. So at family gatherings, dominated by Irish folk, I'd be prevailed upon to sing old favourites like 'Father O'Flynn' ('You've a Wonderful Way wit' Yer!'). I yearned in vain to be taught the piano. Though I like to hear a violin well played, it was never my choice. I just seemed to get stuck with it. My favourite instrument has always been the piano, or keyboard, which I was sadly destined never to learn properly.

Music-making seems to have run through the English side of the family. My uncle Frank, whom I barely remember, had played the organ for services at St Marie's Church, and my father was quite a competent amateur pianist. He was never backward in coming forward on social occasions, when the genial side of his personality emerged, and he had quite a repertoire. He was much in demand at family get-togethers. When some lady vocalist among the visitors was prevailed upon to 'oblige', with a number such as 'Pale Hands I Loved', 'When Rooks Fly Homeward', or another old drawing-room ballad, my father would oblige too – as accompanist. He was not averse to performing solo either, and was much taken by the Viennese waltz form, in which he worked up quite an attractive swing. Johan Strauss's 'Blue Danube' was one of his favourites, and even as an old man he could work his way, partly from memory, through all its variations. It's good I recorded him doing it. His popular showpiece was a tune called 'The Fairy Wedding Waltz', full of upwards and downwards glissandi, which he was pleased to play on request with gnarled fingers well into later life. My son, as a young boy and never a musician, was dazzled by those dramatic runs and trills.

In those early days, my brother, as the eldest, was designated to learn the piano. The family upright, with its yellowing, chipped or badly indented keys, had seen better days. It resided in the dining room, so tiny that at mealtimes the table had to be pushed against the piano to make room for all of us to sit down. It was pulled back when my brother sat down at the keyboard for his regular lessons, conducted by the head of the household. Though he still enjoys playing, and is a better sight-reader than I, the path of learning was sometimes hard for Peter at that stage, as he strove to work out from a frayed music book such airs as 'Woodstock Town' (the tune of which I remember to this day). But he never seemed to get the hang of tunes in the key of G.

'F sharp!' my father would cry out in irritation, as Peter once again failed to negotiate correctly the closing bars of some tune or other in that key. 'F sharp! I told you!'

The imprecation was sometimes accompanied, perhaps appropriately in view of the note in question, by a sharp rap on the back of the head. Poor Peter! It was hard going. Meanwhile I lurked in the background, eager to have a go myself. But it was decided (and one never questioned such decisions) that with Peter working on piano, I should learn something different. As a result, when I started at grammar school and it was known there was an orchestra there, I suddenly found myself with a violin, bought in Bury Market Hall at a long defunct music stall. I seemed to be stuck with it for years – though not, happily, for life. To add insult to injury, when my sister Patricia began to grow up, my father decided to teach her, not me, the piano. I was the odd man out.

Incredibly enough, it was only decades later, in retirement in Wimbledon, that I finally got a proper piano teacher. I was lucky enough at the local public library to spot a card on the notice board with a phone number. This turned out to be that of a charming and extremely talented young American piano student at London's Royal Academy of Music. Simone Dinnerstein, being a practical American, was giving lessons to pay some of the bills. She wanted to know what I could play, and I found myself playing Gershwin's 'Embraceable You' – perhaps not the best choice at a first meeting with a young lady. Nevertheless she took me on, sorted out some of my left-hand problems, and got me reading music as well as extemporising. I was later delighted to be invited, along with her friends and parents, who flew in from New York, to her performance of Beethoven's *Emperor* concerto at London's Festival Hall. Simone now performs around the world, and recently topped the classical charts in the United States for a Bach recording. What wouldn't I have given for such a teacher when I was ten or twelve years old! Or even five, as she had been when she started. I heard the other day on Radio Three that the great film composer Erich Korngold wrote his first symphony at eleven, by which age the great Mozart was also well into his stride.

One of the benefits of attending a Catholic school (or a punishment, according to how you look at it) was learning Gregorian plainchant, which we all sang at services in the lovely old wood-panelled chapel. You were a bit thrown out at first when confronted with a four-line (as against five-line) stave, and all those strange square and diamond-shaped notes, quite different from the circular blobs with tails in the music we played in the school orchestra. But you got used to it, and I suppose it improved your sight-reading.

Those were great times for the movies. There were no fewer

than six full-size cinemas in Bury, not mentioning the old and now outmoded Star Picture House. To our delight, my mother took a part-time job at the box office of one of them, the Scala Cinema. This was doubly lucky for us. It meant we got in to see movies for free. And secondly it showed Warner Brothers' films, their top star the devilishly handsome Irish-Australian Errol Flynn, always the conquering hero in swashbuckling films like *The Sea Hawk* and *The Adventures of Robin Hood*. We loved, or hated, the supporting casts: bluff and hearty Alan Hale as one of Robin's trusty lieutenants, villains played by the rather sinister Claude Raines and the arrogant Basil Rathbone. There'd be hisses among the youngsters in the front rows when the latter appeared on screen, with his sneering lip. We all knew from the start he'd never win that sword fight with Errol Flynn up and down the wide winding staircase of Nottingham Castle. I must surely have been impressed too by the lushly romantic scores of a composer I'd never then heard of, Erich Korngold. But if Flynn was our hero, casual and self-assured, and a big hit with the girls, Humphrey Bogart was the God – tough, laconic of speech and quite unsentimental. Excellent casts there too, especially in the Dashiell Hammett and Raymond Chandler adaptations, notably the lisping, slightly creepy Peter Lorre and fat and fleshy Sydney Greenstreet in *The Maltese Falcon*.

Yes, at the end of the day, the man was Bogart – who, as we increasingly noted as we got older, always got beautiful women too, without apparently trying, like the dreamy Ingrid Bergman or sultry Lauren Bacall. My brother and I would walk home, dazed by Flynn's acrobatic exploits, up dreary Lord Street (factories all the way) and York Street (factories half the way). Or trying to look as tough as Bogart, hands in our raincoat pockets, ready to give a snappy reply to anyone foolish enough to cross our path. They didn't know there were guns in those pockets.

It was only in post-war years that I came to appreciate Bogey was more than a tough guy. He had that special mixture of hardness and vulnerability in films like *The African Queen*, and the crazy menace of his Captain Queeg in *The Caine Mutiny*. He's reported to have been asked once how he managed to portray

Queeg's paranoid personality. 'Simple,' said Bogie, 'everybody knows I'm nuts anyway.'

If I believed in ghosts, I'd surely see them now when I drive in summer along the leafy road to Worcester. Gangs of schoolboys, picking plums in the orchards beside the road, or bathing on warm evenings in the river Avon. We were a happy lot, as well we might be, having exchanged smoke-ridden Lancashire for this sunnier, fruit-laden vale. More like a Garden of Eden, it seemed, when we arrived on the train from Manchester, bikes stacked in the luggage vans. Our kitbags and suitcases had been brought down beforehand. After pedalling along the quiet country lane from Evesham station we'd find the tents already pitched in what looked almost like a country village. Bell tents for the boys, bigger tents for the masters and a large marquee for use as a dining room and recreation centre. We were there to help the war effort. The vale's fruit industry (today almost defunct, alas) needed help. I'm sure Father Wiseman had also decided a visit to the Midlands would broaden our horizons. Every morning we trooped off to Stokes's orchards on the hillside to pick plump Victorias and Yellow Eggs. We worked off ladders, propped precariously against the branches, throwing the fruit into large baskets, then clambered down and poured them into 72 lb crates. It was piecework and we didn't earn a fortune, but we were doing a job the men at war couldn't. Sometimes, boys being boys, we'd stick a small basket covered with leaves and branches under a tree and creep out from our tents at dead of night to reclaim it. Fifth row, second tree along. The following day we'd cycle to nearby Fladbury Station (now also just a memory) and post the package off to addresses in industrial Lancashire, for our mothers to make into pies. Even in wartime, the baskets always got there. I'm sure the farmers knew what was going on, but our schoolmasters didn't, otherwise there'd have been trouble.

For a change from stews cooked by two of the Brothers and ladled out from the communal dixies, we'd cycle into Evesham to eat at the 'British Restaurant', a wartime innovation, and maybe walk up to the Regal Cinema along the street to see one of those 'Road' films, with Bob Hope and Bing Crosby. The songs, I thought, were great and I realised even at that age that the lyrics were in another class. The cleverest line, we all agreed, was in *The Road To Morocco*: 'Like *Webster's Dictionary*, we're Morocco-bound.' We thought that fabulous. Hope and Crosby, of course, had become one of the most famous double acts in film history. And we were all very much impressed by the female star, the dubiously named Dorothy Lamour. None of us schoolboys knew the songs were by the aristocratic-sounding Jimmy van Heusen. (He'd changed his name too, from the rather dull Chester Babcock.) Many years later I'd learn to play some of his brilliant creations on piano. 'Here's That Rainy Day' is one of them.

'How old are you lads?' asked the landlord suspiciously at the Chequers Inn in the village of Fladbury, but he still sold us our first pint of cider. And the best thing at weekends was to cycle along the country lanes, quiet in wartime, to Worcestershire's ancient cathedral towns and see the reality of golden stone abbeys and castles we'd only read about in our architecture lessons. The Vale of Evesham seemed then little short of fairyland. Nothing ever lasts, though. On retirement half a century later, I happily left a flat in Wimbledon to come back and settle. The plum trade's virtually disappeared, and alas, no one seems to know why. Traditional English lassitude, perhaps. It would take a wiser man than me to say. And it's perhaps as well there are no summer camps any more in those riverside meadows. In what passes for summer nowadays, they've twice been deep underwater.

Schoolboys en masse, as everyone knows, are an ignorant bunch. I always remember that memorable actor, Francis L Sullivan, declaring in the film version of Dickens's *Great Expectations*, 'I've a long experience of boys – and you're a bad lot of fellows'. Dead right! Why, when a new and much-heralded music teacher asked us fifth-formers what we'd like him to play on piano, did I request Chopin's devilishly difficult 'Revolutionary Prelude', which I'd recently heard on the radio? The poor man did his best to oblige, but his performance wouldn't exactly have graced the Albert Hall. And how could we as sixth-formers have placed a mouse in the desk of a rather timid history master, to whom for some reason we'd taken a dislike? Youths home in like predators on any sign of weakness. I'd never be a teacher. With the same poor man, we went to ridiculous lengths with another elaborate trick, masterminded if I remember rightly by my cousin, Kevin.

Ten of us taking sixth-form history lessons customarily took our place in advance around a long table in the school library, symmetrically lined with rows of bookcases, with a window at either end. We decided it would be a good lark to shift all the books from one side to the other and move the teacher's desk to the other end. When he did a double take on coming through the door and asked why the room had been changed around, we miserable creatures looked theatrically puzzled and cried, 'It's always been like that, sir!'

He tore his hair out as he left the room, probably deciding conscription couldn't come too soon for any of us. Another teacher had to escort a gang of us by bus each Wednesday afternoon after school for swimming lessons at Bolton's miserably named and dankly smelling Moss Street Baths. As the Bury and Rochdale gang, who all used the same train, were not crazy about swimming, and much preferred to go for an ice cream at Tognarelli's before catching an early train home, we'd hide on the top deck as the rest of the class got off the bus, jubilant at not being spotted. In truth, the teacher doubtless knew exactly what was going on, and was only too glad to see the back of us. No wonder that after graduation I turned down with grateful thanks an invitation from Father Wiseman to teach English Literature at Thornleigh College.

Many of my friends left Thornleigh at sixteen. Some of us stayed on for two years, preparatory to the university entrance exams. Under Fr Wiseman's tutelage, one's education broadened, taking in more of music and literature, as well as some of the country's deeper social history, not just the usual parade of kings and queens, the exact sequence of whom I never could remember. The work I specially recall was *The History of the English Common People*, by socialist authors G D H Cole and Raymond Postgate. I still have it on the shelves. It dealt with themes still highly relevant today. In the 1945 post-war election, we'd all rooted for Labour. We didn't have a vote yet, but knew how we'd use it if we had. Nearly all of us from working-class backgrounds, we knew nobody wanted a return to the Hungry

Thirties. In retrospect, it seems curious that a man with the stature and intelligence of Winston Churchill, who'd won the nation's deep respect in so many other ways, seemed surprised when the Tories were thrown out.

Fr Wiseman, sensing some of us had a feel for language, had a small group of us work through a slim volume – paper-backed under wartime publishing restrictions – called *Interpretations*. This book demonstrated, in a series of extracts from prominent authors, how a scene or a story could be written up in a variety of styles, and asked us to do the same. (What better introduction to the life of a journalist?) And I was introduced through this erudite man to writers and composers I'd never heard of. Notably, 'Saki' (H H Munro), whose subtly menacing stories, however dated the social milieu they reflect, still delight. On the downside, such sophisticated writing only helped widen the growing divide between me and the folks at home. My mother would have been disconcerted, I imagine, by the eerie closing pages of Saki's brilliant 'The Music On The Hill'. And they'd both surely have been shocked if they'd ever actually read the novels of Evelyn Waugh and Graham Greene, both ostensibly good Catholic authors. I was also introduced to the works of Gluck, one of whose best known titles, 'Che farò?', from *Orfeo and Euridice*, were the first Italian words I ever heard…

…apart from 'Mussolini', of course. But neither strutting Italian dictators nor stiffly saluting Nazis with curious moustaches cut much ice with schoolboys far from the conflict, though the gas mask drills, air raids and glowing red skies at night over Manchester had shown us it was all for real. We – and perhaps the British population at large – never wanted to take the enemy seriously. Hitler was portrayed as a bad joke rather than a permanent menace. Accordingly, to the 'Colonel Bogey' tune made famous years later in *The Bridge on the River Kwai*, we schoolboys used to sing in groups as we marched along (when parents weren't about):

> 'Hitler
> Has only got – one – ball.
> Goering

Has two, but they – are – small.
Himmler
Has something similar,
But poor old Goebbels
Has no balls
At all!'

Much later of course, I would find, when covering war crimes trials in Germany, or when an art dealer in Tel Aviv rolled back his sleeve to show me the tattoo on his arm, that Hitler and his henchmen were not such a joke after all.

My parents were exemplary Catholics, though my Dad's father (never referred to) was actually Church of England. Being Catholic – or 'Cat-licks' as our Protestant playmates called us – was a complete departure from the family tradition. A search of old marriage and baptismal records shows that until the time my father came into the world, the Chadwicks of Bury had always been Anglicans or Nonconformists. Back in the late eighteenth century, the family were members of Bury's Unitarian Church; then for some reason in the Victorian era we switched to St Paul's. Then, I assume, my Catholic English grandmother must have insisted her children were brought up in that faith – as was usual in those days. There must have been marital trouble later. We'd always assumed our English grandfather was dead. He was never mentioned in our presence. Amazingly, I was in my fifties before Dad disclosed that long ago our grandfather had in fact, as he put it, 'gone off with this 'ere lady to Blackpool'. Where, presumably, they died. I'd always wondered why our pals seemed to have lots of grandparents, while we had none. The other two, of course, were by now in America.

My father, perhaps because of these earlier family ructions, remained throughout his life a staunch member of Catholic institutions such as the St Vincent de Paul charitable society and the Knights of St Columba. Into the latter's ranks he would vainly try to drag me. And it was not surprising that my brother and I suddenly found at the age of seven or eight that we were to become altar boys. One didn't query such things. One just did it.

We were duly kitted out with black cassocks and white lace-edged surplices, and before we knew it had become regular minor actors at the divine services. It meant being on the altar at St Joseph's for Sunday morning Mass and evening Benediction twice a week. First you had to learn the Latin responses to the priest (there was no English vernacular in those days). Some of the phrases I recall to this day (*Ad Deum qui laetificat juventutem meam* etc.). This unorthodox introduction to the Latin tongue, learned phonetically round the kitchen table with our father as teacher, would help us considerably later when we started studying Latin at grammar school. The responses were spoken by my father verbatim and with accuracy, though he didn't understand a word of Latin. His Latin accent was probably more 'correct' than his English.

Being an altar boy could be quite entertaining. I liked the music and the rituals. I liked the smell of the incense, sprinkled by the priest from a metal container called, and shaped like, a 'boat' for some reason, on to glowing charcoal in the thurifer, which was usually carried, lightly swung, by the head altar boy. The hymns, a few of them Catholic versions of the great nineteenth century Anglican hymn book, were attractive, and certainly better than the pop stuff masquerading as Catholic church music today – in England, that is to say. No self-respecting German congregation would wear it.

We altar boys would assemble for High Mass in the sacristy. There, on their first arrival, the latest recruits, in a strange initiation rite, were pushed by the older acolytes down under an iron grating into a dusty cellar and made to stay there for a few minutes – just so they knew who was boss. This was the head altar boy, a seventeen-year-old entrusted with a key to the sacristy safe where the altar wine was kept. If absent, he had to delegate responsibility, on which occasions the safe might be opened and we'd all have a guilty swig from the bottle.

After a while, you were allowed to do more at Mass than just kneel with your hands joined on the lower step of the altar. If you were the chief altar boy of the day, you used a small felt-topped hammer to hit a bell three times to mark the Consecration of the Host. On Easter Saturday morning, we'd be roused soon after dawn for the traditional rituals. A procession around the church, broken by prayers and hymns, sung vigorously if tunelessly by our parish priest, Father Weardon, climaxed with the ritual blessing of the baptismal font by the church porch. The pale light of early morning filtering through the stained glass windows into a chilly and almost empty church rather appealed to my sense of drama.

In the Lancashire of old, the 'Whitsun Walks' – church parades around the town centre – were a big event, in which we schoolboys grudgingly took part. We'd no choice. From times past, townspeople had gathered along the pavements each Whit Friday to watch the Protestant marchers pass by. Each church, and there were many then – Anglicans, Methodists, Primitive Methodists, Baptists, Unitarians, Congregationalists – had its own music, ranging from small concertina groups to fully fledged brass outfits. Crowds lining the pavements two or three deep had from time immemorial, it appeared, skimmed pennies on to the road towards the feet of any friends, workmates or relatives spotted among the marchers. Schoolboys scrambled to pick the coins up and get back in step, while older walkers pretended not to notice and ignored the charitably intended missiles.

On Whit Sunday afternoon, it was the Catholics' turn. My father, needless to say, was out there in white gloves as one of the 'marshals', keeping the troops in order, histrionically beckoning here, frowning at some laggard there. As small boys, we wore well-ironed white shirts and shiny shoes, and were told to keep our socks pulled up. After the morning walk, there'd be a field day. Farmers on the outskirts of town would rent a field out for an afternoon glut of sports, ice cream, meat pies and cakes, while a brass band played. As small boys, I guess my brother and I enjoyed it with the rest. As teenagers, we'd make any excuse to avoid the walk and the festivities. Times were changing. We were, I'm afraid, also becoming just a bit snobbish. 'Where are your two lads this afternoon?' our father would be asked – or so he said. 'Off in t' countryside somewhere,' he'd reply – and, I imagine, rather sullenly. He was clearly disappointed in us.

There was a growing resistance to parental authority and church affairs. No sooner had we escaped successively the ritual

Sunday morning tour of Irish relatives, then five years as altar boys, than we were dragooned into service at St Joseph's as 'Outdoor Collectors'. After the eleven o'clock mass on Sundays these would tour different areas of the parish, knocking on doors, ringing at doorbells, in search of a weekly contribution to church funds. Peter and I were inevitably conscripted for the exercise. At least we could use our bikes, and we split our 'round' into two sections.

You certainly got to meet a variety of people. Kindly and rosy-cheeked old ladies who always had the money ready. Grumbling husbands, still in their vests and clearly unwilling contributors to this extra poll tax, over and above whatever they'd put in the collecting plate at Mass (if they'd been there, which some of them obviously hadn't; I suppose that's why the priests dreamed up the 'Outdoor' lark). In older Catholic homes, you didn't do badly. It was more problematical when you turned your bike into the council estate of red-brick semis, where if they did open up (and there were times you knew they were there, but didn't), the response would be grudging. 'Just wait a minute while I find something in my purse,' they'd say week after week, as if surprised to see you on the doorstep. Usually it was just a copper or two. I didn't blame them. We'd write it all up in our little books and hand over the takings at the Sunday evening Benediction. As we moved up through the school grades, we pleaded more homework demands and eventually managed to escape from the exercise.

The scene: a long, barely furnished and uncarpeted room above the Cooperative Society Stores in Bell Lane, Bury. In earlier days, when there was less money and less education about, it had been one of the Co-op's Reading Rooms. That was in the heyday of the movement, founded a few miles away in Rochdale.

Brother Sentinel, addressing me from the half-open entrance door of the room: 'Honoured Chief, a brother seeks admission.'

Me (Chief Squire), from the top of a conference table: 'Test and admit, Brother Sentinel.'

Honest, that's how it was. That was me giving the orders. It was a meeting of the Squires of St Columba (Bury branch, sorry,

Council). At sixteen, I was the Chief Squire (my brother had earlier held the post), and such were the arcane procedures, complete with secret passwords, that characterised our regular meetings. The Squires were the junior wing of the Knights of that ilk, and my brother and I had somehow become members. It ran in the family. Dad, most years, seemed to be the Grand Knight, past Grand Knight, or about-to-be Grand Knight again. He was also a leading member of the Society of St Vincent de Paul, which took him out of the house in the evening on many worthy charitable missions. He liked organisations, preferably when he was in the driving seat, and had a talent for writing it all up in his neat, immaculate script. I think my mother just wished he'd spent more time at home.

The Knights seemed to have happily adapted the secretive procedures of lay organisations like the Masons. They did much good work. It was just the mumbo-jumbo I didn't like. We Squires were supposed to be Knights in the making. We also used the room for social evenings, when a mixed lot of sixteen- and seventeen-year-olds danced to 78 rpm black shellac records, mainly Victor Sylvester strict-tempo stuff. The only one I remember was Spike Jones and his City Slickers playing 'Cocktails For Two'. The tune started off as a straight dance-band number, but after Spike Jones and his boys had got their irreverent hands on it, with all the whistles, motor horns, falsetto singing and other adornments, it would never be the same again. Other than that, it was quickstep, slow foxtrot, waltz. Everyone observed the necessary decorum.

As Chief Squire, I got dragged into other things. In the post-war years, Bury not only had a Town Council but a Youth Council, and somehow I was elected Catholic representative. We earnestly debated matters of the day and sent delegates to attend weekend conferences at which even larger social and political issues were discussed. I can't remember exactly what, but they must have been important, I guess. I chiefly remember that my fellow representative from Bury was an attractive dark-haired girl, whom I'd like to have known better.

What busy bees we all were after the war. And how did I keep getting involved in these things?

Mother had always made most of the running at home. Soft-spoken and reserved, unlike her more ebullient Irish sisters in Bolton, she'd never been loath to administer punishment (when thought appropriate, with an old walking stick). My brother and I had lined up and dutifully held out our right hand in turn when caught on the kitchen roof, climbing up a drainpipe to get in through the bathroom window, or similar transgressions. And it was she who, towards the end of the war, when property was going for a song, saw that now was the time to make a move. She'd spotted a large house in an attractive location opposite a pleasant park in much better-sounding Walmersley Road, and it was she who handled all the hassle with bank and solicitors and the rest.

The physical logistics of moving were left to our father to organise. My brother and I were enlisted to transfer a flat-topped handcart loaded with household goods and smaller furniture to the new house. Though we were blazered fifth-formers by this time, at a school considered definitely upmarket, and at the same time derided by some of our old mates at St Joseph's, we'd no option but to assist. It wasn't the 'moonlight flit' beloved of Lancashire comics. Our historic move was quite above board, but it might, on reflection, have been better accomplished after sundown.

In the full glare of a fine summer evening, my brother and I, pushing the shafts of the cart, negotiated a crafty route along the mile-long stretch from one house to the other, using the maximum of backstreets, of which there were mercifully plenty in old Lancashire towns. There was just one main road to cross, one of the town arteries. We braced ourselves to face the music as we trundled the cart, with its noisy iron-shod wheels, across the tram tracks, fearful that one or other of our schoolmates, walking, cycling or riding a tramcar, might spot us and jeer. Mercifully, no one did – not that they ever told us, anyway. We hadn't, needless to say, been wearing those blazers.

The two-up and two-down days were over. We were now installed in a fine house of three floors facing a large park, with a capacious cellar for ghostly pranks, and empty attics where yesteryear's servants used to live and sleep. My brother and I used the larger of these empty upper rooms for practising our cricket strokes with an old tennis ball, until dissuaded. The old Victorian-style kitchen had a big iron firegrate and oven and an old-fashioned clothes hanger which you pulled up with a rope to put the washing on. There was a row of bells on the wall, which would have jangled in former days to say who in the sitting room or one of the bedrooms desired attention from the servants. Our new next-door neighbours were an ex-army solicitor on one side, and on the other a senior schoolmaster who'd somehow survived the wartime Arctic convoys to Murmansk. They all welcomed us warmly. Like many immigrants before and since, I suppose, my mother knew what was needed. My father would have gone on living at 12 Wash Lane till the bulldozer arrived.

Chapter 3
I MEET BEOWULF AND SIR GAWAIN AND TAKE A DISLIKE TO FRANK LEAVIS

It took an intervention in Parliament to get me to university. Father Wiseman thought I was Oxford material and had me take an exam for St Antony's College. The test papers didn't throw me too much, but I can't say I was hanging on the result. Anyway, I didn't make it, and I can't imagine anyone without connections did so in those days. I wasn't really bothered. Universities have never held any great mystique for me.

So instead of Oxford it would be Oxford Road, Manchester, the local seat of learning.

Then the trouble started. Bury Education Authority suddenly reneged on the scholarship it had already awarded, because seven years earlier my parents – understandably wanting me to have a Catholic education – declined to send me to the local high school. And without help, they couldn't afford to finance me for three years at university.

The stalemate was broken by Father Wiseman. He first complained to the Education Minister, Labour MP Miss Ellen Wilkinson, who declined to intervene, then lobbied Bury's Conservative Member, Mr Walter Fletcher, who was happy to.

The powers that be backed down. My father received a rather curt note from Bury's Director of Education, asking him to call round at the office. So my thanks go to the late Father Wiseman and Walter Fletcher, Bury's Jewish MP. But it's strange to think that a working-class boy's future had to be referred to Parliament. I later discovered that the university's textile merchant founder, John Owen, had made the proviso that it should be run on non-sectarian lines. So much for the new Labour world.

Father Wiseman had been a major factor in my education. A learned and urbane man, his Catholicism was an integral part of his life. After his big contribution to Catholic education in East Lancashire, he left for Africa, where he was equally active in a missionary role. The last I heard of him was a letter to my brother from a remote outpost fifty miles from Pietermaritzburg. He wrote:

> In Natal Province, we don't see anything of the civil unrest you hear about on the BBC news – but I think a lot goes unreported. There is a very light control of the media.

In the spring of 1988, when he'd just celebrated his eighty-third birthday, the old, rather languid charm emanates from his prose. ('I garden no longer – I pay someone to do what's necessary.') But he was still saying daily Mass at seven thirty, he reported, adding, 'I don't know what they will do when God calls me.' Which would be no more than a few years later.

So there'd be no dreaming spires. Manchester had taken a pounding from the Luftwaffe. Those buildings that hadn't been blown up, or knocked down in the post-war clean-up, mainly bore the soot-blackened look that followed decades of industrialisation. Coming from another such grey and grimy town, that didn't bother me. It was reward enough to be spending three years reading language and literature. Better than working in an office, or the mills.

But it would be inaccurate to say university was a momentous time for me. To start with, I wasn't around campus very much. I wasn't living in nearby digs, like most of the year's intake. My parents couldn't afford it. So I travelled each day by no fewer than three buses to reach the hallowed halls of Owens College, as the university was still affectionately dubbed, after its founder. Not much different from going to school. I was seldom there in the evening to sink a pint or two with friends, and though there were lots of pretty girls at lectures, I was hardly ever around to make any overtures, successful or otherwise.

I was also highly immature, yet some of these often conceited eighteen-year-olds were not much to my taste. The annual Rag Day, when undergraduates cavorted around the streets of Manchester, ostensibly on fund-raising missions, carried for me uncomfortable undertones of ancient student privilege. I sternly regarded those who took part in such capers as what would now be called 'wankers' and absented myself. I confess I may have got it all wrong. But being at that time of a rather serious bent, perhaps because of tensions at home (and how it all changed when I started working for a living!), I found myself much more at ease with the ex-servicemen now arriving at the universities with post-war education grants and a considerably greater knowledge of the wide, wide world.

Apart from a few ex-Thornleigh mates who were now reading history and architecture (alas, one of them, my close friend Tony Hampson, a great footballer, died tragically at the age of nineteen), I really only remember the names of one group. All, like myself, reading English Language and Literature; they were young men in their twenties (one an ancient twenty-nine, for goodness' sake!) like Wilf Kimber, Johnny Molloy, Rushton and Green. The surnames still trip off the tongue, the first names not always, I'm afraid. The accepted leader of this group, who often congregated in the cafeteria between lectures and allowed me into the magic circle, was a young ex-Navy man called Frank Kennedy, who would enjoy a formidable career as colonial officer, diplomat and Chancellor of the University of Central Lancashire, later to be knighted. They were a most congenial group, had a lot of humour, were not politically fanatic and seemed to know quite a lot about music. All except poor Green, castigated by Kimber on one occasion when challenged to define the mood of the first movement of Mozart's G minor symphony. 'Joyful, I should say,' said Green.

'Rubbish!' retorted the man from Barrow, pointing out the note of anguish in the music, and of course he was right. Why does one remember such trivia?

Members of this group also played in the English Department soccer team, for which, though much the youngest (and who else wanted the job?), I found myself honorary unpaid fixtures secretary. We usually finalised the line-up during Anglo-Saxon lectures.

In the first flush of it all, I'd joined the Socialist Society ('SocSoc', as it was cosily nicknamed). Well, I'd welcomed the election of a Labour Government after the war as warmly as anybody – the Conservatives had precious little going for them, when one looked back at pre-war days in Lancashire – but enthusiasm rapidly waned as I realised university politics was all about slogans, hot air and empty resolutions. Which broadly remains my view of politics to this day, although – or perhaps because – I spent a lot of time with Reuters covering the political scene.

It did teach you one thing, though: how to pack a meeting to get what you want. This was a technique we members of the English Society soccer team usefully employed when we needed a full set of football kit. We all turned up at a meeting of the Society and railroaded through a resolution empowering the expenditure of Society funds on a set of shirts. I was happy to rush off on the bus to a sports shop in central Manchester to buy them before there were any second thoughts about this procedure. Shameful, really. As far as I remember, the shirts were in Blackburn Rovers colours. Our performances on the pitch at nearby Platt Fields were mixed, I have to add.

Luckily, university days coincided with a golden period of cricket at the county ground, Old Trafford, not far down the road. The war had taken its toll of sportsmen, but now emerged the sparkling opening partnership of Cyril Washbrook, later rewarded with a massive benefit collection, and the stalwart Winston Place, who both scored more than 2,500 runs in 1947. Taking time off from lectures, I saw some great performances from the two men, regarded as the finest opening pair in the country, and witnessed the emergence of a young fast bowler called Brian Statham, who'd become an England regular, and the impressive slow bowling stars Malcolm Hilton and Roy Tattersall. And I haven't even mentioned batsmen like Jack Ikin and Australian Ken Grieves.

My interest in languages had got off to a good start at Thornleigh. Now, as well as plunging into Old, Middle and Modern English language and literature, I'd embarked on two years of French language and literature, a further year of Latin and a short course of Italian. All this would come in useful decades later when I was one of the Reuter team covering General Assembly sessions of the United Nations in New York and had to plough through dozens of printed texts of speeches that we didn't have the manpower to cover directly. Experience told us to ignore the first two or three pages of Latin rhetoric. The lead of the story was usually in the third or fourth paragraph from the end.

The other day I unearthed a sheaf of yellowing exam papers and notes which had been gathering dust for years on the top shelf of a wardrobe. I was reminded of what I'd taken on at eighteen. We were obviously expected to come up with the goods at the end of the first year, when exam tasks included doing unseen translations from Cicero and selected odes of Horace, and our thoughts on such subjects as 'the economic significance of the expulsion of the Jews in 1291'. If I had any valuable thoughts about that at the time, I've quite forgotten them now.

Looking through bundled up old lecture notes, some in pencil, some in copperplate writing in ink, and still tied together with the original string, I see I was also expected to know about ridge-and-furrow farming in mediaeval England. I'd quite forgotten ever knowing anything about it when I came to live here in Worcestershire half a century on. Almost eerily evoking my student past, such ridges and furrows are still there to be seen in the old manorial field next to my Evesham home, which itself adjoins a thirteenth-century tithe barn. I tramp across those long grassed-over ridges on my regular afternoon walk.

Anglo-Saxon, or Old English, isn't much practical use to anybody, of course – but to hell with practicality! I'd always been, and remain, fascinated by the northern countries of Europe, home territory of the mythical Beowulf. It's a fascination that many in our own age apparently share, Old English scholars or not. At least, they flock to cinema versions of Beowulf the Great's epic struggle to the death, in a world inhabited by elves and trolls, with the monster Grendel, himself a descendant of Cain the murderer. Beowulf ends twelve years of Grendel's pillaging by lopping his head off. Quite grisly stuff!

Long before writing *The Lord of the Rings*, the great J R R Tolkien (a grand-nephew of whom runs a garden centre just down the road here) called *Beowulf* the most successful Old English poem. It was, he said, 'written in a language that after many centuries still has essential kinship with our own northern world'. Which may have helped, at least psychologically, when I had to learn Danish (and later Swedish) in Reuter assignments to northern Europe. The stamping ground of the heroic Beowulf and the Jutes and Geats of that time was what we now call Denmark and Southern Sweden.

Anglo-Saxon verse doesn't exactly trip off the tongue. As in Latin, gender, tenses and much else besides are indicated by word endings, rather than the easier ways we have of doing that sort of thing these days. Middle English was slightly more comfortable going. For most of us the story of Sir Gawain and the Green Knight remains the best remembered for its colourful vignettes: the mysterious Green Knight, galloping out of King Arthur's Christmas court, his own lopped-off head incongruously gripped in his hand; Sir Gawain's bleak winter journey to the castle in North Wales; his attempted seduction by the lady of the castle – this was definitely a brisker and sexier read! It was nice to know too that its anonymous fourteenth-century author, contemporary with Chaucer, likely hailed from the northern counties – maybe Lancashire – where most of us students came from. Southerners of the time, we learned with satisfaction, would have found the poem almost unintelligible. Nice to know that the exploits both of Beowulf and Sir Gawain are being filmed these days for a new generation.

I would have another stab at Old and Middle English years later, when my turn came at Reuters, where I was then languishing back at head office, for sabbatical leave. Most colleagues taking these breaks understandably went off and lazed in the sun somewhere for a couple of months, and few believed what I said I'd been doing. By that time, seven years covering the Middle East was enough sun for me. But I was relieved to find that for my chosen subject there are now excellent translations and language aids that just hadn't been written half a century ago. Back in the fifties we had to graft.

Politics seems to get into anything, even poetry. The big name being bandied about in scholastic circles in those immediate post-war years, I found, as a wet behind the ears scholarship boy, was Frank Leavis. I was never an admirer, I'm afraid, finding his approach to literary criticism tiresomely mechanistic. It's heartening to know that these days there are many of the same mind. At the time I entered Manchester University in 1947, the founder of the 'Cambridge School' of literary criticism was about halfway through his contentious career, busily promoting the concept of literature as some sort of religion, and literary criticism as a kind of moral vocation.

The very name of the magazine he edited, *Scrutiny*, seemed sternly to suggest that literature was not something to be taken lightly, and this I found slightly ridiculous. The man from Downing College preached a somewhat sombre set of values, had little time for levity. His favourite Dickens novel was *Hard Times*, that bleak little tale from nineteenth-century industrial Lancashire, shorn of the colour, melodrama and joy which makes most of Dickens's novels so appealing to many. Certain lecturers in Manchester's English school appeared to be fully paid-up members of the Leavis movement, preaching *The Great Tradition*, his seminal work, as if it were some sort of Bible. The Cambridge coterie seemed to regard the real world about us, with what Leavis called its 'technocratic drift', as a regrettable distraction from the Holy Grail of Literature with a capital 'L'. Why, I ask myself today, as with failed political movements like Nazism and communism, did it take so long for the bubble to burst? For an eighteen-year-old from England's industrial North, the Leavis movement seemed rather absurd.

Eventually, university days were over. I'd handed in my seventy-page thesis, proudly entitled 'An Examination of the Literary Theory and Criticism of Matthew Arnold'. Three days before my twenty-first birthday, I attended the degree ceremony at the imposing Victorian Whitworth Hall in cap and gown. I was now a BA (Hons). Only six of the fifty-four in my year were awarded Firsts; my soccer colleagues Kennedy, Kimber and Rushton got Top Seconds like myself. I didn't feel too bad about it. Firsts were for swots, one said unkindly.

I was still only twenty, so what to do next? Many of them went straight into teaching, which didn't appeal, though my old headmaster Father Wiseman offered me a job as a junior master. Although I'd have been returning to Thornleigh in quite another role, I thought I'd be taking a step sideways – and anyway I was uncertain if I could deal with sixth-formers not much younger than myself. The University Appointments Board was publicising all sorts of jobs for graduates. I looked at the documentation, and these seemed mainly to be junior managerial training posts at undoubtedly fine firms like Pilkington Glass. But it just wasn't for me. I wanted to do something with words. There didn't seem to be much available in publishing. Meanwhile, I had a stab towards a Master's degree, supporting myself as best I could while reading and writing notes on my chosen subject, 'Satire in the English Novel'.

To earn some cash, I did Christmas relief work at the local post office, where I might have got the sack after somehow mistaking one of two very similar-looking streets for another, and putting scores of Christmas cards through the wrong letter boxes. I realised the error when an irate householder pursued me down the street, but I made good my escape. Then I got myself a temporary clerking job at the local National Insurance office and was turned off such places for life. We spent the days shuffling papers around in shabby, almost Dickensian, office surroundings in a street long since built over as a supermarket. A couple of months of this were all I could take. I abandoned the MA project and decided it was about time to spare my parents any more expense. I walked into a phone box, rang the office of the *Bury Times* and asked to speak to the Editor.

My name had already been seen a few times in the *BT* – on the letters page. In a national debate about church school funding, the same sort of Labourites who would have denied me my scholarship money still couldn't understand why Catholics wanted their own schools. Since I (or rather Father Wiseman) had won that particular battle, and I seemed to have some talent for putting words together, I found myself deputed to put the Catholic case, which I tried to do with all the moral certainty of a twenty-year-old. I said that hard-up England should be spending its money on good teachers, not swimming pools and modern gymnasia, which seems fairly obvious. And I entered the fray in a rather futile philosophical dispute about logicality (the French) as against practicality (the Brits). I apparently favoured the latter.

Looking back at it in these days of national decline, I'm not so sure the French haven't done better. Their high-speed trains have already been running for a quarter-century, while ours still limp along at half speed, between leaves on the line and broken points. I find myself rereading almost with disbelief, in an old copy of the *Bury Times*, another rather pompous letter of mine lauding Britain's unwritten constitution as against other political systems. But then, university students always know all the answers, don't they? Well, now that I was applying for a job on the *Bury Times*, I could at least say I'd already appeared in print.

Chapter 4
CRIME AND CRICKET, MUSIC AND DRAMA –
IT'S A HEADY MIXTURE

Climbing a flight of twisting wooden stairs from the lobby of the *Bury Times* – now buried under a vast shopping centre – I heard the clatter of typewriters and smelled for the first time the aroma of newsprint. I knew this was the place for me. In the upper corridor, a young man in a smart belted raincoat and leather gloves hurried past, on the way, I could only assume, to some exciting story. Editor Wilf Ainscow sat me down in his office, peered quizzically through owlish glasses, long familiar to all who followed the fortunes of Bury Football Club, which he reported as 'Ranger', and asked why I wanted to be a reporter. I was, it seemed, the first university graduate to apply.

I told him about my thesis on Matthew Arnold, the nineteenth-century poet, at which his eyes glazed over. Otherwise I must have said the right things, for he offered me a six-month trial at three guineas a week. The *BT*'s Ramsbottom reporter was leaving shortly to join the *Bolton Evening News*, and I could take over his job. We'd see how things went. Meanwhile, I was told to learn Pitman's shorthand, get myself a typewriter and learn how to use it. The small black-lacquered 'Empire Aristocrat' was the first typewriter I ever had. To this day I still use Pitman's – less than accurately – to write down phone messages. And I'm still a less than ten-fingered typist.

Arriving for duty the next Monday morning at the ripe old age of twenty-one – most of my new colleagues had started work at seventeen or eighteen – I walked into a long narrow room lit by a row of windows stretching all along one side. Individual desks were set about the room and various reporters were clattering out copy on noisy typewriters. Their stories were then passed through a sort of hatch to the paper's sole subeditor, Ruby Greely – who, I was to learn, never missed a mistake of fact, grammar, spelling, possible libel or good taste.

At one end of the room a young man lay stretched on his back across a large table, hands clasped behind his head, holding forth on the joys and perils of hard-nose reporting. This was apparently a familiar occurrence and was the chosen posture of a regular visitor, Joe Horrocks, scion of a long line of Horrickses from the moorland village of Hawkshaw. Until recently the *Bury Times* News Editor, he'd joined the *Daily Express* in Manchester, to the great admiration of those left behind in Cross Street, whom he regularly regaled with reports from the front. Joe believed news could be bright as well as truthful, and he wasn't far wrong. He also believed, like our subeditor, in attractive presentation and punchy headlines, and, to his credit, Editor Wilf Ainscow welcomed new ideas.

In years long past, *Bury Times* front pages – like those of most local papers in England, where dullness tended to be equated with honesty and respectability – had been virtually unbroken grey columns of small print, with little to attract the eye. It was one of the first weeklies to brighten up the product. Happily, in the decades since I worked for the *BT*, even 'quality' national dailies like *The Times*, *Guardian* and *Telegraph* have accepted the need for punchier visual packaging. Overseas for Reuters, I always aimed at graphic reporting. I groan when I see the bleak front pages of papers like Germany's *Frankfurter Allgemeine*. Not my meat, exactly. But that's another story.

You couldn't call yourself a reporter until you'd done Police, Fire and Ambulance. Since the fire station was on my route to the office, I volunteered to take care of the morning calls, otherwise done by phone. The brigade was run with a certain panache by Chief Fire Officer John Heap, as colourful a character as any of those New York firefighters, and a man of standing in the community. Mostly the logbook contained nothing much more than a house chimney fire, 'dog rescued from drain' or 'cat from roof' (though some of the latter incidents demanded agility and not a little courage to resolve). Everyone knew John Heap and his team, and it was not just schoolboys who stood and stared when the gleaming red engines, bells clanging, firemen standing beside the ladders running along the sides, sped out from the station.

I confess I too rather enjoyed this sort of scene, and found something exciting in a big factory blaze (which seemed to happen with some frequency in those days, maybe with insurance claims in mind), stepping around the coiled hoses and water puddles on blocked-off streets, smoke and flames belching from the windows of a cotton mill or warehouse. A far worse scene came about one Saturday evening when a wooden bridge across the line at Bury Railway Station, crammed with football supporters, suddenly collapsed, throwing scores of people down on to the tracks. It was all hands on deck, and I'm sure that helping to cover actualities like these helped years later when I was reporting scenes of injury and devastation in the Middle East. At least you knew how to start.

A year or two earlier, I'd been immersed in two extinct languages, Early and Middle English, and the doings of the legendary Beowulf and the monster Grendel, the brave Sir Gawain and the mysterious Green Knight. Those vanished ages seemed a long way off in the bleak post-war climate of industrial Lancashire. The challenge now was to report how ordinary twentieth-century folk were taking on their particular dragons. In my new bread-and-butter world, police stations provided regular items for the bi-weekly paper, whose Wednesday edition was often hard to fill. The desk sergeant read you out the routine items and, if you were lucky, put you on to something more interesting. Then there were the twice-weekly courts, when local magistrates meted out fines for lesser offences and sent graver misdemeanours on to the Assizes. From time to time, you were happy to join an identity parade, for which the police investigating bag-snatchers or the like often had to scout around the neighbourhood for volunteers. You received a useful five-shilling fee – 'And don't worry if the old lady picks you out, we won't be charging you with assault!'

As well as writing up real crime, I contributed a first fictional story, 'Nathaniel's Father Christmas', whose two main characters were a sly old petty criminal and a pompous magistrate, both obviously drawn from experiences in court. And I bought my first car at Bury Police Station, a black Wolseley 10 saloon, previous owner Chief Detective Inspector T E Musgrave. HG 5564: I remember the number plate, fifty years on, whereas I've forgotten many since.

To supplement our income from the *Bury Times*, we reporters, with the consent of management, also operated a freelance operation, the Bury Press Agency, supplying snappier bits of local news to the morning papers, regionally based in Manchester. We'd take it in turns to make the nightly late night round of calls to the dailies, reading out condensed versions of local stories to highly bored copy takers. ('Is there much more of this?' one man would frequently groan.) I remember phone numbers like Blackfriars 1234 (Kemsley Newspapers), Blackfriars 2345 (*Manchester Guardian*), Blackfriars 8600 (*Daily Mail*). Target papers also included the *Express*, *News Chronicle* and *Daily Herald*. The two last sadly long defunct, the *Herald* a pillar for years of the Labour/trade union movement, the *News Chronicle* a vehicle for good news-feature writing, one of whose specialists, George Vine, would become a colleague of mine years later in Germany.

On a Monday morning soon after, I took a bus from Bury's Kay Gardens, named after John Kay, the inventor of the flying shuttle, sitting alongside the young man in the raincoat. He was called Norman Pickles and sounded very professional. The gloves somewhat detracted from the Bogart image. It wasn't a fashion I adopted.

Ramsbottom, now apparently an upmarket retreat for media stars from Manchester and the like, was then still a place of mills and chimneys, with an unfortunate name. At that time, some vulgar local fellows were still calling it 'Tup's Arse' – a name which may derive from a Middle English word for ram. More respectful historians say that originally the name probably meant 'the valley of wild garlic'. The town itself is overlooked by the rounded slopes of Holcombe Hill, on the western shoulder of which stands the 200-year-old Peel Tower, a monument to Robert Peel, the early nineteenth-century parliamentarian, prime minister and one of Bury's proudest sons. Never mind the accusations by some biographers that he was cold and priggish. The man who repealed the protectionist Corn Laws, opening the way to Victorian free trade, is rightly honoured with a statue in

Bury town centre, the focal point for many a church parade or Armistice Day gathering. And as a reporter I would trudge with the rest up the hill to the commemorative two-century-old Peel Tower for the traditional Good Friday service.

Apart from the town of Ramsbottom, my first reporting beat also included the rather more pleasantly named villages of Holcombe Brook, Summerseat, Shuttleworth and Edenfield – to name a few – spread over several miles of undulating countryside. A stone cottage beside the road from Bury to Ramsbottom had been the home of John Kay, one of those many northern inventors, engineers and entrepreneurs who created much of the wealth that would later allow the descendants of nineteenth-century mill owners to live cosseted lives further south. With few buses operating on useful routes, I mainly walked, which could be a bleak business when winter winds swept down from the moors. It didn't do my health any harm, though. I don't remember anybody being seriously overweight in those days. Obesity would be a doubtful benefit of the greater prosperity to come. Then, people in the middle and working classes (as they still seem unfortunately to be categorised) ate what they needed, when they needed it.

Norman Pickles took me round the contacts, beginning with the usual Police, Fire and Ambulance stations, and I soon began to pick up the routine. Up a typically steep street of stone houses near Ramsbottom town centre was to be found the *BT*'s local office. Not our office at all, really, but the headquarters of the local Weavers', Winders' and Warpers' Association (whose separate and distinct roles in the production of cotton goods I am ashamed, as a life member of the National Union of Journalists, never to have completely understood). The union's general secretary was Councillor Gilbert Holt, ex-Mayor, elder of Shuttleworth Baptist Church, chairman of the constituency Labour Party and a genial, almost Pickwickian presence in town. Very much what would now be called Old Labour, and, like many Labour Party members of that period, considerably more down to earth than many of them today. But British through and through.

I remember the day I arrived at the office on the morning of 6 February 1952. Gilbert's first words as I walked through the doors were, 'Eh, John, the King is dead.' There was genuine sadness and affection in his voice. He had no class hang-ups and I don't think he had any enemies. He gladly let *BT* reporters use his desk and phone. He knew everybody in town and was a priceless source of news. In the general parliamentary election which followed shortly afterwards, he also provided local credibility to one of Labour's new-style post-war parliamentarians. A handsome ex-RAF officer and son of a former Labour Party minister, Tony Greenwood, with his Oxford background and an upmarket accent so markedly different from most of his constituents, mirrored changes in the party after World War Two. Somehow (not Tony's fault), I preferred the earlier generation.

An old diary shows that in the first twelve months of working Ramsbottom I reported fires, mill closures, town council meetings, church events, off-road motorbike racing and the death of a young man in a mine accident. And holiday trips to Blackpool. I'd soon forgotten ever being shy. I'd talk to anyone, and still do, for which I'm sometimes rebuked.

In the then less than fashionable village of Summerseat, I discovered a few people were still living in cottages with earthen floors. In one such, I interviewed a man known in those less politically sensitive days as 'Blind Dan'. He'd, maybe rashly, disclosed to friends and neighbours that his sight was unexpectedly coming back and was more than ready to tell his story. But when it appeared in the *Bury Times*, I was not thanked. Sadly, by revealing the near miracle, he'd lost some social benefits. Some weeks later I was chatting to a regular contact who worked at the local National Insurance offices (reached at the top of forty-two stone steps). As it happened, Dan also had to attend there to collect his money. I was chatting with my contact at the counter when a burly figure appeared at the top of the stairs and with a face like thunder approached with heavy tread. I made good my escape, as they say, before he might be tempted to throw me down those forty-two stairs.

You often had to interview the bereaved. On one such occasion, I called at a two-up two-down terraced cottage, window blinds drawn as was the custom, and was let in by the widow. The good ladies were seldom uncooperative, rather flattered in fact that the sad event would 'go in t' paper'. I sat down in the gloom in the cramped front room and proceeded to interrogate her. Then, resting my left hand beside me, I felt it cold and drew it hastily away. Unwittingly, I'd sat on the bed where the deceased was laid out, it being an old custom to put the corpse in the front room for the neighbours to have a look. Our hands had icily touched.

You quickly learned the ropes and the pitfalls. My old scrapbook also records a minor furore over a plague of foxes. Lambs had been torn open and 150 head of poultry destroyed, a farmer's wife told me on the phone. The marauding animal, she said, was 'as big as an Alsatian'. All farmers were alerted and the local hunt called in to patrol the area. It was beginning to sound like something from *The Hound of the Baskervilles*. We printed the story anyway (even the eagle-eyed Ruby let it past). The farmer castigated his wife. Foxes, I was informed, don't grow as big as Alsatians. Now I knew. I never rang that farm again.

The *Bury Times* was an old and venerable institution. Its first front page on 7 July 1855, though dominated, as all newspapers were then, by adverts, also carried 'the latest intelligence' from home and abroad – some of which would probably have emanated from the recently founded Reuters news agency (the firm I would later join). The ads reveal a thriving town. After-school learning was available at the grandly named Athenaeum (membership ten shillings a year), which announced 'in consequence of the abolition of the newspaper stamp a more liberal supply of daily papers'. Adult education seemed to be thriving. A day class for ladies in French was advertised, and a young men's class in German. The local Freemasons announced a banquet, 'tickets six shillings, exclusive of wines and liquors'. There were classes in dressmaking, and a Miss Nuttall advertised her boarding and day school at nearby Ramsbottom. Foreign news included a report (received at 1 a.m. that day!) that a great fire had destroyed 2,000 houses in Constantinople. In the Crimea, England's Lord Raglan, a hero then, today a controversial figure blamed for the sufferings of British troops, had been laid to rest 'with all the pomp that circumstances permitted'. His name is better known locally today as a pub in the outlying village of Nangreaves.

At the time I joined the paper, it was a few years short of its centenary. My second employer, the *Bolton Evening News*, had been established by the Tillotson family in 1867. Today, after changes of ownership and format, the two papers are part of an American company owning no fewer than 300 of Britain's local newspapers. Is this good or bad? As with football clubs, airports and public utilities alike, it seems to be par for the course anyway in today's Britain.

My career choice didn't altogether please the folks at home, who thought scholastic success should have led to something 'more academic'. They said I should have taken that job offered me at my old school. When they saw I liked what I was doing – and they began to see my name in print (or even just the initials) – they stopped worrying.

The editorial staff were a great bunch. Frank Thomas, also a keen cricketer and hockey player, had taken over the News Editor role when Joe Horrocks left, later becoming Editor. He'd have made a great Reuterman. I was considerably impressed by one feature he'd written. He and a photographer climbed a steeplejack's ladder to the top of an old and very high mill chimney, awaiting demolition. This produced an excellent story and splendid panoramic views. But I was glad no one suggested an encore.

Next in seniority in the reporters' room was Chief Reporter Alan Greenhalgh, a likeable but strangely discontented chap, fond of ending his paragraphs with a pregnant row of dots, clearly intended to convey a deeper significance to what he wrote. Ever ready to buck authority, he would often cry, as we gathered for a Friday night pub crawl, 'Let's get the bloody van out!' And so we'd cram into the woefully (and perhaps fortunately) slow old two-stroke Austin, meant to be used solely for delivering bundles of newspapers, and head for pubs in outlying villages, rolling up every weekend until we got tired of the place and tried some-where else. For serious after-hours drinking, though, our favourite watering hole was Bury's old town centre Trevelyan

Club, where up a flight of steep stairs you could, if you were known and accepted by Harry behind the bar, drink to a late hour. There was also, importantly, a snooker table upstairs. Taxis home often had to be rung for.

There were Lancashire characters aplenty on the staff, and I think Wilf Ainscow was all in favour of it. As well as adeptness at snooker, Henry Rushton from Bacup was famous for his bar-style piano playing. 'Parting Of The Ways' was his favourite number. We'd get together at regular Union meetings, usually held in a pub's back room, the latest young recruit sent out afterwards to bring fish and chips for all. Except for Harold Knott from Radcliffe, who would usually opt for a meat-and-potato pie. 'I like summat grayssy [greasy],' he'd say. John Bradbury, a sometimes lugubrious colleague from Higher Blackley, was an expert both on grand opera (frequently breaking out into falsetto song) and racehorses, regularly reading *Sporting Life* and crossing the sea for the Irish bloodstock sales. When I later opened a Bury office for our friendly rival, the *Bolton Evening News* (they're now part of one firm), I took John on as my assistant. He sometimes disconcerted passers-by by arriving at our town centre office on horseback.

Some of these entertaining colleagues I would run into from time to time later during my Fleet Street days. Roy Heron from Northwich, an almost lethal fast bowler when we played Lancashire Fusiliers' teams at their splendid Wellington Barracks ground, joined the national news agency, the Press Association, housed in the same classic Lutyens building as Reuters. He's still writing in retirement, and tends to win seniors awards at his local golf club in Kent. Directly across Fleet Street at the *Daily Express*, Brian Hitchen, whose first *BT* job as a seventeen-year-old had been collecting church paragraphs in the village of Ainsworth, later made a big name for himself and a reputation as a hard-core right-winger among the red tops. Brian and I once worked in New York at the same time and had an enjoyable time riding around Manhattan streets in his shiny red Ford Mustang.

The late Barry Gill, a Bury High School boy, would become familiar on TV as a motor-racing commentator. I'd often see him at European Grands Prix I was covering for Reuters at places like

Monte Carlo or Hockenheim in Germany. My car-crazy young son would eternally thank Barry for introducing him behind the scenes at Sweden's Anderstorp to eminences like Graham Hill and Sweden's Ronnie Peterson. On the whole, Wilf Ainscow didn't have such a bad bunch.

After two years in Rammy, I returned to head office and was given the Music and Theatre column, much to my liking, though it meant a lot of evening work on top of the normal dayside diary. But by then I was used to irregular hours and the nine-to-five routine never suited me. Fortunately I've never had to do it.

With little TV to distract, the post-war years had seen an explosion of self-made entertainment. This was in addition to the local repertory theatre, the Hippodrome, where one of Coronation Street's up-and-coming actors, Peter Adamson, cut his teeth. In the mill towns, amateur dramatics and music-making were also big. The strains of Handel's *Messiah*, of course, had always rung out at Easter and Christmas time from churches and chapels both sides of the Pennines. Elgar and Stanford were also on the regular menu of amateur orchestras. The local Musical Circle trotted out Edward German's 'Merrie England' for Coronation Year, but that piece didn't survive long in the repertoire. Gilbert and Sullivan were beginning to look very old hat, and Edwardian musical comedies such as Lionel Monckton's *Our Miss Gibbs* and *The Quaker Girl* were giving way to bright and breezy musicals from across the Atlantic. A go-ahead music teacher at the Church Central School, Harry Spencer, bravely took on some new music and his pupils impressively performed Benjamin Britten's *Let's Make An Opera*.

Almost every church or civic society seemed to have a dramatic group. For a couple of years, many of my evenings were spent driving to outlying villages on cold and wet winter nights to sit through sometimes less than sparkling productions in draughty school halls. Terence Rattigan (*The Deep Blue Sea*) was frequently on the menu; so was Yorkshire's J B Priestley (*An Inspector Calls*), as well as old warhorses like Arnold Ridley's *Easy Money* and *The Ghost Train*, and R F Delderfield's *Worm's Eye View*. More ambitious groups took on Christopher Fry (*Ring Round The Moon*) and Oliver Goldsmith (*She Stoops to Conquer*). And I carried the news in my Saturday column of what, I said, 'looks to be a most intriguing thriller by Agatha Christie, *Murder On The Nile.*' I couldn't possibly have imagined that half a century later we're still seeing the film and TV versions. Christie's *Mousetrap* was still running the last time I checked in the West End.

The local Stage Society occasionally tried to up the stakes by trying out plays like Dennis Cannan's *Captain Carvallo*, but what most people wanted after a hard day at the office (or factory) was a good laugh, intended or otherwise. Notions like the suspension of disbelief hadn't got around all the villages yet. One youth, infuriated as a rather hammy actor playing news photographer Henry Ormonroyd in Priestley's popular comedy, *When We Are Married*, made heavy weather of searching around the stage for his lost camera, shouted from the front row, 'It's in t' corner, can't yer bloody see?'

My overall brief was not to be too cruelly critical – 'They're only amateurs after all' – and I largely accepted editorial policy. But I decided to go for broke when I wrote, not quite in as many words, that the local Operatic Society's leading lady in the musical *Hit The Deck*, who'd been more or less a fixture for years, was too old for the part. I'd also questioned their choice the previous year of the Maschwitz/Posford play *Goodnight Vienna*, which seemed to me to have only one good number – the title song. I took my gingerly worded column ('the Society should think twice about deciding to substitute experience for youth') with some trepidation into the editor's office. Local papers have to consider customer relations, and their editors are usually prominent people in town.

To his credit, the great Wilf Ainscow quickly scanned my piece, handed it back and said, 'Fine. Put it out.' When the review appeared in print that weekend, the not-so-young lady was understandably miffed. I was cold-shouldered in the pub that these very superior (as they believed) amateur actors – and we journalists – patronised. But the following year they cast a sixteen-year-old girl singer in the title role of Jerome Kern's *Sally*.

She was wildly applauded for songs like 'Look For The Silver Lining' and the show was a sell-out. 'JC' – as I signed off my pieces – was exonerated.

Cricket was big in Lancashire. As well as the Old Trafford games, the county boasted two excellent weekend leagues. Local elevens, mainly working-class people, were boosted by professionals from Commonwealth countries who brought a touch of glamour to the mill towns of Lancashire. Over the years there came a stream of cricketers from the West Indies, Australia, New Zealand, India, Ceylon and Pakistan. West Indian Learie Constantine had been among the first of those to exchange West Indies sunshine for the grey skies and damp streets of the textile towns.

I only realised years later that I'd witnessed a golden age. The three Ws, as they were called – good-humoured Everton Weekes, big and burly Clyde Walcott and the elegant Frank Worrell (all subsequently knighted), were at the top of their game. At nearby Bacup, I remember a scintillating series of boundary shots by Weekes. He delicately cut the first ball from the Ramsbottom fast bowler through the slips, who rearranged themselves. The next one he edged slightly further out, again eluding the slip fielders. Came the third ball, and he cut it even wider for another four. Poise and delicacy mixed with strength, and all with a sense of humour. He smiled almost guiltily as the last of the three consecutive shots hit the boards.

In Ramsbottom, I interviewed the newly arrived Gul Mohamed. No one seemed to know whether he represented India or Pakistan, though his name gave the game away. He already had a place in the history books with a record 577-run partnership in first-class cricket. This small but brilliant left-hander, also a useful bowler (you had to be when taking one of those professionals' jobs), arrived on a chill April day. I interviewed him in the front room of a stone-walled cottage in Bolton Road West, where he was boarding. He sat huddled in an armchair, feet drawn up beneath him, a blanket around his shoulders. Despite a roaring coal fire in the grate, he was clearly unimpressed by our foul weather. But, aided and abetted by local stalwarts like captain Ronnie Bowker, he played many a scintillating innings and took many wickets.

'Ramsbottom Put Big Burden On Mohamed', I see from my fifty-year-old scrapbook was the headline I put on one of his early games, and that would be the shape of things to come. The flamboyant left-hander was at his best when aggressive, but I wrote in a later report:

> Supporters are beginning to wonder when he will curb his impatience for boundaries until he has stayed at the wicket long enough to get settled in. Attempting these high slashing square cuts at such an early stage of the game is obviously risky.

But that was his way, and brilliant centuries by both him and Walcott one Saturday, I wrote, provided 'sparkling entertainment for a large crowd who will not see brighter cricket all season'. Well, that's what the pros were expected to do (not unlike English football's Premier League footballers today, actually!).

Down at the Ramsbottom ground near the railway station, I covered home games from a sort of fine leg position up in the box alongside a young scorer called Elliot Kershaw. As well as writing up the match at length for our midweek edition, I covered for five Saturday evening papers – the *Bolton Evening News*, Blackburn's old *Northern Daily Telegraph* (NDT), *Lancashire Evening Post*, *Manchester Evening News* (still thriving under the editorship, I gather, of Joe Horrocks's son, Paul!) and *Manchester Evening Chronicle* (defunct).

You had a timetable in front of you with a list of calls to each paper and needed your wits about you. Sometimes, looking down from the scorebox as you dictated an update, you'd see someone bowled out or hitting a six out of the ground and were able to report it 'live'. It was often the wicket or shot that provided a new headline. After the match, down by the railway station I could pick up the first edition of the *NDT* and read what I'd written. Evening papers came in several editions in those days. It was enjoyable work, and an invaluable exercise in quick thinking. So I knew what I was doing when, years later, I joined the Reuter team at the 1972 Olympic Games or covered a European Athletics Championship in Gothenburg single-handed. It's all part of the same game.

I never got to cover the other big game, football. None of us reporters did. Gigg Lane, where the 'Shakers' then played in a much higher league, was the unchallenged preserve of our Editor, Wilf Ainscow – or 'Ranger' as he was pseudonymously called.

(Why they bothered with such devices remains a mystery, for everyone in town knew who he was.) Wilf's other sporting passion was golf, which he also kept pretty much to himself. Blanket coverage of the town's two big golf clubs was sacrosanct. Whichever reporter was assigned to cover the annual dinner of Bury Golf Club, with all the attendant speeches and a bit of gossip, was expected to come back with a full notebook. One year, a newcomer was given the task – unwelcome to most of us – and breezed into the office the following day to tell Wilf there was 'no news in it'. Wilf must have visibly paled at the statement. He spent a considerable time that day phoning all the speakers and when the lengthy story finally appeared you'd never have known he hadn't been there himself.

Having most Saturday afternoons off meant I could play soccer in winter and cricket in summer for St Joseph's in the so-called Sunday School Leagues – though such schools were by then largely confined to a few Nonconformist churches. Playing surfaces for both games were indifferent, usually fields hired from a local farmer, bumpy and seldom level. In cricket, a fast ball might rear up to alarming heights. In soccer, if you started off playing downhill on a sloping pitch you had to make sure of slamming in a few goals in the first half, for it would be hard work defending after the interval. One pitch bordered a quarry. If someone blasted the ball into touch, it was up to him to climb down and get it.

Supporters of professional football (unless they happen to be following Arsenal or Manchester United) must be eternal gluttons for punishment. That certainly goes for the Gigg Lane crowd. Every Saturday evening while I was abroad, assuming I could get to a radio, I'd listen for the football results. Back in England I still do. At the end of too many seasons, my old hometown club has seemed to be facing extinction, short of money, gates dwindling, selling the best players to pay the housekeeping bills. At last, in 2009, they finished in the top ranks.

This lead paragraph taken from a *BT* sports page will sound familiar to Bury fans:

> Defeated at Gigg Lane, Bury's position in the Second Division table becomes ever more threatening and if the closing weeks of the season are not to see another backs-to-the-wall struggle for safety, a big improvement is needed at once.

Guess which season. Last year? The year before? 1953. That was 'Ranger' speaking. Plus ça change – except for the gate receipts. For that home game, lost to Blackburn Rovers in January 1953, 25,577 people passed through the turnstiles. These days, with rival attractions just down the motorway, the poor old Shakers are lucky if they attract 2,000. Most clubs in the bottom league face the same problems. All the big money in English football seems to end up with the big clubs – where hardly a Brit ever gets in the team – and their grossly overpaid players.

Half a century ago, the Saturday match at Gigg Lane, Burnden Park or any other Lancashire mill town was the week's big event. A century back, my father as a boy lived in a street near the ground. With many supporters arriving by bike, he or another lad would grab a handlebar, ask to look after it and stack it with others in the front garden. They could tell from the roar of the crowd if the home team had scored. The size of the tip might depend on the result. The lads themselves never saw a match until they were older. Then they joined in Gigg Lane's sarcastically named 'Gentlemen's Rush', when the gates were thrown open for free for the last twenty minutes.

The local soccer scene gave me an idea. Controversy, I'd soon realised, was a good way to sell papers. So I wrote a provocative piece lamenting what I called a sad decline in amateur soccer. Wilf liked it. Under the headline 'An Indictment of Modern Youth', I hit out as an anonymous member of a local side at 'the easygoing, apathetic attitude of many of our youths'. (Sound familiar?) I put the question:

> Are 1955's teenagers getting soft? They would be most annoyed if anyone suggested it. Certainly some of our post-war generation talk tough, even if the phrases are mostly imported. And they try their hardest to look tough. Shoulders [of jackets] are squarer than they ever were.

Provocative stuff. I quoted club officials who complained that schoolboys brought up in what I called 'the brave new world of super gymnasiums, velvet-smooth playing fields and shower baths' preferred cinemas, milk bars and dance halls to turning out on a rough field on a rainy Saturday. Readers were invited to give us their views. Letters poured in from amateur club officials and players in Bury and surrounding villages, some supportive, some decrying my article – which was the whole idea. We kept the story going for a month. Even Wilf was impressed. I missed this sort of thing when I later started working for Reuters.

Traditional jazz was in the air. There were scoffs when Alan Toft and I disclosed we were forming a band. Alan had for some time been making interesting bass-like sounds in the reporters' room by hitting the edge of a vibrating door with the flat of his hand. He may be the only jazzman ever to have played a door. I'd taught myself rudimentary jazz piano on the family upright. Brian Hitchen's only musical contribution in the reporters' room was a popular song of the day, 'I am a Bandit from Brazil', the first line of which he sang tunelessly and ad nauseam, until restrained. And he did turn out to be rather a bandit in Fleet Street!

Knowing little more than the three basic blues chords, we got the beginnings of a traditional jazz group together, Alan teaching himself trombone as he went along. 'You've got to play a bloody instrument these days to talk to Toft and Chadwick,' our group leader, Alan Greenhalgh, grumbled when we gave the pub crawl a miss. Despite our own limited abilities, we advertised in our own paper for other instrumentalists, and one evening at Radcliffe Conservative Club a band was formed together with three trad-minded schoolboys from the area.

They included trombonist Arthur Taylor and seventeen-year-old Doug Whaley, already a considerable talent, who'd first learnt cornet with a Lancashire brass band. Blessed with a remarkable technique which could also handle Haydn's trumpet concerto, Doug would become leader of the group we called The Cotton City Jazzmen and later led the Oxford University band. Our regular menu of blues and stomps was much as it remains today in traditional jazz circles, and the band we created was still playing, with a more contemporary line-up, until last year when it folded, at the Grant's Arms in Ramsbottom.

Our menu, inevitably, was mainly twelve-bar blues (the chord sequence easiest to get a grasp of) and numbers learnt from 78 rpm records and the first LPs by masters like Louis Armstrong and Jelly Roll Morton. It was the height of Britain's trad revival, when its addicts would almost come to blows with the boppers. The saxophone (though the instrument had been played for decades in American bands) was almost a dirty word to trad men. Arguments even broke out between our own ultra-traditionalists, including Doug, and those like Alan and myself who were quite keen to try newer jazz styles. There seemed to be a trad group in every town, playing in pub cellars and upstairs rooms. For our own band, we settled on the Brunswick, a now-demolished pub near my old school, St Joseph's. We bought a battered and no longer used piano for a few pounds from a nearby working men's club and wrestled it up narrow stairs to the pub's upper room, the headquarters of Bury Jazz Club for years to come. We swapped dates with similar groups in Rochdale (The Wolverines), or in Oldham, Burnley and Bolton, and played at a Manchester jazz spot called the Thatched House. There I heard for the first time a talented young trombonist with an Oldham band who'd later attain world status, Roy Williams. Only Doug Whaley, still playing today despite health problems, would soar into that sort of league.

Our optimism knew no bounds. We were once unwisely booked for a weekly session at a Bury dancing school whose owner clearly expected something in the strict-tempo Victor Sylvester mode. After young couples strongly protested at our undanceable selection of downtown blues and stomps, we were hurriedly paid off and told never to return. In a rare upmarket date, we performed at Accrington Arts Club, whose members included fur-coated ladies who'd clearly never seen or heard anything like this before. Our ever-optimistic frontman, Alan Toft, purported to give a brief lecture note before each number, outlining the differences between the various styles. To me, all our numbers sounded pretty much the same. At least the audience didn't walk out, and one of the ladies said afterwards they all thought we were 'jolly good'.

Alan Toft and I became unexpectedly embroiled in local politics, not altogether to the Editor's liking, when we campaigned to allow jazz groups like our own to perform at the prestigious local arts venue, the Derby Hall. Only Musicians' Union members had been permitted to play there since the war, and Labour members were determined to keep it that way. The Town Council debate on the matter, covered by our 'neutral' colleague Frank Thomas, was more amusing than educational.

'The band sets the tone of the dances,' fumed a leading Labour Party firebrand, Councillor Fred Spencer. 'Some people like this Dixieland music and skiffle groups', he was good enough to admit. But, he warned darkly, 'They are likely to attract young men in long jackets and shoelace ties.' Oh my goodness! It was a curious stand for a Labour man. The Conservatives and Liberals had the ban removed by twenty-two votes to eleven.

Alan and I, ironically enough, were both members of the National Union of Journalists – you had to be when you worked at the *BT*. We followed up our victory at the Derby Hall by organising a charity Press Ball for the NUJ's Widows' and Orphans' Fund of that time. For this, we booked the biggest venue in town, the old army Drill Hall, more like an aircraft hangar than a concert location. And, nothing if not ambitious, we booked both the Humphrey Lyttelton Band and the Johnny (as it was then) Dankworth Orchestra. I don't think this double was ever matched. I met Humph at the BBC studios in Manchester, where he'd been recording, and drove him to the concert venue. Then I met Dankworth's singer and wife-to-be, Cleo Laine (with dog), as she stepped off the train from Manchester and escorted her to the hall. The two bands, regarded then as widely different in jazz philosophy, produced some marvellous music and in the final numbers played together to great effect. The ball was a sell-out, raising over £1,000 – a mighty sum in those days.

The reporter's life was good for social contacts and there were plenty of attractive young ladies about. Maybe it was the dubious glamour of the press that did the trick. Covering the local summer Carnival, I got a date with the Carnival Queen and, in the unlikely context of an inquest I was covering, was captivated by a dark-eyed French nurse who'd been giving evidence. We took country drives in my little Standard Eight car, she came for Sunday-afternoon tea with the family, and, after she'd completed her assignment in England, I went to Paris to meet hers in an apartment near the Opera. Her mother was nice, but I don't think her father liked me. It all fizzled out, as these things do, and back in Lancashire I met a pretty young dental assistant. There were more country outings and again I met the family. Meanwhile, after some happy years at the *BT*, I moved to the *Bolton Evening News*, setting up a branch office for them in my hometown. It was much the same work: routine reporting, feature writing, sports and theatre.

The urge to travel persisted and my first impulse was to go north. I took the meagre travel allowance of the time (£40) with me to Norway, flying with a company called 'Hunting Clan' from Manchester's Ringway Airport to Newcastle, then on to Stavanger. It was the first foreign town I'd ever seen, and its neatness was a revelation. I watched a Catalina flying boat, long one of my favourite aircraft, practise landings and takeoffs as I waited for a coastal steamer. We sailed north to a rainswept Bergen, then I stayed overnight in a town called Voss. High mountains rose steeply from a deep and dark fjord. It might have been a setting from *Beowulf*: the landscape was intimidating, and in the middle of the night, overpowered by this eerie, almost intolerable stillness, I had to dress and go down to reception to assure myself I wasn't the only human being left alive on the planet.

On the train across the central plateau to Oslo, with the aid of a *Teach Yourself Norwegian* book bought in Manchester, I chatted with a girl with the implausible name of Aud (pronounced Owd) Beck. It sounded like a country stream in Yorkshire. She wrote it out for me, along with her address: neither of us ever wrote.

Inspired by my first outing abroad, I travelled with friends by train the following year to Austria, staying at a farm near Innsbruck. We got regularly tipsy in the local pub, where closing time was when the Axams village policeman arrived. We loved the family at the farm, but never did get to like the goat meat. I'd much enjoyed these first tastes of Europe, though, and it was a round trip by car the following year to Copenhagen by way of

Belgium, Holland and Germany, that sparked off my career at Reuters.

Before leaving, I'd suggested to my subeditor at the *BEN*, Harold Miller, that I should write a series of holiday pieces and post them back along the way. He was keen on the idea. A trio of us flew my car (there were air ferries for cars then) from a small airport near Southend. On the seafront in Ostend they were celebrating the annual blessing of the boats by the local Archbishop and the place was packed. I interviewed people, wrote it up and sent it away. One evening at Scheveningen we heard both classical piano by England's Clara Haskill and jazz piano at a cellar club. In Amsterdam we admired Rembrandt portraits at the National Museum, but never could find the old master's house in a maze of streets. There was a quick dip in the Zuider Zee en route to North Germany, where we were much impressed by the autobahns. From Denmark, I reported from Hans Anderson's fairy-tale island of Fünen, and in Copenhagen we took in a concert at the Tivoli Gardens and sampled free beer at the Carlsberg Brewery. In hotel rooms before dinner I knocked out a series of features on these events. They received prominent play, and when I later got the job at Reuters, they told me these pieces had done the trick. I was one of only two people taken on from seventy-two applicants – and the first graduate from a redbrick university.

It hadn't been my first bid for a prestige job. A few months earlier I'd chatted with editors at the *Guardian* in Manchester and liked the rather old-fashioned, clubby ambience of the newsroom. But there wasn't a vacancy at the time, and I really wanted to get out of England. Reuters (luckily I'd seen their ad in the *Telegraph*) seemed a likelier place to achieve that. I took the train from Manchester for the interview.

Emerging from Blackfriars tube station, I had my first look at the British newspaper world. Ludgate Circus and Fleet Street were much as I'd imagined: noisy, bustling with traffic, everybody apparently in a desperate hurry to get somewhere else. I'd already seen pictures of Reuters' headquarters, the impressive eight-storey building designed by Lutyens, but its gracefully arched entrance was quite unforbidding. Slightly more intimidating was to walk into a room on the seventh floor, to be interviewed by six or seven much older people sitting round a conference table. But I'd fortunately made a good impression already, it seemed, with my clippings. To the inevitable question, 'Why did you apply for the job?', the only possible answer was that I wanted to be a foreign correspondent. They were very supportive, asked me a few more general questions and then told me I had the job. I was invited to go downstairs to the fourth-floor newsroom and talk to the head of the English Desk, which handled domestic news. Someone said, 'Mr McLurkin, the Chief Reporter, is expecting you.'

The late Renauld McLurkin was a man I got to like a lot, a Scot who spoke his mind but was always considerate. I sat beside his desk in the middle of the crowded newsroom. I liked the bustle, the noise of clattering typewriters and teleprinters, a certain sense of urgency. Sheafs of papers which I assumed contained stories were zinging along by old-fashioned pneumatic tubes along the ceiling from one desk to another. I heard scraps of conversation, minor arguments and laughter from nearby desks. It was new but reassuringly familiar – not too different from the *Bury Times* newsroom, in fact. But we didn't talk much about what I'd been doing in Lancashire. Mac knew all that, he'd done the same thing himself in Scotland. Then I nearly put my foot in it.

'What sort of interests do you have outside journalism, John?' he asked. I'd expected it coming. He knew about the travel. I mentioned sport and told him I was interested in jazz. He asked almost absent-mindedly, 'What sort of jazz do you like?'

'Well,' I said dubiously, 'there's a pianist called Jelly Roll Morton. He's long dead now.' I added, 'You've probably never heard of him.'

Clang. Mac was as much of a Jelly Roll fan as I myself. Propped up on the piano stand of his Battersea flat, I would see later, was a copy of 'Buddy Bolden's Blues'. Mac, like me, had been trying to play the great man's New Orleans classics for years.

Chapter 5
THE ICELANDERS GET STROPPY: WHAT ABOUT OUR COD AND CHIPS?

> Fires, explosions, floods, inundations, railway accidents, destructive storms, earthquakes, shipwrecks, street riots of a grave character, disturbances arising from strikes, duels between and suicides of persons of note, social or political, and murders of a sensational or atrocious character.

This was a note to correspondents back in 1883 from our founder, Paul Julius Reuter, telling them what was wanted. Apart from the duels, not much different from today in other words. Though when I started at 85 Fleet Street, it all seemed a bit laid-back at first. To someone who'd once trudged the wet streets of Ramsbottom to fill a large page every week, this looked like a doddle. On the UK desk, I'd condense or rewrite three or four average-length stories a day, mainly coming in from Reuter stringers or Britain's Press Association, the domestic agency.

Then they sent me out on diaried events in or around London. I must have turned in acceptable copy and was encouraged to do colour pieces.

The first of these followed a press trip to England's south-west coast, from which we were ferried out over the bay by motor launch and climbed up a swaying rope ladder to board a large Dutch passenger ship. Aboard, we interviewed families returning from what's now Indonesia – an early sign of the decolonisation process that would soon be into full swing also for Britain, France, Belgium, Portugal and just about all of the other colonial powers. In another sign of changing times, I took the train to Scotland to report local demonstrations against plans to station US nuclear-armed submarines at a base in Holy Loch, south of Glasgow. (The base was nevertheless established and would not close down until 1992.)

Then the story broke of Princess Margaret's romance with the handsome, but unfortunately divorced, Group Captain Peter Townsend, and not only the British media were interested. I found myself riding in a London taxi in the middle of a line of press cars snaking round Piccadilly Circus in pursuit of the couple. An Italian cameraman was standing up through the roof of a Renault Dauphine just ahead, snapping away as we went. Complete madness. There was nothing to film, and the couple shook us all off. Then I flew to Belgium on the same story – my first foreign assignment. The couple seemed perfectly happy to be run to earth and gave us enough friendly quotes for a story. My mother was pleased to see me in a front-page picture standing, notebook in hand, just behind the Group Captain. But it wasn't a branch of journalism I'd have wanted to pursue for life.

At head office it was a five-day week, something new for me, and there was lots of free time. The worst of the three daily shifts was the overnight, which meant going into the office shortly before midnight to emerge bleary-eyed at seven or eight in the morning. I'd get a lot of night work later, particularly in the Middle East, where a big story could mean staying up for twenty-four hours.

Working nights had its humorous sides. Another *Bolton Evening News* man, sports reporter Fred Shawcross, had got a job at one of the Fleet Street dailies and, both strapped for cash, we decided to share a flat. This was in Primrose Hill, in a large house owned by a canny man from Northern Ireland, Jack Montgomery, who'd seen the potential in London property post-war. Fred and I shared the basement flat, with just one bedroom. As hardy Lancastrians, we decided we could live with it. Luckily, our working hours seldom coincided, so the bed was usually only singly occupied. To save money, I rode the long journey to Bolton one weekend in the sidecar of Fred's motorbike. In pre-motorway days, it wasn't the most pleasant experience.

Another old friend from Lancashire, trombonist Arthur Taylor of the Cotton City Jazzmen, was now studying at London University, and was a member of its jazz group. I went along to a Monday night 'hop' in Gower Street to find this little swing band had no pianist, and I was invited to join. We generated quite a good beat, I think. The best night was when alto star (the late) Bruce Turner, one of England's top jazzmen, who'd made a big name with Humphrey Lyttelton's band, came along as guest in the front line. I was thrilled, if slightly nervous, to play behind him on Duke Ellington's uptempo classic 'Perdido'. But my jazz-playing days would soon be over for a long time to come. Working overseas for the next quarter-century, I didn't even have a piano, even if I had the time, and whatever meagre jazz skills I'd learned soon began to evaporate.

There was also football and cricket. Reuters Editorial ran teams in both sports, and I got to play in friendly matches on various muddy pitches in the London suburbs. On the cricket field, I seemed to be one of the few who knew a bit about bowling. Our principal fast bowler was teleprinter operator George Boanas from Yorkshire, as burly as Freddie Truman, with a wicket count almost to match. On one occasion, we were the only two bowlers in the eleven and had to slog it out, alternately bowling from each end, until all ten wickets were down: five each. A Canadian colleague joined us on a few occasions in what was to him an exotic English game, dressed for the part in immaculate flannels, spiked boots, protective gear and gloves. Poor Don, I remember, rarely survived more than a few balls.

The post-colonial scene figured prominently in the news, not least on Reuters' Diplomatic Desk – 'Dipdesk', as we called it. This quiet oasis in the newsroom seemed just a professional and social cut above us general reporters. It was presided over by the tall and urbane John Earle, who as a member of Britain's Special Operations Executive (SOE) had parachuted into Yugoslavia in World War Two. Now he wrote crisp and elegant copy about the international diplomatic scene. His sidekick, a recent young recruit called Nick Herbert (who also batted for our Reuter cricket team) was the scion of an East Anglian newspaper family. The formidable Pamela Mathews had the stentorian voice and upper-crust accent of an old-fashioned girls' school headmistress. The quartet was completed by the jovial figure of Pakistani-born Mohsin Ali, who seemed to spend most of his days shuttling between 85 Fleet Street and the Foreign Office, excitedly returning with purportedly exclusive information about the diplomatic news of the day – and I'm sure at least some of it was.

Mohsin, to new recruits' awe and respect, was rumoured to have been a Spitfire pilot in World War Two. Well, he never contradicted the story. Some people said he'd actually had a perfectly honourable but slightly less glamorous role in the Indian theatre of war with RAF Transport Command. But I never asked. He certainly possessed an encyclopaedic knowledge of the many tortuous resolutions and agreements that world diplomats had drawn up over the years.

I would have to learn about Foreign Relations and World Problems myself. I began to be assigned to the small team of desk men and correspondents sent to cover diplomatic conferences in Geneva or elsewhere. With John Earle and other seniors handling the big stories, I was usually asked to write background colour pieces and find 'human interest' angles behind the diplomatic wrangling, which wasn't too difficult.

The ministerial line-up at such conferences in the post-war period was the United States, Soviet Union, Britain and France, plus a representative each from West and East Germany. The two latter delegates would sit at separate tables, located a short distance away from the ends of the arc-shaped table occupied by the main participants. The American delegation would be headed by a man called Christian Herter, the Soviet side had the better-known Andrei Gromyko at the helm, the cast being made up by Britain's Selwyn Lloyd and France's André Couve de Murville.

Any significant newsbreaks at these gatherings, as relayed by official or unofficial sources, would be reported ad hoc by the wire services, to be fleshed out later in what were called 'Nightleads' or 'Leadalls'. Dayleads – jargon for a forward-looking story intended for the morning papers (the leading ones would also have their own correspondents present) – would be a considered story on the day's events, with some speculation on what the following day might bring. So our evenings would often be stretched beyond midnight, and we snatched a snack and a drink as time allowed.

Our competitors included teams from the American agencies Associated Press (AP) and United Press International (UPI), also headed by experienced diplomatic writers. The main competition in Europe came (and does, I would think, to this day) from Agence France-Presse (AFP). Separate 'sidebars', as the jargon had it, would be aimed at specific regional markets. The overall lead, or 'Upsummer' as we called it, was usually written by John Earle. There'd be contributions to this from the separate briefings given by the 'Big Four' diplomats and those of the two German delegations. Of course, other news breaks might occur in the course of the day and merit 'Urgent' bells on the wire.

During the course of the day and evening, bits and pieces from the team were assessed by Desk Editor Ronnie Cooper – another Reuter stalwart who'd come into the news business the hard way. He was completely unflappable. At one of those Geneva conferences, which regularly produced so many words but so few results, Mohsin dashed into the office, as was his wont, brandishing a sheaf of papers and crying, 'I've got it! I've got it!' – meaning the final communiqué. 'Well, get it away, get it away!' he shouted excitedly.

Ronnie remained impassive at the keyboard, his fingers failing to move. He replied calmly, 'I'll get it away, Moshin, if you'll just tell me what it says.' But despite his idiosyncrasies, everyone loved Moshin. From the fifties to the seventies, an international conference wouldn't have been the same without him.

There was a minor panic one evening when the news got around that the usually taciturn Mr Gromyko had unexpectedly called at the American delegation office. This was on the top floor of a building in central Geneva. A small crowd of us stood on the pavement, chatting and stamping our feet for an hour in the expectation of getting a rare story out of 'Grim-Grom', as we called him. The Soviet Foreign Minister eventually emerged and seemed, unusually, to be smiling as he got quickly into his car and drove off. Had there been some major breakthrough? We surrounded a Soviet official who didn't seem in too much of a hurry to leave.

'What have they been talking about?' people shouted.

'No discussion,' said the Russian, smiling with obvious relish. 'Mr Gromyko has just been visiting the dentist on the fourth floor.'

Up around the Arctic Circle, trouble was brewing. The Icelanders, whose quarter of a million people had rarely made the international news pages since World War Two, decided they'd had enough of their fish being taken away by other countries and declared a twelve-mile limit. The Brits had been happily fishing there for centuries. So had fishermen from Norway, Sweden, Germany and Russia. Now, with the foreigners employing much more efficient equipment, fish stocks were running low, said the islanders. So from 1 September 1958, any trawlers crossing the new line would be forcibly expelled.

It was bad news for the trawlermen of Hull, Grimsby and Fleetwood, who'd fished for cod, plaice and halibut around Iceland since time immemorial and always had amicable relations with the Icelanders, whose seamen, after all, were their sort of people. And what was going to happen to England's fish and chips?

Adding insult to injury, as Britain saw it, Iceland's communist Fisheries Minister, Ludvik Josepsson, flew to Moscow and agreed to sell more of its fish to Russia instead. Moscow gave the islanders a $1 million loan to extend their own fishing fleet. It all snowballed rapidly into a major international dispute. The government of Harold Macmillan said Britain couldn't possibly accept the new fishing limit – though it had recently let the Russians get away with a similar thing. But nobody trifled with Moscow.

In those typically British Ealing Studios films of the fifties, the little men challenged authority. In *Passport to Pimlico*, a London suburb declared independence. In *Whisky Galore*, Scottish islanders seized on a shipwrecked cargo of spirits and defied the customs men. It all came right in the end, of course, and order was restored. This is how the political and military bigwigs seemed to see this Icelandic challenge to the status quo. They went into slightly comic crisis mode. The *Daily Telegraph* solemnly reported on its front page, 'The attendance of the Earl of Selkirk, First Lord of the Admiralty, in cabinet discussions is taken as evidence of the government's determination.' Were we supposed to draw breath?

I suppose you have to see it in the context of the time. It was only two years since the Suez Crisis, when Britain and France, in collusion with Israel, took on President Gamal Abdel Nasser's new Egypt, only to be rebuffed by Washington. Britain's imperial past was slipping away, the African and Asian countries one by one winning independence. Things were changing. But the problem up in Iceland must have seemed a trifling matter that the Navy would soon deal with. The fishermen of Northern England were given the go-ahead to cross the twelve-mile barrier, protected by the Royal Navy. From Hull, Grimsby and Fleetwood, trawlers sailed north a few days before the deadline with secret orders. In Reykjavik, the Icelandic premier resolutely declared, 'Fishing is our lifeblood. Without it we perish. There can be no question of compromise.' It sounded a bit like Winston Churchill. It was stalemate.

In the best traditions of the Royal Navy, a task force of five warships was assembled, to be led by the 2,200 tonne frigate *Eastbourne*, armed with two 4.5-inch guns, two 40 mm Bofors anti-aircraft guns, and depth charges (were they expecting enemy aircraft and submarines?). Yorkshire trawlerman Frank Pitts and colleagues had received sealed orders from the Admiralty, to be opened once they were at sea. One hundred big, high-powered trawlers manned by 2,000 fishermen set sail, ready to move across the twelve-mile limit at the 1 September midnight deadline.

Savage cartoons in the Icelandic press depicted a top-hatted John Bull as the bully boy of the North Atlantic. The other Nordic countries stood solidly behind the Icelanders. The row was a godsend to Moscow, always miffed at the US presence on the island. The war was threatening NATO unity.

Well, I'd always said I liked the North, so it was my own fault that Sid Mason sent me. I joined a task force of British journalists covering what was becoming a juicy story. I was lucky enough to be allocated to the flagship. At Tilbury dock, I climbed aboard the *Eastbourne* completely unequipped in all the rush for what was obviously going to be a cold and rough trip. Reuters didn't possess any seagoing kit, and I hadn't had time to buy any. I didn't even have a thick sweater. I went to war in a lounge suit. On *Eastbourne*, I joined *Daily Express* troubleshooter Frank Goldsworthy, an older journalist who'd covered all manner of conflicts, and two cameramen, Charles Treslove of the *Express*, and a newsreel cameraman with the exotic surname Cave-Chinn. The four of us shared two cabins below deck, and I got my first taste of how stuffy and uncomfortable a naval vessel can be. Pitching and rolling, it would be home, however, for the next three weeks. The 200 crew members were used to it.

As we steamed 1,000 miles up the North Sea towards the battle zone, we were fed a few more details which only helped to prompt the unspoken question, Can all this be serious? Three good fishing zones off the north-west, south-west and south-east corners of the island were labelled 'havens', in which the armed frigates would shepherd the British trawlers. The 'havens' were code-named 'Spearmint', 'Butterscotch' and 'Toffee Apple'. It was all rather hilarious. We only needed Biggles and his chums to join the fray…

The other member of the Reuter front line reporting duo was George Bishop, more often seen driving vintage cars. I'd ridden through the streets of London in the passenger seat of his green Bentley. Later he would become Editor of *Motor Sport* magazine, the enthusiasts' bible. He was not at all happy at being selected to cover the other side of the story aboard the Grimsby trawler *Coventry City*. As we approached the coast of Iceland and I saw the way these tubby vessels bobbed up and down in the waves, often disappearing from view, I felt glad they'd given George that job. One day, I spotted the *Coventry City*. At my request, the First Officer called down from the bridge to the heavily sweatered trawler skipper and asked through his megaphone, 'Is George Bishop of Reuters aboard?' Upon which a bearded and bedraggled figure emerged from the trawler's nether regions, making my shared cabin seem a very comfortable berth. George gave me a less than spirited hand-wave. He was clearly not in the mood for conversation.

It was bad enough aboard the *Eastbourne*. In triangular patterns among the trawlers, you'd just got used to one kind of movement when we turned about on another tack, with a different but equally queasy effect. The pressmen were not the only sufferers. Seasickness pills were issued daily to all crew members, who could take them or not. Even our commander, Commodore

Barry Anderson, who'd learned all about heavy seas on Antarctic sailing ships way back in his career, admitted he still suffered. You'd never have guessed it from his robust and cheerful manner. The stocky and ever confident Anderson was the perfect man for the job. He'd first gone to sea at fifteen, then joined a Nordic shipping line as an apprentice before gaining his master's ticket sailing between Liverpool, Brazil and Argentina. He spent the Second World War chasing U-boats in the Irish Sea, then the Dunkirk evacuation and the landings in Sicily and Salerno. En route, he'd learnt Norwegian, Danish and a little Icelandic. He also knew some of his new adversaries well.

But I think he overestimated us reporters' qualities as seafarers. One day we came up with another Navy ship, the *Russell*, with whose skipper Commander Anderson had decided to have a chat. How was this to be accomplished? Up on deck, we journalists watched fascinated as a line fastened to the forecastle of our ship was fired across the bows of the other as we steamed along in parallel about thirty metres apart. After a couple of empty grabs, sailors on the other ship secured the line. It was then connected to a strong cable carrying a pulley. A second line passing through this was grasped by a dozen hefty sailors, who hauled it, tug of war style, from the one ship to the other. I watched with interest as, first of all, a couple of mailbags and other stuff were passed across. Then our doctor, who had a patient to see, went over, using what they call a jackstay. We watched the technique with interest as he thrust crossed ankles into a sort of stirrup. The idea is that you then rest the buttocks on a canvas strap, press your weight downwards and hold tightly on to the rope – and hope for the best. You're not actually connected to anything. It looked distinctly hairy to me. Anderson followed, but before going across suggested that we press men would perhaps also like to have a go – or words to that effect. To him, clearly, this was all good sport.

The *Times* photographer was wise. He stayed aboard the *Eastbourne* and filmed the proceedings. Frank and I, foolish enough to accept the challenge, were duly fitted with life jackets. Frank went ahead of me. I looked with some dismay as the seas rolled through the gap between the two ships, racing along in parallel at thirty knots. A more than usually high wave rose up and clipped Frank about the ankles. He didn't look very seamanlike. To begin with, he was still wearing his raincoat – he had no special Arctic kit either. But it was too late to back out now. The honour of Reuters was at stake, I told myself, feeling like a man going to the gallows.

Half the ships' crews, it seemed, were lined up on either side to watch. The jackstay was pulled back along the line to the *Eastbourne*, I grasped the rope tightly as directed, thrust my feet into the stirrup and then swung downwards towards the water. The first bit seemed to go quite quickly, as I was smartly tugged away from the side of the *Eastbourne*. There was some swaying in midstream as I reached the low point of the traverse. Suspended in mid-air, I stared astern, one ship to the left, the other to the right, and tried to ignore the surging waters beneath. The second stage of the operation was accomplished mercifully quickly, and I stepped with relief on to the destroyer *Russell*'s deck. One of the sailors looked at me, shook his head and said in a cockney accent, ' 'Ere, I've been in the Navy fifteen f—ing years, and managed to get outta doin' that. And you f—ing well volunteer for it!'

They told me later that if I'd dropped, I wouldn't have survived the cold before a rescue boat arrived. We were between Iceland's west coast and the shore of Greenland. And who would have paid compensation? As far as I know, I wasn't insured by Reuters. It could never happen today.

Sporadically, the crazy war continued. The tiny Icelandic gunboats carried proud names I remembered from the sagas, like *Thor* (693 tonnes) and *Odinn* (a puny 72 tonnes) but they were no match for even the trawlers, let alone the Royal Navy. The Icelanders resorted to pelting British fishermen with dried cod. The *Loch Fleet*, fishing off north-west Iceland, radioed that she was retaliating 'in like manner'. Trawler crew on the *Stella Campus* used potatoes and broom handles to repel Icelanders who tried to board them. The British trawler *King Sol* rammed the *Odinn* as she came alongside and tried to damage the trawler's fishing net. 'I went astern into him,' reported the Yorkshire skipper gleefully, 'and made a right nice mark on his bows.'

It was all becoming faintly ridiculous. Even the very patriotic *Telegraph* couldn't take it completely seriously. Its correspondent on board HMS *Russell* reported with more than a touch of mockery:

> The annals of British sea history will be enriched by the engagement between the Fleetwood trawler *Loch Fleet* and the *Odinn*, one of the greatest 'battles' in the Anglo–Icelandic dispute.

Aboard the *Eastbourne*, between such skirmishes, there was not much to do apart from feel seasick, so Goldsworthy and I, spurred on by Commodore Anderson, started a ship's newspaper, which was printed out in the ship's wire room and eventually went into five editions. We invited contributions from all quarters and the paper, consisting of five or six sheets clipped together, was a big success among officers and ratings alike.

There were plenty of contributions from 'below decks' and the paper demonstrated that there's plenty of creativity at all British levels if anyone ever bothers to ask. Frank did the editorials and later wrote generously in his memoirs, 'John Chadwick proved to be a genius in compiling crosswords.' I did them twice-weekly, angled on topics such as sport, literature and jazz. They were highly popular. And we were soon to acquire Icelanders on the editorial staff. This came soon after the crazy war reached a nasty climax.

The Icelanders had finally figured how to get aboard one of the trawlers, by putting *Thor* on one side and the *Maria Julia* on the other of Grimsby's *Northern Foam*, trapping it between them. Ten Icelanders quickly climbed aboard. The radio operator locked himself in the wire room and radioed for help. The English crew were told by the *Eastbourne* to 'resist vigorously and immobilise your ship, but no shooting or force'. We steamed for the spot in dense fog at twenty-five knots, and a naval boarding party was sent across the water to regain control. But *Thor*'s captain refused to take the men back and they were brought aboard our ship.

'British Navy Turns To Piracy', screamed the communist *Daily Worker* next day in its front-page banner headline. But from the *Eastbourne* I reported, 'The nine Icelanders, mostly in their early twenties, were given a friendly welcome and within an hour were eating a hearty dinner.' And this was the atmosphere which prevailed during their enforced ten-day stay. The following morning, the *Thor* came alongside and its captain asked by loudhailer, 'May we speak to your prisoners?' Anderson replied, 'We have no prisoners. Presume you mean our Icelandic guests?'

I watched as Hrafnkell Gudjonsson, first mate of the *Maria Julia*, conferred with his countryman by radio telephone. The Icelanders, wearing woollen caps, clustered around by the rail. But Anderson was not for backing down, and I reported:

> Last night the two Icelandic officers watched an American film with British officers after a roast beef dinner. Their men smoked, chatted and played cards with British naval ratings and became good friends with a guitar-playing skiffle group.

But at top level the diplomatic deadlock continued. In Reykjavik, 1,000 protestors threw stones and smashed windows of the British Embassy and threw red flares into the garden. Inside, according to the Associated Press, Ambassador Andrew Gilchrist sat at the piano and played Chopin. Even the august *Times* said in its editorial:

> The game of cops and robbers off the Icelandic coast does not seem to have extinguished the reciprocal good humour which is the saving feature of this sad dispute. It would be ludicrous if it were not already serious – and liable at any moment to become tragic.

Eight miles off the coast of Iceland, meanwhile, we were getting to know the nine Icelanders, who, having been welcomed aboard, were smoothly absorbed into the class system prevailing. Their officers dined in the wardroom, the others below decks. Frank and I drew on their talents for our ship's magazine. We even tried to help heal the wounds. I wrote in a background feature:

> The Icelandic coastguard service, with which the Royal Navy is tangling in this unfortunate dispute, has a long and honourable record for saving seamen of all nations and last year saved sixty-two British trawlermen.

I launched a largely comic 'Learn Icelandic' column for the benefit of our own sailors – *skip* for ship, *fiski-batur* for fishing boat, *takk* for thank you, and *'Vad heitur du?'* for 'What's your name?' One of our guests, entering into the spirit of things, explained how Icelanders run words together. *'Hadstarettarmalaflutningsmannsvinnukendundirbujxateya'*, he assured us, meant 'the elastic in the panties of the housemaid of the lawyer of the high court'. We editors saw no reason to doubt it.

The niceties were preserved. We didn't attempt to talk politics to the Icelanders, nor would the Navy, on whom we depended for communications, have transmitted such a story anyway. The Icelanders, though invariably polite, were pretty tough young men you wouldn't want to trifle with. Like tall, lanky Olafur Gudmundsson, for example. Of him, the *Northern Foam* skipper Jim Crockwell, a pretty tough bird himself, said later, 'That guy with the blue cap. If anybody could have struck me dead with one look, it was him.'

After three weeks at sea, I felt I'd seen enough of the rugged coast of Iceland from every possible angle. And our 'guests', with worried families back home, were dying to get back. For the Navy and the British Government, they were becoming a headache. Since the Icelandic authorities wouldn't let them back aboard any of their vessels, they'd have to sail back with us and be put on a plane to Reykjavik.

Their eventual release was as controversial as their capture and took the Icelandic Government – and maybe Whitehall – by surprise. It was all engineered by Anderson, who'd taken the Icelanders into his confidence. I remember the final scene vividly. It was two o'clock in the morning, and from the rail of the *Eastbourne* I could see the harbour lights of Keflavik a mile away. The British ship had switched off all its lights but for a faint glow from the masthead. Down in the water bobbed a whaleboat, donated by the Navy. The nine Icelanders, wearing lifejackets, shouted their goodbyes and rowed away into the darkness. On the bridge, we followed the faint blip on the radar screen until it stopped and we knew then that they were safely home. Captain Anderson ordered the frigate about and raced hell for leather out of the bay. We'd been three miles inside territorial limits. There was further uproar in Iceland and a few raised eyebrows in London.

Anderson's view: 'What else could we do? They wanted to go home, so I gave them a boat.' There was a diplomatic storm, of course, and the British Embassy in Reykjavik was dutifully stoned again. But the crazy war was virtually over. Later, Anderson would give an alternative version of the 'prisoners' episode. After the skipper of *Thor* refused to take the nine Icelanders back, said Anderson, 'He agreed I should take his men on my ship. To save his face in Iceland, I "captured" them.'

For me, there was a nice sequel, which made a good feature story, but it didn't happen for thirty years. Back in London as World Desk Editor after decades abroad, I wanted to track down some of those Icelanders and a little belatedly talk things over. What happened to that whaleboat? What did they really think of the Cod War? And the swashbuckling Commander Anderson and his personal brand of high seas diplomacy? With the help of Reuter colleagues in Reykjavik, I traced two of them and decided to sail up there for a chat. After covering the Cod War, I couldn't possibly have flown. The vibes would have been quite wrong. So I took the car by sea, via Shetland.

Iceland's snowy peaks glinted across the water as we approached the south-east port of Seydisfjördur. Fjords indented the jagged coastline. In one such, the first Irish settlers had landed 1,200 years earlier. It was the first time I'd ever seen the island on a clear day. 'Spearmint,' I said aloud, standing at the rail of the *Norrona*, startling another tourist. I'd suddenly remembered the Navy's code name for this stretch of water, like something from a Peter Sellers movie. Somewhere close by, three decades earlier, we'd taken the Icelanders captive.

Seydisfjördur, tucked away inside one of the fjords, was an attractive multicoloured jumble of wooden houses under the cliffs. Everyone was out by the harbour, it seemed, to welcome these now peaceful invaders. I bumped off the ship in my Audi and consulted a huge map of the island to see exactly where I was. A big arrow gave me the answer, accompanied by the words *Đu*

Ert Her (You're here). It hardly needed my rusty old Anglo-Saxon to understand. They were the same words the Icelanders would have used a millennium ago – and not too different from the English of that time. While other languages have been changing, Icelandic has been preserved as in aspic, and today's schoolchildren can read tenth-century literature, elsewhere the preserve of scholars.

I was in Beowulf sort of country as I drove for the first time along the jagged edge of Iceland's southern coast. The road took me round countless inlets and along the edge of the mighty Vatnajökull glacier, which covers a great deal of the country, all the way to Reykjavik. There, I checked in at the Seamen's Hotel. It seemed an appropriate choice for the occasion – and was a bit cheaper than some of the others. I'd hardly opened my suitcase when there was a ring at the door. I opened it to see Olafur Gudmundsson, one of our Cod War prisoners. He'd been generally described by one of our sailors at the time as 'stroppy' – as he'd every right to be. Now a commander in the coastguard service, he was still wearing a navy blue peaked cap set at a familiar rakish angle. 'You look younger than you did then,' he quipped.

'Well, I'm not seasick any more,' I responded. From then on conversation was plain sailing.

His house was at the edge of the sea, outside Reykjavik. A British Land Rover, encouragingly, was parked outside. We talked about the war long gone and consumed a fair amount of the hard stuff. So much so that by two or three in the morning we were talking not about fish, but fairies. People in Iceland believed in them, I was assured by the lady of the household. Could I be dreaming, or was I drunk? I asked myself afterwards. No, I discovered. Two years earlier, Reykjavik City Council apparently drew up a chart of the main dwelling places of elves and spirits. A road connecting with a city suburb was accordingly routed around a site where the elves were said to live. I'd remember this years later, when a bypass in Ireland was made to curve round a reputed home of the Kerry fairies. Clearly, these people on the outer fringes of Europe know more than we about such matters.

At an earlier stage of the evening, Olafur had shown me his

scrapbook from the Cod War. He said of the conflict, 'The British were stupid. If they had handled the matter in a different way, we could have come to an agreement. As it was, we scored a big propaganda victory. Of course the British backed down in the end.' Of Captain Anderson: 'He became something of a legend in Iceland. Did you know he came back many years later in a minesweeper on a friendly visit? He helped us clean up some old anti-submarine nets the British put down during the Second World War.'

In another green suburb, I was equally relieved next day to see a set of British golf clubs in Hrafnkell Gudjonsson's hall, and he and his wife greeted me no less warmly. During coffee and cakes, he took down a book recording Iceland's fishing disputes over the centuries. It said trouble with British fishermen went back to the year 1408. His view of the 1958 conflict? 'I think you lost the war because public opinion was against you.' What about the 'prisoner release'? As I'd suspected, the Icelanders hadn't unanimously accepted the offer of a whaleboat to get back home.

'Captain Anderson called me to his cabin to make the offer. I protested. I said, "You know better than I that if you go into Icelandic waters without permission, you are breaking international law." He said nothing.' And, Hrafnkell admitted, 'The men's urge to get home was strong.' What about the famous whaleboat? Hrafnkell said, 'I suggested we should give it to young people to teach them rowing.' Olafur tried to track it down and reported later, 'It was kept at the coastguard station for many years. They just forgot about it. Then they gave it to a youth club in Keflavik, but it deteriorated after standing on the ground for many years. I don't think it exists any longer.' Nor the old grievances, one hopes. We live and learn.

And what happened to my old Reuter colleague, George Bishop, after his queasy ordeal on the trawler? He'd long left the firm and it was nearly forty years before I renewed contact. Ever a Bentley enthusiast, it was one of his entertaining columns as Editor of *Car Magazine* that helped me track him down. He got letters from all over the world from people who said they'd been reading his stuff for twenty or thirty years. 'Nice to hear from you after forty years', he wrote back in a typically amusing letter.

I was always a bit peeved that I got pushed on to the trawler while you were swigging pink gin in the wardroom of the *Eastbourne*, for which occupation I thought I was better qualified.

As for his motives in leaving the agency:

I'd had ten years of Reuters, where I couldn't say it was raining without giving a source … I've been living in Cornwall the last twelve years, which is God's own country. I can hear a pin drop unless the neighbours are cutting their blasted grass. I have a large deck at the rear of the cottage where I sit in the sun and say, 'Who needs the South of France?' We have one bus a week, no shops, no pub, no nothing.

We arranged to meet when one of us could make the long journey, but it never came off. A great character, George. He should have been in films.

And now, half a century later, we're in dispute again with our North Atlantic friends – this time not about fish, but hard cash. But this one can't be settled, as the Cod War was intended to be (though in the end wasn't) with gunboats. (Have we any of those left, by the way?) Dozens of town councils and hundreds of private investors foolishly put their money into Icelandic accounts and now, with Iceland in a financial crisis, couldn't get it out. The Prime Minister brusquely told Reykjavik we wanted our money back. It all smacked of Margaret Thatcher and her angry demand from the European Union – which was no doubt her successor's intention. But what were they thinking about, all these private investors and institutions? Now the Icelandic parliament has agreed to repay to Britain some 2.3 billion sterling compensation for all those foolish savers. An unfortunate (to my mind) corollary of this may be that the proud North Atlantic Island is sucked into the eager embrace of the European Union. No doubt the profligate translation factory in Brussels would be more than ready to employ yet more staff.

Surely the writing had been on the wall for years. How could a tiny island of 300,000 people, whose primary exports were fish and energy, get all the money to buy whatever their entrepreneurs fancied in England, from prestigious toy shops to football clubs? Where has common sense disappeared to? It's not the first time I've asked myself that question. It's all about greed, on both sides.

There's another rather curious footnote to it all. It's reported that big Icelandic trawlers are again turning up at Grimsby – the port from which the British armada set off with the naval escort all those years ago. Now, in the wake of the financial crisis, the Icelandic skippers can't sell their cod at home, so are bringing it to Britain. I'm sure that country's fishermen at least are more than welcome in our east-coast ports. There's a long tradition of friendship, as well as good business, between Yorkshiremen and the Icelanders.

Chapter 6
GRILLED SAUSAGES AND CARLSBERG –
AND I TALK WITH THE KING

News Editor Sid Mason, summoning me to his desk, said, ' 'Ere, cock, you made a good job of the Cod War. You know a bit o' Norwegian, don't you? How would you like to be Reuters' man in Copenhagen?' To which there could only be one answer.

Mikkelbryggersgade. No, I couldn't pronounce it at first, either, though I learned to. I just showed the address to the taxi driver, who dropped me off at the front gate of Denmark's own news agency, Ritzau, named, like Reuters, after the founder. It was in a side street just a block from the majestic Town Hall Square. An area full of twisting little streets and charming old houses and shops, many of which happily survive to this day. (In fact, a former Danish ambassador friend of mine lives in one of them.) But the Town Hall Square today, alas, is not what it used to be, cluttered up by a tourist office of monstrous design. The square, with all the cyclists and yellow trams, looked better, and more human, the way it was. And the next couple of years would be one of the most pleasant times of my career.

From a flagged courtyard inside the Ritzau gates you took a noisy old lift or mounted a few stairs to the second floor, where the newsroom and offices were located. Then the good Danes showed me my own quarters, a cosy little office on the top floor, windows overlooking a courtyard and lots of green copper roofs.

My predecessor wasn't there at the time. Carol Coghill, daughter of Oxford Professor Neville Coghill, of *Canterbury Tales* fame, was out of the country. Until my arrival, our secretary-translator, Annelise Kring, had been taking calls. She took me down the corridor to meet my opposite numbers. Poul Nielsen, of Danish-French descent, represented Agence France-Presse (AFP). The Deutsche Presse-Agentur (DPA) office was headed by Ernst-Siegfried Hansen, from the German-speaking part of Jutland. For two years they would be my friendly competitors – and later guests at my wedding.

Mrs Kring took care of phone calls while I tried to get my tongue round this most impenetrable of European languages, the formidable task immediately facing me. My smattering of Norwegian had sufficiently impressed Sid Mason to give me the job, but it was clearly not enough. The ancient connections with the old English I'd studied at university were not particularly useful either. The Nordic languages, with the striking exception of Icelandic, had moved on a bit since then. Danish and Norwegian are more or less the same when written, but are pronounced quite differently. As the Danes always tell you proudly, 'Ours is not a language, it's a disease of the throat.' No easy way out. There was never much trouble in interviewing. The Danes usually speak English as well as you do. But reading the local newspapers is the first priority for a journalist overseas.

My first caller, after I'd hung up my coat, was the Ritzau boss, Gunnar Naesselund-Hansen. He greeted me warmly, promised every help from his own reporters and wire-room staff and then handed me my first sheaf of what were called the *grønne blader* (green sheets). These contained printouts of all the foreign and domestic news which had been put out by the Danish agency during the past couple of hours. Mr Naesselund told me a messenger would be delivering these to my office every couple of hours. If something more urgent happened, the Ritzau desk would phone me. 'I suppose you read Danish,' Naesselund added as he was leaving my new office. Not exactly, I told him. 'You'll quickly learn,' he said.

Well, I had to. Over several weeks in Copenhagen, I would plough through the 'green sheets' and the newspapers with the aid of my *Teach Yourself Danish* and a dictionary. I set myself the task of learning twenty new words a day. It became a joke among colleagues at Ritzau, who would gently prod me. 'Have you learned your twenty words today?'

Luckily, as everyone knows, most Danes speak excellent English and are, along with the Dutch, the most fluent masters of our language. To begin to get some grasp of their own spoken word, I'd sit for hours in the office every night. Even when working on a story I'd have the radio playing constantly in the background, soaking into my head this exotic sound (it gradually moved from being ugly to being, well, let's say offbeat). It had to be done. Gradually I began to get a smattering of it.

Then there was the strange numbering system. It's all right until you count up to the forties. Forty-five, quite cutely, becomes 'five and forty'. But fifty, for some reason, becomes the equivalent of 'half sixty', which in Danish is itself shorthand for 'half three-times-twenty'. *Halv fiers*, translated, is 'half four-times-twenty'. Even this doesn't explain things exactly. But I needn't go on. You get the hang of it eventually. Even today I still remember our Reuter office number in the late fifties as Palae 5309, becoming in Danish *tre og halv-treds nul ni* (three and half three twenties). Something like that, anyway. You just had to learn the sound of it. Once learned, never forgotten. Swedes living just across the water in what used to be the Danish province of Skåne have an infinitely simpler system. The number fifty-three becomes *femti-tre*, much easier on the brain.

Carol Coghill, I was told, was calling round to meet me a couple of days later. She'd sent apologies for not being there on my arrival. Her mother was Swedish and she'd spent most of her young life in that country, so was one up on me on the language front. She'd not however had much experience of working journalism, and preferred to move to Paris to do other things. Brilliant, but a little eccentric, I'm sure she wouldn't mind me saying. She was to arrive from the French capital a couple of days later, and she'd already been in touch with one of the messengers at Ritzau, who asked to drive with me to the airport. I wondered slightly why he wanted to come along, but would soon find out.

Copenhagen's Kastrup, as it was then known, was infinitely different from today's massive and glittering terminal. Smaller, cosier, much more relaxed. The Ritzau man and I stood in our side of the arrival hall as passengers approached from Customs on the other side of a glass-topped screen. The Ritzau man picked out Carol as she approached, waved and moved closer to the barrier. The next thing I knew, a small hairy bundle was being hurled over the screen, to be neatly caught with the adroitness of a cricket slip fielder by my Danish friend. It was Carol's pet dog. She couldn't be bothered with such things as quarantine. Some things were certainly simpler in the old days.

Nobody could be more informal and friendly than the Danes at Ritzau. We foreign correspondents had more or less a free run of their newsroom. It was not unlike the old *Bury Times* or Reuter set-up: a forest of desks, with typewriters rattling away. Next door was the wire room, where stories from Ritzau reporters and us foreign correspondents would be 're-punched', as we called that now defunct process, for transmission to head office. They were like Reuters teleprinter operators in London. But not completely the same. Instead of our very male, and sometimes rough-spoken, Fleet Street colleagues, the operators sitting at these machines were all girls. Things were clearly going to be different.

With accommodation scarce after the Second World War, I booked in for the time being at a comfortable pension close to Copenhagen's attractive lakes. Walking to the office took me close to the once-notorious Shell Building, Gestapo headquarters during the German occupation and finally bombed by British Mosquitos streaking low over the rooftops in one of the most spectacular raids of the war. My fellow 'lodgers' were a lively mixture of students and businessmen from Norway, Germany and England. We ate at seven (me when I could make it) in a communal dining room.

The German described scrabbling for food among the ruins as a boy after the Air Force bombed Düsseldorf. Everyone at the Danish news agency had lived through the wartime occupation and still held the British in high regard, which made my own job easier. There'd been a few collaborators, of course, but the Danes had bravely saved many Jews from the concentration camps by ferrying them in small boats across the Öresund to neutral Sweden. Maybe the Brits, if occupied, would have had a similar mix of people – impossible to know. Meanwhile, the English social scene, judged by some of its representatives in Denmark, didn't seem to have changed very much. The young man from British American Tobacco, who never wore anything but a pinstriped suit with waistcoat, was typically snooty, though friendly enough.

'NOSOP,' he murmured confidentially at the communal dinner table one evening, describing some other guests he'd met at a Copenhagen party.

'NOSOP?' I asked.

'Not Our Sort Of People,' he explained.

I gathered this was the jargon among London debs and their squires. NSIT, I further learned, meant 'Not Safe In Taxis'. Well, all I can say is: NMWAA – Not My World At All. I preferred these lovely young ladies from Norway and Sweden, unimpressed by English snobberies.

My first big story took place in the icy northern waters close to the Cod War scene. Ships and aircraft, I learned in a tipoff from the Ritzau news desk, were searching for a 2,875-tonne freighter, the *Hans Hedtoft*, missing on its maiden voyage after hitting an iceberg south of Greenland. I followed the hopeless search for the vessel, with ninety-four passengers and crew aboard, with more than usual interest. After mysterious flashes of Morse code, nothing was heard from the stricken vessel. Coastguard ships raced to the area. Also taking part in the search was the Icelandic Catalina flying boat which had shadowed us during the fishing conflict. It all seemed very real to me; but no trace was ever found of the ship. I got in ahead of the opposition and the story was well played in the British press.

Another story might have come straight from an Agatha Christie novel. The bodies of four dead men, two Frenchmen, an American and their guide, missing for three months, were found in the Nubian Desert near their abandoned car. Two of the bodies showed signs of violence, and the guide had been shot dead. It was a mystery worthy of Hercule Poirot's attention, but this one was never solved. The theory was that the men died fighting for what remained of their water. I exclusively interviewed a Danish engineer, Herman Nielsen, who'd met the party in the desert while driving from Wadi Haifa to Aswan on the way home to Denmark. He'd offered them a five-gallon can of water but, he said, they declined the offer. It was perhaps a fatal decision. He was the last to see them alive.

I was making my mark, albeit in stories of death and disaster. Head office's monthly report showed me eight minutes ahead of the Opposition on the death of Danish Prime Minister H C Hansen, adding, 'Copenhagen had one of the month's best brighteners – a man who lived in a haystack for ten years.' I'd realised the fairly obvious, that big news would be hard to find in tiny Denmark. The snippets we'd been sending about political affairs rarely made foreign newspapers. But nobody seemed to have been writing any feature stories, and the country was full of them. People like to be entertained as well as informed. 'The Man Who Lived In A Haystack' was followed by 'The Pet Lion That Roared At The Landlord' (who'd come to collect the rent). 'I got the cub for photographic purposes when it was six weeks old and it was such a sweet little thing,' said the tenant. 'I just couldn't let it go.' The lion was removed to Copenhagen Zoo. Another flat-dweller, it was discovered, was keeping snakes and mongooses. 'You have to keep them well apart, though,' he sagely observed, 'otherwise they'd fight. The mongoose usually wins.'

Amazingly, even anacondas, brought in from Brazil by seamen, were found in a few households. Their owners said they mostly lived in the bath. Also discovered were pet kangaroos, wild cats, apes, racoons and alligators. The owners of vipers said the big problem was keeping them supplied with frogs. I was beginning to wonder what sort of country I'd arrived in. After such exotica, Carol Coghill's smuggled-in dog wasn't even in it. Head Office's Features report for October 1959 put me in top place. In just a month, I'd also written about the world's northernmost airport in Greenland, the opening of a new SAS skyscraper hotel opposite Tivoli Gardens, and plans to link the two main Danish islands with the world's longest bridge (it now exists).

All this stuff got excellent play around the world. The best way of reporting Denmark was to write not less but more. The Danish press itself was… well, different. Remembering British libel laws learned back at the *Bury Times* from subeditor Ruby Greely, I looked twice at one headline in a paper from Jutland: 'Murderer Acquitted.' I had to laugh.

It wasn't all work and no play. Many an evening I'd join in a pub crawl with the reporters from Ritzau, a marvellous bunch I remember with great affection – Jens Bang, Bengt Nielsen,

Mogens Bryde and the rest. These were talented people. Bengt had written a popular satirical novel, *Why Did Little Brother Laugh?* Mogens, who'd later become the Danish news agency's man at the European Union headquarters in Brussels, introduced me to the music of Buxtehude – the seventeenth-century Danish composer and virtuoso organist, whom the young Johann Sebastian Bach reputedly walked 200 miles to hear.

Sports Editor Allan Larsen's sister, Inge, was one of the teleprinter operators and I got a date with her. News Editor Anker Nielsen later became Denmark's press attaché in London, where I'd meet him again a quarter-century later. There were some late nights at a rowdy drinking place called Lauritz Betjent. And in a pub with the boys in the harbour area, Nyhavn, I was trying to knock out a jazz number on the battered piano one evening when a heavily muscled seaman came chasing into the pub through the back door and out by the front, pursued by a policeman. At the tables, nobody moved a muscle and drinking continued. It was that sort of place.

One annual event was unmissable – the annual Carlsberg Lunch for journalists, a four-hour orgy of good food and drink, after which we'd all roll home in taxis. We'd already have downed a pint or two at the bar in the entrance hall before going into the dining hall. There, one of a hundred waiters asked you what you'd like to drink. Everything, we were told, was available – wines, whisky or whatever. 'How about a Green Tuborg?' I asked mischievously. The two breweries (now merged) were as competitive as Hertz and Avis. 'No problem,' said the waiter, and it was on the table moments later.

There were some good jazz clubs, where I became a fairly regular visitor. One was Vingaarden, where you heard down-to-earth blues and boogie from black American 'Champion Jack Dupree'. For a smoother, more sophisticated brand of jazz, I could walk down Strøget, Copenhagen's renowned shopping street, after work to the more upmarket Montmartre. Here the star attraction was American tenor sax star Stan Getz, whom I was lucky to catch during his self-imposed rehabilitation stay in Scandinavia. It followed a bad period he'd had in the States with narcotics, culminating in a ludicrous and abortive attempt to rob a drugstore. I'd often share a drink during the intermission with the quiet, sometimes prickly figure sitting moodily at the bar. Alongside him on the stand were Sweden's rising piano king, Jan Johansson, and the lyrical American bassist/cellist Oscar Pettiford. They delighted the regulars with all the old show tunes, some boppish new ones, and the blues. Sometimes incorporating old folk melodies from the region, it was jazz with an agreeable Nordic tinge.

Denmark was certainly different where the law was concerned. Alarmed one evening by the sound of a crash down in the street, I looked out from my window at Pension Berg and saw a man had badly bumped my car while trying to park. I'd only had my white, bottom-of-the-market, three-geared Ford Anglia a couple of weeks, but with Denmark's crippling 100 per cent purchase tax it had cost me about £1,000, big money in those days. I dashed downstairs, berated the culprit and returned. Ten minutes later there was a ring at the bell and a policeman stood outside. Good, I thought, he spotted what happened. No such thing. The other driver had made an official complaint. 'He says you shouted at him,' said the copper. I was learning about Scandinavia. The Nordics were just a few decades ahead of us.

With Copenhagen much closer than Stockholm, I was often sent to cover sports events on the Swedish side of the Kattegat. There was no bridge to Malmö in those days, not even the fast hydrofoil boats which were later introduced. Getting across to Sweden meant a ninety-minute ferry ride. En route to cover an international soccer match, I once missed the boat, finally sliding into my seat in the stand about five minutes before half-time, when my first scheduled call to London, with half-time score and brief summary, was due. I got a quick fill-in from helpful Swedish colleagues and just made the call in time. London never knew the difference. Knowing little about the game, I also had to do some quick thinking when sent to cover a European golf championship across the water, won by Peter Thomson, I seem to remember. Amazing what you can pick up quickly when you have to! And there are always locals just dying to help.

An American chap from high society, it was announced, was going to marry a Danish girl. A big wedding was planned for

Roskilde Cathedral. For some reason, it was big news across the Atlantic and I was pressed to get in ahead of the opposition, mainly AP, when the knot was tied. I'd taken on a young Australian, Geoffrey Dodd, as a part-time assistant and took him along a day in advance. A big hotel just off the main square directly faced the cathedral. I booked a front second-floor room, from the window of which, the next day, I could look down to the church porch, where a crowd of onlookers had gathered. Geoff emerged from the cathedral as soon as the rings were exchanged and gave me the big wave. Standing by the window on an already opened line, I gave London the 'snap' they wanted, and we were way ahead of the opposition. Long before mobile phones, there were many other ways of doing things.

I joined the reporting team in Geneva for another foreign ministers' conference, convened over tensions in Berlin. The Western powers were refusing to sign a peace treaty until Germany was reunited through free elections, insisting that the four-power occupation should remain until Berlin was the capital. That seemed a long way off. The Russians pressed for separate peace treaties with the two halves of the divided country. The four powers failed to reach agreement and we all returned home. Tensions remained in Germany when I was sent to help out in Berlin. Unfortunately my secretary, whom I'd asked to get me on the first available plane, booked me on a Polish Airlines flight, which I realised would land at the East German airport of Schoenefeld – and I had no entry visa. Bizarrely, I was the only passenger on the flight. The Poles were most hospitable and there was quite a drinks party in the sky as we flew over the Baltic.

The visa problem remained, however, and my in-flight companions soon disappeared when we landed. Queuing at the arrivals desk, I made for the most friendly looking of a line of immigration officers, tentatively clutching a wad of West German marks in my hand, in case needed. But when I said I was reporting the fair for Reuters, they waved me through; a policeman sat beside me on the bus into town and instructed the ticket collector not to charge me. With no Berlin Wall at that time, I just took a taxi from the bus depot into the West. Three decades later, when I was heading the reporting operation in Germany, the Wall had long since gone up, and when I visited our correspondent Mark Brayne in East Berlin, getting through controls was not by any means as easy. Then – in a flash, it seemed – the Wall was gone and remarkably quickly forgotten. Post-war Europe had gone through some strange contortions before Mikhail Gorbachev in Moscow saw that the game was up.

The word came from London that general manager Sir Christopher Chancellor was coming to Copenhagen for contract negotiations with the Danish news agency. I was advised to be at the airport when he arrived. Sir Christopher was a redoubtable figure, with a massive reputation for steering Reuters into smooth waters after the war. The agency had been living from hand to mouth in the early fifties, but Chancellor turned the ship around. I was at hand as requested at Kastrup Airport when the great man arrived, accompanied by Tony Cole, his burly Scottish deputy, and I shepherded this impressive pair out towards the long queue for taxis.

These were mainly glittering black Mercedes, though I noticed that down the line a battered relic of pre-war days had somehow got into the action. It surely wasn't going to get to the head of the queue, though, was it? Surely? But as the line rolled relentlessly nearer, it became clear that this wheezing wreck was indeed the one into which Sir Christopher would be bundled. We rattled in virtual silence into town. After Sir Christopher had retired to his suite in the splendid Hotel d'Angleterre (where else?), Tony took me aside to teach me the facts of company life at higher level, where you don't queue for taxis, you order cars in advance. I was clearly not accustomed to the good life.

So I made sure to be at the hotel promptly at nine each morning, when the General Manager's day began. A morning chat would first take place in Tony Cole's room, where I was already at hand. A knock on the door heralded Sir Christopher's arrival. The Reuter boss would walk in behind an outstretched copy of *The Times* and then sit down to peruse its principal pages, shooting sharp questions at Cole from behind the paper, to elicit how Reuters was doing on this or that world story. Tony, obviously already well briefed by head office as to the state of the Reuter wire, would respond smartly. Now there were social/business calls to be made and, on the first day, a visit to the Ritzau family's home.

We surely cut a strange sight in this highly Social-Democratic capital. Chancellor's elegantly tailored black jacket and striped trousers were not something the Danes saw every day. He strode briskly in front, the massive Tony Cole doing his best to keep up. Chadwick (as I was always addressed by Sir Christopher) brought up the rear, carrying a bunch of flowers, as commanded, for Mrs Ritzau.

Once the MD had left for London, things relaxed. Cole, who would succeed Sir Christopher on his retirement within a year, had learned journalism in much the same sort of environment as myself. Business done, he liked to get out in the evenings. He had what seemed to me a gargantuan appetite. We were walking down Strøget one evening when he spotted one of those Nordic institutions – a hot dog stand. Danes (and some other Scandinavians) are as addicted to hot dogs as Brits to fish and chips. In Denmark they're called *pølser* (in Sweden, *korv*), and I too had got to like them. They come boiled or grilled in different sizes and with tomato ketchup or mustard – or both. Wrapped in paper, they're usually consumed beside the kiosk. On a chilly night, a street corner hot dog stand and the customers standing in a pool of light around it, form a familiar Nordic tableau. It somehow makes many a chilly night slightly cosier.

'Let's have some,' said Tony. So Reuters' future boss and I stood in the cobbled square, munching shiny red sausages. 'I like these,' he said. 'We must try them again'. And so we did, several times, before his business in Copenhagen was done. And he'd already dined substantially, I imagined, in the considerably more elegant surroundings of the Angleterre.

There were no forbidden areas with Tony Cole. He enjoyed the atmosphere of Copenhagen by night, the lights from dozens of small shops casting a warm glow over the street. He told me he collected old lamps. I'd just written a feature on the subject and knew where the antique shops were. I remember him standing out on the pavement on a cold November evening, watching like a tennis spectator at Wimbledon as inside the dimly lit shop, half a floor below pavement level, the proprietor and I haggled back and forth over the price of a pair of Chinese lamps which had taken his fancy. My boss also wanted a bargain. Eventually I looked up through the window and signalled the price had been negotiated, at which Tony came bounding down the steps. He was delighted with his purchase. He rewarded me by letting me carry the bulky parcels back to London for him on my next trip home!

I was soon to meet the third man in a row to accede to the Reuter throne, following Tony's sudden death of a heart attack at his desk in Fleet Street. Gerry Long was very much the gourmet, and I doubt if he'd ever have dreamt of eating sausages on the street. At the time I met him he was European Editor, based in Bonn, where I'd called for a few days indoctrination before flying on to Copenhagen. Now Gerry arrived for contract talks with the Danish agency. He'd had a fairly rapid rise within Reuters, which he joined after wartime service and a spell in Army Intelligence in Berlin. A fellow northerner, son of a postman, he'd by this time acquired quite an upmarket accent and manner to go with it. I found him easy enough to get on with. We often ate together, drank together, went one evening to the cinema.

He was outspoken in his views of the agency, clearly ambitious and dissatisfied with his present role. Because of Reuter stinginess, he said – however seriously I couldn't judge – their fourth child, born in Bonn, had had to sleep in a bottom drawer, converted into a bed. He told me he'd had a good offer from the *Daily Express* and now wondered if he shouldn't have taken it up. It was strange to recall all this a year later in New York, when the news came through, after Cole's death, of Gerry's appointment to the top job. I was the only one in Reuters North America who'd ever met him. Even the New York boss, Julian Bates, never to be a great favourite of mine, was constrained to ask me what sort of a man the new chief was.

Head office seemed to like my coverage, expanded from an unproductive preoccupation with Danish politics, not exactly the world's favourite topic. My features were getting good play. I covered the annual 'Viking Games' at nearby Frederiksund and, a little further up the coast road at Elsinore, reported a slight problem with the old ruins. With a touch of poetic licence, I gave the story a snappy five-word intro, 'Hamlet's Castle Is Falling

Down'. Well, some of the ramparts were crumbling away. The widely used story didn't do the Danish tourist trade any harm and may even have helped speed up the repairs. Then head office came up with the annual request for Christmas brighteners. I contributed a story about a farmer and his wife with nineteen children who'd won the annual prize for the biggest family in Denmark.

Then, having been told that Danish royalty were very accessible, I rang the castle in Jutland. I asked the man who answered, a very friendly secretary, I assumed, how the royal family would be spending Christmas. We chatted pleasantly about this and that. The King, I was told, would be cooking the Christmas dinner himself.

'That's interesting,' I said, 'and where is the King at the moment?'

'This is the King speaking,' was the laughing reply. You'd hardly have got past the switchboard at Buckingham Palace. Yes, some things were very definitely different in Denmark.

My next encounter with a head of state would be in Finland. The Soviet leader, Nikita Khrushchev, was to visit Helsinki on the occasion of President Urho Kekkonen's sixtieth birthday, and we always pulled out the stops on such occasions. They asked me to back up our Stockholm correspondent, Elizabeth Kitson, and I was happy to do most of the legwork. I was at Helsinki's impressive Saarinen-designed central station as the small tubby figure of Khrushchev, familiar from television and the papers, stepped off the train from Moscow, to be greeted by top officials and a small girl with flowers. After the political talks, Khrushchev went a-visiting, calling at several factories to chat with the workers. Most of the foreign reporters had called it a day after the formal arrival. I followed, along with the Finnish press, and with their help interviewed some of the overalled workers Khrushchev had talked to. To my surprise, he'd told one group the Soviet Union would in a few days time be launching a new sixty-ton Sputnik into space. It was clearly the story. We were well ahead with Khrushchev's arrival (Reuters 2103, AP 2147), and sticking around had paid off. London reported 'substantial usage for the space story throughout Europe, the United States and the Far

East'. The Sputnik duly soared into orbit a few days later. This is what agency journalism is about.

It was the age of the Angry Young Men, as a new crop of novelists and playwrights had been brand named in Britain. Yorkshireman John Braine, author of the best-selling novel *Room At The Top*, later to be successfully filmed, came to town on a lecture visit. I interviewed him in the lounge of the Grand Hotel in the Town Hall Square. Coming from roughly the same northern milieu, I'd admired his work and envied his success. But before I could tell him this, he got in first by saying, 'How on earth do you get a good job like this – Reuter correspondent in Copenhagen?' We shared a laugh.

I later interviewed Shelagh Delaney, the young author of one of the other 'kitchen-sink' plays and novels which were much in vogue in England at the time. Then, another writer, as much in the news for his drinking as his writing, arrived in town. Ireland's Brendan Behan was the author of the tragicomic play *The Quare Fellow*, which revolves around a prisoner facing execution in Dublin's notorious Mountjoy Prison. He was, fairly predictably, more than a little tipsy. It didn't matter. That was part of his image.

A senior editor from *The Times* visited Stockholm a few months later and I showed him around. The day before he left, he asked if I'd be interested in joining his paper. He suggested I call round at Printing House Square for a chat when I was in London, which came shortly, as my two-year Copenhagen assignment was up. By then I was married to a girl from the Swedish university town of Lund – one of the lovely students I'd met at Pension Berg. In London, it looked like I'd be stuck for some time on Central Desk, as it was then known, which didn't appeal very much. I called round at *The Times* as invited and was offered a job. But I'd have to serve three years in London, they said, before being considered for a foreign posting. When I disclosed this to the bosses at Reuters, they suddenly found a place for me on the United Nations team in New York. Suddenly, I had a very tough decision to make, especially with a child on the way. But I decided to take up the Reuter offer (the firm had been very good to me), and in the early summer of 1961 Marianne and I sailed from

Gothenburg aboard the Norwegian liner *Stavangerfjord* for the New World.

Chapter 7
WORLD WAR LOOMS, KENNEDY'S SHOT, BRITAIN BATTLES THE COLONIES

Naively, I suppose, I'd thought of it as one big adventure. Images of Broadway and a vast country beyond, stretching to the Rockies, New Orleans and Hollywood, had been duly imbibed via music and the movies. The seven-day Atlantic crossing, prolonged by a day while engine trouble in the forty-year-old liner was fixed, only sharpened the sense of anticipation. Up to that year, I'd only met a couple of Reuters North American staff at those international conferences in Europe. My simplistic image of America had traditionally involved tough guys like Humphrey Bogart and George Raft, film stars Bing Crosby, Grace Kelly and Marilyn Monroe. On the musical side, there was George Gershwin, Louis Armstrong and Jelly Roll Morton. Skyscrapers, gleaming transcontinental trains and big limousines. Such were the symbols for many of my age group of 'The American way of life'. It had all been sparked off much earlier, of course, by the comics, with their cowboys and Indians, and gangster films. And the young Americans who arrived with their suntans in Lancashire during the war seemed to wear much smarter uniforms than anything the British Army provided. They generally seemed a friendly and outgoing lot, compared with us dour Lancastrians. Such were my simplistic reference points, even as a thirty-year-old, as we sailed to America.

It was much the same too, I think, for many in the Nordic countries where I'd spent the past two years. For many Swedes and Norwegians, America had traditionally meant a gateway to a better life. I was lucky enough not to be a cash-strapped immigrant with a job to find at the other end; like my maternal grandfather, for instance, when he arrived with half of a large family in the wake of World War One. A pity both my grandparents had passed away, and the family was now scattered around the States. I always meant to look them up, but with work pressures, lack of cash, skimpy holidays and soon my own family, I never got round to it. Nor did I imagine, as the *Stavangerfjord* tied up in the Hudson River, that the United States would soon be plunged into a world crisis of alarming dimensions.

We'd all read and heard a lot in Europe about the new President, John F Kennedy. His election had been welcomed by liberals and those on the left of the political spectrum. The handsome young senator struck a chord in Europe with his talk of a New Frontier, and seemed to have a positive attitude to social and employment reform. On the foreign front, albeit in his own hemisphere, he was not so sure-footed. He was soon in trouble for ordering the disastrously failed invasion of Cuba, the new communist state on his doorstep. And big dark clouds were gathering in relations with Moscow.

New York, I soon realised, is not everyone's meat, especially in the middle of a humid summer. After the initial thrill of working in one of the world's most vibrant centres, I began to wonder if we'd done the right thing. Reuters' overall editorial boss in New York, (the late) Julian Bates, was not, I'm afraid, one of the world's most charming people. He went out of his way from the start to let me know he hadn't recruited me himself, as with most of his New York team. He'd had me foisted on him, as he obviously saw it, by London. It wasn't a very auspicious start to life in the New World. The flat allocated to us in Leonia, New Jersey, had not yet been vacated by my predecessor in the UN team. So we found ourselves stuck in the second-rate Tudor Hotel on 42nd Street, with no air conditioning and a child shortly to be born. To add to our discomfort, although I was there specifically to join the UN team, Julian, in overall command of the Reuter operation in the city, stuck me on the overnight shift at the central New York office the second week I was there.

Returning sleepless to a sweltering hotel room after working all night, I was hardly the best company for Marianne. Julian clearly thought the UN was a cushy number. He'd recruited most of the other staff himself and gave them the principal reporting assignments, such as space shots at Cape Canaveral. I'm afraid,

120

historically, he doesn't rank among Reuters' more engaging people; fortunately he was one of only two or three such that I met during a fairly long career.

With the United Nations General Assembly on its summer break, I worked out my first couple of months in the central bureau. We were quartered a couple of floors up in the old New York Times building in West 43rd Street. Photographed from the air, or from one of the neighbouring rooftops, as it often was for magazine pictures, the Times building, long since demolished, had almost the romantic look of an old French chateau. At ground level, close to the background blare of traffic in Times Square, it was not quite so appealing. At night, with the presses rolling, delivery vans roaring up and departing, the atmosphere in the side street from where the papers were disgorged was hectic – not unlike those narrow streets off Fleet Street as it used to be. Almost a madhouse. You'd have been a fool to try to park thereabouts.

I'd arrive from New Jersey via the Port Authority bus station a few blocks away, itself a hectic, echoing, fume-ridden location which always filled me with gloom. The Times building itself was a bit worn out inside, even in the sixties. Perhaps I'd been too long in Scandinavia, with its contemporary architecture and furnishings. The Reuters editorial was the usual jumble of desks and teleprinters, two executive offices opening off it. The other was occupied by manager Kim Rodgers, a friendly American who couldn't have been more different from Mr Bates. At least he showed some friendly interest in how the two of us were settling in.

There was a good mix of experienced journalists from England, notably (the late) Ronnie Batchelor, our intrepid chief reporter on that side of the Atlantic, desk chief (the late) Mike Charvet, who'd also followed the traditional path of British journalism, and Dick Wilson, an affable American from upper New York State. Our sociable and good-humoured teleprinter operators were Ritchie, a New Yorker of partly Italian descent, and Yngve Anderson (understandably called Andy for ease of pronunciation) from Sweden's Åland Islands. I think everyone did their best to keep out of Julian's way.

American politics at home and abroad were covered by our Washington team, seasoned veterans led by Irish-American Pat Heffernan. I wasn't unhappy not to be involved. I knew precious little of the US political scene, which I still find bewildering today. And their elections, with those seemingly endless 'Primaries', can be rather a bore. At least the last tussle, with a black American for the first time in the race, injected a bit more sparkle to the process.

I saw the young president John F Kennedy for the first time when he arrived from Washington to address the General Assembly in September 1961, days after the death of UN Secretary General Dag Hammarskjöld in a mysterious plane crash during a peace-seeking mission to Northern Rhodesia (now Zambia). There was trouble on all international fronts, and some people feared another world war was in the offing. Relations between the two superpowers had been strained since the Russians shot down a US spy plane which had taken off from a NATO base in Norway. Summit talks in Paris between Soviet leader Nikita Khrushchev and US President Dwight D Eisenhower had collapsed. Kennedy, Eisenhower's successor, was scorned as a youngster by the often boorish Khrushchev at more unproductive talks in Vienna.

Strains intensified as Khrushchev pressed for concessions on still-divided Berlin, where the continued presence of Western forces was for the Russians a thorn in the flesh. When the Americans declined to play ball, Moscow had its communist ally, East Germany, build a wall across the city to emphasise the political divide.

I'd seen Kennedy in action on the domestic front when he addressed America's labour union confederation, the AFL-C1O, whose tough delegates are no easy meat. We reporters, sitting below the stage, were given printed copies of his speech in advance. But Kennedy, interrupted by heckling after a few sentences, tossed the prepared speech aside and gave them as good as he got, stabbing his forefinger in that very characteristic way to emphasise his points. I decided that this Kennedy guy was no soft touch. He was much less rough and ready – an expert in altering his demeanour to suit the audience – but equally outspoken, when addressing the General Assembly. At the time, there were crises in Africa, the political tug of war continued in still-divided Europe and the East–West nuclear arms race threatened a world conflict. After formally saluting Russia's 'brave cosmonauts' – he had little choice, as they were ahead in the game – Kennedy said outer space must not be driven by old-style imperialism – code language for 'No bases on the Moon, please.' He said events of the next few months might well decide the fate of man for 10,000 years. A touch rhetorical, perhaps, but in an atomic age, with the Cuban missile crisis shortly to erupt, the hyperbole was maybe justified.

Meanwhile, a story was going the rounds that the beautiful socialite Jackie Onassis, seldom seen by the general public except at his side, was not actually the first wife JFK had ever had. There'd been another hasty marriage, which was rapidly annulled and given the hush-hush treatment, it was said. I gathered that Reuters had been pointedly advised not to touch it, or we might regret it, and I'm not sure whether further details ever emerged; but the old story is still going around on the Internet. It's part of history now anyway. There were much darker days ahead in the Kennedy story.

With our Washington bureau handling the domestic political scene, there were precious few bits and pieces left to be garnered that summer at the New York office. We mainly plucked stories from the Associated Press 'A' Wire, but there were relatively few angles of interest to the outside world. The biggest out-of-office stories were covered by Ronnie Batchelor, a veteran of the Arnhem landings in World War Two. He'd established himself as an excellent on-spot reporter and would cover stories like the first space shots from Cape Canaveral. He also produced rapid copy on sports events, notably boxing, dominated during the fifties and sixties by colourful characters like Jersey Joe Walcott, Rocky Marciano and a white(!) Swedish interloper called Ingemar Johansson.

Keen to make a mark, I decided, as in Copenhagen, to contribute colour pieces to the file during the news-thin weeks before joining the UN bureau. I tackled the human side of the big fight game in a 'Where Are They Now?' piece on America's top boxing legend, who two years after retirement now faced money problems on a gigantic scale.

> Joe Louis, who rose from the humble surroundings of a cotton-picker's cabin to fame and riches as the world's heavyweight champion, lives today haunted by the knowledge that he can never pay off a million-dollar tax backlog which is a legacy of his fighting career.

In the post-war world, the name Joe Louis still epitomised the big fight game. People remembered his merciless two-minute four-second despatch of Germany's Max Schmelling, who'd been reported to have disparaged black Americans. Now the German had offered financial help with the Brown Bomber's tax problems. Singer Frank Sinatra also offered funds. My feature story won wide play worldwide.

There was one story I wouldn't have wanted to cover, and I forget who, if anybody, drew the short straw. An elegant gilt-embossed card had arrived at the New York office inviting us to an execution. I forget the name of the unfortunate man. It was an aspect of the American scene I could never come to terms with. Gas chambers and the electric chair were still widely used at the time to dispatch the worst criminals – and for that matter, hanging was still the method used in Britain. I don't think Reuters took up the invitation.

By this time Marianne and I were living in a one-bedroom flat in the pleasant suburb of Leonia, New Jersey, away from the noisy bustle of Manhattan on the far side of the Hudson River. It was a quiet area with wide streets, trees and gardens, which many of the Europeans tended to go for. We were succeeding Noel and Muriel Hudson, an English couple whose house I would also inherit in Cairo in days to come. One of the good friends they bequeathed to us, American Helen Fuhrman, kept a motherly eye on Marianne as the weeks sped by. Luckily, she called round at my request one day in July when I'd had to leave home and take the bus to work. Our next to useless doctor had told us not to worry, that the baby was not immediately due. But a couple of hours later, then at work in the New York office, I got a call from Helen's husband, Michael, to tell me I was now the father of a baby boy. Julian Bates didn't think it necessary or appropriate to let me have the rest of the day off. And we changed doctors.

So now we had a beautiful baby boy, christened Nils Peter to reflect his Anglo-Swedish heritage. As soon as she saw the situation, Helen had called an ambulance, which drove to Englewood Hospital, siren blaring. Marianne still had another hard time before being admitted, having to answer myriad questions about our national background and ability to pay. After seeing the child, I celebrated, appropriately I think, by calling at a nearby foreign car dealer's and buying a Volvo Amazon, a sporty Swedish car I'd always fancied in Copenhagen but could never afford. It was one of the quickest purchases I ever made, taking just a bit longer than buying a hot dog. I asked the salesman, 'How much is the Volvo Amazon in the window?'

'Twenty-five hundred dollars,' he said, 'but let you have it at twenty-three.'

Well, it was still more than I could afford, I said, after explaining I'd just come into the country. I pretended to look instead at two fairly crappy English cars, which I won't name, each marked a good $500 cheaper.

'Tell you what,' the salesman said. 'You can have the Volvo for twenty-one.'

$400 knocked off in five minutes. That's salesmanship for you. So this was the bright side of the American way of life!

I drove the car away without paying a cent in cash. All he had, after checking my credentials, were two post-dated cheques for $100 each as part of a three-year deal. I was still paying off the balance from Sweden, where I shipped the car when my New York sojourn was over. I thought it was an appropriate way to celebrate my half-Swedish son's arrival. And he, because of where he was born, now enjoyed the benefits of a US passport.

In an era of long bonnets, mammoth tail fins and cheap petrol, American friends thought we'd got ourselves 'a cute little car'. I suppose they were right. 'Well, waddya know,' said one New Yorker kindly, arriving at our flat with his English wife in a very long gas guzzler. 'Windshield wipers and everything!'

So instead of taking buses, I could now drive to work at the United Nations when the new General Assembly session started.

It was an easy drive over the George Washington Bridge and down the East River Drive, with a brief incursion into Harlem. Then a simple turn-off at Forty-Second Street and a ramp brought you down into the UN garage, where you enjoyed press parking facilities. So simple at that time. With only sixty or so member nations and no terrorism threats, such luxuries were possible. Things have changed slightly since.

Nobody at head office had told me about the cost of medicine in the United States. You had to pay on the nail. That's why they took all those particulars from Marianne before allowing Peter to be born. And I confess I'd never thought to ask about natal expenses. So my son cost us $600 – quite a sum then. He turned out to be well worth it! I paid the sum back to the New York office in two instalments. I made a protest to head office and as a result, they agreed almost reluctantly, it seemed, to pay medical costs in future for correspondents posted to the States, though not for the spouse. This didn't benefit me, but it did others later. London should have told me about the lack of medical care in America, and our union should have taken the matter up. Only that same year did Kennedy urge Congress to approve Medicare for 14.2 million Americans aged sixty-five or over. Four years later, it was finally agreed.

After the cramped and somewhat shabby office in West 43rd Street (all newsrooms were at that time), the splendid UN building, when I finally got there for the start of the autumn session, was certainly different. The spacious main lobby, its famous Foucault pendulum swinging from the lofty ceiling, made an impressive entrance. The Reuter office on the third floor, one of a string of newspaper and wire service offices along the corridor, was not large, but had wide views over the East River, busy most of the day with hooting ferries and small boats. Sometimes a seaplane bringing some Wall Street banker from his Long Island pad would drift in to land downriver. The view was wide, light and airy. It was a pleasant environment, one of the best I've worked in. And a far cry from West 43rd Street.

I met for the first time Mike Littlejohns, our chief UN correspondent. He'd become a byword among other reporters of many nationalities, whom he usually shamed by his wide range of contacts – and immaculate shorthand. He'd been covering the place long enough to know the UN backwards. Get to know as many delegates as possible, he said. Covering committees was one thing. But the speeches didn't say everything. There was much to be learned lobbying after the day's sessions, amid the chit-chat and gossip of the multi-ethnic Delegates' Lounge. With its long bar, it did a roaring trade.

Of the various United Nations forums, the Security Council, bringing in top statesmen from around the world, was and remains the most prestigious, and the bitter rows therein grab most of the headlines. For many other countries at that time served by Reuters, the Fourth (Colonialism) Committee was the main news source. With Britain, France, Portugal and other countries still clinging to vast areas of the world's surface, their populations crying out ever more vociferously for independence, it was bound to be so.

Somewhat to my surprise – I'd been used to moving around a lot – it was a largely sedentary job. With so many committees to cover, we rarely moved from the office. Most days would find three or four of us sitting silently with headphones clasped to our ears, making notes. Not very glamorous – almost like a school-room at times. Shorthand helped us get the juicier quotes down accurately, and I was surprised to find how few other journalists knew it. Some of them considered themselves too grand. '*Ich bin kein Reporter, ich bin Korrespondent,*' as one German put it. But reported speech, without quotes, makes for a very dull story. All of us at Reuters were accustomed to reporting the English way – one thing I think the Brits get right.

Once the General Assembly with its myriad committees got into gear each autumn, it was all hands on deck, with more reporters moved from the central New York office to UN Headquarters at the other end of 42nd Street. Gerry Ratzin, with Russian learned during national service as well as French, was one of them; emigré Brit Tony Goodman and Australian Alan Barker were also in the action. Few urgent stories emerged from the committees. The day's main story, usually from the General Assembly or Security Council, was usually written by Mike, with two or three new leads as fresh material emerged. They were long hours. As the doors of luckier news offices along the corridors closed one by one, the wire service men were still at work. Stories still had to be 'freshened', as the phrase was, for a Daylead or Overnighter, which we took it in turns to write. I was invariably late home, which didn't do domestic life much good.

The Fourth Committee sounds dull, but often wasn't. One of the big issues of the day was decolonisation, with some of the sharpest exchanges between opponents and defenders of the status quo in Africa, the Middle East and elsewhere. The related Trusteeship Council, set up to oversee the interests of about-to-emerge nations, was another battleground. Britain and Portugal still held sway in large chunks of Africa. South African delegates fought off increasingly bitter attacks on its apartheid system. The native black petitioners, as they were called, were often backed by a British left-wing cleric, the Reverend Michael Scott, whose deadpan voice droned through many an early autumn afternoon. Scott, revered by Africans (the Namibians named their capital after him), was long and lanky, straggle-haired, usually carrying a briefcase stuffed with background papers: a truly British product. He'd been jailed once in South Africa for supporting the Passive Resistance to Apartheid campaign. With no official role in the Anglican Church, and not even a parish of his own, Scott was regarded either as a hero or a confounded nuisance – which is how he would have wanted it. Britain was ever in the firing line in an increasingly hopeless struggle to retain a foothold in the last of those pink blobs on the globe. Apart from the merits of the case – and decolonisation has been a mixed blessing – Britain couldn't afford an empire any more. The world had changed, but in London the penny didn't seem to have dropped, even with the Suez fiasco.

A few decades later, decolonisation has been of limited benefit to vast tracts of black Africa under the continent's new dictators. We used to laugh at the Hutus and Tutsis, comical names we'd only just heard of, fighting it out in the heart of Africa. Four decades later, in Rwanda, they're still at it. The departure of the British from swathes of East Africa hasn't made life better in some places either, with dictators like Zimbabwe's Mugabe in charge. (And I well remember many Sudanese, when I reported from that country later, saying, 'It was better when the British were here.') Not that I support colonialism; but the big changes in the Dark Continent haven't made life universally better. An opinion I couldn't have expressed when writing for Reuters, of course. We were strictly impartial as the battles raged.

Among the star orators, and a leading scourge of the old brigade, was India's V K Krishna Menon. Grandson of a Rajah, son of one of India's richest men and a graduate of the London School of Economics, he'd been fighting since the twenties for Indian independence. He joined the Labour Party, became a local councillor in the London district of St Pancras and was later made a freeman of the borough, an honour shared only with one other voluble man of words, George Bernard Shaw. After independence in 1947, Krishna became India's High Commissioner in London, and for ten years led its delegation to the UN, preaching non-alignment, criticising the United States, supporting Communist China, giving some people apoplexy. He had an unparalleled gift for phrase-making. 'You tell us we're going to go to hell!' he once shouted back at a heckler at a London rally in the run-up to Indian independence. 'Well, we reserve the right to go to hell in our own way!'

When the word got around that Krishna was to address the General Assembly, there was a rush for seats. With his acquiline nose and piercing eyes, he once made the cover of *Time* magazine. There were always fireworks when 'the old snake charmer', as some Western delegates called him, was around. He broke the record for the longest unscripted speech in the history of the General Assembly, a peroration on Kashmir which lasted five hours, followed by three hours more the following day. I enjoyed his verbal tussles with Pakistan's erudite Muhammad Zufrullah Khan in the perennial Kashmir debate.

Today's delegates should be relieved that 'Mephistopheles in a Savile Row suit' – another label put on him – is no longer around. After listening to thousands of words at the UN on this apparently insoluble problem, I'd get an on-the-spot indoctrination into the Indo–Pakistan conflict a few years later when I was sent to cover the 1965 war. And the political battle over Kashmir has turned into terrorism.

A few European politicians also enlivened the scene. Denmark's energetic foreign minister, Per Haekkerup, was one such. With my Copenhagen background, I got to know him well. When news was scarce, you could usually rely on Haekkerup to come up with a new 'Nordic Initiative', whatever the issue. When you checked it out with the Swedes and Norwegians, they weren't always happy to be lumped together with the Danes, while Haekkerup got all the publicity. But he got Denmark on to the Reuterwire and into the papers. Which, you could argue, is what being a politician is about.

As Peter grew, we used the skimpy American two-week leave to drive south to Washington, Williamsburg, West Virginia and the Carolinas. One restaurant waitress thought this blonde Nordic baby so beautiful (he wasn't overweight like many American kids) that she insisted on carrying him into the kitchen 'to show the other girls'. I got badly sunburned on a North Carolina beach. We almost managed to suffocate the child by leaving him in the locked car while shopping. And we drove over a couple of snakes straggling across the road in a place called The Great Dismal Swamp – the name might have come from a Sherlock Holmes tale. The following winter, Marianne's sister, Barbro, flew over from Sweden to babysit and we travelled north on an overnight Greyhound bus for a ski holiday in Canada. I discovered just how difficult skiing was. I hadn't been brought up in Scandinavia. Marianne had no problems, but the overlong pair of skis I selected made it hard to execute even a simple snow-plough stop. For decades I thought it was just my own clumsiness, until a surgeon told me I had 'restricted movement' of the hips. Well, we live and learn.

New York takes some getting used to. The brusqueness of people's street manners, the gratuitous rudeness of some of its citizens. The bus drivers who don't answer, don't even look at you when you ask where they're going. Maybe it's because most of their passengers act the same way. I remember once getting into a taxi outside the United Nations building, and asking the driver. 'Could you take me to the Port Authority bus station, please?'

I feared the worst. What had I said wrong, I wondered as a

thick-necked head turned slowly round from the driver's seat. But he simply said, 'If you ask like that, I'd gladly take you anywhere.'

So there you are. Nobody says 'Please'. At the other extreme, at the same taxi rank outside the UN, I was gratuitously abused by a driver and went round to the front of the cab to take his number. He snarled from the window, 'If you don't get away from there, bud, I'm gonna run you down!'

I decided discretion was the better part of valour.

There existed – maybe still does – a sort of Taxi Court, where you can air your grievances. They always ask complainants first whether they're prepared to attend the court and give evidence. At that stage, most people decide to let it go. The fearless Ronnie Batchelor, however, not one to avoid a scrap (he'd fought at Arnhem, for God's sake!), said he'd most certainly attend. We feared for his life as the day of the hearing arrived, but he came back to the office smiling. The driver had lost his licence for ten days. 'He looked daggers at me as he walked out,' Ronnie reported. I can imagine…

The last time I was in New York, in the nineties, most taxi drivers seemed to be new immigrants, with only a rudimentary grasp of the spoken language – and sometimes of the streets. Returning to my Manhattan hotel late one evening after visiting my former piano teacher in the wilds of Brooklyn, I discovered that my driver was from Sudan. 'Khartoum,' he said. When I mentioned towns like Juba, Malakal and Wau, he said, 'You know more about Sudan than I do.' I also had to point out the way back to the hotel.

The international scene continued to deteriorate, the cold war to intensify. Washington and Moscow seemed frozen in their entrenched positions. The United States had slowly overtaken the Soviet Union in the space race after a nasty fright over the sputniks. Soviet missiles were powerful enough to be aimed at Western Europe. The Americans could now strike anywhere in the Soviet Union. Neither side was in the mood to back down. New York newspapers started running sales pitches for bomb shelters. These looked pitifully incapable of withstanding an atomic fallout. One might as well, in the words of a British *Beyond*

The Fringe satirical sketch of the time, 'Jump into a brown paper bag'. We began to think about flying Marianne and the child back to Sweden.

With diplomatic progress blocked on most fronts, Khrushchev's decision to place missiles in Cuba, his new ally, was bound to send shivers down the spine. After two 'conventional' wars, costly enough in lives, property and industrial resources, the last thing anyone wanted was a confrontation between the superpowers. The outlook seemed bleak. The provocative Soviet move followed Washington's own misguided attempt to neutralise its new communist neighbour by sending in an invasion force of Cuban refugees. The landing was a disaster. But Cuba's ruler, Fidel Castro, clearly thought another attack imminent.

In the summer of 1962, the Russians, spotting a chink in the American armour, got Castro's permission to erect missile sites on the island and duly sent in the weapons. After a week's intensive talks in Washington, Kennedy ordered a naval blockade of the Caribbean country to prevent any further missiles coming ashore, and demanded that the sites already there should be dismantled. Moscow initially denied the existence of the rockets, and it was in the middle of this dangerous stalemate that an historic confrontation took place at the United Nations between US Ambassador Adlai Stevenson and Russian Ambassador Valerian Zorin. It would be Stevenson's finest hour. I was lucky enough to watch it from the press gallery above the Security Council.

The two fighters in the ring both had impressive careers behind them, and with world peace at stake there was a capacity crowd in the chamber. Some Americans had doubted the erudite Stevenson's capacity to tough it out with the stolid, bald-headed Russian, but they couldn't have been more mistaken. Armed with photographic evidence of the missiles, America held all the cards. Zorin, it appeared, hadn't been authorised to back off from the official Moscow line that the missiles simply didn't exist.

Not mincing his words, the American told him, 'Mr Zorin, I do not have your talent for obfuscation, for distortion, for confusing language and for doubletalk' – it was not the sort of diplomatic language usually heard at the UN! – and continued, 'we do have the evidence, and these weapons must be taken out.' He added caustically, 'The other day, Mr Zorin, you did not deny the existence of these weapons. Instead, we heard that they had suddenly become defensive weapons. But today, if I heard you correctly, you now say that they do not exist – or that we haven't proved they do exist.' Then came the knockout blow.

'Let me ask you one simple question. Do you, Ambassador Zorin, deny that the USSR has placed and is placing medium and intermediate-range missiles and sites in Cuba? Yes or no – don't wait for the translation – yes or no?'

Zorin: 'I am not in an American courtroom, sir, and therefore I do not wish to answer a question that is put to me in the fashion of a prosecutor.'

Stevenson: 'You are in the court of world opinion, and you can answer yes or no.' And in a phrase that sent the authentic thrill down the spine, he shouted over to the silent Russian, 'I am prepared to wait for an answer until Hell freezes over.'

It was a masterly piece of theatre. With the Russian looking more and more uncomfortable, Stevenson had an easel set up and presented aerial photographs showing Cuba, before and after. There for anyone to see were the missiles, there were the partially assembled Soviet llyushin 28 bombers. 'One of these missiles,' the US delegate said, 'could be armed with its nuclear warhead in the middle of the night, pointed at New York and landed above this room five minutes after it was fired.'

At this point, the Assembly President tried to calm the atmosphere and halt the exchanges, but Stevenson told him, 'I have not finished my statement.' And turning again to Zorin, he said, 'I asked you a question. I have had no reply.'

He left it there. The point had been made. Game, set and match to the Americans. Moscow removed the weapons and missile sites. The dramatic encounter, lasting less than an hour, had prevented a world conflict. Khrushchev wouldn't survive in office more than a year or two longer.

The following year I had an unexpected meeting with one of our own top politicians. In January 1963 the news came from London of the sudden death of Labour Party leader Hugh Gaitskell. Harold Wilson, a grammar school boy from Huddersfield and the youngest-ever Oxford don at the age of twenty-one, was a main contender to succeed him. The other was George Brown, whose unpredictable social antics in New York and elsewhere hadn't endeared him to some party members or the general public. Wilson happened to be in New York at the time. I tracked him down to his hotel near Central Park. He was out shopping, they told me at the desk, so I sat in the lobby until through the revolving doors came a now familiar figure, complete with pipe and tartan-collared Gannex raincoat, both of which had become trademarks. Wilson was the man who'd memorably observed that 'a week is a long time in politics' – and so in this case it had turned out to be. His folksy reference, amid economic problems, to 'the pound in your pocket' is still recalled to this day. He had the common touch. 'You'd better come upstairs, lad,' he said, and we took the lift to his room.

We were both northerners – he supported Huddersfield in the Football League and had heard of Bury FC. We didn't stand on ceremony, therefore. I sat on the bed while he composed a few well-chosen words at the desk. 'Will this do?' he asked, handing me his handwritten tribute.

'Fine,' I said. 'Might I just suggest…?'

'Do what you like with it, lad,' he said, and I put it into better shape: the only time I ever subedited a future prime minister's copy. Wilson, who was the Left's chosen candidate to succeed Gaitskell, was duly elected, and a few months later, after a general election, became Prime Minister.

The political atmosphere in America remained tense. It wasn't much of a life for Marianne, and it would do her good to see the family back in Sweden. We arranged a sea passage in the late summer of 1963. I'd stay for the rest of the year, I told London, but would then like some time off. In the event, it was for a year, spent in Sweden.

The United Nations factory reopened in the autumn of 1963, and the Reuter team dutifully reported the usual debates, charges and countercharges. For me, it was all beginning to be slightly predictable, and I wondered how Mike Littlejohns could have stuck it so long. With the flat empty, I hung around the UN building even more than usual in the evening and took the opportunity to hear some jazz in Greenwich Village, sometimes along with a young black (sorry, Afro-American) American working in the press department called Rudi Skeete. Bright and punchy swing was on the menu at the Room at the Bottom club, where the De Paris brothers, Sidney (trumpet) and Wilbur (trombone), played New Orleans stuff with a few trimmings. Naturally I got all the band's autographs, and a picture of the club still stands on a bookcase here.

I'd been a little surprised by the way some people stared at Rudi and me as we walked together in Lower Manhattan. I got a further taste of the conservative fringe after letting a beard grow – for the first time since the Cod War. Hard to believe nowadays, this provoked some hostile reactions among New Yorkers. 'Hello, God!' shouted one chap provocatively as I passed him on a Manhattan side street. 'I think you mean Jesus Christ,' I couldn't help replying, and walked on, leaving him to figure out the theology. Maybe I'd tempted Providence.

My American assignment ended against a background of tragedy. It was just another averagely busy morning at the UN on 22 November 1963, when one of our friendly competitor colleagues from UPI next door stuck his head in the doorway and said, 'Hey, you guys. Kennedy's been shot.'

It hadn't been on our own wire yet. Mike stayed on at the UN, the rest of us hurried to the central New York office. Within minutes I was stopping people in busy Times Square and 42nd Street for reaction. Most of them hadn't yet heard the news, but the story was spreading like wildfire. Radios and TV sets were switched on in shops and stores, people just piling in from the street to watch and listen. I'd gathered a lot of quotes even before we knew the inevitable – that President John F Kennedy was gone.

For two days we were all working almost around the clock. Allowed to take the Sunday off, I awoke in mid-morning and immediately switched on the TV. I thought I must be watching an old movie as the picture cleared from fuzz to sharp black and white and a burly man wearing a Stetson emerged from a small group of people and advanced on a young man I recognised as suspect Lee Harvey Oswald. Holding a pistol out in front of him in a curiously stiff manner, he shot Oswald in the stomach. I couldn't believe I'd seen a murder live on television. Still clearing my brain, I picked up the phone and rang the office, for I didn't know if this was live or a repeat. Dick Wilson, on the desk, assured me Reuters already had the story. An extraordinary day, an extraordinary weekend. After that, nothing I did in New York sticks in my memory. By the end of the year I was flying back to Sweden to spend Christmas with the family.

The final chapter in my own reminiscences of the Kennedy era came eighteen months later on 14 May 1965, by which time I was back at head office. The scene was a pleasant tree-shaded bank beside the Thames. Under a historic Runnymede dateline, I was dictating an Urgent first paragraph: 'The Queen and people of England today dedicated this small corner of their land to the memory of John F. Kennedy.' As the Urgent flashed on to the world wire, my story continued:

> The late American President's widow, Jacqueline, and their two small children, Caroline, 7, and John, 4, watched the ceremony in a sunlit glade close to the spot where Englishmen won their civil rights bill, the Magna Carta, from King John seven centuries ago. Queen Elizabeth and Mrs Kennedy stood together, reading some of the President's most stirring words in defence of freedom, inscribed on a gleaming white granite plinth in a three-acre stretch of parkland which Britain has given to the American people for ever. The memorial stone, a seven-ton, clean-carved piece of Portland granite from the same centuries-old quarries which helped to build St Paul's Cathedral, carried the stirring words from the late President's inaugural speech of 20 January 1961: 'Let every nation know, whether it wishes us well or ill, that we shall pay any price, bear any burden, meet any hardship, support any friend, oppose any foe, in order to ensure the survival of liberty.'

Being first with this story was the best personal tribute I could have paid to JFK.

Chapter 8
INDIANS AND PAKISTANIS GO TO WAR, BUT VIGILANTES ARE THE DANGER

I took a taxi to the battlefront. Everybody did. It was the only way to get there and it made a good Intro, used just once. My driver, understandably, didn't like getting too close to the action, and I could see his point. The upper branches of the trees along the main road from Lahore, heading east, where the Indians were, looked decidedly shredded.

I paid him off in smelly Pakistan notes, and walked the last 200 yards to where I could see soldiers clustered among some dilapidated farm buildings and a tent. The welcome, from a major of about forty, was meant to be reassuring. 'Come right in,' he said, pointing the way to a sort of field office, where an assorted collection of maps and binoculars lay on a simple trestle table. 'Good to see you, old man,' he said, in a lingo and accent I guessed had been acquired at Sandhurst. 'Come in and I'll put you in the picture.'

It was 1965 and, less than twenty years after Partition, the two countries were at daggers drawn again. It was mainly about the disputed territory of Kashmir, the area I'd heard so much about in those Colonialism Committee debates at the United Nations. Now for the first time I was hearing about the Rann of Kutch, a barren area in the Indian state of Gujarat, whose marshy borders were claimed by Pakistan. Not a name on everyone's lips exactly, but the Indians and Pakistanis were squabbling over it (and still are).

A tribunal set up by Britain's then Prime Minister, Harold Wilson, had awarded 350 square miles of this wilderness to Pakistan. The country's rulers decided to go for a bit more, believing India would not be able to defend itself against a quick military campaign. But a small group of saboteurs was soon dealt with by the Indians, who understandably got stroppy. As pre-war tensions built up and a full-scale conflict seemed imminent, Ronnie Batchelor flew to Karachi, and thence to Rawalpindi by local airline. By the time I was sent out to reinforce, the Indians had crossed the international border, the real war had officially begun and internal flights were suspended.

I got a preliminary fill-in on arrival from our resident correspondent in Karachi, Ralph Shaw, married to a local lady. He operated from a spacious villa in a good residential area of Karachi and a permanent office at the Pakistan News Agency. The military told us flights north were not likely to resume, and there was no question of getting on a military aircraft; so there wasn't much choice. I'd been told to link up with Ronnie in Rawalpindi, and the only way to get there now was by train. Karachi itself was noisy, hot and dusty and I couldn't imagine the train would be any more enjoyable. It wasn't.

For the first sixty miles or so, as we trundled north across an arid landscape towards the Punjab, it was comfortable enough. I had another of those friendly but very pukkah army officers as company, and in our first-class compartment you had room to stretch your legs. Things changed as we approached Lahore, about halfway to my destination. I only knew the city from its connection with Rudyard Kipling, who'd been a newspaperman there in the days of the Raj. As we approached the outskirts, the train ground to a halt and stayed there.

My military companion disappeared in search of information and returned with the news that the city was being bombed by Indian planes. After being stuck on the line for some hours, we rumbled into the railway station. It was the nearest thing to a madhouse, with refugees besieging the train – any train – to get out of there. The Indian forces were now reported close to the international airport. The United States had requested a temporary ceasefire to get its own nationals out of Lahore. With the city threatened with capture on the very first day, the situation didn't look good for Pakistan.

It didn't take long for our compartment, meant for six, to fill up with families desperate to get out of the city. As day turned to night and a second day dawned, the compartment became increasingly hot and stuffy, and I held on to my seat by the window. In the crush, two men were lying up on the luggage racks. There was no food to be had, and only a few swigs of water from a communal bottle which the major had managed to rustle up somewhere on the train. In the end, a journey which should have taken a little over a day took nearly two. By the time we got to Rawalpindi, I was exhausted and hungry – and feeling more than slightly ill. It was that bottle, I concluded afterwards.

Well, it had been my own choice to get back into reporting. After the stresses of New York, Marianne had been more than happy to be back in Sweden while I took my year's sabbatical in the pleasant university centre of Lund, her home town, in the south of the country. Marianne was absorbed into the family, and between various outings I tried to do a bit of freelance writing. But subjects were few and far between, and articles hard to sell, which depressed my mood. The in-laws couldn't have been more helpful. They organised a nice flat for us. We had sea trips in her parents' converted fishing boat, quaintly called *Stanley*, across the Sound to Denmark. Sometimes we'd fish (cod again!) with long lines draped with hooks.

There was a great extended trip, if a bit rough on the stomach, across the Baltic to north Germany in the tubby little boat, with its cosily upgraded saloon and sleeping quarters below. We'd stop at picturesque little Danish towns. The first thing you saw was the inevitable church tower on the skyline. As you sailed in, the cluster of little houses took shape and, stepping ashore, we'd stock up with food and petrol. I'd been reading a lot of Hammond Innes at the time, and this seemed like his sort of territory. It was hard to imagine these pretty coastal towns had been under German occupation a few years earlier. Across the Sound between the two countries, intrepid Danes had smuggled Jewish people risking arrest by the Nazis to safety in neutral Sweden. Ashore, we had nice trips in the newly acquired white MGB sports car, our now three-year-old son Peter full of excitement in the back seat. Even at that time, he was car crazy.

But, after nearly a year, I was getting restless, and with that work ethic ingrained in most northern Brits, I suppose, I felt I should be doing something more than this and earning some money. But I was in a minority of one when I talked of going back to London and rejoining the fray. Understandably, Marianne, like many women before and since, had had enough of being a Reuter wife and rebelled at the idea of changing homes again. To cut a long story short, we agreed to disagree. Marianne and Peter stayed in Sweden. The MGB was hoisted on to a ferry in Malmö and I began the trip back to England to rejoin the Reuter merry-go-round. Which seemed, somehow, to suit me.

But the first months were hard. Every evening into my mind came the image of my small son reciting the bedtime prayer he'd learned by heart:

> Gud som haver barnen kär
> Se till mig som liten är
> Vart jag mig in varlden vänder
> Står min lycka i Guds händer
> Lyckan kommar, lyckan går
> Du förbliver Fader vår.

(freely translated)

> God for whom each child is dear
> Keep this small one free from fear
> Where'er I go by land or sea
> Always my protector be
> In our joy and sometimes pain
> You our Father should remain.

Ronnie was by now ensconced at Flashman's. But with more pressmen finding their way into Pakistan, some by road, others via Afghanistan and the Khyber Pass, the hotel was filling fast. They put a single bed for me in Ronnie's room, and yet another when old *BT* colleague Brian Hitchen arrived, now working for the *Express*. It was getting to be like a school dorm. Shortly afterwards, I was gripped by the half-expected stomach problem, which meant frequent trips to the bathroom. All rooms had been blacked out in a panic about enemy bombers (which never arrived).

When stricken again in the early hours, I was groping around in pitch darkness to find the bathroom door. Half-dazed with lack of sleep, my hands came into contact with something I could swear hadn't been in the room the night before. My hands were feeling slowly along this object when there was a loud scream, and Hitchen, along whose recumbent form my fingers had been slowly groping, rose bolt upright and screamed: 'It's a f— cobra!' The situation resolved itself. It was the nearest he got to injury during the conflict.

As pressmen congregated around the hotel entrance next morning, clamouring for taxis, a convoy of cars arrived. An uptight Englishman with all the hallmarks of a natural born leader at a time of crisis approached, saying he was from Lahore and was evacuating wives and children. The cars were packed with luggage, at the back and on the roof. 'We're heading out of the country!' he cried. 'You people getting out too?'

An unsympathetic spark from Fleet Street replied laconically, 'No, mate. We just got in.'

For the first day or two, until trips to forward areas were arranged, we were dependent on army briefings, which understandably always emphasise the successes and ignore the setbacks. Ronnie and I made what we could of it, compacting the communiqués and adding what descriptive colour was available. We knew our colleagues across the border would be presenting the other side of the picture from Delhi and the desk back home would make a comprehensive and unbiased report from it all. It's difficult to get a clear picture of ground fighting. You're largely dependent on what the military tell you, but it was clear the conflict had resolved itself into two main battlefronts: the region south of Kashmir, known as the Rann of Kutch; and the area around Lahore. It was decided Ronnie would cover the northern front, while I moved back south. In the north, the fighting would climax later in what we called the Battle of Sialkot, in which India's 1st Armoured Division came under heavy Pakistan fire and withdrew. Conversely, Pakistan's much vaunted 1st Armoured Division tried to capture Amritsar, but was heavily defeated, losing or abandoning almost one hundred American-made Patton tanks.

It was hard for outsiders to get exercised, or even know, about the disputed Rann of Kutch, inevitably called by ruder names by the indomitable Fleet Street cameramen. ('Well, it's just a lotta bleedin' sand, innit?' said one.) It's a vast area covering 10,000 square miles, once part of the Arabian Sea and still flooded every year during the monsoon. This salty and inhospitable region is a resting site for migrating birds from Siberia, and a wildlife sanctuary for wild asses, foxes, jackals and gazelles. Few of us knew that at the time. We were inclined to agree with that cameraman.

The Lahore front had seen heavy fighting on both sides of the border, with Indian and Pakistani forces launching attacks and counter-attacks along the line of a canal which formed the de facto boundary between the two countries. In this area, interestingly, both sides were partly officered by veterans who'd fought with the British in World War Two. Initially the Indians crossed the canal and threatened Lahore – that was the time my train had been halted – but were later driven back by Pakistani armour and infantry. I based myself at Faletti's hotel, the local equivalent of Flashman's, and it was from there I headed in my taxi for the front along the road passing the old Bata shoe factory, and then met up with the brisk Sandhurst type and his men.

A posse of Italian reporters and photographers arrived. The Pakistani officer said the Indians had been driven back across the frontier and he was eager to show us the results of the latest fighting. We piled on to a couple of open trucks and the small convoy headed east, past shattered buildings. Emaciated cows stood listlessly in the arid fields to either side, a large buzzard perched expectantly on the back of one of them. We heard a series of screaming noises like express trains going past. 'They're shelling our rear lines,' the accompanying officer explained helpfully. 'Not to worry. It's over our heads.'

We came to a straight stretch of dusty road. Facing us was a line of burnt-out tanks, presumably from an unsuccessful Indian attack. One of the Italians jumped down and raced over to the nearest tank, climbed up on the tracks and peered inside the turret. 'There's a dead driver here!' he shouted down. 'No head.'

I took his word for it. Two other photographers ran a short

distance into the field alongside, trying for a better shot. Our accompanying major shouted loudly, 'Mines, mines!'

The Italians stopped dead in their tracks and moved very slowly back to the road, stepping into their own footprints.

All I'd known about Lahore before coming on this assignment was that in the days of empire, Rudyard Kipling, at the age of sixteen, got his first newspaper job there with the *Civil and Military Gazette*. Now, two countries that were once one under the British Raj were battling it out with sophisticated aircraft in the sky above the city. It made good copy, like watching one of those Battle of Britain movies, as jet fighters of the two nations dived and circled, leaving vapour trails across a deep blue cloudless sky. The Pakistanis, better armed with American-built F86 Sabre jets and F104 Starfighters, would claim later to have shot down over one hundred Indian aircraft on various fronts. The Indians, who claimed they'd destroyed over seventy of the enemy, while losing only thirty-six, were flying British Hawker Hunters and French Mystères. These were post-war estimates. It was impossible to get precise figures at the time, and I don't suppose anybody really knows to this day.

At ground level took place some of the fiercest tank battles since World War Two. The Pakistanis had better machinery, with American-made Pattons and Shermans, and more up-to-date artillery, but some post-war analysts said the Pattons, scores of which were abandoned, proved too sophisticated and were generally outfought by the Indian armour.

Within five weeks, with close on 7,000 deaths overall, the war reached a stalemate. It ended with a United Nations-sponsored ceasefire and little change in the status quo. Pakistan was awarded just 10% of its claim to the Rann of Kutch, the overwhelming part of which remains with India. Kashmir remained intact, as it does to this day. (But the dispute has not gone away, and the end of 2008 saw further carnage over the issue after Muslim militants arrived in power-driven dinghies in the harbour of Mumbai – once Bombay – and attacked multiple targets in India's now rich financial centre. Only two days earlier, Pakistan's President Asif Ali Zardari had said he was ready to end the fifty-year-old dispute over Kashmir. Clearly not all Muslims were of the same mind.)

After the bulk of the foreign correspondents left, including Ronnie, I was asked to stay on for a few weeks to do some follow-up features, and to cement relations with our friends at the local news agency. Taken by the army by truck up into Kashmir, I finally got to see what this remarkably beautiful hilly region was all about. Now I could understand what had exercised the minds of both Krishna Menon and Zafrullah Khan in those endless and ultimately fruitless debates at the United Nations. The disputed area remains divided, the two halves still administered by India and Pakistan, the latter's share known as Azad Kashmir. How long before the next eruption?

There were still a few political stories to be written and one or two features. I got a ride up country to the Khyber Pass and visited the fine museum at Peshawar, a town now reportedly coming under the control of Islamic militants. Back in Rawalpindi, close to where the future seat of government at Islamabad was still being built, I knocked out my pieces on a portable typewriter at the now almost deserted Flashman's, sending them off via the Pakistan News Agency office a few hundred yards down the tree-lined street.

After handing in my story to the wire room, I stayed chatting with colleagues at the agency late one evening, then closed the outer door behind me and walked down the path to the front gate. I immediately wished I'd called in daylight.

In the gloom, I was accosted by a ferocious, ragged-clothed man, clearly not of the same social class as my very literate opposite numbers inside the building. And he was holding a rifle. As he continued to make threatening gestures, I hopefully took out the official press pass from my breast pocket and showed it to him. When he looked at it upside down, I realised there was little point in pursuing the conversation. The worst thing would be to argue – or make a run for it.

For a minute or two we made noises at each other which neither of us understood before I got away and continued up the street, only to be waylaid at the first junction, this time by a group of three Pakistanis. One of them was whirling one of those long bamboo lathi sticks like a helicopter blade over my head, shouting words which sounded uncomfortably like 'American' and 'spy'. I remembered such alarms had been going the rounds, presumably emanating from government quarters. I was never quite sure how the Americans got into the act, but they usually do, or are thought to.

I talked my way out of this confrontation too, only to be threatened once again in the last hundred yards by a man lurking in the shadows with a rifle. Reaching the sanctuary of Flashman's, I told myself it was maybe time to leave Pakistan. The story was dying anyway. The next day I got the recall from London.

Chapter 9
'KEEP YOUR HEAD DOWN,' THEY SAID,
'AND WALK IN THE TANK TRACKS'

All I brought back from Karachi were five words of Urdu (*ek*, *do*, *din*, *shah*, *panch* – the numbers one to five, roughly and phonetically reproduced) and a lot of unusable banknotes. Expecting to be in Pakistan a week or two longer, I'd rashly changed a wad of sterling into local currency just before the recall message and was now stuck with it. Back in Fleet Street, bank tellers looked at me with polite disdain when I tried to change it back. And I needed every penny I could get. I had a monthly support payment to make on behalf of my son. The rest of my salary, still grandly denominated in guineas under an antiquated union agreement, was by no means as lavish as it sounded. I eventually had to sell my beloved white MGB sports car, but not before using it to tour the country and write a series of feature stories on all the World Cup venues.

I criss-crossed the Midlands and Pennines on a ten-day tour of all the magic addresses – Old Trafford, home of Manchester United, Goodison Park (Everton), Villa Park (Aston Villa), Hillsborough (Sheffield Wednesday) and Roker Park (Sunderland), finishing up with a flourish with Wembley Stadium itself. It was my old colleague Ronnie Batchelor's idea – he was now heading the UK Bureau – and very much my sort of thing. I tried to convey not just the atmosphere of the ground, but its history, and what the town was about – steel, coal, cotton or whatever. Club officials were enormously helpful as I drove from Birmingham to the north-east, and finally to the soccer showplace in London. The series went down well with clients across the world. Another plum assignment was a visit to the Concorde factory in Toulouse, where I had the pleasure, as a long-standing aircraft addict, of sitting in the pilot's seat of the prototype of the plane which would for a time revolutionise civil air transport. I never could afford to fly the Atlantic in the real thing. That would be the privilege later of Reuter MDs. And it's too late now, anyway.

If the World Cup had been a most enjoyable job, my most odious one was the trial of the notorious 'Moors Murderers', Ian Brady and Myra Hindley. This unsavoury story centred on the drab Manchester suburb of Hyde, from whose streets local youngsters had been vanishing without trace. The mystery started to unravel when early one morning a young man called David Smith rang the police from a call box in a state of terror, saying he'd witnessed an appalling murder. At first, they thought he was just reliving a nightmare, but it became all too real, as he described how Brady hacked a young lad to death. The living-room walls were sprayed with blood, he said, as the axe descended again and again. Brady, who'd invited him to the house, had him help clear up the mess. Then, as soon as Smith could get out, he ran home. Still disbelieving Smith's story, the police drove to an unremarkable semi-detached council house, where they unlocked an upstairs bedroom door and found the body under a bed, wrapped in a blanket. There were also two loaded revolvers, a book detailing Nazi atrocities in World War Two, and tape recordings of various victims' last screams.

The story snowballed long before the trial, revolting the nation, as a string of unsolved mysteries were re-investigated. The search spread to bleak Saddleworth Moor, where more bodies were found. By the time I arrived in Hyde for the eleven-day initial magistrates' hearing, the atmosphere in the shabby little Lancashire town had changed from initial disbelief to rage as the extent of what was already being labelled the crime of the century became clear. The atmosphere on that December day was ominous. Thunder rolled and lightning crashed as I arrived at the magistrates' court. An aggressive-looking crowd, already fed lurid details by the press, had gathered outside. With 'Guilty' verdicts assumed, if this had been the Wild West the pair would have been lynched.

Press places were relatively few, but I had a ticket and took my place in the dark-panelled courtroom. The eleven-day hearing, after which the case went to Chester Assizes, which I also covered, included sickening evidence I'd prefer to forget, like the cries replayed in court of a tortured girl pleading for her life. A great deal of it was unreportable. A child's mother screamed at Hindley across the court from the witness box, but I saw no signs of emotion, let alone shame, from the hard-faced peroxide blonde or the sallow, emotionless Brady, sitting beside her. The pair got off lightly, most people thought, with life imprisonment. If the trial had taken place a few months earlier, before the death penalty was abolished in Britain, they'd surely have gone to the gallows.

I drove to Oxford to cover a surprise return to the stage by screen idol Richard Burton. The handsome Welshman, renowned for films like *Camelot* and *Night of the Iguana*, had agreed to play Christopher Marlowe's Dr Faustus in an Oxford University Dramatic Society production directed by his former tutor, Professor Neville Coghill.

'Was this the face that launch'd a thousand ships?' Who better than Burton to orate the mellifluous lines? And when it became known that glamorous Elizabeth Taylor, who'd married Burton a year earlier after a stormy love affair and two divorces, was going to be along too, the performance became a must. American papers especially were clamouring for cover.

Burton, staying at the same hotel as we pressmen, joined us at the bar. He only took leave of us late one evening after Liz peeped round the door of the lift across the hall and shouted, 'Richard, Richard!' There was no resisting such an invitation – or was it a veiled threat? There'd be many ructions before the pair finally called it a day and the hard-drinking Burton died comparatively young. In retrospect, the Edward Albee film adaptation that year, *Who's Afraid of Virginia Woolf?*, in which the pair brilliantly and savagely portray a bickering married couple, was perhaps as much fact as fiction.

In London, I usually worked the evening shift, when it was my job to organise the news file and check (or if necessary rewrite) reports coming in from various assignments. I had a slight problem one evening when an impressive young reporter returned with a story about a Pakistan opposition group who'd been holding a public meeting in London. I'd bumped into him occasionally around Swiss Cottage Tube station. Leather jacket, cords and desert boots seemed to be his trademark. This particular evening, he'd turned in an engrossing report, but it read more like a radio or cinema script than a Reuter story. Not quite as objective as I'd have liked, but with a good feel for atmosphere. Sadly, I had to turn it down for the late night schedule.

The reporter shortly afterwards left Reuters. Maybe he'd decided we were not really his scene. After a short spell with the BBC, he wrote a thriller admirable for its precise background detail and dramatic touch. The book was *The Day of the Jackal*, by Frederick Forsyth. And I'd turned his story down!

I was living off Finchley Road in a leafy avenue called Netherhall Gardens. Looking for a flat, I'd answered an ad and was pleased to find the owners of the house were a well-known TV newsreader, Robert Dougal, and his wife. They welcomed a tenant also in the news business and became good friends. They also had a very pretty au pair from Salzburg, whose delightful home city I'd later visit. Meanwhile, being permanently strapped for cash, I had to earn more. I spoke with Stuart Underhill, the amiable Canadian who'd now become news manager at Reuters.

The best place to earn more was abroad. I'd done my punishment for my year off. Stuart talked with our Chief Correspondent in Italy, John Earle, who put me on his payroll. I'd known him since those endless European conferences. I'd be a sort of floating presence, working shifts like the others, but available for 'fireman's duties' – which usually meant covering a war. But it was time I had my own bureau again, and in the end it didn't take long, though there'd be a busy year meanwhile.

'Come sarei felice si avessi questo gatto!' (How happy I would be if I had that cat!) It's a curious phrase that somehow stuck after a year of Italian at university. It was better to have students plunge straight into everyday conditionals and subjunctives than ploughing through present, past and future tenses until they get

bored with it all. In my case, at any rate, it sparked off a liking for the rhythm of the language, and I had this at least to build on when I arrived in Rome in the early spring of 1967.

I'd had one brief 'work experience' in the Italian capital a few years earlier and liked the place. I can't remember writing much at that time, but I do remember riding pillion round the sunny streets of Rome on junior reporter David Willey's Vespa. The latter seemed to be the smart fashion accessory of the time. David, understandably, seems to have decided later that staying in Rome was a better bet than Reuters, and I don't blame him. I still hear him occasionally, reporting Vatican affairs for the BBC.

I expected my own second visit to last a year or two, though it didn't turn out that way. I was glad to be out of London, earning some decent money and working in an attractive city under a good boss. John Earle was now in charge of the bureau after quitting the Diplomatic role. Married to an Italian, he knew the place intimately. In fact he was conversant with the whole area since his wartime days with Britain's Special Operations Executive (SOE), the top secret organisation set up to promote resistance to the German occupiers. He'd parachuted into Yugoslavia as a British liaison officer; not that he would ever have talked about it. It was only years after joining the firm that I learned that our Diplomatic Editor had done some brave things in the war. So had many of the older correspondents and editors. But no one ever spoke of it.

I found myself a small old-fashioned flat in the Via dei Greci, an attractive little street five minutes from the office and just a few doors away from the famous Accademia di Santa Cecilia, one of Italy's most respected musical centres. I took a one-year lease, arranged with one of those formidable widows, of which there seemed to be great numbers in Europe at the time, who'd inherited property (or properties) and liked to know what sort of people they were getting. I underwent close inspection by the lady and her lawyers before a contract was signed.

The third-floor living room and small bedroom opened on to a paved terrace, with stone flower boxes, from which you had marvellous views of old churches and a jumble of red-tiled roofs and terraces. An attractive place in the cool of an evening, the stillness only disturbed by the sound of bells. In fact I'd fallen asleep on the sofa one drowsy day and awoke to a strange sight, seen from a distance of a few inches. A column of ants was making its way methodically along the polished top of the coffee table to some point in the flat's shadowy interior, the parallel return route equally well defined. As I sprang up, both lines of ants quickly regrouped and scurried back across the table top, down the legs and out on to the terrace, where they'd presumably emerged from plant pots to investigate the interior and now returned to base. It all added to the exotic nature of the place. But I kept the door shut in future.

After two years shuttling between leafy Hampstead and a hectic head office, broken by assignments up and down the country, Rome was a much calmer place to live. My flat was only a short walk to the Reuter office, a suite of first-floor rooms with a balcony opening on to the renowned Spanish Steps, with all its Keatsian connections. There were good restaurants aplenty within easy reach, and I took especially to Tuscan cuisine.

Using audio tapes, a dictionary and the newspapers to expand my rudimentary Italian (to me the most mellifluous of all European tongues), it wasn't long before I could hack my way through the *Corriere della Sera* and the Italian agency ANSA's newswire. It's a charming language, if not always the most precise. I'd got used to airy phrases and circumlocutions while ploughing through the printed texts of Latin delegates at the United Nations, which seemed aimed to impress rather than inform.

The trickiest thing during my first evening shifts was taking calls from stringers in far parts of the country, whose regional variants I often found a bit hard to grasp. But the callers were always helpful when they realised they were dealing with a tyro in the language. People always appreciate it when one tries, however imperfectly, to learn their language. Perhaps the most important thing I learned, after nearly tripping over it in a story, was that in Italian 'Monaco' doesn't refer to the place where they run a Grand Prix, but Munich, Germany. Many people have been caught out.

Brought up in a typically Catholic environment, I'd somehow pictured Italy to be much the same… the Vatican and all that. It was a surprise to discover – and it made an excellent feature story – that some five million Italian men, women and children were living, as we used to say in Lancashire, 'in sin'. Latest figures showed that an estimated 20,000 illegitimate babies were being born every year, while about half a million secret abortions were taking place, with the loss of many mothers' lives. Under Italian law, wives couldn't divorce their spouses. A fiery battle erupted in the press. That very ascetic-looking Pope, Paul VI, called the country's mounting divorce rates 'a sign of moral decadence', not to mention a violation of Italy's 1929 concordat with the Vatican. But he was fighting a losing battle, as left-wing members of parliament clamoured for change. The Church was gradually losing its grip. A long ban on birth control publicity was lifted, and sex education in the schools given the go-ahead. As a Christian Democrat Senator told Parliament, 'We can't go on telling our children that babies are brought along by storks…'

A few Swedish phrases helped to break the ice when I interviewed a visiting American film star, red-haired Ann-Margret (Olsson). A sex symbol of the period, she'd starred in hit films like *State Fair*, *Cincinnati Kid* and with Elvis Presley in *Viva Las Vegas*. Born in Sweden, she'd lived in America most of her life, but seemed to appreciate a short conversation in her native tongue. I remember her rather aggressive American agent, however, was not too pleased to be left out of things.

The idyllic Roman days were not to last, however, and within a few months I was booted north to Geneva, where decidedly less glamorous GATT trade talks had begun. The Kennedy Round, as the talks were called in tribute to the late President, was a tortuous and esoteric series of negotiations aimed at slashing world tariffs, breaking down farm trade restrictions and helping the developing nations. Sixty-six countries representing 80% of world trade were taking part. Ron Cooper rang me from London a couple of days into the talks to say they 'couldn't make head nor tail' so far of our coverage by a relatively junior non-English reporter. Could I go up there and try to sort things out? I did, though I don't think the man involved ever quite forgave me for showing him how the job should be done. Hardly had I done it than I got another call from head office. They wanted me in

Monaco (the real one this time) to cover the Grand Prix. At Reuters, you had to be a jack of all trades.

It was my first visit to the principality, and the job promised to be a pleasant one. The city was bathed in hot sunshine and crowds were thick around the famous twisting track between the houses. A holiday atmosphere pervaded the harbour, packed with the yachts of the wealthy. Motor racing fans were there in tens of thousands, and the harbour reverberated to the sound of high-powered machinery, including the mighty Ferraris. Unhappily, with the race almost over, tragedy struck on the eighty-second lap.

Italian driver Lorenzo Bandini had started his career as a mechanic and progressed into sports and rally cars, driving for Cooper, BRM and the world-famous Ferrari, for which he was now at the wheel. Running a close second to Denny Hulme, Bandini lost control in the tricky harbour chicane when his nearside rear wheel struck a guard rail and sent him skidding. From the press stand I saw the car roll over, crash into straw bales lining the track and burst into flames, Bandini trapped beneath. The marshals were quick to get the car upright again, but the Italian was badly burned. They lowered him into a boat in the harbour and he was whisked to hospital. Instead of reporting a race, I was reporting a tragedy. Head office sent me back to Geneva, where three days later I learned Bandini had succumbed to his injuries.

It had been a hectic year so far, but was about to become even busier. With war threatening between Israel and the Arab countries, another call from London told me to change locations again. I booked a flight to the area quickly, in case airfields closed. My indoctrination in the noisy world of Middle East politics began in June 1967 on a plane over the Mediterranean. My fellow passengers, who'd also boarded the plane in Switzerland, were without exception young and not-so-young Jews from Europe and the United States, singing patriotic songs which got ever louder as the plane descended across the eastern Mediterranean towards Tel Aviv. I might just as easily have been heading for Cairo. The Israelis were faster and more efficient in issuing a visa.

It was a pointer, I suppose, to the way the Six Day War would go, with a quick-on-its-feet Israel – portrayed as David in much of the Western press – triumphing over a lumbering Arab Goliath. Egypt, Syria and Jordan would like to have driven the Israelis, whose presence in the region was still unwelcome to most Arabs, into the sea. But their rather decrepit armies proved no match for the well-equipped and highly motivated Israeli forces led with spirit and dash by the man with the eye patch, General Moshe Dayan.

Reuters, still at that time very much Fleet Street's poor relation, covered the war, almost unbelievably today, with just two reporters and a desk man. Patrick Massey and I drove separately each day to various fronts, from the Suez Canal to Jerusalem, the West Bank of the Jordan and the Golan Heights of Syria, filing from phone boxes, shops or private homes, wherever we could get a line. There were no mobile phones in those days. Our resident Israel manager/correspondent, Arye Wallenstein (Wally to all and sundry), and his wife, Shula, took down our dictated reports at their home in Dizengoff Street, Tel Aviv – which was also the Reuter office – and passed them on by teleprinter to London. The war would change all that.

Amid the cheerful, curly haired, apparently undisciplined but obviously committed young soldiers, one of whom always seemed to speak at least one European language as well as Hebrew, it was easy enough to get an interview. Almost as easy to find yourself in the firing line. One colleague was shot in the head while rashly peeping over a parapet during the Israeli onslaught on Jerusalem; another was killed by a mine. 'Keep your head down,' the soldiers told you, 'and always walk in the tank tracks.'

And I'd learned in that earlier war in Pakistan the danger signals against driving too far down apparently empty roads. Torn branches, tank treads in the tarmac, a too eerie silence are the warning signals. I sheltered one day with a group of reporters in a farmhouse in the middle of the Huleh valley as Israeli and Syrian guns exchanged salvoes across our heads like baseline sluggers in a tennis match. I could understand why the Israelis wanted to neutralise the Heights. Their farming settlements in the valley had been sitting ducks for Syrian military up on the top. They'll never give that territory back, I thought (and they haven't).

Driving up the twisting road to the crest the day after it was captured, I saw the effects of the Israeli onslaught. Dead Syrian soldiers sprawled clumsily at their firing posts. I thought how young and small they looked – but at peace. Despite the war's short duration, which gave it its name, I got to report all fronts, from the West Bank of Jordan to the deserts of Sinai. I noted the difference in Sinai between the ebullient Israeli solders and the long lines of Egyptian prisoners, obviously peasants, squatting in line in the sand. They'd thrown off their boots as an unfamiliar encumbrance. Clearly expecting something bad to happen, they broke into a chant.

'What are they singing?' I asked the Israeli conducting officer.

'They're singing "Long Live Moshe Dayan",' he said with a rather satisfied smile. The prisoners needn't have worried. They were all sent back across the Canal

Managing Editor Stuart Underhill, in a general order to all Reuter bureaux, called our coverage an outstanding success. 'We more than held our own against fierce competition and our reputation for fast, accurate reporting must have been greatly enhanced.' At the company's annual luncheon in London later, Reuter Chairman John Burgess would pay tribute to our 'gallantry and professional skill'. Our cover of the war had been magnificent, he said. Well, I'm sure everybody's reporters received similar plaudits.

Back in Tel Aviv, after the fighting was over, I started my political education in the ways of the Middle East, which would continue over eight years. From Cairo, via London, the Reuter teleprinter churned out the report that President Gamal Abdel Nasser had offered to resign. The story said he'd reluctantly been restrained by cheering crowds. Wally chuckled disbelievingly, the ever-present cigarette smouldering between his nervous fingers. He was a 'Sabra', born in Palestine, unlike some of these nouveaux arrivistes from London and New York. He reckoned he knew what to believe or disbelieve.

Pat Massey went home, and I was asked to stay on for a while, so that Wally could take a well-earned break from his labours. But no sooner had London agreed to his request than violent earthquakes shook Turkey and they rescinded it. He stayed in Tel Aviv and I was on the move again. In Istanbul, I teamed up with old friend Arthur Chesworth of the *Daily Express*. The worst of the quakes, we were told, had been in the mountains in the east, so it was to Erzerum, with a couple of Fleet Street photographers, that we flew. We knew the name from that John Buchan novel, *Greenmantle*. I seemed to recall the true Brit hero Richard Hannay of *Thirty-Nine Steps* fame, pinching a staff car from the Turkish soldiers with his fellow adventurers and driving over the hills to Erzerum for the climax of the tale. So it seemed a likely sort of area. We contacted the military and were soon sitting in the back of an army truck, grinding up gravel tracks into the mountains.

Meanwhile, back in Tel Aviv, Arye Wallenstein was getting increasingly restive, bombarding London with requests for some time off. The following exchange of service messages, leading off with a half-protest by Wally, and all in lower case, as was the custom, gives some flavour, I think, of wire service jargon of the period:

> prodesk exwallenstein: desk indicated earlier that chadwick or another staffer expectable telaviv midweek.
>
> prowallenstein exdesk: chadwick presently uncontactable remotest Anatolia but trying move him telaviv fastest.

Remote was about right. Preliminary reports said a town called Fem was at the heart of the quake. It seemed a snappy little dateline for a story. Halted by a landslide, our small group jumped down off the army truck, clambered over the debris and continued on foot along the roadway on the other side. There were no immediate signs of devastation and we began to think we were on the wrong track until we reached a small miserable-looking village – more of a hamlet, really. And this was Fem. Hardly the regional semi-metropolis we'd geared ourselves up for. No picturesque ruins, no rescue workers, no weeping survivors, no people at all, dead or alive. Just a collection of rough stone houses, the roofs collapsed. The villagers had left. No picture, no story. We'd wasted a day. It happens.

Dusk was falling as we trekked back down the mountain. A mounted figure loomed up in the gloom. The rider on top, wearing a strange pointed hat and understandably perplexed at seeing a bunch of westerners in the heart of the mountains, made menacing guttural noises and waved a long stick around. Our Turkish colleague (luckily we had one) calmed the situation. Back on the other side of the landslide, the army truck dropped us off at the nearest town, from where we trekked by a combination of overnight train, rural bus and decrepit taxi to the city of Erzincan, reached about breakfast time. By this time, we'd seen a lot of Eastern Turkey, but got nothing to report. Arthur and I would laugh about it in later days. The 'Men of Fem', he liked to call us. We were like overgrown schoolboys – which reporters, I guess, often are.

But my quick return to Tel Aviv still wasn't to be. A two-day papal visit to Turkey was about to happen and, being on the spot, with a knowledge of Italian, in which most of the official handouts were written, I was asked to stay on in Istanbul and cover it. Poor Wally, he must have been smoking sixty a day by now! I didn't mind all this activity – I was getting around and that was what I'd asked for.

There'd been some anxiety about the papal visit in view of the earthquakes, but the last of the tremors seemed to have died down by the time the austere figure of Pope John Paul VI stepped down from the plane on 25 July, accompanied by the usual retinue of prelates and followed by battalions of noisy Italian pressmen. After celebrating Mass in the Catholic cathedral, the papal party moved south to Ephesus next day to see the ancient Roman amphitheatre, where the Pope was to celebrate another Mass at the historic Shrine of the Virgin.

I'd got used to Italian-style news reporting during those London days when we were chasing Princess Margaret. It was much the same thing here. As the long convoy moved south, the papal limousines leading, the Italian press cars constantly switched about, trying to get in front of each other. When the most ambitious of their drivers realised he was now at the head of the convoy and overtaking His Holiness too, he quickly braked and drew back in a swirl of dust to squeeze in just behind the Pope's car. What's the rush? I thought.

There was big competition on the story from the American and French agencies, and as we drove back to Istanbul I knew it would be hopeless trying to get London or Rome by the usual channels. Nuyan Gigit, a journalist at the leading daily paper *Hurriyet*, who was our occasional correspondent in Turkey, had told me there was a telex machine, little used, at the newspaper's sister publishing house. We drove round there, and lo and behold in a back room stood the telex. And, despite a thick layer of dust on the top, it worked. I got through to Rome, which passed the story on to London. We were a couple of hours ahead of the opposition on the Pope's first full day in Turkey. Someone at the Rome office asked: 'When are you coming back?' I replied, 'I wish I knew.'

Next day His Holiness was being shown around the magnificent Santa Sofia, built by the Emperor Constantine in the year 325. It had earlier been a pagan temple and would later become a mosque, but these were ecumenical times and the Turks were gracious hosts. The Pope was escorted into a small museum almost filled by a glass-topped table. Hands joined in prayer, eyes gazing down at the holy relics, the Pontiff was a picture of saintliness. But one Italian newsman with a big camera wanted a better angle. '*Scusi, Papa,*' he murmured, placing his hands on the pontiff's shoulders as he squeezed irreverently behind him.

The Pope's closed eyes and pained expression said it all. But he seemed to be used to it. The pontiff flew back to Rome with his entourage the following day, and the day after, one Istanbul daily carried the banner headline, helpfully translated for me by Nuyan Yigit: 'POPE LEAVES, EARTHQUAKES RESUME.' The Turks do have a sense of humour.

Eventually, Arye Wallenstein did get some time off. I returned to Tel Aviv and took charge of the bureau for a few weeks. When Wally returned to base, I flew to England for some holiday time myself, calling briefly at Rome to pack a suitcase. Then, at my hotel in London, I got a call from head office. 'You know the ropes at the UN,' said Stuart Underhill. 'Like to go there for the General Assembly? The Middle East is going to be the big story, and you were there for the war.'

Well, it made sense, and I'd no objection. 'But I wish you'd told me before I left Rome,' I said. 'I'd have brought a few changes of clothes!'

The famous (or infamous!) Resolution 242, still the source of endless debate between the affected parties, was drafted by Britain's Lord Caradon, scion of a distinguished line of politicians and civil servants. As Hugh Foot, he'd done sterling ambassadorial work pre-independence in Cyprus, Nigeria and Jamaica. After a fairly innocuous preamble, the Resolution, briefly summarised, called for withdrawals from territories occupied by Israel in the Six Day War and an end to belligerency, affirming the right of all states in the area to live in peace within secure and recognised borders. These demands might appear fairly obvious. But, ever since, they've been interpreted and reinterpreted ad infinitum by politicians and lawyers, usually depending on which side of the Arab–Israeli divide you live in – or support. The devil lay in the detail. The resolution called for the 'withdrawal of Israel's armed forces from territories occupied in the recent conflict'. But did this mean a total pull-out, or only a partial one? Great minds were at loggerheads over the issue, and the battle of semantics has raged ever since. Not for six days, but well over forty years.

The problem arose when the English text was translated into French, also an official UN language. The phrase which caused the trouble (and may to some minds have been deliberately ambiguous) became in the French version '*retraite des territoires*', which can mean 'all' or 'some' territories. It depends on what you want it to mean. I would be reminded fairly often of its various interpretations when reporting from the Middle East in the decade to come. The 'land for peace' formula prescribed by Resolution 242 would be partly implemented in a 1979 peace treaty between Egypt and Israel. The latter pulled back from the Sinai Peninsula, Egypt withdrew its claims to the Gaza Strip, and Jordan its claims for the occupied West Bank, since when the River Jordan has become the border. Syria, the other main Arab protagonist in the Six Day War, continues to claim the Golan Heights. To the present day, the Resolution's demand for a 'just settlement of the [Palestine] refugee problem' remains unimplemented.

Britain's then Foreign Secretary, the mercurial Labour MP George Brown, pooh-poohed what he saw as verbal quibbles, saying, 'Before we submitted the Resolution to the Council, we showed it to Arab leaders.'

Caradon, chief author of the text, said later, 'I would defend absolutely what we did. It was not for us to lay down exactly where the border should be.' He said the 1967 border was never a satisfactory one, merely the line along which the troops had to hold their fire when the 1948 Israel–Arab conflict came to an end. To me, the phraseology always seemed rather a cop-out. The verbal and legal battle will doubtless continue ad infinitum. The UN gave a Swedish diplomat, Gunnar Jarring, the unenviable task of getting 242 implemented. Egypt, Israel and Jordan recognised his mission, Syria did not, citing complete Israeli withdrawal as a prerequisite. So the Jarring mission, to no one's surprise, was terminated seven years later, and has given way to equally fruitless peace conferences ever since.

Amid the war of words, there was a lighter side to New York that autumn. I attended the first night of the film version of *Camelot* on Broadway, my story well displayed in London's evening papers. The heavily drinking Brown was also making a very visible impact on the New York scene – and in newspapers on both sides of the Atlantic. It started when he fell off the gangplank from the plane bringing him to New York. I covered his subsequent meeting with US Secretary of State Dean Rusk, and he looked fit enough as he arrived. But he was back on top form at a party on the *Queen Mary*, docked in the Hudson River. He was pictured on the front page of the *New York Post* dancing the Twist with a voluptuous young lady in a curious knees-bent crouching position. Such episodes were also making headlines back home. It wouldn't be the last time I came across our Foreign Secretary in familiar form. There would be drunken episodes in Europe and the Middle East, and he'd once invite me to breakfast in Cairo.

The English satirical review *Beyond The Fringe*, then at the height of its success, was also playing in town that autumn. Walking across from the UN building for a lunchtime perform-ance, I was struck as I walked through the doors of the club by the sound of swing piano being very expertly played. I glanced at the programme they'd handed me and read halfway down the page,

'Intermission Piano by T Wilson.' I thought I'd recognised a master touch. But didn't they know his first name, for God's sake? And we were in his own country! At the interval, I tried to make amends by offering him a drink at the bar, where I found him just as elegant and well mannered as his playing.

For jazz, New York at that time was certainly a good place to be. One night I caught a great two-keyboard act at the famous Village Vanguard. Willie ('The Lion') Smith was playing his own brand of stride piano, bowler on head, cigar in mouth, in a 'cutting contest' with the very competitive, if more sedate, Don Ewell. I got them over for a drink and a chat and they signed my record.

Another night I took a taxi to a downtown club in search of the controversial Thelonious Monk, whose appearances were as unpredictable as some of his chords. Quite another pianist than Wilson, Monk was famed not only for his apparently disjointed keyboard approach, but for standing up in mid-number and doing a short dance around the platform – or for not turning up at all. To my great regret, this was one of the no-show nights. Well, there are always the records.

Then came the phone call from head office. How would I like to become Chief Correspondent in Cairo? Fine, I said, but will the Egyptians let me in? They must know I've been covering the war on the Israeli side. It proved not to be a problem. The Egyptians had seen my reports from Tel Aviv and had no objections. So in January 1968, I was heading back across the Mediterranean again, after stopping off in Rome for the rest of my baggage – and a few necessary inoculations.

Chapter 10
'NO COMMENT,' SAID THE EGYPTIAN SPOKESMAN, 'BUT DON'T QUOTE ME'

The evening heat was soporific, the air a little dusty. On the placid surface of the Nile, a felucca slid slowly upstream. Far across the river, like the cover picture of a science fiction novel, the setting sun was an orange ball between the points of the two pyramids, making a perfect geometric design. In a couple of minutes the picture would be gone.

Ahead of me, the road was a noisy jumble of clapped-out cars, horse-drawn carts with fat rubber tyres and the occasional unwary cyclist wobbling uncertainly along the gutter.

I'd been in Egypt a couple of months and was on the way home from the office in downtown Cairo. I'd learned to brave the traffic. My predecessor had himself driven about by Elefteri the Greek, who was sorely affronted when I dispensed with his services. I'd felt it ridiculous to be chauffeur-driven in a battered, beige and not really beautiful Ford Cortina. Elefteri, I gathered from others in the office, thought he'd lost face. I, in my ignorance, had imagined he'd be glad to be rid of taking the boss around day and night. I'd felt guilty after attending diplomatic receptions to find him asleep over the wheel. I still had a lot to learn about the Middle East. I went on paying him the same money – but clearly for him life would never be the same again.

There were other things I'd have to learn. I'd decided I should have an Egyptian driving licence, though no other foreigner I ever met had even bothered. Elefteri parked the Cortina at a corner near the test centre, leaving me in the passenger seat while he fetched a policeman from the licensing office. The officer signalled me to drive around the corner into the side street. I thought this a bit odd, but did so and expected him to get in the car now to see how I went on. He simply said, 'You've passed.'

Up in the police boss's office, we chatted amiably about everything but cars. He said, 'Before you go, please stand up a moment.' Which I did, but, before leaving, politely asked why. He chuckled. 'I just wanted to make sure you had two legs.' Which surreal incident left me puzzled for weeks.

I was now boss of thirty-one people, the only Englishman in a team including Muslims, Christians, Greeks, Armenians and Nubians. Cairo is truly a melting pot – and there were only seventeen million Egyptians at the time I arrived, compared with treble that number today. The place seemed overpopulated even then. God knows what it's like now.

Reuter headquarters was in Sharia Sherif, a small cul-de-sac off one of the main streets. We had an extensive second-floor suite of rooms, curving round a central courtyard. Rubbish and what else had been thrown down into the central well from infinity, it seemed. No wonder the windows overlooking the yard were kept firmly closed.

They'd been glad to see me, as there'd been a managerial gap since the Six Day War. My predecessor had bequeathed me not just the Cortina but his family villa in the suburb of Ma'adi. I'd have preferred to stay in town for convenience, but the lease still had eight months to run and Reuters didn't believe in wasting money. So, for the time being, I had a spacious house with an impressive front porch and a large garden behind, with coconut trees and masses of grapes of various colours. Enjoying a gin and tonic on the veranda in the evening, you could stretch out a hand and pluck a lime from the tree to go with it, a party trick which never failed to amuse. A staircase off the hall led to three bedrooms, far more than I needed. I'd also inherited a servant-cum-cook.

Abdou, a tall handsome Nubian with skin like polished ebony, was more than happy to stay on. Looking after just one sir was a lot easier than doing the housework and errands for a whole family. All we foreigners in Cairo had servants. There was no shame in being a cook – or embarrassment in employing one. It was a good steady job, and the servants, mainly from the Upper Nile, were a community unto themselves. They passed the word around when one of the effendis was due to leave, and the job wouldn't go unfilled for long. And they were usually excellent cooks, a blessing for me, the most mediocre of kitchen practitioners. Abdou knew all the English dishes. Maybe today's, I speculated while driving south, would be his excellent steak and kidney pie.

I first set foot in the office in January 1968. Cairo was still sunk in gloom after Egypt's humiliating defeat in the Six Day War. Only later did I realise I'd arrived on Gamal Abdel Nasser's fiftieth birthday. The event, which would normally have been a cause for celebration, was ignored. Belief in the revolutionary hero, el Rais, had been severely dented. As his eventual successor, Anwar Sadat, wrote years later in his memoirs, 'The Egyptian citizen no longer believed a word about the war. He had lost all hope.'

I remember a taxi driver pointing to the tall TV mast in the city centre. The top of it had housed a popular revolving restaurant before the war. Now it was closed indefinitely. 'The last revolution is over,' chuckled the driver. Egyptians can always crack a joke.

The atmosphere in our dusty offices, unrelieved by air conditioning, remained cosily British. Senior Egyptian staff recalled the spy Kim Philby's visits in the years before he defected in Beirut to the Russians. 'A very nice English gentleman,' said office manager Shafik Bishai, 'but often very drunk.' I could have lain back to be cosseted, I suppose, filing the occasional heavily censored despatch, while endless cups of tea or black coffee were brought to my office on a copper tray. 'Sweet or unsweet?' 'Medium,' I'd reply. Or, '*Mazbout*', as I learned to say. Or, '*Wahad shai, b'doun shekker.*' Tea without sugar.

We had four local reporters, who became good friends. Progressively for those days, the senior local journalist was the charming Samiha Tawfik, whose husband Ernest was also the local Reuter doctor. Bahgat Badie and Fouad Gawhary were Christian, Assem Hassan the only Muslim in the team. They were all friendly and helpful, with a good grasp of Reuter principles, sometimes harder for them to apply than for me, a foreigner. Me the authorities could always kick out. The locals had to watch their step in a fairly controlled state under the auspices of the so-called Arab Socialist Union (ASU). The socialism lay in the name rather than the practice.

Nasser had become a remote figure, far from the image familiar to anyone who'd followed the Egyptian story through recent decades: the growing discontent with British control; the sporadic street riots; the excesses of an increasingly corpulent King Farouk, eventually despatched aboard the royal yacht into exile; the hero worship of the young Nasser and his fellow officers, who'd finally kicked the British out.

The son of a postal worker, Nasser had fought as a soldier in the 1948 Palestine War, which ended with the emergence of Israel along a narrow strip of the east Mediterranean coast. He'd led the army coup which toppled Farouk and dislodged General Mohamed Neguib as Egyptian leader. Nasser had escaped death by inches when five bullets were fired at him during a mass rally. (His eventual successor, Anwar Sadat, was not so lucky in a similar incident.) He'd turned to the Russians when the West refused to aid the construction of a giant dam at Aswan, blocking the mighty River Nile. His status was further enhanced when he nationalised the Suez Canal. It was the final kick in the teeth for the old imperial powers. Until the disaster of the Six Day War, Nasser had everything going for him. Now living in virtual seclusion, he was still a revered figure, if increasingly remote. I remember wondering later, now living in the suburb of Zamalek, why the road near my flat had acquired overnight a glistening new surface of black asphalt. It turned out that Nasser was due to visit the Indian Embassy, just up the road.

He'd not lost his oratorical flair. Periodically we'd be treated to one of his major speeches. They could ramble on for hours, veering from historical references to hopes of better things to come, but with few facts and figures. My Egyptian colleagues were a first-class translation team, listening in turn to the stream of Arabic, turning the highlights quickly into English, which I would then scour for nuggets of real information. Head office always expected a quick-fire production – but you had to hold your fire. Useless getting bogged down during the first fifteen minutes. You had to wait for a worthwhile lead. When some newsy paragraph was passed to my desk, usually in Samiha's excellent handwriting, I'd start the story off, then lead it once or twice as more interesting things emerged. It was a matter of news judgement and holding your nerve. Leave it too long, and you could be beaten on the story. Start the story off too quickly and you'd be bogged down in verbiage. Reporting Arab leaders is not the same as reporting Westminster.

Communications with head office were by today's standards laughable. In Israel, a basically Western society, we could file directly to London by telex from manager Arye Wallenstein's home. The process in Cairo was rather more roundabout. Phone connections to and from Europe were useless and calls censored. Reuters had a close working deal with Egypt's Middle East News Agency (MENA). Stories typed in our own office would be taken by one of our many messengers to the MENA offices a few streets away, headed by the very friendly Mohamed Abdel-Gawad. Our story would be read and sent on by MENA's foreign desk, senior members of which also acted as unpaid censors, knowing pretty well what might make the authorities unhappy. They were very helpful, but had their own careers to think about. We never stretched good relations too far. One always had to think of the long term.

The incoming Reuter wire from London, carrying the world news file, also arrived via MENA. And, believe it or not, there was no direct line between London and Cairo, only radio transmission. Our incoming world news service often arrived unreadable. Much of my time was spent on communications, not news. Local clients included government ministries, Cairo newspapers and other media, and several embassies. There were frequent complaints. The problem might lie at Reuters' own radio centre outside London, but more likely it was in Cairo. The Italian Embassy, for some reason, was the most unlucky. After a phone call from them, we'd despatch an engineer yet again to investigate. The problem was often traced to a defective cable in one of those holes in the road, and the necessary baksheesh was needed to speed up repairs. I'd asked Shafik when I first inspected the accounts to explain the entry headed 'Sundries'. Now I knew.

Egypt seemed a century behind Israel. For us, still distributing our world news service directly to clients and servicing their equipment, getting half a dozen new Siemens 200 printers was a gift from the gods. But importing such goodies from Europe was an all-day exercise. I'd drive to the airport with Shafik to clear them through customs. We did the rounds of officialdom, a stamp here, a signature there, until everyone had had his say, signed his name – and had a small wad of smelly banknotes pressed into his hand.

We had three main competitors, America's Associated Press (AP) and (now defunct) United Press International (UPI) and Agence France-Presse. AP's Joe Dynan was a hardbitten but straightforward sort of guy who clearly didn't like Egypt a lot and didn't think much generally of the Ay-rabs, as he called them. AFP correspondent Jean-Pierre Joullain would become a good friend. More and more we'd converse in French, at his prompting, and I didn't object. 'I think you've had an order from Paris about this,' I once joked. 'You're correct,' he admitted. 'We'd occasionally play golf at the course out near the Pyramids. My closest friend, also an occasional golf partner, was Ireland's (the late) Mike Dennigan. After the problems of the day, we'd meet in the Aladdin Bar. An order for '*Itnin birre*' (two beers) was usually the start of an evening session. You didn't have to specify the beer. There was only one, Stella, which came in green pint bottles. Every tenth one or so was flat, quickly replaced without protest.

Across the Suez Canal, after their overwhelming victory, the Israelis were lying low for the moment. The only gunshots I heard out at Ma'adi were from policemen killing off the hordes of yapping stray dogs that made nights a misery, the only aerial attacks the sharp buzz of mosquitoes homing in on a new and unwary foreigner. My face was a mass of white splotches before I realised that wire-mesh screens across the windows were not a luxury option, but a necessity. Until I could get them fitted, I'd developed my own rough-and-ready method of killing off the aerial marauders, which was to stand underneath and splatter them where they lurked on the ceiling with a crisply hurled paperback. Effective, but rather a mess to clean. I was lucky that Abdou would see to that.

In addition there were, of course, the cockroaches. Shortly

after arrival, feeling thirsty one night, I got up and went down the stairs in semi-darkness, feeling my way to the kitchen. The moment I grasped the door handle, I knew something other than my hand was on it, and when I switched on the light inside, cockroaches streamed away from all points with a faint rustle towards the outer door. I didn't bother with that drink, after all.

Maybe my northern English upbringing made me rebel against the post-colonial flavour of the Reuter office. When I first arrived, our eight messengers (no less) stood in line at the salute. I banned saluting. It worked, except for one sweet-natured man called Saleh, who couldn't bring himself not to offer the traditional salaam as he knocked at my office door each morning and entered with the small cup of Turkish coffee. Eventually, I told Shafik to let him know I'd have to fire him if he went on saluting. He stopped.

Shafik told me one day it would shortly be my task to 'distribute the sweets'. Sweets? It was the Muslim feast of Bairam, when it had been the tradition since time immemorial at the Reuter office to hand each of the more menial staff a beribboned white cardboard box containing a selection of sticky confections bought at Groppi's, long the favoured coffee shop for foreign visitors and the local bourgeoisie. The next time round, I asked Shafik how much these exotic concoctions cost, and wouldn't the recipients – who I knew by now had large families to support – rather have the money? He smiled and wisely shook his head. 'I think they are preferring the sweets,' he assured me.

'Well, just ask them, will you?'

He returned after a quick poll in the corridors. 'They would prefer the money,' he said.

The war had been a disaster for Israel's Arab enemies, and for Egyptians a severe test of faith in the man who'd driven the foreigners out in the first place. But it was a long time now since the airy phrases of the revolution. Nasser, once regarded as almost a saint, had been swiftly outwitted by the Israelis, his air force wiped out on the ground while the politicians and generals were still exchanging pledges of victory, blatantly broadcast to the population until it was too late to deny the truth any longer. Egypt had not just been defeated, but flattened.

The Suez Canal, now the virtual frontier between the two armies, had been blocked since the war, leaving fourteen foreign ships, including four British vessels, stranded in the aptly named Great Bitter Lake halfway along the strategic waterway. We were allowed to go and view the vessels and interview the skeleton crews left aboard. The freighters *Port Invercargill* (10,500 tonnes) and two slightly smaller ships lay forlornly at anchor. The crews served three-month spells, relieving the tedium of blistering summer heat or winter sandstorms with film shows, deck football, beer, darts, and fishing contests. But with a re-escalation of the conflict in the spring of 1970, with shells falling a few hundred yards away and dogfights going on above, it became clear the lake would become a ships' graveyard. The men's three-year vigil ended that summer, when the last of the British ghost crews were flown home and the ships abandoned, to be declared 'total constructive losses' by their insurers. 'It's a pity to see them go,' said an embassy official. 'It's been a strange little era.'

The Israelis occasionally rubbed salt in the wounds. They once showed their prowess by having a jet fighter fly behind a civil airliner approaching Cairo airport, then peel off to dive on the Nile, shattering windows for miles along the waterfront with its supersonic boom. The Egyptians were humiliated. They didn't allow us to report the incident, not even to say anti-aircraft guns had fired at an enemy plane.

'You cannot say it's an enemy aircraft and you can't even say it's a plane,' said the censor, rejecting my third attempt to get a story out. 'You can say our guns fired at a target.'

'What do you mean – a barrage balloon?' I expostulated.

It was truly Wonderland, without Alice. But there was tragedy as well as farce. We reporters were taken to see a village school near the canal hit by Israeli bombers which got the wrong target. The bodies of the small victims were laid out in the hall. It looked, and smelled, like a butcher's shop.

One night, in the early hours, Israelis commandos took out a power station at Nagh Hamadi on the Upper Nile. The first we knew of it was on the Reuter wire from Tel Aviv. I rang government press spokesman Mahmoud Anis, every inch the old-fashioned English gentleman, for confirmation or comment. He asked angrily, 'Do you realise what time it is?' He did ring back a few minutes later, however, to announce triumphantly, 'Well, I got the official statement for you. The army says, "No comment".' But, he added, 'Don't quote me!'

Meanwhile in Cairo, life went on more or less as usual. The rich remained rich, the poor got poorer. The bourgeoisie went to Groppi's for coffee and cakes. Belly dancer Zoheir Zaki danced in the nightclub of the Hilton, and Egypt's favourite singer, Umm Khalsoum, sang her melancholy laments of life and love, a musical genre that left me cold. More to my taste was the Cairo Jazz Band, created by young Colonel Saleh Ragab, musical director for the Egyptian Armed Forces. A trumpeter and drummer himself, he'd raided every military band in Egypt, brought the star performers to Cairo and sat them down in front of American big band scores. With Cairo and Washington still in diplomatic deep freeze, he was taking quite a chance. He invited me to the Aladdin bar one afternoon and told me sadly that the experiment might be over. He'd been called before top brass to explain what was going on. 'What is this *jazz*?' he was asked. 'Is it some kind of religion?' But the big band survived and, with the help of Germany's Goethe-Institut and their jazz expert Hartmut Geerken, even produced an LP full of American wartime classics like Glen Miller's 'American Patrol'. Saleh pushed his luck even further by labelling one track 'Freedom for Iratilim' (read the last word backwards). Nobody twigged it. But this was one story I had to self-censor. I told it years later in Britain's *Jazz Journal*.

I became good friends with Hartmut and his wife, and another German couple, Bert and Dolores Puttkamer, all very much into jazz, though I didn't always share their modernist tastes. I was even more pleased when Bert flew down his young cousin, a beautiful nineteen-year-old Birgitta, from Hanover for a holiday in Egypt. I squired her around Cairo, and later visited her in Düsseldorf. Hartmut was an excellent amateur pianist, familiar with everything from Beethoven sonatas to Bartok's 'Mikrokosmos'. I was occasionally roped in for some light-hearted exploratory modern music-making at their Heliopolis home. The Germans were very much into what came to be called Free Jazz. Well, I didn't even mind banging a hammer (or my head) on a wall if that's what Hartmut decided should be my role in such a session. It was all fun.

A more professional avant-garde experience was provided by the black American bandleader and keyboard artist Sun Ra and his idiosyncratically named Arkestra. They performed in Cairo – to largely mystified audiences. He was assured of a more sympathetic hearing when invited to give a private performance with his band at the Geerkens' spacious villa. This too made a nice one-off story for *Jazz Journal*. Jazz in Cairo seemed to be largely in the hands of the Germans, in fact. My opposite number in the German press, Peter Fuchs, was a charming chap, married to an Egyptian. In World War Two, he'd defied Nazi strictures condemning American jazz by taking a wind-up gramophone and a few 78 rpm records to the Russian front. We were sitting in his lounge, listening to some old big band tracks when the news came on the radio of Louis Armstrong's death, a sad day for jazz lovers. We played some of the old All Stars tracks in tribute.

For some time after arrival in Egypt, I was serving two masters. Reuters had long been in partnership with the partly Foreign Office-funded Arab News Agency – recently renamed Regional News Services. Its London-based boss was the genial, pipe-smoking and blue-blazered English journalist Tom Little. A veteran of the region, he would periodically descend on the office during one of his regular tours of RNS offices in the area, vainly seeking an interview with Nasser, whose biography he had once written; but the Egyptian leader, perhaps understandably, didn't want to know. Very few people got to see El Rais. The nearest I got, though my application was permanently pending, was Foreign Minister Mahmoud Riad, a sombre man who demanded written questions in advance and when you finally got into his office only came out with routine platitudes.

Hoping for some better insights into high-level thinking, I took the lift one day to the glittering top-floor office of the boss of *Al Ahram*. Mohammed Hassanein Heykal, traditionally described by the media as 'a close friend of President Nasser', cracked his knuckles and let me admire his ultra-modern furniture. The glass-topped table, said this leader of democratic Arab Socialism proudly, was designed by Princess Margaret's husband, Anthony Armstrong-Jones. But of hard news there was none. Every Friday he'd produce a flowery piece of rhetoric about Middle East politics which Western diplomats and press scoured for hints of meaning. 'Rely usual Heykal daylead,' London would say in a reminder message every Thursday evening. Sometimes it was hard to oblige.

Officials were keeping note of you. I knew my own journalists were periodically phoned by the intelligence service and asked what the Reuter boss was doing and whom he was seeing. I had no direct contact with them, though I was infrequently called to the Foreign Ministry when they discovered we'd reported something they didn't like. This couldn't happen very often, because every word we wrote or spoke on telephone was censored. Increasingly so, after the link with RNS was terminated.

There were ways of getting stuff out. You could 'pigeon' a piece to London, Rome or Paris in the pocket or briefcase of compliant airline passengers, who seemed to get a schoolboyish thrill from the adventure. But this was a practice easier for occasional visiting journalists than for those of us with a permanent presence and local clients. The Egyptians knew what was going on and sometimes winked at it, not wanting to drive the Western press out altogether. I reckoned I could risk it two or three times a year for a really good story, which would be put out under a London dateline, attributed to those ubiquitous 'travellers' arriving from foreign places. Next day I'd be summoned to the Foreign Ministry to explain how the story got on the wire. I'd feign ignorance, of course, but they were not fooled. 'OK, throw me out,' I said in effect. For my Egyptian staff, the stakes were much higher. I couldn't risk their safety or jobs. And, besides, Reuters had business clients in Egypt.

Despite communications and censorship problems, Cairo was chosen as one of four key news centres to launch a new radio service initially aimed at America's Mutual Broadcasting Service. Twice a week I was asked to provide six rather ridiculous three-line snippets for American breakfast news bulletins, plus a 100-word in-depther – if that's not a contradiction in terms.

This had been set up by my former boss in New York, Julian Bates, now back at head office. I'd never done radio before, but the BBC's Brian Barron, newly arrived in Cairo from the Gulf, gave me a couple of quick lessons. Actually, writing such items was the easy bit. The worst part of it was a mad car dash through the Cairo heat and traffic to the censor's office (four floors up, lift seldom working) to have it stamped, then another scramble across town to the radio transmission centre.

There, if you were lucky, your pre-booked call to New York came through more or less on time, with a censor listening in. The Americans at the other end, not always quite in tune with Middle East politics, were rather put out if you declined to answer follow-up questions of the 'Is Nasser in danger of assassination?' variety. Things seldom went smoothly in these broadcasts, and one 95°F day I roundly berated a poor technician about it. As I left the building, I was informed by the director of operations, 'You are now banned from this building.'

'Good,' I said. 'Thanks.'

He waved a hand dramatically. 'For life!' he shouted after me as I made for the exit.

'Thanks very much!' I called back as I left the building.

It was the heat that did it. Needless to say, Egyptians being as they are, we were all the best of friends again within a week.

Most of the Western correspondents had it easier, operating from the then peaceful, cosmopolitan and censor-free Beirut, flying into and out of a noisy, depressed and overpopulated Cairo as infrequently as they could get away with. My old buddy from Turkey, Arthur Chesworth, arrived from Lebanon for the *Daily Express*, and I found him on the sun-baked terrace of the Cairo Hilton.

'Back to Balfour again,' he complained wearily as I joined him for a beer. With his very English brass-buttoned blazer, he'd presented an easy target for a group of Palestinian student activists, who blamed all their troubles on the British politician who back in 1917 famously declared in favour of a new Jewish homeland in the area. The young men vanished in a flurry of scuffed winkle-picker shoes as I approached. I'd had the same sort of treatment, many times. I was escorted once at my own request by the same group in a car with closed curtains (though I always knew pretty well where I was) to a suburban villa, to meet Fatah boss Yasser Arafat. There was little useful content in his replies to my questions, just the familiar windy propaganda. The *Daily Telegraph*'s doughty war correspondent, Clare Hollingworth, widow of a British ambassador to Egypt, flew in from Cyprus and stood with me, gin and tonic in hand, on her balcony at Shepheard's Hotel. Bleakly surveying the jumble of rooftops below, replete with lines of washing, rabbits, cats, and even the occasional goat, she blinked in her characteristic way and declared with a shudder, 'God! Haven't they let the place go down!'

As it transpired, the story which caused the biggest hullabaloo of my time in Egypt was sent out on the open wire, via MENA. Nasser's successor, Anwar Sadat, referred in one of his speeches to the deaths in an Israeli air strike of six Soviet soldiers manning anti-aircraft missile batteries eighteen miles south-west of Cairo. Officially there were no Russians in Egypt, though they'd virtually taken over and modernised the army after the 1967 debacle. I got the story away quick, and it went out subsequently just as rapidly on the world wire from London. Then all hell broke loose. I was rung by the hapless Mahmoud Anis and asked to withdraw the story. Naturally I refused – and in any case the news had gone round the world by this time. They pestered me for a couple of days and then gave up. I had the honour later of a laudatory editorial in the *New York Times*, which said, 'Egyptian censorship was too slow to prevent Reuters from reporting President Anwar el-Sadat's revelation. Only Reuters reported fully what the President had said.' A nice pat on the back for me and the translation team in the office. But the poor part-time censors at MENA got a rocket from the authorities.

Since the Six Day War, there'd been an obsession about bridges. Carry a camera within 200 yards of a bridge, much less take a tourist photo of the Nile, and some black-uniformed (or white in summer) policeman in his heavy boots would quickly be on the scene. They had some reason to be cautious, it transpired. Suddenly the news went around that one of our colleagues, the jovial Ali Mahmoud, a local AP reporter, had been arrested on espionage charges. We all trooped along to the trial, where informality reigned. Ali and an alleged accomplice (their car had been bugged) sat in the dock. But his friends in the press were allowed to go over, chat and hand him cigarettes through the bars. He did serve a short stretch in jail, but the whole affair seemed semi-serious, and on emergence from detention he was quickly re-absorbed into the reporting scene.

Truth, I found, was a flexible concept. News filtered into the Reuter office one day of a large political demonstration in the city centre. By the time I got out there to investigate, the marchers were gone. I called at the MENA office to check. 'Yes,' said Abdel-Gawad, 'a few hundred people were on the street.'

'Oh,' I said, 'I heard there were over a thousand.'

'OK,' said Mohamed, 'a thousand, if you like.'

Another street incident nearly turned extremely ugly after two young hostesses from Austrian Airlines who should have known better were spotted strolling down one of the main shopping streets. Nobody seemed to have told them that miniskirts, then at their shortest, were not a good idea in the Arab world. A half-hysterical bunch of young Egyptians pursued the girls down the street and, by the time they sought refuge in a shop, whose owner locked the doors, the incident had turned into a near-riot, eventually quelled by baton-wielding policemen.

There were other examples of differing cultures. One night I was phoned at home to be told one of our messengers had been killed in a traffic accident, by no means uncommon in the half-lit and chaotic streets of Cairo. I gathered what information I could about his circumstances and reported back to head office the following day, giving them as much detail as available, since the amount of his family's compensation might well depend on that. But nobody at our Cairo office seemed to know how old he was. When I pressed for a date of birth, I was asked somewhat impatiently, 'What difference does it make? He is dead.'

A strange case I came across, quite unpublishable at the time, was that of a Czech news agency colleague, son of a World War Two fighter pilot with the Royal Air Force and partly educated in England, who suddenly disappeared from the Cairo scene. A year later, he just as suddenly reappeared with his wife and invited me over for dinner. In the sitting room he explained. He'd approached the British cultural attaché a year earlier about getting the necessary papers to work in England. They'd told him, he said, that they might be able to fix things – on conditions. The Czech authorities got wind of all this and recalled Emil to Prague, where they showed him film of himself meeting British Embassy staff. They said he'd be allowed to return to Cairo if he 'doubled up' and started spying for them. I suddenly wondered, as Emil was telling me all this, How do I know if he's been turned? And, by the way, I asked myself, is this room bugged? I was understandably sparing in my comments. The West Germans eventually helped him to defect.

In the late 1960s, the Reuter operation in Egypt still had semi-colonial undertones. For years we'd supplied the news service to a small string of embassies in Cairo. Examining the books on arrival, I noted that every embassy was charged £100 a month, except the British, who paid just £60. I increased the British subscription to £100 like the rest and Tom made no objection. He knew anyway by this time that the writing was on the wall for RNS. Reuters shortly thereafter ended the partnership and announced it was going it alone in the Middle East. It was the only sensible thing to do – and a relief to me.

But with the end of the old lavishly funded Cairo operation, I was ordered by head office to cut the office staff from thirty-one to fifteen. As well as the local office manager and four journalists, we ran a teleprinter maintenance service with trained mechanics, eight messengers and various supernumeraries. Fortunately, at this time there was little real news about, for the staff reductions had first to be sanctioned by an Egyptian Labour Court. This was to prove a time-consuming and not very pleasant job in a packed and sweaty 'courtroom', though I was only there formally as the employer's representative. The vital exchanges of course were all in Arabic, the talking on our side handled by our smooth-tongued lawyer, Maître Kalaoui.

When I'd inquired on arrival about the income tax situation, Shafik told me, 'You should talk with Maître Kalaoui. He is a *vairry* reasonable man.'

'What do you mean?' I asked. 'He can bribe them?'

Anyway, in the hot and stuffy courtroom our legal

representative was at his most eloquent and the staff reductions were accepted.

I suppose I could have left it at that and earmarked the ones to go. But the staff had been universally helpful to me, and I did my best for them now. I persuaded Abdel Gawad to take on some of the Reuter messengers himself. With my own contacts developing around Cairo, I succeeded in getting Australian immigration papers for one man, whose departure was preceded by an office party and farewell presents. Friends at the United States mission arranged a visa for the head of our workshop. I don't think any hard feelings remained. For those who chose retirement I arranged lump sum payments. The break with RNS, which had been opposed by some quarters in London, made things much clearer for our reporting operation.

I was told that when former Soviet leader Nikita Khrushchev visited Egypt he scowled as his hosts showed him one ancient temple after another and finally declared petulantly, 'Now show me something you've built today!' Whatever the truth of that, it did need an international $36 million rescue operation to save the ancient temples of Abu Simbel, unearthed from the sand a century and a half earlier by Swiss orientalist John Burkchardt. In the arid higher reaches of the Nile, the battle to resite them had been fought and won over the past five years.

In the autumn of 1968 I took a hydrofoil 175 miles south from the ancient town of Aswan across the new Lake Nasser to the inauguration of one of the world's most exacting architectural preservation projects. The ancient temples of Rameses and Queen Nefertari had been threatened with submersion after the mighty Aswan High Dam blocked the Nile. Now, after being carefully sawn into pieces, the ancient temple of Abu Simbel had been removed piece by piece and reassembled on a rocky new perch high over the river by the United Nations Educational, Scientific and Cultural Organisation (UNESCO), with money from fifty countries.

A Swedish-led team of 200 experts and 1,700 workmen carried out the daring plan with contractors from Germany, France, Italy and Egypt itself. A whole new town, complete with hotel and club, swimming pool and floodlit tennis courts was built to house the engineers and workmen. Now, after five years, the three faces of the Pharaoh Rameses the Second smiled complacently down from his new perch out over the waters of the lake. In those mobile-less days, I had to make a five-hour journey back to Aswan to report the historic event. After those many thousands of years, it didn't really seem to matter.

Reuters had been in Egypt well over a century, and the relative dearth of hard news in those early months allowed me to do some historical research on our own doorstep. The Egyptian Royal Palace, I knew, had been receiving the Reuter service since 1868. A few years later, we began selling the service to the leading daily *Al Ahram*, then published in French as *Les Pyramides*. The English-language *Egyptian Gazette* signed a contract in 1882, giving Reuters 25% of all sales. In a dusty and long unopened cupboard, I unearthed old documents and newspaper clippings telling us much more. They are now back in the Reuter archives in London.

First find was a heavy leather cash book with a Dickensian look about it. The front cover was stamped in gold leaf, 'Reuters Telegram Company Limited'. Within, in neat copperplate writing and still very legible figures, were the accounts of Reuters, Cairo and the Sudan, from 1876 to the end of 1893. The housekeeping entries were meticulously detailed. Five thousand envelopes cost 15s 10d. Oil for the office lamp averaged one and sixpence (old money) a month. And some time towards the end of the 1880s we seem to have gone into the photographic business, judging from a regular monthly entry of 'potassium – 10d', presumably for the old-fashioned flash camera. Names of subscribers gave a glimpse of a vanished era. The company running the Suez Canal, opened in 1869, was among the first Reuter customers. A railway to the new canal town of Ismailia had been opened in 1893. Our correspondent claimed fifteen shillings for the trip.

I also rescued from the dust – the books must have been trundled from one office to another as Reuters moved about Cairo – a battered collection of newspaper clippings. It was a time of Britain's imperial greatness. The movements of regiments in and out of the country were duly chronicled. Even the pop songs of the era, stirring melodies to be sung 'at the piano', reflected the scene. A London publishing company advertised songs called 'The Departure for Egypt', 'The Gordon March' and 'The Nile Expedition'. The latter expedition, assembled by a Colonel Hicks, was at the time on its way south to rout the Mahdi. Reports by Reuters and *Times* correspondents told the story of the ill-fated venture thereafter.

Reuters report from Cairo on 19 February:

> Colonel Stewart telegraphs from Khartoum that the town of Obeid fell into the hands of the False Prophet on the 17th ultimate. He adds however that serious dissensions exist among the Mahdi's followers. It is reported that the Mahdi's following is composed of 50,000 men, but that very few of them possess firearms.

The Mahdi had made a levy of £400,000 on rich Sudanese merchants. There was also 'insubordination' among the British expedition's Egyptian troops.

Hicks's army, with its 10,000 mostly undrilled Egyptians, was described by Winston Churchill in his *River War* as 'perhaps the worst army that has ever marched to war'. And Hicks himself was eventually to die the following November, encircled by Mahdist troops with sword in hand – a colossal blow to British pride, only worsened by the defeat and slaying of General Gordon later.

Rumours of the poor showing of Hicks's force had obviously been reaching England, and it was in one of those near disasters that Reuters' correspondent almost lost his life. Here's the London *Times* account:

> Brigade Major Thompson of the Cavalry Division brings under the notice of the authorities the gallant conduct of two of his men. Major Thompson was in a perilous position when two troopers, seeing his danger, dismounted, and though breathless they succeeded in putting him on one of their horses and galloped away with him to a place of safety. Mr Roberts, who represents Reuters' agency, was rescued by Garstin of the 9th Bengal Cavalry.

The frayed clippings were maddeningly incomplete. I couldn't find our correspondent's own account – if he thought it worth mentioning. He was apparently still safe in Sudan when Gordon arrived a year later. For when I scoured the accounts book again, I found a small entry: 'Sundry Expenses – Paid to Mr F J Roberts £30' (at last I had his initials!). And in the following month's accounts I read, 'Paid to Mr Roberts for horse – £40.' By then, General Gordon had died, speared on the steps of his palace in Khartoum. The papers I unearthed in Cairo had illuminated one busy period in Reuter history. My nineteenth-century predecessor, Mr Schnitzler, Reuters Agent in Cairo, I subsequently learned, wrote to London at the time about the problem of maintaining his war correspondents. Stressing the need for good horses, he wrote, 'The work of a war correspondent appears to be journalism no longer, but simply horsemanship.'

Reuter clients in those far-off days included the Welsh Regiment, the Nile Field Force, the Soldiers' Club and the famous Shepheard's Hotel, which would be burnt down by a mob in 1952. And the Turf Club, which was still going a century and a half later. Here, some of us British expatriates assembled in the evenings under the watchful eye of Costa, the manager. A Somerset Maugham feel lingered in the air as soft-footed waiters in long white jellabiyas padded with regular trays of beer into the billiard room. British Ambassador Harold Beeley, as well as being a superb Arabist, was acknowledged to be the best potter of a billiard ball in town.

And there were many outdoor sports. Brian Barron and I turned out at left back and left half respectively for the English soccer team. We were once conned into playing at Cairo's main stadium against an Egyptian team who'd been wickedly described by its English coach as 'fairly average'. But he'd been lying. The centre forward, Aly, had a devastating shot. If I'd got up fast enough to block one of his volleys, he'd have taken my head off. They beat us 12–1, letting us saunter upfield just once towards the end of the game to soothe our feelings. Our opponents, we were told after the final whistle, were all from the Army, fighting fit, and Aly was centre forward for Egypt. That coach had been having us on. Barron and I almost collapsed into the nearby swimming pool, where I immediately developed cramp in the legs and had to paddle with my arms to the steps.

At the Gezira Club, expatriates from the cricketing Commonwealth played Sunday matches in often broiling heat. It felt good to turn out on the very cricket field where former England captain and star batsman Wally Hammond played during the war. The Ambassador of Ceylon (now Sri Lanka) donated a cup, presented each year to the winners of an annual battle between sides conveniently called West of Suez and East of Suez. They were pretty well balanced. Our opposition were Australian, Indian, Pakistani and Ceylonese expatriates. We had Brits and West Indians, and co-opted some exiled black South African students. I got to bowl, took a few wickets now and again and wrote up the matches regularly for Monday's English-language *Egyptian Gazette*.

There was golf as well at the Gezira. After emphasising that the rules of the Royal and Ancient Golf Club of St Andrews applied, the official score card mentioned a few slightly unusual hazards, noting, 'All masonry, culverts, water pipes, the dog graveyard and race course fixtures may be treated as immoveable obstructions.' It added, 'A ball lying on ground damaged by hoof marks may be lifted and placed within six inches of where it originally lay, not nearer the hole.' And there was golf too at the Mena House Club, on the edge of the desert, where you stood with your driver on the third tee and just aimed at the large object directly behind the distant flag – the Great Pyramid. 'Easy swing, easy swing,' my Egyptian caddie-cum-coach exhorted, not always to best effect, as I lunged once again at a ball half-hidden in tufty grass.

Back at the clubhouse, I once saw a whole set of irons lying twisted and broken on the floor behind the counter. A beefy American oil worker from the Gulf, it seemed, had broken every one of them across his well-muscled thigh, after one last desperate but unavailing effort to hit a clean shot towards the green.

No, it wasn't all work, and in this heavily censored society there were quiet periods. Barron and I flew down to Hurghada on the Red Sea. It was a quiet fishing village then. Today, I see it's advertised for package tours in the weekend papers. I'm glad I saw the area as it was then. We hired a boat and sailed off with a few bottles of beer towards the islands. The turquoise sea looked very still and welcoming. But the boatman at the rudder waved a warning finger at Brian, sitting up front with one leg languidly trailing in the water. 'Sharks!' he shouted.

'But you told us there weren't any sharks here,' we expostulated.

The boatman smiled. 'Not many,' he replied. How very Egyptian.

I got a good feature story out of the trip, anyway, in the shape of a gnarled ninety-year-old local fisherman and great-grandfather who was still going out to sea. He proudly showed us his tubby, blue-painted boat and had good tales to tell about sharks and a giant squid. I called him Egypt's oldest fisherman, which wasn't too far out, I think.

There were feature stories aplenty to be written. The boys in the office suggested I visit the 'snake village', as they called it. Out in the desert, a few miles from the Pyramids, in the village of Abu Rawash, the snake trade went back generations. About fifty villagers were involved, happy when I visited them at the start of the long hot summer, when sweltering heat forces snakes and scorpions to leave their pits and hunt for food. One of the hunters would scoop them up with a sickle-like weapon called a *mangara*, while another stood by with a sack. At the moment, the villagers were most unhappy because the Egyptian taxmen had threatened them with a new demand for $500 a month as their share of the takings.

As part of their training, Egyptian troops being readied for guerrilla activity behind the Israeli lines in Sinai – still at that time occupied by the enemy – were taught how to catch and eat non-venomous snakes and other reptiles. The villagers of Abu Rawash supplied them. 'We have a special price for the Army,' said the wrinkled seventy-year-old headman and chief snake charmer, Sheikh Mohammed Tolba. 'Twenty-five piastres. It's our national duty.' The normal price for a cobra was about four dollars.

Among the main customers were American serum laboratories, which had bought some fifty cobras and 200 other snakes in the past year.

As the sheikh told me all this, a little girl stood in the sandy street, cradling a snake in her arms, softly caressing its head, while a woman was feeding a batch of baby snakes with milk. 'Most Western visitors are scared,' the chief said. 'I don't know why. There's nothing unnatural about snakes. If it's a cobra, we just remove its fangs. If it's a scorpion, we cut out its sting – unless the customer doesn't want them removed.'

Egyptian snakes, I was told, were never more than about two metres long. Trained hunters could guess their type, size, sex and if they were of the poisonous variety by reading their wriggly tracks in the sand. 'It takes wits rather than courage to catch a cobra,' said Sheikh Tolba. 'You have to grab its head at the right moment. Otherwise,' he added with a wicked smile, 'may Allah have mercy on your soul!' Maybe he was just joking. 'But,' he said, 'this new tax is just too much. We will simply have to scare the taxmen from coming to our villages,' and added, 'I think we have the weapons.'

The story got wide play, not least in the United States, from where I later received the following handwritten letter from a schoolboy in California:

> I fully enjoyed your article on snakes. I collect snakes of all kinds.
> I have two boa constrictors. I really would like to have a defanged cobra, but if I bought it around here it would be over 100 dollars.
> Can you give me any information, please?

There followed a footnote from a lady called Ada Porter, who wrote, '*Mother permits Scott to purchase defanged cobra.*' It was one letter I didn't reply to.

For the average newspaper reader – if there is such a person – ancient Egypt is at least as interesting as the present, probably more so. Anything mentioning Queen Cleopatra would be snapped up by news editors. I got big play in the spring of 1970 with a report that an ancient shrine visited by Cleopatra had been unearthed near the pyramids. Even better for the London papers, the discovery was made by Professor Walter Emery, of London

University, and a combined British-Egyptian team. They'd discovered a stone plaque that was described to me as 'the great lady's calling card' – which made a great headline. Interesting that the discovery of this big underground temple complex was made as Israeli bombers were pounding Egyptian Army camps just a few miles away across the desert. The inscription bearing Cleopatra's name was written in well-preserved black ink in the old demotic language. Another inscribed stone bore the name of Alexander the Great, known to have visited the nearby Pharaonic capital of Memphis in November of the year 302 BC. The sixty-six-year-old British professor had been taking part in digs in Egypt for forty years. He described the find as 'undoubtedly one of the most important discoveries in Egypt in the present century'.

I won even more space in the papers when the tomb of the boy king Tutankhamen was sent to London to be put on display. Calling one evening at the Cairo museum, half a mile from the office after a tip-off, I was amazed to find myself in a small room with just one archaeologist and a helper, who were almost casually wrapping up the sarcophagus for despatch to Britain. Before it was sealed, I gazed at the impressive gold funerary mask from just a few inches away, a private view of a cultural icon which would later that year – and again years later – be viewed at a much greater distance, and at a price, by hundreds of thousands in Britain and around the world. A few days later, the crated sarcophagus was flown by a Royal Air Force Comet jet airliner to London. An air crash didn't bear thinking about. But in death, at least, the boy king had good fortune…

Khrushchev was right, sort of. The country that built the pyramids had to import Russian engineers to build the Aswan Dam, a huge structure that would revolutionise the economy downstream. Communist bigwigs were much in evidence at the official opening. Compared with today's obsession with security, I still have a photograph I took of Nasser and Yugoslavia's Marshal Josif Broz Tito from a few yards away. You could hardly imagine getting that close to the bosses today.

It was a festive occasion. Pigeons, deputising for doves of peace, were released from baskets at the appropriate moment.

Some of them fluttered down again behind the assembled masses and were promptly grabbed by men in white jellabiyas, who no doubt had them for supper. Egypt's lean and wiry fellaheen had a healthy fat-free diet. Not so some of their leaders. And Nasser, unlike his successor Anwar Sadat, was to die not from an assassin's bullet but in his bed, struck down in his early fifties by a heart attack, the scourge of Egypt's overweight leaders.

I was out of the office at the start of a planned drinking spree with colleagues after an exhausting Arab summit meeting. Nasser had played a key role in reconciling Jordan's King Hussein and Arafat's Palestine guerrillas. Now we journalists were planning to relax. Luckily I'd given Bahgat, manning the evening desk, the phone number of a New Zealand colleague at whose flat the carousals were due to begin. Bahgat's message was terse and disturbing: 'You'd better come in. They're playing solemn music on the radio, so it must be somebody big.'

Neither of us guessed just how big. Thank God I'd left contact numbers, otherwise my career might have ended there and then. But it was annoying, because of our poor communications, to be beaten with the first newsflash on Nasser's death by our Beirut office, which was able to monitor Cairo Radio and had a direct teleprinter line to London.

Almost as irritating was reading Beirut's first lead, which had Nasser 'bestriding the Arab world like a Colossus' – that all-purpose cliché which I would have hoped had died a merciful death. My own factual Snap, finally issued under a Cairo dateline, said simply:

> President Gamal Abdel Nasser, father of the Egyptian revolution, died tonight, leaving his 33 million countrymen bewildered with grief. The 52-year-old soldier turned politician was struck down by a sudden heart attack hours after he had brought peace to Jordan. He died surrounded by his family and grief-stricken aides at his suburban villa on the outskirts of Cairo.

I commented:

> It is difficult today for anyone here under middle age to imagine Egypt or an Arab world without Nasser, the soldier-president

who has dominated Arab affairs for nearly two decades. As if reluctant to accept the news, crowds of youths raced round the streets, endlessly repeating the name of the lost leader. But the main reaction was of numbed disbelief. Most people who heard the news on street radios went quietly home, weeping openly and tearing their hair ... Massive demonstrations can be expected when the news has fully struck home.

This proved an understatement.

Asked by London for an immediate 'Think-piece' on Nasser's likely successor, I named the obvious candidates, including Sadat, and couldn't understand why London didn't issue the story. Actually, it never left Cairo. The censors, when I later protested, said they thought issuing such a story within hours of Nasser's death was in bad taste. And who, on reflection, could argue? *Autres pays, autres moeurs*.

A hysterical anti-foreigner wave broke over the capital. A crowd surrounded my car on the way back home, thumping on the roof and windows. I revved up my faithful Cortina and got through. The masses poured into Cairo from the provinces, some of them falling off the crammed rooftops of trains, for one of the most extraordinary state funerals ever. Amid the universal press coverage, in which Reuters won a large share, it was nice later to see that my old friends at the *Manchester Evening News* devoted a whole front page to my bylined report of a funeral that nearly turned into a riot. 'CAIRO MILLIONS WEEP' was their banner headline, which said it all. In a day I'll never forget, the nation went wild as the man they'd called 'The Boss' was finally laid to rest.

I wrote:

If any proof were needed of Nasser's hold over the Egyptian people, this was it. Original plans for the procession completely collapsed and all attempts at maintaining order were swamped by a fighting, struggling sea of humanity. Today's funeral was almost certainly Cairo's biggest mass demonstration in its 1,000-year history. The lament 'Nasser, Nasser' rang out on all sides from dawn into the heat of the afternoon. Women tore their hair and scratched their faces. Countless hundreds fainted and were passed spreadeagled over the heads of the crowds to overburdened first-aid units. Thirty-foot-high trees along the Nile cracked and crashed to the ground under the weight of humanity clinging to them for a better view. Some half a million people were jammed into the main station square, with its giant granite statue of the ancient Pharaoh Rameses. The coffin was nearly toppled from the gun carriage on which it was carried, as a howling mass fought over each other's bodies to get to the coffin and touch it, and the crowd almost bore the coffin away.

Some fifty leading foreign dignitaries were ignored by the crowds and finally took refuge from the crush in a small park safely away from the mob. Mass demonstrations and deaths took place too in other parts of the Arab world. Soviet Prime Minister Alexei Kosygin promised continued aid to Egypt and warned Israel not to pin any hopes on a political vacuum in the region. In Cairo, the big reaction had set in by early evening, seen in the sullen faces of workmen clearing up the wreckage and the slumped figures of mounted policemen slowly plodding back to barracks. 'There will never be another like him,' many people in Cairo were saying. It was one of the biggest stories I've covered. And Egypt never had a leader of similar stature. In the years ahead, the country was to develop along other lines.

Among the foreign guests had been Britain's ebullient George Brown, whom I was to see again for the first time since his New York antics. I was at home when Bahgat wisely rang me from the office and alerted me to a MENA story containing a quote from George which seemed highly dubious. I rang Shepheard's Hotel and was connected. The Foreign Secretary had clearly been drinking. When I told him the statement that had been attributed to him, he exploded. 'It'sh absholutely untrue!' he said. 'Come round for breakfast. I'll explain tomorrow.'

When I met him the following morning in the hotel lobby, Brown, well known for his dislike of old-style British diplomats, almost shoved a couple of junior flunkeys aside before ushering me on to his balcony and giving me breakfast. 'Let's get away from these chaps,' he said very audibly. Then he gave me the correct quote, which was much less dramatic and in fact hardly worth reporting.

Chapter 11
'SURE, IT'D BE A NICE DAY IF IT WASN'T RAININ' ' – A MAN I MET IN TIPPERARY

My fellow passenger on the ferry to Belfast looked a bit like Shell, the old derelict memorably played by F J McCormick in that marvellous film *Odd Man Out*. He tries to help an IRA boss, mortally wounded in an abortive bank raid. With the title role played by James Mason, it was a box-office hit and remains one of the finest black-and-white movies I've ever seen. With director Carol Reed at the helm, it had to be good. He'd go on to make two more winners, *The Fallen Idol* and *The Third Man*.

My eighteen-year-old brother was doing national service in the Irish Fusiliers at Ballykinlar Camp, and I, in the sixth form at Thornleigh, was taking a trip across the water to see him and the sights of Belfast. The old man had me trapped on deck, both of us travelling steerage from Liverpool on a cold and blustery night. He gave me a lengthy treatise on the political situation in the divided island, and it was clear which side he was on.

'Make no mistake about it, son,' he assured me sotto voce as we steamed up Belfast Lough in the early morning between shores which seemed a sharper shade of green than anything on the Lancashire side of the water. 'By Christmas, the Six Counties'll be ours!'

Well, half a century later we're still waiting. Maybe the nouveau-riche Irish Republic lost interest, though hard times have arrived in the past twelve months.

My brother had already paid the Irish relatives in Tipperary a visit – shedding his British Army uniform before crossing the border. As boys, we'd heard about Clonmel, though not very much, from my mother, always reticent about her own background as an Irish immigrant and disinclined to talk politics. Her rather more voluble sisters in Bolton, the next town to Bury, were never quite so discreet. We'd hear occasional references during our regular visits there in the thirties to 'Mr de Valera', who despite his Latin-sounding name and American citizenship was, we gathered, the leader of the new Irish Republic. Nothing was ever said about the Post Office siege in Dublin, or about Michael Collins and the civil war in which he'd been ambushed and shot. We never knew about Patrick Pearse, one of the leaders of the Easter Rising, or the poem he wrote in 1916 on the eve of his execution. Things like that weren't talked about. Opinions seemed divided among the relatives about Mr de Valera, though he was mostly thought a good thing and would stay in power for decades, becoming President. But every March, a few days before the seventeenth of the month, a sometimes soggy package would arrive from Clonmel containing a green bunch of shamrock. We'd wear a sprig of it in our buttonholes, like many of our school friends, but didn't know quite why.

I assumed it was something to do with being a Catholic. We gathered as small boys that Ireland was a very Catholic country – which seemed fairly obvious, anyway, from the number of Irish priests and nuns in Lancashire. We found some of our Irish relatives a bit heavy going. My brother and I didn't care over much for those visits to Bolton, where the five sisters, gathered at one or another of their homes, seemed to spend most of the time arguing, mainly in loud voices. There was rarely any sense of relaxation at those periodic conclaves of the Ryans and their spouses, and it was nice to get back on the bus to Bury, fortunately six miles distant from the eye of the storm. My mother seemed the quietest of the five – though she'd prove to have greater ambitions for us kids than our rather dour Lancastrian father. It was often a relief to be back home, away from the squabbling. We didn't say so, of course, except to each other.

Yet I'm sure it implanted in me as a kid the firm conviction that Irish people were perhaps best taken in small doses. I thought maybe they were all like that, slightly crazy. Fortunately, this did not prove to be altogether correct.

When the war with Nazi Germany started, we understood that Ireland was neutral – though this didn't seem to square with the fact that our Irish uncle was fighting with the British Army in Burma, and once turned up in Bury wearing one of those big jungle hats, which we thought pretty smart. But then we'd only just about got used to seeing him in photographs wearing a long cassock. Somewhere along the way, he'd lost the faith, it seemed; or perhaps just decided he didn't want to be a priest. Maybe he'd been pushed into it in the first place. That seemed to be the sort of place Ireland was. Uncle Ned, as we called him, gave me a biography of the Anglo-Irishman Norman O'Neill, one of the most famous theatre composers of the thirties, now virtually forgotten. I have the book still.

My knowledge of Ireland expanded over the years, but mainly on the musical and literary side. After my infantile solo perform-ances at those Sunday evening concerts of 'Father O'Flynn' – a tune and words that I actually found rather clever – I got to recognise other Irish songs, and the voice of John McCormack, rightly idolised by the Irish, in numbers like 'The Bard of Armagh'. This plaintive song, when sung by him or other popular tenors like Robert White or Clonmel's own Frank Patterson, can still bring a tear to the eye. Irish literature came next. In my late teens, notably at university, I got to know the short stories which writers in this small country across the Irish Sea seemed to turn out in remarkable abundance. By my twenties, tales by writers like Frank O'Connor, Sean O'Faolain, Daniel Corkery and Mary Lavin figured high on my reading list. I was not surprised years later, on regular visits to the Republic, to find the first two named were both Cork men of about the same age.

There was all the flavour of a foreign culture in such stories, and I was intrigued by the small but distinctive differences between the spoken and written idioms of the two countries. Irish English, I would later find when talking to my very first taxi driver across the water, seemed rather exotic – and a bit more user-friendly, if you know what I mean. Put a question to an Englishman, he'll probably reply with a blunt 'Yes' or 'No'. An Irishman might say, 'It is, mind you,' or, 'Now, I wouldn't say so exactly.' The Irish, it seemed, seldom used simple affirmatives or negatives, turning them instead into a short sentence – more oblique but often more agreeable. As has been stated more than once, the Irish have a way with words. It's what Hal Boyle, of Reuters' principal American rival the Associated Press, once called 'turning your prose to poetry'.

We'd had a certain amount of Irish history at school, and knew the island's fortunes had fluctuated wildly over the centuries, the main culprits – apart from occasional coastal raiders from the Mediterranean – being the Brits. As far back as the twelfth century, the Welshman Giraldus Cambrensis had been pretty scathing about the folk he encountered on an island which he sniffily considered next door to barbaric. As he said:

> Although they are fully endowed with natural gifts, their external characteristics of beard and dress and internal cultivation of the mind are so barbarous that they cannot be said to have any culture.

That's telling them. Moreover, he wrote in wonderment, these Irishmen rode bareback and went naked and unarmed into battle. But, he added graciously, they were more expert than anyone else at throwing stones and missiles at their enemies 'when everything else fails'. Well, a man's gotta do what he's gotta to do.

Oliver Goldsmith, writing several centuries later, presented a different picture. In a report for the *Weekly Magazine* in 1759, he was more generous about the natives. In a cottage warmed by a turf fire, he reported, was a girl 'as beautiful as an angel and excessively cheerful'. And, he added:

> I was permitted to send to the neighbouring alehouse for a shilling's worth of beer, which the daughter ran and fetched in a moment. Which soon threw us all into tiptop spirits.

A gloomier tale came from a visitor during the days of the English-imposed Penal Laws, illustrating both the privations of the period and an admirable native resilience in dealing with them. Regular schooling was forbidden to Catholic children, and when not so much as a cowshed could be obtained for a school-room for the children of Irish peasants:

> The worthy pedagogue selected the first green spot on the sunny side of a quickset hedge, which he adapted for his purpose, and

> there under the scorching rays of a summer sun and in defiance
> of spies and statutes carried on the work of instruction.

(I must confess I never witnessed many scorching summers during the years I holidayed in Ireland.)

It was in the late fifties, newly affianced to the young Swedish lady met in Copenhagen, that I first toured the Republic by car. At that time, the worst thing you might still see were a few kids with bare feet on the streets of Dublin. But I wasn't on a reporting mission. We were on holiday and it was the beauty of places like Glendalough, Killarney, Bantry Bay and the Ring of Kerry that we wanted to see, not the still rather shabby centre of Dublin. At that time I was still reluctant to introduce a foreigner – as well as myself – to family forbears in Clonmel whom I didn't even know. I remembered those family squabbles back in Lancashire and half feared the same high-octane sort of encounter here. Or maybe, if they were devout Catholics, they wouldn't be happy at the pair of us, still unmarried, sharing a hotel room…

With our holiday time limited, anyway, I decided not to plunge into a family visit unannounced and maybe awkward for all concerned, and instead just to enjoy the sights and the scenery. We toured the south-west peninsulas, standing on wind-blown cliffs where the next bit of land to the west was America. My penchant for exploring intriguing country lanes, often little more than tracks, led us into a farmyard on one occasion, raising some objections from my passenger. Along the way, we did stop briefly in my mother's hometown and lunched at the riverside Clonmel Arms – now, alas, defunct.

By then, I'd been looking at travel books. Clonmel was clearly not just some obscure spot on the map but had a good bit of history about it. The town's darkest yet most glorious days came in 1650, when England's military ruler, Oliver Cromwell – of whom political views in England seem strangely ambiguous to this day – laid siege to the town after putting down insurrections in most other parts of the island. Big guns were levelled at the town walls, and there was heavy slaughter as the English forces were driven back with the loss of around 2,000 men. It was the biggest defeat of Cromwell's career, one still celebrated that side of the water. Daniel O'Connell, who'd much later dominate Irish politics in the slow road to independence, put it this way in an early nineteenth century speech to Parliament in London: 'We are an imperishable people.' The Great Famine which followed would, however, test Irish mettle to breaking point.

'People went to sleep at night with the potato fields looking green and healthy; when they got up the next day, every stem in the fields was ruined by the disease,' wrote Maire ni Grianna in her memoirs of the Great Famine.

This set off a transatlantic exodus, after which one emigrant wrote home that he was under 'the constant apprehension of our crazy old vessel going to the bottom'. Some of them doubtless did. Three-quarters of a century later, in slightly greater comfort, my own grandparents with five of their children would sail the same route, to arrive safe but fairly poor in New York.

Clonmel was not short of local heroes, I found. Writers Laurence Sterne, of *Tristram Shandy* fame, and George Borrow, author of the picaresque *Lavengro*, had both lived there as boys, while the Victorian novelist Anthony Trollope spent time there working for the Post Office. Charles Bianconi, another local hero, was the entrepreneur who launched a famous coach service in the eighteenth century, based on Clonmel's Hearns Hotel. Illustrations from the time show that these were not the jaunting cars most people associate with Ireland these days, but roomy and elegant carriages pulled by two pairs of horses. They monopolised transport in Ireland for the greater part of the nineteenth century.

My first visit to Ireland had left strong impressions, and a few years later, at the age of thirty-six and now divorced, I became a property owner there. Maybe my Irish ancestors had been spiritually getting through to me. Also, my young and growing son had never been far from my thoughts during those intensive years in the Middle East on either side of the Israeli–Arab divide. I spent all my holidays with him, taking him skiing each winter to Norway, France or Austria. For the summer break, I'd long toyed with the idea of buying a place of my own, so why not in Ireland? There, he could spend time with me in a stable setting, as against short breaks in England or European ski resorts.

So I flew over to Ireland in 1971, took a train to County

Tipperary and finally met all the relatives. They couldn't have been more welcoming, and there was none of the high-voltage squabbling that I remembered from boyhood days in Lancashire. And so the pleasant vale of Clonmel ('Honey Meadow' in Irish) would be my holiday destination for years to come, and Peter loved it. My mother's cousins and their children, delighted when I decided to buy a property in Clonmel, were enchanted by this beautiful fair-haired boy from Sweden. I'd soon discovered that the Irish of Clonmel were considerably more laid-back than the relatives in England. My annual, sometimes biannual, visits became a richly rewarding experience for both my son and myself. We felt very much at home.

Dickensian recollections were triggered off again when I first called on solicitor Arthur Morris. His office, as shadowed and cluttered as I expected an old-fashioned lawyer's office to be, was up a flight of slightly creaking wooden stairs in a nineteenth-century terraced row of houses near the railway station, the entrance approached by a short path through a small and rather neglected front garden. Arthur, who'd been recommended to me by my cousin Syden Bolger, proved a mine of information and a very good friend. He also introduced me to young professionals at the very convivial Clonmel Club. There I met architect Joe Anthony, from nearby Carrick-on-Suir, a few miles further along the vale towards Waterford. He'd later design my house. I'd had a preliminary look at a few existing properties, but they were usually too poky and close to traffic. Further out in the country, I was shown a newly renovated former farmhouse on a hillside, but it was thumbs down. I found one room extremely eerie and would never have felt happy living there. Likewise an old cottage in the woods, approached by a bumpy track barely wide enough to drive a car, and almost hemmed in by undergrowth. There seemed too much history about such places (and who knew what it might be?) to ever feel at ease. I could imagine ghosts lurking in the woodwork.

On my next visit – from Egypt – I decided instead to have a new house built and found the ideal setting a mile from the town centre in a field which sloped gently down to the River Suir. Eight plots were being sold. In happy contrast to the gloomy aura of houses I'd looked at and rejected, here was a hitherto untouched sunny meadow, golden with tall summery ryegrass, a line of trees separating it from the river. I didn't take long to make a decision. I told Joe Anthony roughly what sort of house I had in mind, and together we sketched out a rough plan. Shortly afterwards, back in the Middle East, I received a more professional printed plan from Joe for a single-storey house (I hate the imported Indian word 'bungalow', of which there are thousands in Ireland). Principally, I wanted the lounge to be large and airy with tall windows most of the way round, and that's what he gave me. I like light and space.

Back in Cairo, I received in the post shortly thereafter from Arthur Morris a charmingly old-fashioned document, headed 'Memorial Of An Indenture'. This informed me that the landowners of the field…

> thereinafter and hereinafter called 'the Vendor' of the One Part and John Chadwick, of Marlfield Road, Clonmel, in the County of Tipperary Reuter Correspondent (thereinafter and hereinafter called 'the Purchaser') of the Other Part WHEREBY after reciting as therein it was witnessed that for the consideration therein (receipt acknowledged) the Vendor as Beneficial Owner did thereby GRANT AND CONVEY unto the Purchaser ALL THAT AND THOSE part of the lands of Inishlonaught formerly known as Abbeyslonaghty being part of the Marlfield Demesne situate in the Barony of Iffa and Offa East and County of Tipperary being part of the lands described in and conveyed by the therein before recited Indenture of Conveyance.

Gosh! I guessed this extraordinary document meant I was now owner of the strip of land I'd earmarked in that lovely meadow beside the river. The Barony of Iffa, indeed! I wonder if they still use this sort of gobbledygook in today's Ireland. I found it quite impressive. I felt I was almost becoming a part of history. Then in June 1972 I received word from the architect that construction of the house was 'now advancing very rapidly and should be finished within the next month or so'. Or so… The painting of the exterior walls would be under way in two weeks time, I was also told. When I picked up my now eleven-year-old son at Dublin airport and we arrived by train in Clonmel, the house remained unpainted, surrounded by planks and the odd wheelbarrow. It didn't really matter. The house was liveable in, and with the help of my cousins down the road we were not short of the necessaries. I'd get used to the Irish pace of things, not unlike what I'd experienced, first in Italy, then in Egypt, from where by this time I was now reporting. A year later, I learned that the garden wall was still not completed and the exterior of the house remained unpainted.

In Cairo, they always tell an impatient inquirer after progress, '*Bookra, inshallah*' (Tomorrow, please God). In Ireland, I was to find, things were much the same. And I'm reminded here of one of those excruciating jokes with which George Vine used to regale Reuter colleagues in Bonn over end-of-the-day drinks. He was fond of accents and had developed a pseudo-Irish one all his own. 'In Spain, we say *manyana, manyana*,' the visitor says to the Irishman. 'Do you have a similar expression here in Ireland?' After pondering the matter a little, the Irishman replies, 'I don't think we have a word that conveys quite the same degree of urgency.' I hope George, who now spends much of his time in County Cork with his Irish wife, will be forgiven for that one.

As an absentee house-owner, I made regular visits over the next three years and eventually had the place shipshape. I later took over to Ireland an old baby-blue Opel I bought during the 1972 Olympics. It would do sterling service for years, until I bequeathed it to the local postman, John Hallinan, who did the gardening during my long absences. My second cousin, Syden, toured the household stores with me and helped me with curtains, carpets and the other necessaries. Her husband Dick, a convivial and good-looking man who seemed to know most people in town, introduced me to a few of the pubs, notably his favourite, the Clonmel Inn, where I found myself considerably outpaced by the regulars. Dick, like most of the habitués, downed pints of draught Guinness separated by doses of Paddy, the local Irish whiskey. I never could stay that pace and settled for a lower speed of intake.

It didn't seem to make much difference to Dick's driving habits. We left the pub one Saturday night and crossed the road to where his car was parked, facing the pavement. Dick (who I knew didn't have a driving licence) unfortunately chose forward gear, at which we lurched towards the kerb and bumped into a mailbox. At this point, a policeman emerged from the gloom. I feared the worst. Prosecution? Court case? Heavy fine? Loss of licence? (And we'd still have to walk home.) The policeman drew near, but said, 'Oh, it's you, Dick, is it? Away home wit' you now!' And we motored on.

In such a relaxed environment, I had no qualms when teaching my son to drive in Ireland. Already a car/motorbike fan, he first learned how to execute a three-point turn in a parking lot down by the River Suir near the village of Marlfield. At thirteen, I couldn't hold him back any longer and this small figure, who then could hardly see over the steering wheel, was allowed to drive the Opel for a couple of hundred yards now and then on quiet country roads. That's how Ireland was. He's never looked back since, and there's no chance of you ever getting to drive a car – even your own – if he's around. No surprise that his first job was with Ford, the next with Yamaha.

I had a large number of cousins, how far removed I never quite worked out. Syden's brother Billy, a familiar and almost elfin-like figure around town, who flitted in and out of all the pubs at weekend with his raffle tickets, lived with the Bolgers. His brother Joe, still remembered for singing '*Panis Angelicus*' as a choirboy at St Mary's Church, lived a block or two away. Another brother Eamon lived up the road towards Marlfield with his family. He was fond of starting ambitious property projects which seldom materialised. I'd receive an urgent cable, wherever I was with Reuters, inviting me to join some new deal on a fifty–fifty basis. 'Take no notice of him, John,' his wife Vourneen said when I rang, and I didn't. Their imposing but slightly crumbling old mansion stood on a bluff overlooking a bend of the River Suir. Here I was taken one day to meet Great-aunt Kathleen. The atmosphere was like something from a Sherlock Holmes tale. Across the lounge, the old lady sat near the fire in a high rocking chair. She regarded me with little warmth as I was led across the room to meet her.

'From England, are ye?' she said, grasping the top of her stick.

'And ye dare to come to Ireland?' Despite protestations from other family members, the conversation didn't progress a great deal further.

My mother was delighted when she first saw my house, just half a mile from the terrace in Irishtown where she'd been born and a dozen kids somehow raised. For several summers thereafter, my parents were able to spend a few months in Ireland, and her youngest sister, from an English convent, also joined the crowd sometimes. Sister St Peter was very popular with my son, who was never, as a true Swede, one for angry words. 'She is so calm and kind,' he pronounced. It was his biggest compliment. Apart from my mother and the nun, calmness was not a Ryan characteristic.

Once the house was comfortably furnished, I had my piano shipped over from Sweden, where I was posted in the early seventies, and there'd be Sunday evening family get-togethers. My son, a big Peter Sellers fan, was showing a remarkable gift for accents and impersonations and would dress up as various characters from history or literature. His speciality was a cruel impersonation of the artist Toulouse-Lautrec, for which he shuffled into the lounge with his knees in shoes. My contribution would be a few show tunes on piano, until I was firmly eased off the stool by the hips and shoulders of my increasingly eccentric father, perhaps fortified by one too many Paddies down at the Clonmel Inn. He'd play a couple of Viennese waltzes, of which 'The Blue Danube' and 'The Merry Widow Waltz' were his favourites, and, if there was anybody present with a voice, one of those Edwardian ballads. As he entered his eighties, the accuracy of his playing was somewhat affected by the badly crooked third finger of his right hand, which he'd broken years earlier on some building site but never had treated. 'It'll be all reet,' he said. It wasn't, with the result that some Fs got to be F sharps and D naturals turned into E flats. Nobody in Clonmel seemed to notice.

When working in Bonn, I bought two small Honda motor-bikes and took them over to Ireland. My son and I had long rides through the woods or over the fells, where we sometimes pitched a tent for the night. Or we'd take the car to the scenic south-west peninsulas facing the Atlantic and camp there. It remains my favourite part of Ireland. Killarney, the Ring of Kerry and Garnish Island, with its lovely subtropical garden, became regular destinations. Irish weather, as is well known, changes three or four times a day, but we got used to it.

There was no prior warning in the late summer of 1979 of my mother's death and, perhaps happily, she died in her sleep. I'd said goodbye to my parents the day before, then flown back to Germany. At the office next morning, I received the sad phone call from my brother, and an hour or two later was flying back to Ireland. As I drove over the hill into Clonmel, the valley was suddenly suffused by a warm flood of sunshine and an air of complete peace. One of the few mystical experiences I've ever had. Catherine Chadwick (nee Ryan) was buried beside her Irish relatives a few days later. I'd taken the last rose of the summer from the garden and placed it in her fingers. It was more than just a sentimental touch.

Chapter 12
UP THE NILE AND IN NEXT-DOOR LIBYA, TWO MORE SOLDIERS GRAB POWER

From across the border in Libya, the news trickled through in September 1969 that a young army officer called 'Gaffadi' had taken power. He was a complete unknown. We didn't even get his name right for twenty-four hours. But he was soon visiting Cairo to pay his respects to the revered Nasser. The Libyan leader frowned, we were informed, when he saw the wine glasses on the prepared banqueting table, insisting these were removed. For some Egyptians, not averse in the main to the odd alcoholic drink, at least in private, it was a first black mark against Gadaffi. And I could never get into the place to write about the new Libya. It was impossible to obtain a visa.

A few months after the Libyan coup, another hitherto unknown army man took control in Sudan. We called him 'Mineiri' for a day or two, before we once more got the consonants in the right order. I flew south on my first visit to Khartoum, and, having checked into the hotel, trudged into town in mid-afternoon in search of news.

It all seemed strangely quiet. Just an empty, sunbaked street and, in the far distance, another solitary figure approaching from the opposite direction. We converged, like protagonists in a Western film, and I recognised *Financial Times* correspondent Richard Johns. He'd had the same misplaced optimism as I. Apart from the two of us, the town was dead. Every Sudanese official in his right mind would be sleeping, to emerge at sundown. A perfect time for a revolution, I thought, tempting Providence. The temperature, I discovered later, was 46°C. Even those famous mad dogs might have lain panting in the shade.

In the cool of the evening, I visited the recently founded Sudan News Agency (SUNA), with which we'd been cooperating; in fact it was one of the main reasons for visiting. I found the agency's jovial and energetic boss, Abdel Kerim, operating from an outdoor office at the rear of a large villa near the university. Carpenters and electricians were banging, sawing and hammering away. Further extensions were planned, to be built largely by voluntary labour. Two offices were in the process of erection during my visit. I congratulated Abdel Kerim on progress made so far, but – maybe pre-negotiating his next Reuter subscription – he complained of constant financial pressures.

'Well, how are you paying people's wages?' I asked.

He chuckled. 'I smuggle in a few diamonds from Central African Republic.' Was he joking? I'll never know.

If Cairo was scientifically backward, Sudan was primitive, though receiving considerable technical aid, doubtless for long-term political reasons, from both the Russians and the Chinese. In a cupboard at one media office, small transistor radios of Chinese origin were piled high and higgledy-piggledy, though clearly new. When the batteries ran down, they just took another radio from the crate. For another Reuter client, I arranged the purchase of some brand new Siemens teleprinters, but, on my next visit, editors there complained of technical problems. I touched the top of one of the printers and quickly pulled my hand away. In the fierce heat of a Sudan summer, the metal was burning. Have you ever tried lubricating them? I helpfully suggested.

Next, I visited Omdurman Radio, where they complained the Reuter service was not coming through, unlike those of our competitors. In the wire room, Reuters, Agence France-Presse and other agency printers stood in a row. I lifted the top of the Reuter machine, thick with dust, and looked at the works inside. 'You might like to put a ribbon in,' I said politely. For our new radio service, I said I'd like to make a broadcast to London. Of course, they said, showing me into a spacious, rather musty-smelling wood-panelled studio. I suppose the huge lozenge-shaped microphone standing on the desk, of the kind you see in old BBC documentaries, should have made me wonder… I waited for two hours, but the promised circuit never materialised, though they assured me the studio had 'often' been used before. I asked, 'When was the last time?'

'During the Queen's visit,' they said.

Her State Visit had been in 1954. We were now in 1970. I wondered if the studio had ever been opened in the years between. By this time, darkness had fallen, and everyone in the building seemed to have gone home except a young technician. Mission unaccomplished, I rode back into central Khartoum on the back of his motorbike.

My first visits to Sudan were nothing if not diverting. After Reuters' break with RNS, the energetic and sociable Shahe Guebenlian ('Gubby' to friends and colleagues) was now manager for the Middle East and Africa, criss-crossing the continent in a variety of decrepit airliners, from all of which he somehow emerged unscathed. We'd sometimes meet in the Sudanese capital, he flying in from somewhere else in Africa. Gubby could certainly lay on the charm. In one French-speaking West African country, Reuters and Agence France-Presse had been competing for the same news contract and seemed to be level pegging. Then, after a government dinner, Gubby unveiled his secret weapon – his one-legged dance, in which he whirled round at high-speed like a dervish on one foot. How could his hosts refuse him the contract? The French don't do things like that.

The two of us were once invited to dinner at Abdel Kerim's home. We politely listened to one of his anecdotes after the other, but no food materialised. When, well after midnight, after exchanging eye signals, we rose to take our leave, he leapt up and said, 'Oh, the dinner… I forgot!' and dashed into the kitchen. We finally ate about two.

On my next visit, I decided to watch a football match and took a taxi to the main stadium, unwisely joining a large crowd already assembled in front of the main gates and increasingly desperate to get inside. When an official suddenly flung the gates open, a tidal wave of humanity, with me incautiously in the middle of it, swept into the ground. There were shrieks and cries, people tumbling over one another in the crush. I'm going to die, I told myself, but managed to work myself to the fringe of the human cataract. I noticed steel railings running along the sides of the terraced steps. I grabbed one of them and hoisted myself up out of the crush, then worked my way along the girders under the roof to an outer wall, where I climbed through a gap and dropped into the dust outside, my only loss a torn jacket. I took a taxi back into town, where I heard later that one woman died and many others were trampled on and injured. It was my first and last sports date in Sudan. And there wasn't even a story in it.

I'd known for some time, via our Khartoum correspondent, that Germany's Rolf Steiner, one of many white mercenaries operating at that time in various parts of Africa, had been detained in Sudan. I was told unexpectedly during an otherwise routine visit to the Sudanese capital that he was about to be sentenced. A car would be sent to my hotel to pick me up. We drove to a military barracks on the outskirts of town. A few minutes later I found myself, extraordinarily, sitting not in a courtroom, as I'd expected, but as the third man at a small square table, Steiner to my left, the prosecuting officer to my right. The officer ran through a list of charges in English. Steiner, strangely enough, looked perfectly relaxed, made no comments and asked no questions. Then the officer at this 'quickie court' told the German he was to be shot. I almost found all this too surreal to take notes.

'Do you understand the sentence?' the judge asked him.

'Yes,' the German replied quite calmly. Altogether too calmly, I thought; and though I had an exclusive story, I wasn't really surprised to learn a bit later, back in Cairo, that the ex-mercenary had been reprieved and subsequently returned to Germany. I'd always smelt a deal.

It was time to visit southern Sudan. Tensions had been high for years between the mainly black and animist southerners and their Muslim overlords from the north. The Anyanya (meaning 'snake venom') were a separatist rebel army which had been keeping the Sudan military busy in the border region.

En route from Khartoum to the southern town of Juba, I looked down from the aircraft at the inhospitable region of the Sudd, a vast sprawl of interlocking bogs on both sides of the Nile. The name means 'Barrier' – which it certainly had been to explorers dating back to the Romans, when they tried to find the source of the Nile. The tangled vegetation below, with little sign of a river in the middle, recalled for me John Huston's classic film *The African Queen*, in which Humphrey Bogart and Katherine

Hepburn tried to force a rusty little steamboat through such a nightmare region of tall grass, reeds, leeches and ever-shifting islands. I was glad to be looking down from the comparative safety of a Sudan Airways plane.

Mind you, boarding the flight in Khartoum, I'd thought the Russian-built Antonov seemed curiously reluctant to leave the ground (this was apparently one of the plane's less pleasant characteristics), but now we were finally en route to Juba, calling at the intermediate towns of Malakal and Wau.

In Juba, I talked with Sudanese soldiers engaged in an apparently endless struggle with the Anyanya. They said I could have a ride along the border with Uganda on one of the helicopters keeping track of movements below. This seemed like a good idea until a few miles out the engine started making strange noises. We made a fairly rapid descent, and the journey back to Juba was by truck. I'd got a reasonable colour story, but I'd missed the return flight to Khartoum. I asked around the airport and someone suggested I should try the military plane standing out on the apron. Some visiting Russians were aboard, training Sudanese pilots.

The Army agreed to give me a ride back to the capital. I was the only civilian passenger. Apart from me, on the flight were just a few Army men and a medic attending to a wounded soldier lying on a trolley in the aisle, with drips attached. If the take-off was not quite like a rocket, it was pretty steep. The stretcher with its moaning soldier aboard started rolling back down the aisle, where it was finally grabbed and held firm by one of the others. Second air incident of the day – and if take-off was like this, what was landing going to be like? We completed the journey north, circled around Khartoum, and I held the edges of my seat as we began circling over the desert. But the landing couldn't have been smoother. 'How come?' I asked one of the Sudanese officers.

'A Russian landed the plane,' he said with a chuckle.

When Jaafar el-Nimeiry assumed power, my first impression, during an informal chat along with other correspondents in the sitting room of his home, was of a tough but friendly man with a relaxed manner towards journalists, admired locally for his habit of joining in kids' football games in the streets.

*John Chadwick (right), wearing a smart new school blazer,
with brother, Peter, and sister, Patricia, circa 1941*

*Cotton City Jazzmen playing in a carnival tent in the mid-fifties
Author at piano*

Bury Times *editorial staffers, circa 1953*
left to right: Brian Hitchen, John Bradbury,
John Chadwick, Roy Fishwick (photographer)

Off Iceland, 1957
The ship's doctor leads the way across...

...And now I've made it to HMS Russell

Cod War 1958,
Icelandic seamen 'prisoners' on board frigate Eastbourne
Olafur Gudmundsson (centre)

Return to Iceland,
Olafur Gudmundsson with John Chadwick, 1992

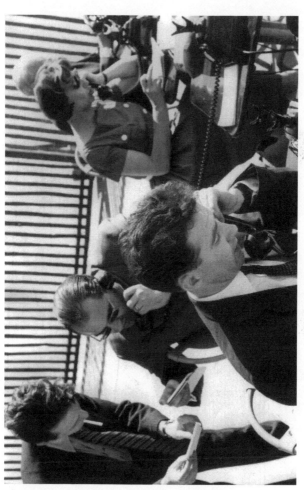

The world press at a foreign ministers' conference, Geneva 1959
John Chadwick in foreground

Son Peter at Copenhagen zoo, mid-sixties

Cricket at Cairo's Gezira Club, circa 1969

By hydrofoil across Lake Nasser en route to Abu Simbel

Cairo office, 1969
Bahgat Badie (left) and Fouad Al-Gawhary

Abu Simbel

Going-away party for Antoun Sidhom (centre), off to Australia

*Egyptian President Gamal-Abdel Nasser and Yugoslavia's Marshal Josip Tito
at opening of new Aswan dam (you couldn't get that close nowadays!)*

*Khartoum; a sombre press conference amid a wave of
executions after an abortive coup against President Nimeiry
John Chadwick second from left, Don North (NBC), Kit Minicleer (AP)*

Son Peter with my father at my house in Ireland in the late sixties

The Reuter pigeon returns to Aachen, where it all started,
and perches on a teleprinter

John Chadwick (left) with Managing Director Gerald Long
welcoming guests at the opening of new Reuter offices in Bonn, circa 1981

Palais des Nations, Geneva
Arriving by mini-Honda

Wig and Pen Club, Fleet St., London. A long-delayed reunion: (left to right) Frank Thomas, editor, Bury Times; *John Chadwick; Roy Heron,* Press Association; *Alan Toft, editor,* Independent Grocer

A harassed World Desk Editor is confronted minutes before issuing the evening News Schedule with three late (and misspelt) offerings from graphic artists Chee Kin, Lance and Kieron (Lance drew the cartoon)

*Approaching Franz-Josef Land aboard Klaudia Yelanskaya
as an icebreaker clears the way ahead, July 1993*

Franz-Josef Land. Our ship is dwarfed by the nuclear-powered Russian icebreaker

A beach in Spitzbergen with sharpshooter/vocalist Alexander Adamlovsky and interpreter Viktoria Gladysheva, July 1993

Getting a story at Kuwait Writers' Club

At home on the back terrace at 'The Stables' in Middle Littleton, Worcs., 2008

Maybe he was too relaxed, for, less than two years after his installation as President, he narrowly escaped death in an attempted communist takeover. For us, the story broke, as happened so often, from sources in Cairo. The first inklings of trouble in Sudan had come in early 1971, when Nimeiry ended his honeymoon with leftist factions who'd supported him in seizing power. Now the honeymoon was over and he threw out some sixty communists from the interior ministry, army and police.

Reporting from Khartoum shortly afterwards on a military parade marking the second anniversary of the coup, I wrote:

> The missiles, the tanks, and the low-flying jets were unmistakeably from the Soviet Union, but this year the red banners of Sudan's traditionally communist-dominated trade unions are noticeably absent from the celebrations.

Nimeiry had thrown down the gauntlet. But the left-wingers took it up, and a few weeks later he was himself deposed by a group of young army officers with communist backup. I was writing another think-piece in Cairo, speculating as to what the new leftist government might be up to, when Nimeiry suddenly returned to power himself in a bloody counter-coup. Nobody knew exactly what was going on. Our own correspondent in Sudan could not be contacted (it turned out he'd actually fled to Cairo when things started getting nasty, but never bothered to tell us). Khartoum Airport was closed to normal traffic. Eventually I got on the first plane from Cairo. Several hours after I'd left, a plaintive service message from London head office arrived at the Reuter office in Cairo. It read: 'ANY WORD FROM CHADWICK? HE SHOULD HAVE ARRIVED KHARTOUM BY NOW.'

Well, I had, but I was under arrest, like hundreds of political prisoners. I'd thought I was being smart taking only hand luggage on the flight and getting the first taxi into the city centre while others were struggling with customs clearance. But my solitary taxi, which seemed to be the only vehicle on the streets, was stopped right outside the white wedding cake palace of the President and I was ordered out. The soldiers looked upside down at my papers, always a bad sign, and prodded suspiciously at my radio, typewriter and tape recorder. I was then marched off at gunpoint, a disconsolate taxi driver trotting alongside, bemoaning his lost fare. I hadn't changed any money yet and couldn't help him. I told him (hopefully) to call round at the Sudan Hotel later.

In the sandy courtyard of the Ministry of the Interior, groups of communist prisoners squatted in the sun. More young men in shirtsleeves were periodically being brought in at rifle-point for questioning, their hands above their heads. Piles of confiscated communist literature lay around. I had time to read some of the titles – *Works of Marx and Lenin* and *Thoughts of Mao Tse-Tung*. Nimeiry obviously knew what he was doing. The university seemed to be a hotbed of communist subversion.

The red sun was sinking over the Nile and curfew hour rapidly approaching as I was detached from the local prisoners, taken to a jail and locked in a small cell. Two hours later I finally got an English-speaking officer there to let me use his phone and ring our local correspondent, Saad es-Sheikh, now back in Khartoum, where he seemed to know everybody – including, fortunately, the officer, who said, 'We are most apologising.' He abruptly ordered the same soldier who'd been guarding me to drive me post-haste to the hotel. I arrived five minutes before the curfew.

'Where've you been?' other correspondents asked suspiciously. They'd been scratching around to get a few quotes from the embassies. They looked sympathetic when I told them I'd been under arrest – but I'd really got the best colour story. And with a monetary consideration or two down at the central post office, I got a cable away to Cairo, for onpassing to London.

I'd always been happy in Khartoum to stay at the old-fashioned hotel, right beside the Nile, with its high ceilings and huge fans. Guests were ferried by motor launch to its elegant front steps before the Second World War from the old 'Empire' flying boats landing on the river. I'd always envied those travellers of old. Right now in Khartoum, things were considerably less romantic.

Reporters from the world media were shown a government guest house, floors deep in blood, where some twenty army officers, victims of the attempted coup, had been slaughtered. The President himself escaped by climbing through a window into the garden. Twenty-eight officers were shot dead. One of four survivors of the massacre, forty-year-old Colonel Saad Bahar, Commander of the 2nd Tank Brigade and deputy commander of the armoured corps, described from his hospital bed how rebel officers came with an army truck to his home and took him to the guest house where some thirty others were also being held.

'When I heard shots outside, I ordered the officers to lie down on the floor,' he told us. 'Suddenly I heard somebody outside giving the order to shoot. They shot first through the door with a sub-machine gun, then they opened the door and began to shoot again and again. One officer lying beside me was asked his rank. He replied, "Colonel." They shot him. They began to shoot the others who were not dead. Then I heard the sound of a T55 [Soviet] tank outside and they fled.' Colonel Bahar said he was just 'very lucky'. The shots missed him.

The coup, in which communist politicians backed the dissatisfied military men, had lasted less than forty-eight hours. My first story to get on the world wire was advertised by head office as the first from any foreign correspondent after the counter-coup. I reported the final street gun battles between the army and the rebels, tanks standing by around the white-walled presidential palace, whose walls were holed by shellfire. Rebel soldiers sheltering in the People's Bank had been killed; seven others walked out and surrendered. The British Embassy and the American Interests section of the Dutch Embassy were also damaged in the gun battles.

The international press now numbered some dozens, mainly holed up in the Sudan Hotel. Over the next few days, they broke up into now familiar camps. Americans, Brits, Germans, Scandinavians and Japanese stuck pretty close together. The French media, with the customary large-size chip on their collective shoulders, remained aloof, constantly complaining to Sudanese officials of unfair favours allegedly shown to the Anglo-Saxons. The Italians, lavishing charm indiscriminately, flitted between one group and the other, picking up whatever they could.

Then the post-coup trials began. Two of the coup leaders condemned to die were Colonel Babakr El-Nur, who'd been named as Nimeiry's successor, and his chief aide, Major Farouk Hamdallah, a former Interior Minister earlier dismissed for his left-wing sympathies. After the initial coup, the two men had prematurely been flying back from London to set up a new left-wing government. They were detained after their plane was forced to land in Benghazi by the Libyan leader, Colonel Gadaffi, and handed over to Khartoum. El-Nur's wife later flew back from London hoping to appeal for her husband's life, but was told at the airport minutes before take-off that he'd already been shot.

Now began a series of executions – shooting for the military, hanging for the civilian plotters. At a series of late-night press briefings, we'd be given the details of the latest firing squad. Seven rebel leaders were executed at an army compound in Khartoum, standing without blindfolds before a firing squad, we were told. 'Was there a lot of blood?' a UPI correspondent from Texas unnecessarily wanted to know. The same man went ballistic later when I was the last man to get on the single phone line to Cairo before it closed for the night. He was next in the queue.

Among the first civilians to die was the usually jovial Minister of Southern Affairs, Joseph Garang, who claimed to be both communist and Catholic. The only black African member of Nimeiry's government, he'd been given the job of ending unrest in the three southern provinces, where the minor civil war had been raging for years.

We were all taken to watch the trial of communist leader Abdel-Khalik Mahgoub, alleged mastermind of the abortive coup, before a panel of army officers in a dusty improvised courtroom at the Shagara Barracks, six miles outside Khartoum. A small, tubby figure with balding head and neat clipped moustache, Mahgoub had been leading a charmed life. Deported to Egypt some months earlier, he was arrested on return but then escaped again. He'd been many times to Moscow and other communist capitals. Now he bowed and smiled to reporters as he was led into the green-walled courtroom. Then we watched him fight for his life, sweating under television arc lights as he rebutted three charges of complicity in the short-lived coup. He told us he was only informed of the trial at noon that day and was given just one hour to prepare his defence.

Dressed in a neat grey shirt and white slacks, the communist leader placed two packets of British cigarettes on the small table in front of him and started making detailed notes with a red pencil. Standing behind him were two burly red-bereted paratroopers, with automatic rifles. Mahgoub was kept sitting for eighteen minutes, perspiring in the stuffy lecture room until the three judges arrived. Their impressive gold-braided uniforms and angry glances at the prisoner already seemed to betray the inevitable verdict.

Mahgoub stood erect as he was asked by the presiding judge, 'Are you the Secretary General of the Communist Party of the Sudan?'

Mahgoub replied simply, 'Yes.' Then, challenging the validity of the court, he told the judge, 'You are well known to be one of the Arab nationalists in conflict with the progressive forces of this country. I have nothing against you personally, but I think you are not competent to judge me.'

He denied repeatedly that he was connected with the coup. 'I knew there was discontent in the country, but I did not organise the coup,' he said. Smoking and sipping water occasionally from a tin mug, Mahgoub was at one stage engaged in a shouting match with the presiding judge, and tempers were rising as the questioning went on. About forty-five minutes after the start, the presiding judge looked at his watch and said it was time to adjourn. There would be a half-hour recess, he said.

As the judges left, a harassed-looking Mahgoub was ringed by reporters. We were his last link with the outside world. Armoured cars stood outside the courthouse as he was marched off a few minutes later across the sandy courtyard. The court never reconvened. They hanged him in an army barracks an hour after midnight.

Information Minister Omer Hag-Musa later told reporters the only reason for taking the later stages of Mahgoub's trial in secret was that state security and relations with foreign powers might be involved, adding, 'His statements made clear that the Communist Party was the architect.'

A few months later, the Information Minister presided over a much happier gathering, when Reuters, along with the Thomson

Foundation, sponsored a training course for Sudanese journalists. Work at the local news agency headquarters was continuing and editorial staff had been increased, but, with few experienced journalists around, Reuters was invited in to help. Don Dallas, a veteran Reuter correspondent and manager, and I were the lecturers. It's not always easy in some countries to inculcate the need for accurate reporting and impartiality, but Reuters did its bit to help. When the Khartoum course was announced, there was a massive flood of applications from would-be reporters and wire room staff. The exotic blend included former army officers and a rather beautiful twenty-two-year-old folklore dancer. I reported back to head office, 'There is tremendous enthusiasm, which our course has undoubtedly helped to foster.'

Well, Sudan has gone through many crises since then, and internal conflict seems never-ending. Maybe, along the way, Reuters helped a bit.

My two terms in Egypt ended in 1972. The job was stimulating and gave invaluable insights into the ways of the Arab world. I showed the ropes to my successor before returning to London. There, Shahe Guebenlian, heading the business side in Africa and the Middle East, asked for me as his assistant, which I became for a couple of months. But before long Sid Mason yanked me out of pen-pushing. I was to fly to Munich to handle the logistics for the Olympic Games. It was an attractive change of pace. But the Middle East conflict had become a fact of life, even in the heart of Europe.

Nasser, Sadat, Nimeiri… they're all part of history. Who would have guessed in 1968 that the last survivor of that string of Middle East leaders would be the erratic President Gaddafi? Yet here he was in the autumn of 2009, celebrating forty years in power with a parade of 1,000 camels, an air display and a party in the world's biggest-ever tent. True to form, he'd blown it with some of the potential high-level visitors by welcoming back to Libya a man convicted of carrying out the terrorist attack on a transatlantic airliner over the Scottish town of Lockerbie. But as his Egyptian hosts quickly discovered back in 1969, Gaddafi was ever unpredictable.

Chapter 13
HOW GERMAN ORGANISATION FAILED TO STOP THE MUNICH TERRORISTS

After four years of heat and dust, I was ready for greener climes. When head office invited me to fly to Munich and set up our reporting centre for the forthcoming Olympics, I jumped at the chance. It would be a very pleasant change, I thought. And so it should have been, but the assignment would end in tragedy. It seemed I somehow couldn't escape the Middle East conflict.

My old colleague Nick Carter had been masterminding arrangements long distance from London for the past eighteen months. Now we needed someone on the spot to see it was all going to plan – and to write a few colourful advance features. 'I'm just a nuts and bolts man, John,' said Nick, though he was much more than that. One of the organisers in Munich glanced approvingly at one of Reuters' detailed requests and said, 'Mr Carter should be working for us.'

Now that the brand new Olympic Centre was complete, my job was to transform the large empty space we'd been allotted into an editorial room. It wasn't too difficult to map out a desk layout and make sure we had everything needed, down to the last telephones, pens, paper, typewriters and ribbons. The others in the advance squad were a trio of technical experts from Bonn, the bearded and impressive Werner van Zoggel and his sidekicks, Hans Bolender and Kurt Langartner, who would set up the new high-speed Siemens transmission system and see that it ran smoothly.

I reported to London:

> The labyrinths of the committee headquarters are like something from Kafka. Everything has been organised to the last detail – identity cards, typewriters with 80 different kinds of keyboard,

refrigerators in the press rooms and sheets for the reporters' beds – which will become West German army property afterwards! There are files galore, each division spawns a multitude of offshoots, each aware of its responsibilities – and apparently not much interested in the others.

Olympic Press Chief Hans Klein told me jokingly, 'We Germans don't know how to improvise. We take refuge in organisation.' Well, up to a point, as we'd tragically learn.

There were enjoyable times at first. The four of us in the advance party could relax over steins of beer in the sunny Englischer Garten, where the talk was mainly about football and the fortunes of Bundesliga teams like Bayern München, Bremen and Hamburg. Our regular Munich stringer, Australian Roley Egglestone, a full-timer for the Munich-based American news operation Radio Free Europe, sometimes joined the gang. He somehow managed to fit Reuter demands into a busy social life. Sometimes he'd already worked a night shift at RFE, and the strain proved too much. We were sitting one evening in a Schwäbing bar when he excused himself. Time went by and there was no further sign of him. I did a quick check of the gents, and could hear from the snoring that he'd simply dropped off. I left, and the episode was never referred to.

Roley had short-rented a flat for me during the run-up to and during the Olympics. Early on the morning after I arrived in Munich, the landlord was ringing insistently on the doorbell, inquiring after the rent, and surprised (it seemed) not to find the attractive blonde student, as she was described by Roley, from whom he'd sub-rented the small apartment.

It was proving difficult to get on with the job. A phone breakdown in the flat (probably due to earlier charges not being paid, I assumed) meant that for a time I had to send all messages to London, via our long-suffering news desk in Bonn, from a public call box down the road – hoping I had enough small ten-pfennig pieces to keep the call going. And one evening was spent keeping a rising flood of water at bay when the plumbing went bust at (naturally) ten o'clock on a Saturday night. At least I got to learn from the phone books that the German word for plumber is *installateur*. Why wasn't I staying at a good hotel? it may be asked.

But those were the earlier, poverty-stricken Reuter days. And I had one heck of a job persuading the tight-fisted man responsible in London to let me acquire a car to speed things up a bit. Finally, I was graciously permitted to purchase a cheap second-hand vehicle – at a cost equivalent to about £80. Registering it proved to be no less complicated than in Cairo.

The Olympic City was an impressive sight. The park, beginning to green over after mammoth excavation and landscaping, was spacious and beautiful. Not everyone liked the 'wet look' steel-and-glass roof on which $60 million had been spent amid screams from some enraged Bavarians, or the rather monotonous greyness of the huge blocks housing the 12,000 athletes. I secured a better deal for our team.

Our sports specialists from London and various foreign bureaux began to arrive, and I saw them settled in. There was only one snag, which shows the Germans do get it wrong occasionally. One of our women reporters objected, on political grounds, to the female journalists being housed in separate quarters from the men. I sorted this out with officials and she was duly accommodated. The things one did for Reuters! I also took care of the logistics for our close client, the Australian Associated Press (AAP), whose boss later told our head office in a letter, 'The ever-smiling John Chadwick refused to allow the Germans' "organise by the rulebook" frustrations to upset him.'

With a Reuter team now numbering thirty journalists, a dozen clerical and technical staff, and a small army of telegraphists under the charge of my old cricketing Yorkshire friend, George Boanas, I reverted to a reporting role and sent a series of 'advancers' to London, mainly about political aspects of the Games. With Germany still divided, one of the main themes was inter-nation rivalry. East Germany and other communist states, led by the Soviet Union, spent a fortune on athletics, for prestige as well as sporting reasons.

There were some lighter moments. As various national contingents rolled in, we saw as many as possible of their flag-waving arrival ceremonies. Having just completed four years in Cairo, I naturally covered the Egyptian team. With the sportsmen and women from Cairo lined up stiffly at attention, the German band struck up with the Egyptian national anthem… or was it? I could see a look of perplexity on the athletes' faces. Which was understandable, for the Germans had got hold of the wrong music and were playing the twenty-year-old anthem of the disgraced and exiled King Farouk. It made a brief 'sidebar' for Middle East clients. Not much organisation about that. If it had been the only foul-up…

When the Games finally opened, Munich resembled a West German capital, as world figures including Chancellor Willy Brandt, French President Georges Pompidou, British Prime Minister Edward Heath and Washington's ace diplomat, Henry Kissinger, flew in.

Among the 7,173 athletes taking part, honours on either side of the Iron Curtain were to be almost equally divided. From the Soviet Union, the petite seventeen-year-old gymnast Olga Korbut caused a sensation on the parallel bars. She later recalled, 'One day I was a nobody, the next day I was a star.' From the United States, the handsome Mark Spitz proved unbeatable in the water, reaping a record seven gold medals for his exploits in the swimming pool – a feat only recently overtaken by another of his countrymen.

A few unsporting stories, including drug scandals, disqualifications and the removal of a gold medal, sullied the scene. But all this was overshadowed when, at dawn on 5 September, a group of Palestinian terrorists broke into the athletes' village. Those identity cards weren't much use, it seemed, against men with guns in the middle of the night. The mayhem that followed would be the darkest day in Olympic history.

The participation of an Israeli team at the Games had been intended as a mark of reconciliation with Germany less than three decades after the grim events of the Holocaust. The Olympic Village was only a few miles away from Dachau, one of the most notorious Nazi concentration camps. There, prior to the opening of the Games, the Israeli fencing coach, Andre Spitzer, had laid a wreath. The West German authorities were trying hard to erase memories of Nazi days and keeping formalities to the minimum – which may have accounted for the ease with which the terrorists got into the Israeli athletes' quarters. The night before, the Israeli athletes had watched a performance of the show *Fiddler on the Roof*, and dined with its star, Shmuel Rodensky.

The Palestinians had a relatively easy job getting in. Wrestling referee Yossef Gutfreund awoke when he heard noises at the door. As masked men burst in with guns, he shouted a warning to the others, but the Israelis were outnumbered and weaponless. Weightlifter Yossef Romano, a Six Day War veteran, was shot dead. The attackers took the others hostage, demanding safe passage to Egypt and the release of over 200 Palestinians in Israeli jails – together with Germans Andreas Baader and Ulrike Meinhof, founders of the terrorist group bearing their name, who were now in jail. Our Games Editor, Ronnie Cooper, later recalled:

> The overnight staffer in the Bonn office picked up a radio report of an Arab commando raid on the athletes' village. He phoned Roly Egglestone, our industrious Munich stringer, who quickly checked the report with police. The longest working day that most of us can remember had begun. The Reuter team streamed out of bathrooms and bedrooms. One batch of sleepy-eyed, unwashed and unshaven reporters was sent to the Olympic Village, where the drama was taking place. But the whole village was sealed off, and it was impossible for reporters to get in or out. Except there's no such things as impossible, and one by one our reporters did get in, in some cases by methods that had better go unreported. It was just good luck when an Olympic Federation official with whom we had special contacts and who bore a striking resemblance to one of our own men walked into the office. We persuaded him to part with his identity card bearing his photograph, and our man was in the Village. An Italian colleague was less successful. He tried a phenomenal leap from a high wall into the Village, but found that man wasn't built like a bird and broke his leg.

The tragic conclusion came later that day when the Germans agreed to let the terrorists fly out of the country and transferred them by helicopter from the Olympic Village to the Fürstenfeldbruck Airport. The mismanaged events that followed did no credit to West Germany's apparently bewildered local and national leaders. There was an ill-judged, almost farcical, attempt at the airport to take out the terrorists. The authorities sent in just five marksmen, mainly weekend rifle shooters with no special training, when at least two snipers for every target were needed. The results were predictable. When they realised they'd been fooled, the Palestinians blew up their escape helicopter and everyone inside it. German officials misled us and other journalists by at first suggesting there'd been some survivors amid the carnage.

I've always thought the Germans played it completely wrong. Had the terrorists been allowed to fly to Cairo with their captives, the Egyptian authorities, never overly enamoured of the Palestinian guerrilla movement, would very likely have let the dust settle, played for time and eventually released both the terrorists and the Israelis. It was worth trying, anyway. It couldn't have been worse than what happened.

The events of that day would permanently scar memories of the Olympics. Up to then the main headlines had been about Spitz and Korbut. The German people, who'd expected so much of the Games, could hardly comprehend the magnitude of the horror which burst on them overnight. Suddenly, instead of athletics, a German orchestra – an unsavoury theatrical gesture to some people's minds – was playing a tragic Beethoven overture in the main stadium, while Israelis wept in the stands. But Avery Brundage, the fiery eighty-four-year-old President of the International Olympic Committee – a man not known for sympathy with the Jewish state or the newer nations – insisted stubbornly, 'The Games must go on.'

Brundage had already been embroiled in a major political crisis before the athletics even started, when black Africans threatened to pull out if then white-ruled Rhodesia took part. 'Naked political blackmail!' he cried. But the black Africans – whose star athletes included Kenya's Kip Keino, later to win the 3,000-metre steeplechase – were adamant. Either Rhodesia goes or we do, they said. The IOC leaders backed down in the end. By thirty-six votes to thirty-one, they decided to withdraw their invitation to Rhodesia's mixed black and white team.

The Africans, jubilant, stayed on, and Uganda's John Akii-Bua took the gold medal with a world record time in the 400-metre hurdles, while Ethiopia's Merus Yufter won the 10,000 metres bronze. Brundage, making no secret of his disgust at the way African and Palestinian issues had clouded the Games, denounced these 'two savage attacks' on the Olympic movement. But while the Arabs – many of whom didn't support the Palestinian guerrilla movement – were mainly embarrassed by the massacre at Fürstenfeldbruck, the Africans condemned the Palestinian raid and called Brundage's remarks an insult.

In an atmosphere of mingled grief, anger and recrimination, the 1972 Games stumbled to a muted close. They might and should have been remembered for the imaginative architecture of the stadium, the powerhouse swimming of Spitz and the athleticism of the elfin Russian gymnast. The Olympics had been intended to erase older memories of Munich – meaning Adolf Hitler and the beer cellar rallies. Now, for most Bavarians, Munich 1972 would replace old memories with equally bitter new ones.

The German hosts were deeply depressed. There was a wave of disgust among the assembled 10,000 sportsmen at the massacre. Many West Germans would gladly have pulled out of the Games, but as host nation they could hardly do so.

Even before the Olympics turned into something between a United Nations debate and a Middle East battlefield, the retiring IOC President had made his own views plain. The Games, which had started off as a leisurely congregation of upper-class sportsmen, he protested, had been taken over by professionalism and chauvinism. Such views received scant support. He was succeeded as IOC boss by an easier-going Irishman, Lord Killanin. And Mayor Jean Drapeau of Montreal, where the next Games were scheduled to take place, said his city couldn't possibly rival the glitter of Munich. Yet, subsequently, showpiece Olympics have taken place, most recently in Communist China.

For me, as my Reuter colleagues flew home to various capitals, there was just the sad job of closing down the office on which so much time and effort had been spent in the last three months. I wasn't left alone in Munich very long. A few days later, in the arrivals hall at Munich Airport, a small fair-haired boy who'd just flown in from Sweden walked a little apprehensively towards me, hand in hand with an SAS air hostess, for a welcome two-week holiday in England and Ireland. At eleven, it was his first solo trip abroad. There'd be many more in the years to come.

Meanwhile, head office, knowing how much my son meant to me, and as a reward for my work in Egypt and Sudan, offered me a two-year assignment to Stockholm, which I was more than happy to accept.

Chapter 14
IN OLOF PALME'S SWEDEN,
THE BIGGEST SIN SEEMED TO BE TAX EVASION

I can't say I fell completely for the Stockholm of the early Seventies, though it's a much more relaxed place these days, with lots of pubs and restaurants. Tourist brochures always show the city in summer, of course, when the waterfront and archipelago are enchanting. But summer doesn't last long and the long straight streets of central Stockholm can be pretty bleak thereafter. From my flat in the suburb of Bagarmossen, a train ride from the centre (Reuters didn't run to expensive city apartments), I travelled to work in darkness and returned home in the dark. As I walked back to the office after lunching with colleagues, night had fallen. If only there'd been some snow! I'd seen on film those winter trails through the woods, lit by atmospheric lanterns, traversed by stern-faced Swedes with ski poles doing their exercises. I'd brought slalom skis along, but never bought a set of the cross-country type. It wasn't worth it. You had to take the train much further north for downhill skiing. And I'd foolishly thought of Stockholm as north!

I'd undoubtedly come to a modern, efficient and comfortable place, with bright, clean-lined contemporary furniture available at very low prices – as long as you assembled it yourself! And I speak as one who over the years put quite a few IKEA products together for Reuter offices in Stockholm, Geneva and Bonn. I know a 'Billy' bookcase when I see one. My home's full of them. I'm sitting in an IKEA chair right now.

My first year-long stay in Sweden in the early sixties had been spent in the more pastoral southern province of Skåne and the charming towns of Lund and Hälsingborg, where manners and speech seemed not too much different from the Danes across the water – who in centuries past, of course, owned the place.

Stockholmers seemed to me a bit uptight, the accent a shade precious, the politicians more than a little preachy. And to this day I still prefer the homelier accents of rural Sweden to the sound of *Upplandsvensk*. My young grandson, brought up in the Stockholm region, once put me firmly in my place by declaring that I was speaking *Skånsk* – the unforgettable accent of Skåne, scorned by some Swedes as the 'Brummie' accent unfairly is in England.

Returning to Sweden after a gap of ten years, I found they'd actually changed the language – at least the way they addressed each other. When I first met my then fiancée's family, her grandparents addressed me in a curiously oblique third person form. ('What thinks Mr Chadwick about that?') You couldn't use the *ni* (plural you) form, considered impolite. Nor could you use the *du* (you singular form) – too familiar. It was difficult navigating between all these versions of a fairly simple word. By the time I returned to Sweden, they seemed to have dropped two of the variants and everybody was calling each other *du*. It made things easier, though the rapidity of the change was rather startling. I suppose it was all to do with being a Social Democrat society.

Reuters had close links and an easy working relationship with the Swedish News Agency TT (Tidningarnas Telegramburo). But, compared with my large Cairo establishment, I now had just a tiny little office on the twelfth floor of a tall office block in Sveavagen, TT headquarters. As in Copenhagen, my near neighbours along the corridor were the French and German wire service reporters. I became good friends with DPA's Dieter Basil and his family, and also got to know the French correspondents well. But the first Agence France-Presse correspondent I met in Stockholm was not, I'm afraid, around for very long. Sweden's stringent drink-driving laws did for him, and after, I was told, almost falling out of his car when stopped by police, he was swiftly removed from the country by mutual consent. We never saw him again.

His successor, Georges Herbouze, I got to know quite well. The Nordic bleakness and the buttoned-up manner of some Swedes didn't please him. Over a restaurant meal one evening, he confided gloomily, 'John – I 'ate Sweden. It does not correspond to my personal needs. I really *'ate* it.' A splendid chap, Georges, but the Swedes weren't always kind to him. A group of us were invited on a press trip to see how the Swedish Army was doing. We were flown many miles north, enjoyed nice rides in snow vehicles pulling very photogenic groups of winter soldiers on skis, and in the evening were treated to dinner at the regimental headquarters. The splendid dining room was replete with past regimental glories, the officers all in dress uniform.

As dinner progressed, the presiding colonel turned to Jacques, sitting on his right as the senior foreign newsman, and asked him, as an expert from a renowned winemaking country, if he knew that Sweden itself also produced a rather good red wine. Georges raised his eyebrows.

'It's called Château Sundswall,' said the Colonel, 'because that's the name of the region.' Georges said he wasn't aware that Sweden was so climatically blessed, but was assured this was a more than usually sunny valley where weather conditions were amenable to vine production.

'Try a glass,' suggested the Colonel, motioning to a waiter.

Georges sniffed, drank, and after some hesitation, said '*Oui. Pas mal. C'est acceptable.*' Only then did the Colonel reveal that the wine was actually a very good Bordeaux! They'd simply stuck a new label on the bottle. They'd played the same schoolboyish joke on other guests in the past. I had word from Georges the following year that he was more than happy to be back in Paris.

Stockholm was full of foreign correspondents, not many of whom seemed to know much about the trade. They included a fair number of political refugees and other young men who'd married Swedish girls abroad and now, living in the North with a press pass, seemed to be thriving. They didn't give the authorities much trouble, reporting-wise. By contrast, Dieter Basil (DPA) and *Die Welt*'s Rainer Gaterman were two very professional and friendly Germans. England's *Financial Times* was represented by Will Dullforce and the late John Walker, the latter a Bentley car addict in earlier days. He and his Swedish wife, Anne, were always most hospitable, as were Will and his Norwegian wife. I think we all, English and Germans alike, reacted rather similarly to the chill conformity of Prime Minister Olof Palme's Sweden, its government cool towards the West, seldom questioning the

Moscow line. Many ordinary Swedes, one found, thought otherwise.

The *Observer*'s Roland Huntford (who also covered the European skiing scene), had for some time been a thorn in the government's flesh. His book, whose title *The New Totalitarians* well conveyed his view of Swedish socialism, considerably irritated the local establishment, which I gathered had once unsuccessfully suggested to the *Observer* that he be replaced. Roland subsequently moved to England, where in a controversial book he similarly challenged the hagiography surrounding Captain Scott of the Antarctic, arguing that the Norwegians led by Roald Amundsen, who beat Scott to the South Pole, simply organised things better. I think Roland, who knew the subject backwards, may have been right. I shared my own office with a young American, Roger Choate, a freelance representing the London *Times*, and later took on another young American, Mark Goldsmith, who proved an excellent and energetic recruit, and later established his own thriving public relations firm.

One most diverting colleague was the late Michael Salzer, a Jewish refugee from the Third Reich who'd fled, first to Britain, where he joined the army fighting the Nazis, then to Sweden after the war. There he lived for decades in a timber-built house on the idyllic island of Lidingö, where he pursued traditional crafts such as woodcarving, spinning and weaving with natural dyes. I was one of many dragooned into collecting driftwood from the beaches of Lidingö, to be dried out in his garden and later transformed into small miracles of practical carpentry. I still have a knife of his creation in my kitchen.

With his distinctive spare figure and beard, and something of the look of a George Bernard Shaw about him, he was fluent in several languages and wrote hundreds of articles for British papers, and a host of others like the *Toronto Star* and *Time* magazine. Born in Hungary and growing up in Austria, Salzer was serving with the Army in Berlin at the end of the war. He managed to get into the ruined bunker where Hitler had committed suicide and in an abandoned room found a stack of gold-embossed invitations to a Christmas Party from Herr Hitler himself. Michael liberated a few of these and generously gave me one of them when he brought these and other memorabilia over to London to be auctioned at Christie's.

Things have changed. In the bleak mid-seventies, living in Sweden was sometimes a bit like being in the Eastern Bloc. Revered by his followers – and by many of similar persuasion elsewhere in the world – Palme was almost sanctified by the Left. The more travelled correspondents in town took a more studied view of the prevailing political philosophy. Palme had the air of a preacher and surrounded himself with a bunch of young men who read from the same hymn book. Mostly in their late twenties, they seemed to know all the answers to the world's problems. If only, they seemed to be saying, the rest of the world were like Sweden! They resembled today's 'politically correct' brigade in England. They didn't seem too much bothered about day to day issues affecting ordinary folk. Such political dogmatists seldom do. Similarly indoctrinated were some of the civil servants. I once had to consult a young female official on some subject or other affecting Reuters. Suddenly she started quizzing, then lecturing me about my income tax position. Was I in the dock? I asked. I referred the matter to Lars (Lasse) Georgsson, the foreign ministry's excellent linkman with the foreign press. He immediately picked up the phone and, while I sat by, tore strips off her. He wasn't the only official who disliked some of these high-handed attitudes.

The biggest sin in Socialist Sweden, it appeared, was not murder, gluttony or lechery – but income tax evasion. It had become an obsession. The leftist *Aftonbladet* ran an annual front page story with the sort of headlines usually reserved in English tabloids for media stars and professional footballers, with a sort of league table showing how much they all paid (or should have paid!) in tax. The joke was that as Swedes finally approached the pearly gates, they'd see St Peter as some kind of government official. Never mind the seven deadly sins, he'd want to know whether they'd paid their taxes.

It wasn't just visiting journalists who were suspected of cooking the books. No less a figure than film director Ingmar Bergman, as much a Swedish symbol as Volvo cars, would a few years later be hounded out of the country by the tax police. He told the newspaper *Expressen* before leaving for Paris that, though a convinced Social Democrat, he could no longer live in his native country. Police had arrested Bergman, the director of screen classics like *The Seventh Seal* and *Wild Strawberries*, during rehearsals at Stockholm's Royal Theatre and charged him with tax fraud. He had a nervous breakdown and spent two months in hospital before criminal charges were dropped – but he was told he still owed taxes on $750,000.

In the surrealistic Swedish world of the seventies, officials had at first demanded he should pay tax at 139%. He told *Expressen*, 'I realised that anybody in the country, any time and in any way, can be attacked and humiliated by a special kind of bureaucracy that grows like a galloping cancer.'

Bergman's was not the only case. One of his regular actors, Bibi Andersson, was also confronted by police on suspicion of tax evasion and held in a cell overnight, after which she decided to film abroad in future. Another Bergman star, Max von Sydow, the unforgettable figure of Death in *The Seventh Seal*, was also questioned and said he intended to emigrate. At a less public level, I was told by a senior editor at the Swedish News Agency that he'd now reached a salary level at which any increase would just be taken back in income tax; in fact he might have to pay more than before. Like many others in similar situations, he asked for a few presents instead. Was this really the Brave New World? Eventually, the Swedes themselves decided not. But it would take time.

The chilling hand of conformist bureaucracy seemed all-pervasive. Shortly after arrival in Stockholm, I called at the bank next door in Sveavagen to check Reuters' long-established office account. I now had a personal account there too.

'I must see your ID number,' said the bossy lady behind the counter.

'I don't have an ID number,' I told her, only to be interrupted halfway through.

'Everybody has an ID number,' she told me. I tried to explain politely that as a foreign national I wasn't obliged to have such a document, but she brushed this aside. I asked for the manager, who quickly appeared and told her, 'Give him the money!' – or words to that effect. I realised afterwards of course that they hadn't backed down, really. They simply didn't want a scene. This was Sweden, 1973 vintage. I was never queried again.

The would-be reformers pressed on, calling for a punitive tax ceiling on salaries, the money going to feed people in the developing countries. Economist Gunnar Adler-Karlsson, a professor of social science, declared no one should be allowed to earn more than $100,000. Another activist, Mrs Berit Rollen, a magazine editor and formerly Palme's private secretary, said piously that she'd set the limit much lower, at $39,000. The professor declared that with every Swedish family aiming for a comfortable flat, plus a car and a summer cottage (or both), it was time for Swedes to sit back and ponder exactly where they and the world were heading.

'We are like hamsters inside a wheel,' he said, 'always running to reach a top that forever eludes us.' He proposed a minimum standard of living for the whole world's population, guaranteeing adequate food, water, health services and a simple dwelling – and at the other end of the scale, a maximum salary.

I stated the obvious in my story. 'The idea looks doomed from the start, even in this egalitarian society.' It was. What would be the next crackpot scheme?

The social scientists were relentless. In an 800-page report, a non-parliamentary group set up by the Ministry of Education advocated sex education for children from the age of seven. After ten years studying the subject, they'd decided kids between seven and ten should know everything about conception, birth control techniques and masturbation. Successive courses up to the age of nineteen, they said, could show film of actual intercourse. Conservative circles reacted fiercely, saying the proposals ignored the susceptibilities of Catholic and Muslim immigrant families from Southern Europe and the Mediterranean.

At ground level were more practical people. A small side street garage in Stockholm job did a prompt and excellent restoration job on the old baby-blue Opel Rekord car I'd bought for a song in Munich, and they didn't charge the earth. As it turned out, I had little use for the car in the end. There were extremely strict drink-driving laws, which I never dispute. And I'd learned from my French colleague's experience. I didn't even think of getting behind the wheel after an embassy cocktail party. For work, I travelled by efficient commuter train. For smaller distances, I bought a bike of sturdy Swedish construction, which is still in the garage – unused after hip trouble, I'm afraid. After Sweden, it served me well for years in Germany. Not all Swedes, by any means, were like the Palme clan.

To investigate the success story at Volvo, Sweden's biggest exporter, I went to see to see the production plant at Skövde, which was streets ahead of anything the Brits were doing. Robots outnumbered humans by 400 to 60, and the scene had a science fiction look. I reported:

> With uncanny precision, the waist-high red robots pick up a car engine block and then move off silently to the first section of the assembly area. After a few twists and turns of power tools, as further parts are added, the robot moves on with a flick of the starting handle to the next assembly point.

Employees, male and female, many of them immigrant Finns and Yugoslavs, were working in pleasant pastel-shaded surroundings. Large picture windows looked out on well-trimmed lawns and soundproofed rest rooms were furnished in best Scandinavian style. Management and workers I chatted to seemed to regard labour problems in Britain with bewildered disbelief. Here, the workers collectively decided what level of production to aim for, and could then vary the pace at different times of day. Managing Director Per Gyllenhammar (years later to become Reuters' chairman) said, 'Old discipline does not work. We are dealing with educated people who are perfectly capable of taking initiatives. That doesn't mean you give up discipline. You replace the old sort with a kind of self-discipline.'

I was genuinely impressed. But somehow I couldn't see it catching on in bolshie-ridden British car-making plants, whose management and workforces carried on regardless in their old ways until the whole industry went to the wall.

Summer came round eventually, and for a short time the plate-glass windows of our office in Sveavagen made it like a greenhouse. You could grow tomatoes in here, I observed to the lads, and then I thought: Why not? Mark Goldsmith and I went down and bought a couple of tomato plants in the market square and placed them in front of the windows. Flooded with sunshine, they thrived, and soon the wall was festooned with snaking green tendrils and ripening fruit. The word spread around the building that Reuters were growing tomatoes and one of Tete's teleprinter operators came up to check. Carrying a handful of luscious fruit back with him, he reported the rumours were correct.

I learnt the arcane procedures surrounding the annual Nobel Prize awards. There was keen competition among the wire services. At an agreed time, we'd all be handed sealed envelopes containing the winners' names, followed by a brief résumé of their work. Our operator sitting at a teleprinter had already punched on the tape under a Stockholm dateline the words, 'The Nobel Prize for Medicine [or whatever] was awarded today to…' *Blank.* Then you tore open the envelope and read out the winner's name, which he punched into the blank space. Couldn't be quicker. So far, so good. But now came the tricky bit – trying to make some sense quickly of an unfamiliar area of research. Best not to go into detail. So when a Professor Albert Claude was awarded a Nobel Prize for cell research, you had to plough quickly through a lot of scientific prose. The ordinary layman wouldn't know about 'differential centrifugation'. It didn't much help to be told that 'by using a centrifugal method we can find the tumours very quickly'. Plus, these brilliant people always seem to be born in one country but work somewhere else. Three men once shared the Medicine prize. One of them was born in Belgium, but had served with British Intelligence. Another was born in England of Belgian parents. The third was born in Romania but lived in the States. Try getting all that in a crisp lead paragraph!

Nobel Prizewinners are clearly not like other people. The exiled Russian writer Aleksander Solzhenitsyn, deported from the Soviet Union and living in Switzerland, finally made it to

Stockholm to pick up his award after a four-year delay. A big news conference was arranged. Solzhenitsyn's answers to simple questions developed into rambling dissertations ranging over politics, economics, religion and much else. He devoted the first two hours to a detailed critique of Marxism, with the aid of a blackboard, several large reference books, quotations from Marx and Lenin – and two translators. He said he'd been 'the object of coercion' since coming to the West, and the Soviet security police (KGB) had tried to provoke him in Switzerland, but he wouldn't say how. 'Let them start publishing my books and then I will go home,' he added. Not the easiest speaker I ever reported. The news conference was scheduled to last six hours, but I left halfway through, otherwise we'd have had nothing at all on the wire that night.

The day after the traditional banquet, when the medals are presented, I had to check a few facts and figures for a follow-up story on Solzhenitsyn. I called at the Nobel Foundation office in central Stockholm. The secretary, busy on the phone, waved me to a chair. I glanced idly around. On the desk in front of me was an open red leather case containing a solid gold medallion. To my surprise, the name inscribed on it was Aleksander Solzhenitsyn. 'Oh yes,' said the official casually when he came off the phone. 'That's Solzhenitsyn's Nobel Prize. He forgot it.' After waiting years to collect it, the writer had left it lying among the dirty plates and glasses. 'We expect him to come round later and pick it up. He may be rather tired today after all the ceremonies.' It was a nice little exclusive. The *Chicago Tribune*'s apt headline: 'Solzhenitsyn Wins No Prize For Memory'.

Another Nobel Prizewinner for literature was West Germany's Heinrich Boell, a pleasant man to speak to, whose short story style I'd always found more modern and less convoluted than some of his countrymen's. But his acceptance lecture, 'The Sense of Poetry', the text of which I had to translate and condense, proved heavy going. Boell called it 'an examination in metaphysical terms of the clash between the view of the world as seen by poets and writers and ordinary accepted points of view'. What he was actually talking about, *'ganz konkret'*, was the conflict in Northern Ireland. This, said the Nobel laureate, could be explained as 'one kind of sense coming up against a completely different kind of sense, which we would simply call unreasonableness or folly'. Well, yes, I suppose so. But that's the German language for you. I'd further discover the problems of translating German prose into readable English some years later in Bonn.

For politics in Sweden, I came to conclude, read politesse. I watched a Liberal candidate defend herself on TV for taking a glass of wine at dinner. The parties had less than riveting slogans like 'Jobs For All' and 'Taxes Must Be Reduced'. One post-Palme leader of the Social Democrats, Ingvar Carlsson, would later proclaim sententiously from the election posters, 'For me, the conviction of men's fundamental equality is the driving force.' Didn't somebody say that before?

The best way to escape the longueurs of Swedish politics was to get out into the country, meet real people and see the scenery. There were two excellent ways of doing this, I heard, and I managed them both. I was urged to ride the historic Inlandsbana, an old railway route forging through forests and valleys from central Sweden to the far north. The other recommended journey, west to east, was the Göta Canal, which winds its way via lakes and rivers between Gothenburg and Stockholm. I did both when I had time and wrote about them.

Looking rather like an old Mississippi riverboat, the tubby old *Wilhelm Tham*, moored at the quayside near Gothenburg's Opera House, was dwarfed by oil tankers and container ships. 'Is that really ours?' asked a fellow passenger a bit doubtfully, as we all lugged our suitcases towards the gangplank. We needn't have worried. Our Swedish skipper had sailed all round the world, through the Panama and Suez Canals, and to Middle East ports I remembered, like Haifa and Alexandria. At the other end of the scale, he'd taken a narrowboat the previous year for a holiday on the Yorkshire canals. No, he didn't find that tame, he told me. 'You just adjust to the circumstances.' Now, supposedly retired, he was having a whale of a time shuttling this century-old ship through the heart of Sweden. 'There's so much to see,' he said, and how right he was.

I was allowed to stand on the bridge as he took our ship

through, or under, a row of bridges along the Göta River, the massive structures lifting up, or swinging aside, to let us through. Conversation at table over a gourmet dinner with Tom and Priscilla, from Massachusetts, and Gunnar and his wife from Stockholm, showed it was not just old fogies who did this trip. Tom flew his own Cessna private plane. Gunnar was a keen rally driver and motorcyclist. Everyone said they just wanted to get away from it all. Me too, after months of Swedish politics. We all agreed not to talk about such matters.

By late evening we were sailing across Lake Vänern and by midnight passing the rather ghostly looking thirteenth-century Läckö Castle. And before seven next morning I was on deck to find we'd now moored in an idyllic little village. Tables and chairs were laid out in summery gardens beside the canal. A heron rose from the reeds, wings flapping, and made off across the fields. Small deer were grazing at the edge of a wood. As the sun reluctantly appeared, we passed through clusters of Falun-red houses and neat, well-kept gardens. Emerging into one small community from a narrow stretch of canal where the trees almost brushed the sides of the ship, we were entertained by singers and an accordionist, who'd been greeting travellers this way for decades, I was told. I was beginning to see where Bergman got some of his film themes.

In the town of Vadstena, we visited the thirteenth-century convent of Saint Birgitta, whose cathedral-like church was kept in immaculate order – by the State, I was glad to hear. As we descended a chain of five locks into Lake Boren to start the 'downhill' second half of the journey, a pair of wild geese, followed by eight tiny goslings, strutted around the grass beside the canal. The young women operating the locks were students from Linköping University, the skipper told me. I wondered how many of our own undergraduates would do it. A beautiful passage followed along a twenty-kilometre stretch where the water was a milky green, the banks lined with maple trees. Bikers and other holidaymakers aboard horse-drawn carts and vintage cars waved to us as they passed by along the canal bank.

The heavens opened, but only temporarily, as we arrived at Söderköping, another town whose name I'd known for years but never visited. The canal was shrouded with ghostly white mist as the water warmed up again after the squall. Families of ducks scuttled for cover, a startled deer ran across a meadow and a dramatic rainbow stretched halfway across the sky. We visited an ancient Viking settlement at Birka, a pleasant meadow sweeping down to the wide bay in which the longships would have been moored. We passed by the king's ship at Drottningholm Castle as we arrived in the capital. The Wilhelm Tham would be off back to Gothenburg in the morning. I'd had a welcome glimpse of another Sweden, the real one perhaps.

Always hunting for feature stories, I drove over to Östersund to board the Inlandsbana. The town is Sweden's answer to Scotland's Loch Ness. It has a monster. At least that's what the locals say, and I hoped the beast might just show up while I was there. Helpful colleagues at the local paper filled me in on the story. Townspeople had apparently been hunting the monster for nearly a century. In fact, Sweden's King Oscar, back in 1894, founded a 'Company for the Capture of the Great Lake Monster'. A team of Norwegian harpoonists was hired and went to work optimistically, using pigs' carcasses as bait. But the monster, if it ever existed, didn't oblige, and the Norwegians went back home. But, to be on the safe side, the authorities put a protection order for the beast under Sweden's Nature Conservation Act. The Great Lake Monster has been rather a money-spinner for the town. A pity it didn't choose to appear while I was there. But I had another story to do.

Early next morning, I was catching the Inlandsbana train north. It was a time of crisis for the line, and the faceless bureaucrats in Stockholm were under attack. This wasn't any old train, but Europe's longest single-track railway. Thrusting 1,300 kilometres from Sweden's central farming region and up through thick forests into the Arctic, it was the main link between small communities along the way – but the government had decided it was too expensive.

Lapplanders fiercely protested. 'After milking our hydroelectric power and timber, the southerners are casting us off,' they said. Posters depicted the Communications Minister as an executioner standing ready at the block. A genial editor at the local paper told me, 'The Minister's just been here to open a bridge, but got straight back on the plane to Stockholm. Otherwise he might have been lynched.' I assumed he was joking.

It had become an international issue. The word had spread, and rail freaks from Europe and America were rallying round. I talked with five British Railways employees who'd flown in overnight. They'd been around the world on trains, one time from Victoria Station to Peking. A sixty-year-old Dutch Railways engineer flourished maps and timetables, inveighing against what he called government madness. An architecture student from Ohio wanted to get as far north as he could in Europe while there was still time.

We rolled off at seven thirty, heading towards the Arctic Circle at a sedate eighty kilometres an hour. From a microphone in the driving cab, where I was allowed to stand, a young lady called Sofi, granddaughter of one of the men who laid the railway, gave us all the facts and figures. Early in the century, work gangs had braved mosquito-ridden swamps to build the railway. The *rallare*, as they were called, were hard-working, hard-drinking men. Local farmers kept their daughters well out of sight.

Traditionally a main communications route for small communities along the way, it was also, unhappily, the line on which the Swedes, neutral in World War Two, allowed the German army to send troops north to fight the Norwegians. 'Some of the German soldiers tried to escape,' said Sofi into the mike. 'They did not succeed.' Driver Lars-Åke, at the wheel, put it more succinctly, sotto voce. 'They were shot,' he said.

He halted the train (it's that kind of railway), to let me get off and talk to one of the men who drove those troop trains in a period most Swedes would rather forget. Long retired, he lived in a cottage in the wilderness beside the line he'd travelled for thirty years. An Alsatian dog lay in the sun and a battered old Volvo stood in the backyard. Hearing the train's hooter, he said, was an event in his day.

A civilised train, the Inlandsbana rattles along its single track at a maximum 90 kph. I left it halfway up the line at Arvidsjaur, where tourism official Peter Berglund was incensed at the threat to the railway. He'd written to the Prime Minister and joined a delegation to Stockholm which blocked the Transport Minister's office with lengths of track. We gathered almost conspiratorially in an old railway coach in the siding, used as a meeting place by the local opposition movement, led by physics teacher Lars Lindström. There were proposals by local communities to buy out the line and run it themselves, he said. He swung open the door of an engine shed to reveal a giant fifty-year-old steam locomotive which he'd lovingly restored.

I was back aboard the next day as the train curved and twisted through Sweden's central uplands, seldom seen by road travellers, but providing easy access to Lapp centres, fishing areas, hiking trails and the massive national parks of the north-west. The miles clicked by and eventually we were 1,000 kilometres north of Stockholm, deep into what they called 'Christmas Tree Land'. A technicolour sunset flared on the western horizon, the tips of a million fir trees sharply edged against a fiery sky. Then darkness settled over Lapland, the headlights illuminating our curving path through the forest. Our driver suddenly hit the brakes. A family of reindeer had wandered on to the track. We had time to stop. But hundreds of reindeer and elk are killed each year, and the Lapps who herd them scrupulously are compensated.

Ten miles short of our final destination, the town of Gällivare in the far north, we nearly hit an elk. Suddenly he was standing there in the headlights, 200 yards down the track. Majestic, four-square across the rails, staring us down. Lars-Åke hit the horn and brakes simultaneously. The elk ambled off the track, taking his time. The *Guardian* gave the story full-page treatment.

Could things be hotting up in the political arena? After four decades in power and apparently there for eternity, the Social Democrats had now become increasingly under fire. Conservative, Liberal and Centre parties were alarmed at measures they branded 'Socialism by the Back Door'. If Palme could be ousted, a non-Socialist coalition looked likely.

It was in this atmosphere that Palme launched a new attack on Washington. I'd called at the office one quiet Saturday afternoon in December to check the local news agency file. One brief report said that Palme, at a weekend rally, had compared American bombing raids in Vietnam with the worst twentieth-century atrocities, such as Guernica, Babi Yar, Lidice and Treblinka. Familiar by this time with the Palme rhetoric, I filed a short story to London without thinking too much about it – typical Palme, I thought – and flew off for Christmas in Lancashire. There, I was amazed two days later to get an urgent call from head office telling me to get back to Stockholm. All hell had broken loose when the Reuters story was published. The United States had recalled its ambassador from Stockholm.

This was not for the first time. Palme had a long track record of anti-Americanism, though he'd studied in the United States before taking the familiar route through student politics into government. He'd once led a Vietnam protest march against the US Embassy, after which Washington withdrew its envoy for the first time. Now he'd done it again. Swedish officials were rather pathetically blaming the trouble on Reuters. Back in Stockholm, after confirming with the Swedish news agency that I'd translated their story correctly, I called on the head of the government press office to give him a chance to say the same thing to my face. He never mentioned the matter.

Anti-Americanism was a comparatively new phenomenon in Sweden, and certainly by no means universal. There were historic relations between the two countries. King Gustaf the Third was the first monarch to recognise American independence. Several million Swedes emigrated to the United States in the nineteenth and early twentieth centuries, and large Swedish-origin communities remain to this day in the Midwest.

Palme's style had never been to the liking of conservative Swedes and there was fresh outrage now. Conservative leader Gösta Bohman said all the government had achieved by its rhetoric, disliked particularly in the provinces, was to freeze relations.

The government hastily dropped plans to introduce another controversial piece of legislation downgrading the position of Sweden's Lutheran Church. After forty years in power, the Social Democrats were encountering some serious opposition.

In the course of a few days in September 1973, there was an

unprecedented surfeit of news from this usually tranquil country. King Gustaf Adolf died at ninety, mourned by the whole nation. The government was forced back on the ropes after a unique dead heat election. And, in a bizarre incident which would add a new phrase to the language, a young gunman walked into the Kreditbank in central Stockholm and demanded money.

When two policemen arrived, Jan Erik Olsson opened fire, injuring one of them. In the first comic touch of a bizarre story, the other cop was ordered to sit down and sing. He obliged with 'Lonesome Cowboy' – maybe that was the only song he knew. Olsson then took four hostages and demanded three million kronor in cash, together with guns, bulletproof vests and a fast car. He also wanted his friend, repeat offender Clark Olofsson, brought along. Then the two men barricaded themselves and the hostages in an inner vault. In a phone call to Palme, Olsson threatened to kill them.

Over the next six days, the strange train of events continued. Olofsson walked around the vault singing a popular song of the moment, 'Killing Me Softly'. One of the female hostages, Kristin Enmark, phoned the Prime Minister and asked him to let the robbers leave. Eventually, the police drilled through the ceiling from an apartment above, fired gas inside and freed the lot. Both men were jailed. But, while serving his ten-year sentence, Olsson received admiring letters from several women and became engaged to one of them. The hostages said they'd been more frightened of the police than the robbers and refused to testify against them.

Since then, whenever captives develop bonds of affection with their captors, it's been called 'the Stockholm Syndrome'.

Meanwhile, Sweden acquired a new King and parliament. Twenty-seven-year-old Carl Gustaf inherited the throne. The new Queen was Sylvia Sommerlath of Germany, whom he'd met at the Olympic Games. Some of his countrymen were now questioning such institutions as the monarchy. But a greater number of Swedes protested that Sweden had gone far enough to the left, with government intervention in banks, businesses and private lives. However, the opposition parties failed to make the breakthrough and Sweden's most crucial election in years ended in a dead heat, each side winning 175 seats.

Palme refused to quit, the opposition declined to push and it was decided that issues in parliament would be decided by a 'Yes' or 'No' vote drawn from a hat – or actually a ballot box. Critics ridiculed the idea, talking of a 'Bingo Parliament'. For a time, the lottery was not needed as clear majorities emerged, one way or the other. Then the first dead heat occurred and the ballot box was called for. Amid high excitement, the Speaker read out the result. The government was defeated. Two hours later there was another lottery, again going against the government. Next day, Palme had his revenge when the ballot went his way. By now, people were calling the system a farce. I reported, 'Most Swedes seem to have decided gambling is for racetracks, not parliament.'

Finally, under a constitutional change, the number of parliamentary seats was reduced to 349. By then, the ballot box had been used eighteen times. Strangely enough, government and opposition blocs had won nine times each. What could be more Swedish!

After a political stalemate lasting months, the Liberals agreed to back the government, and I wrote:

> It's a smiling Mr Palme who has gone off for the autumn recess.
> He has come out the winner of Sweden's 'Bingo Parliament' and
> shown himself to be one of the astutest politicians in Europe.

Svenska Dagbladet, the Conservative paper, seemed to agree. But it cautiously used a photocopy of my bylined story, rather than its own.

The Social Democrats had had a fright. Palme assured citizens there were no plans for sweeping new nationalisation measures. 'It is not an ideological goal,' he said, amid scepticism. Two other declared aims – the creation of a republic and a thirty-hour week – were only long-term projects, he added. And he admitted there was no public demand to abolish the monarchy. But he'd weathered the storm and would remain unchallenged leader of Sweden's Social Democrats until 1986, when he was gunned down by a still unidentified assassin in central Stockholm.

I'd only come across him once again, in the early eighties, when, as Chief Correspondent in Switzerland, I attended a news conference at the UN's European headquarters in Geneva. The

Iran–Iraq war, which had raged for years, showed no signs of abating, and the Swede had been sent by the UN to Baghdad and Tehran on a mediation mission. Fifty or sixty of us gathered in a conference room at the Palais des Nations to hear the results. Palme began by observing, 'Well, I've met the leaders of both these countries – and they're both very nice men.' The rest of what he might have meant to say was drowned in a wave of tittering and guffaws from the hacks.

Palme may have meant well. His name is commemorated to this day in dozens of street names in Europe and the Third World. Britain is not among them.

I remember when the Öresund Bridge linking Denmark and Sweden was just a project for the future, providing an occasional feature story. Now it's there, making it a quick car journey across. In the old days, your car had to be lifted by crane on to a passenger ship between Malmö and Copenhagen. The ships, followed for a while by hydrofoils, made travelling just that bit more exciting. You had the definite feeling of swapping one country for another, however close. And the language was different at the two ends.

Today, the Öresund seems to be one big urban belt presenting, as well as shopping opportunities both sides of the water, a quick route for criminals. A big influx of immigrants into the region has brought cultural changes which are not to everyone's liking. The Danes finally decided things were getting out of hand and reduced the flow. The Swedish authorities are less proactive and seem to be alienating some traditional voters. It's really up to them to decide how Swedish Sweden will remain.

In the old days, I liked the town-and-country mix of Skåne, and to my pleasure my son and family choose to live in another rural spot between Stockholm and the ancient university town of Uppsala, where he studied. Next door is the old family farm. Deer are not too far away, wild boar live in the woods and once I filmed an elk with her two young ambling in line across the next field. From the forest we selected a Christmas tree and the old village church had a Christmas Day children's service. The kids sitting around the crib seemed to be enjoying it, some of the old hymns were sung, and I was touched when the priest took the congregation through that old prayer my son used to recite each evening as a child. It had stuck with me throughout the years.

Chapter 15
GUN BATTLE ON A TEL AVIV BEACH,
CHRISTMAS IN OCCUPIED BETHLEHEM

'I only arrived in Israel last night,' a Brazilian tourist told me in despair as machine-gun fire rattled along the waterfront. 'I'm catching the next plane out.'

I'd hadn't been in Tel Aviv long myself. After a cinema show one evening, I'd strolled back along the seafront towards my hotel. I leaned for a few moments against the low stone wall bordering the beach. In the semi-darkness, I could hear the waves break gently on the sand. What a place for a surprise attack, I thought. But the Israelis must know that better than me, I told myself.

They apparently didn't, for a few weeks later Palestine guerrillas did come ashore around midnight a hundred yards from where I'd been standing, sprayed machine-gun fire at the same cinema and then holed up in a cheap hotel across the road. I was about to go to bed when New Yorker Bob Gary, the Tel Aviv evening desk man, rang to say there were reports of shooting down by the beach. Martin Fletcher, cameraman for our newsreel associate Visnews (later Reuter Television), had given us the tip-off. 'I just happened to be having dinner in a restaurant nearby,' he told me later. 'I could have been miles away.' And luckily I myself was at home, half asleep.

We didn't know at that stage whether or not it was Israeli gang warfare. There'd been a wave of violent crime in the country. Hand grenades had been tossed into a discotheque. There was a huge traffic in drugs between Israel and the West Bank, plus a big rise in domestic violence. As one expert in the Welfare Ministry put it, 'The husband comes back from army reserve duty and has a weapon next to his bed.'

While Bob put a first brief story together, I dressed and hailed a taxi. I hadn't even hired myself a car yet. Immediately the driver heard the address, he baulked. He'd obviously been given word over the radio not to go down there. I got him to drop me near the American Embassy and walked the rest of the way. The sound of firing marked the spot. I went as near as I could before being stopped by soldiers a block or so from the Savoy Hotel, where something was clearly happening, nobody knew exactly what. Half an hour later, with troops pouring in, the whole area was cordoned off and I couldn't have got into it at all.

Troops and police were dashing in all directions. They looked at you suspiciously in the darkness. Sub-machine-gun fire rattled over the rooftops. A young man dressed only in pyjama trousers was gesticulating to a mixed group of police and young night revellers. When he'd run out of steam in Hebrew, I asked him to say the same thing in English. He was our first eyewitness. He lived near the Savoy, and after hearing noises outside, went out and found himself facing gunmen down the road. They fired one shot at him and he fled. His mother and sister were still in there. At that point there was a stream of machine-gun fire across the street, and we all made for the wall nearest the direction the tracers were coming from. A line of orange flares went up along the beach. Nobody knew anything. All was confusion. I ran to the nearest hotel and persuaded the night desk clerk (he'd been in the British Army) to keep the switchboard open.

He was still there, grumbling, at eight the next morning, while refugees including an old woman and her son (more eyewitnesses for my story) and two weary streetwalkers tried to sleep on chairs in the lobby. Reporters, army officers and police all scrambled for the single phone. Our night teleprinter operator, American Mary Lee, swiftly took down my dictated copy as the story developed. Bob Gary and our local boss, Arye Wallenstein, had been fighting their own battle – with the censors.

I continued filing through the night, Bob tying the story together. Getting close to the hotel meant persuading an Israeli soldier to take you through the barriers and lead you, running with head down, along the beach behind the sea wall, in case the guerrillas started taking potshots. The soldier in front of me suddenly stopped and waved me around a dark object on the sand, an unexploded device the guerrillas had left.

As the night wore on, it became clear the end would be bloody. Officials were saying nothing. We had to glean information from wisps of conversation on the military car radios. Then I saw a platoon of commandos running in from a side street, obviously ready for action. One of them was an older man, without a steel helmet. Soldiers held journalists back eighty yards from the hotel. A few minutes later there was a racket of machine-gun and automatic fire, and shortly afterwards a massive explosion. Silence, and then another short burst of fire. Then as dawn broke over Tel Aviv's shabby red-light district, the soldiers came filing back from the hotel, helmets off, some smoking, one chewing an apple. The older man wasn't among them. We heard later he was a senior officer who'd joined the assault group at the last moment and died. So did seven guerrillas, who must have known from the beginning it was a suicide mission. And several tourists from Germany, Switzerland, Holland and Somalia, who'd been taken hostage. Their bodies were found in the rubble.

One hostage who survived was a young Israeli woman, Kohava Levy. 'I was on my way home when one of them grabbed me and pushed me into the hotel, then up the stairs to the top floor.' She was then ordered by the Arabs to shout out their demands to the Israeli troops ringing the hotel. 'They started shouting all kinds of orders at me and kept arguing with each other,' she told us. 'They had laid packets of explosives on the second and third floors of the hotel, threatening to detonate them if their demands were not met. They wanted a plane out and the release of other terrorists in our prisons. And they were still trying to decide their final terms when the Israeli troops moved in. I just lay down and slowly crawled to a dark corner. The next thing I heard was an Israeli soldier asking, "Are you alive?" '

The Israeli Navy later intercepted a small sailing vessel from Lebanon, where the raid was believed to have been launched. It was seen as an attempt by Yasser Arafat's Palestine Liberation movement to embarrass both Israel and Egypt at the start of new peace efforts by American Secretary of State Henry Kissinger.

Ever since the Six Day War, the Middle East had been big news and the Reuter operation considerably beefed up. Up to the war, it consisted of that back room in the Wallensteins' flat in

Dizengoff Street. Now, Wally was managing a much larger team, with Reuters not just reporting from Israel, but selling the incoming world service from London to an increased number of clients, including government, press and radio, as well as Arabic-language papers in Jerusalem.

I'd arrived to find the editorial team working in a dismal and almost windowless office in the *Maariv* newspaper building. Thankfully, Wally soon acquired a large villa in a pleasant residential area of the city. Our team of about a dozen included four reporters, teleprinter operators and support staff. Wally didn't so much report any longer as preside. He took care of client relations, office management and finances. Day to day news coverage was handled by the reporters. All were Jewish, fairly naturally, but this would lead to some acrimony when I took overall charge later after Wally's death.

The editorial team reflected Israel's origins and continuing breadth of intake. The two eldest and most experienced staffers, Hugh Orgel and Bob Gary, were from London and New York respectively. Our sports correspondent, Jack Leon, was from Manchester. Part-timer Zvi Zipper had emigrated from the former Southern Rhodesia and lived with his family, appropriately enough for Israel, in a house in an orange grove. Other members of staff were from Germany, Lebanon and Argentina. And apart from Wally himself, we had two Sabras (born in Israel). One of them, teleprinter operator Arik, an engaging young man who'd served in the army but not particularly liked it, applied to become a reporter and I arranged the transfer. Then a young lady called Rivka Fried joined the outfit, adding considerable youthful glamour to the scene.

Wally remained manager of this multinational team, while I was in charge of editorial matters. The latter had been made clear by Managing Director Gerald Long before I left London. If there were any dispute about it, I should inform head office immediately. And I had myself insisted on this being clarified before re-entering the Middle East political minefield. The chief problem, which had become increasingly obvious to head office, lay in respect of the now occupied West Bank of the River Jordan and the Gaza Strip, from which a less than satisfactory report had been coming since the end of hostilities. Wally was a committed Zionist, and this I respected, but the Middle East had moved on since the Six Day War. And with close to a million Palestinians now living under Israeli control, apart from those in Israel itself, things had to change. Wally accepted this and, in asking for me as head of the editorial, must have known I'd run things differently. But sometimes I seemed to be walking a tightrope.

Minor attacks by Palestinian guerrillas were an almost everyday occurrence. They often seemed just as amateurish and suicidal as the beachfront raid, but were a harbinger of things to come. One day, an Arab was shot dead after he emerged from an orange grove near a road junction and hurled grenades at Israeli soldiers. His rusty old British-made Mills bombs didn't go off. The soldiers just threw them back and shot him. The same afternoon, explosives went off accidentally in two West Bank villages. Another explosive charge was found in time under an Israeli bus. That was just one day. The attacks would become much better organised, and lethal.

Such sporadic incidents had been largely written up from Israeli army handouts. No one from the Tel Aviv office seemed to have visited the two occupied areas, the West Bank and Gaza Strip. West Jerusalem, on the Israeli side of the city's dividing wall, was as far as anyone got, leaving the large towns of Nablus, Ramallah, Bethlehem and others virtually unreported. Nor was there much interest among our local staff in going there. Admittedly, in view of their Israeli citizenship, they might have had problems. London had apparently decided that a complete outsider, with no religious or political axe to grind one way or the other, was needed. With four years' background knowledge of Egypt, my earlier stint in Israel during the June War, and the diplomatic wrangle at the United Nations in New York which eventually produced Resolution 242, the Reuter bosses must have agreed with Wally (with whom I'd always got on well) that I was a suitable choice to change things.

The presence of a million Arab citizens displaced during the early 1948 war within Israel itself added to the lopsided nature of reporting the country. The majority of them identified themselves as Israelis by citizenship, Palestinians by nationality. And Israel's occupation of the West Bank and Sinai emphasised the dichotomy by easing contacts between Palestinians within and outside its borders. This inevitably increased political activism among Israel's Arab citizens. Suspicions about their loyalty were emphasised shortly after I arrived, when two Arab residents of Lydda, near Tel Aviv, were jailed for planning to kidnap soldiers and steal their weapons. In another such incident, an Israeli soldier was killed. Understandably, Arab Israelis were not required to do military service, and to this day only a handful of them volunteer. They ran their own town councils, of course, and the election of a communist mayor in the unlikely setting of Jesus Christ's reputed birthplace, Nazareth, made a nice little offbeat story.

In the occupied West Bank itself, our report had to improve. Wally had taken on as part-timer a Jewish refugee from Iraq, Shafik (Hebraicised to Shefi) Al-Jaby. He was conversant with the political scene among the Arabs. None of our full-time staffers were apparently interested in visiting the West Bank, euphemistically labelled the 'Administered Areas'. One of them, the ex-New Yorker, declined to use Shefi's stories at all. According to Shefi, he'd told him, 'I'm a Zionist and didn't come here from New York to see stories like this being reported about Israel.'

Well and good, but in that case he should perhaps have sought employment elsewhere in the Israeli media. Wally was no fool, and knew this sort of situation couldn't continue.

Before I arrived, Wally had ordered me a new car, a shiny green Ford Consul. It would cover quite some distance in the couple of years to come, from the Lebanese border to Sinai, the Huleh Valley, the Dead Sea and the Gulf of Aqaba. For me, the best part of reporting the Middle East was the travel, which didn't seem to interest any of my Jewish colleagues very much. But then they were not exactly in the first flush of youth. Most stories in recent years had carried a Tel Aviv dateline, and mainly relied on Israeli official sources, plus occasional contributions from our Arabic-speaking reporter. Head office had read the signs right. There was more now to covering tensions in the area than having an office in Tel Aviv and reading army communiqués. There were no barriers at the time to travelling to the West Bank, but our reporting had become fossilised. It was high time to get around a bit and test the temperature.

On visits to Jerusalem I'd stay, not at relatively modern hotels like the famous King David, scene of a bloody attack by Jewish terrorists in the run-up to Israeli independence, but at the much more charming American Colony, just over the dividing line. It's a rambling old-fashioned place with golden stone walls and small gardens; a place much liked by diplomats. It was a good starting point for tours of the West Bank towns, and I'd also drop in at the city's two Arab-language newspapers, which received the Reuter service at bargain rates. Next stop would usually be Ramallah or Nablus, but over time I investigated the scene at most of the West Bank towns – including Bethlehem, of course, whose Christian Mayor, Elias Freij, dressed and spoke like the proverbial English bank manager, and was always agreeable and most helpful.

'Tea – or coffee?'

Well, I was clearly back in the Arab world. For my first forays into the occupied areas, Shefi would alert the local dignitaries in advance and there'd be the old routine, familiar from Cairo days. The brass-topped table, the tea or coffee arriving in tiny cups on copper trays, the elaborate courtesies. The last thing to do was to start quizzing them on political matters the first time you met. We'd sit in the office, or their home, Shefi sometimes along to interpret, though the 'notables', as they were referred to, mostly spoke quite adequate, even florid, English. If they were a bit miffed that no senior Reuter staffer had come to call since the Six Day War – now eight years back – they didn't show it. After a few visits, I began to win acceptance, and once they knew Reuters would stop by on a fairly regular basis, they obviously felt freer to talk. There are two sides to most stories, and we were correcting an imbalance. The highly complex and volatile situation had been partly brought upon themselves by the Arab countries, of course, with their combined onslaught on Israel in 1967, when Nasser declared that 'our basic goal is the destruction of Israel'.

At this stage, the Israelis had only been in the occupied territories for seven or eight years. Their settlements, though much resented, were comparatively small, and the situation had not frozen in the way it would. Driving out of Tel Aviv, leaving the green and well-tended acres of Israel for the arid slopes of the West Bank, to speak all day with Palestinian mayors and ordinary folk, then driving back into Israel to write and send the story, sometimes threatened schizophrenia – but one got used to it. They were two different worlds on either side of the invisible Green Line.

In a foretaste of days to come, about the time I arrived in the region a twenty-eight-year-old Palestinian living in Lebanon had been captured after crossing into Israel. The first the news agencies knew of it was when the full text of an Army interview with the guerrilla was broadcast on television. He admitted, 'Our mission was to take hostages and to free prisoners held in Israeli prisons.'

Q: If, for example, citizens had tried to prevent you from carrying out the action, what would you have done?

A: Anyone trying to prevent us would be murdered.

Q: If you had succeeded in taking hostages and the Israeli authorities did not accept your demands, what were your orders then?

A: To murder the hostages and blow ourselves up, together with them.

This was clear enough, though naturally it told the story from Jerusalem's viewpoint.

The Israeli press system was familiar to any Western journalist. Government and Army spokesmen and staff were quick and efficient. In Egypt, I'd tried for three years without success to interview President Nasser. Here, when Prime Minister Yitzhak Rabin and Foreign Minister Shimon Peres flew up to the northern front, they invited a small group of agency and broadcasting media to join them on the helicopter. We were rung the night before and told to be at the military airport north of Tel Aviv at six, never searched, then flown up to the Lebanese border. We could report what we wanted. If the helicopter had been shot down, Israel would have lost at one fell swoop its two top ministers – as well as half a dozen reporters. Ironically, years later, it would be not an Arab but a disaffected young right-wing Israeli, unhappy about peace moves with the Arabs, who assassinated Rabin.

The last time I'd reported from here was in wartime. In what now passed for peace, Parliament and its institutions were relatively open. The country had a lively choice of newspapers of various political persuasions. In marked contrast to Cairo, I could interview whom I liked and report as I wished, including stories from the occupied territories which contained views from the Palestinian side. There was censorship only on real security issues. As we had our own direct line to London, stories could not be vetted – or killed – as in Egypt. If some specific military or security issue were alluded to, we were honour-bound to call the censors and check. I only remember one occasion during two years in Israel that I felt this necessary, and after I'd read out my story they requested only a very small excision. Other news agencies worked with the same ground rules – and punishments. When United Press International (UPI) broke the agreement, they were made for three months to submit every word of copy to the censors, a most time-consuming routine.

As desired by London, I wrote many of the main political and action stories myself and, as in Egypt, tried to broaden the scope of the file with more detailed and personalised 'think-pieces', as we called them. Across the West Bank, traders went on strike after the imposition of an 8% value added tax. Arab mayors said the traders had no intention of paying it. Major Freij told me, 'From a cultural point of view, it is altogether foreign to the local mentality to try to impose bookkeeping on small traders who have had a different way of life for centuries. Some of these are small shopkeepers, getting up at four o'clock in the morning to sell a little milk and bread. Do the Israelis think these people can write everything down, or afford a clerk? It is ridiculous.'

In Nablus, Mayor Bassam Shaka said, 'This sort of tax and bookkeeping is obviously for developed societies. The Israelis make no attempt to study our lifestyle and the day to day problems of enforcing such a law.' Later, the Israelis backed down and said they would exempt anyone with an annual turnover of less than $80,000.

All Israelis were not by any means hardliners. Some of the country's most sophisticated thinkers even at that time had severe misgivings about the way events were shaping up. And these included Israelis of impeccable background. I interviewed Arie Eliav, an ex-minister and former secretary-general of the Israeli Labour Party. A former Jewish underground fighter in the days before statehood, he was now campaigning for a peace settlement with the Arabs and Israeli withdrawal from the occupied territories. In a hard-hitting book which sent shock waves through the establishment, he said Israel's leaders were steering the country to disaster. The jury is still out on that one.

Eliav had been in at the birth of Israel. In 1947, under the code name Arthur, he captained an ancient ex-American Navy ship from Sweden to Palestine with thousands of survivors from the Nazi holocaust aboard. After first being repelled by British troops trying to prevent further Jewish immigration, his passengers eventually entered the country. Now he described Israel's continued occupation of Arab lands captured in 1967 as a tragedy, both for the Arabs and for Israel. 'We have put them in a kind of limbo. You cannot hold a people under occupation indefinitely,' he said. In an interesting forecast of events of later decades, he said the change that had to come would have to be imposed from outside, mainly the United States.

Eliav asked, 'Do we want thousands more killed? Our young people have been brought up on the categorical imperatives of land and blood. People here are living on hawkish slogans. Tanks we have, guns we have. What we have to regain is our moral raison d'être.'

Three decades on, it seems clear that, despite continued unease among intellectuals, Eliav was talking to the wall.

Another Israeli with impressive credentials was calling for a change of tack. Professor Yigael Yadin, former operations officer of the Haganah pre-independence underground army, played a central role in the 1948 War of Independence, later organising Israel's standing army under compulsory military service. A man of relaxed temperament, which some observers correctly predicted could not fit in the hurly-burly of Israeli politics, Yadin advocated a pragmatic approach by Israel to a settlement with its near neighbours, declaring on television, 'Israel cannot absorb within its borders a million and a half Arabs who, if given complete democratic freedom, would make Israel lose its Jewish identity.'

Scorning the right-wing theme of 'maximum borders' based on the biblical state of Israel, he said, 'I am attached to the Bible like most other people, but we must be realistic.' And rejecting the official view of the Palestine Liberation Organisation as simply a terrorist group, Yadin said the Israeli Government should be ready to negotiate with PLO leader Yasser Arafat.

A further voice of sanity, it seemed to this humble observer, was the editor of the *Jerusalem Post*, Ari Rath. In those days, Reuters had no office in Jerusalem, only in Tel Aviv. After being pointed in his direction by Arye Wallenstein, I found Ari kind, courteous and down to earth. He allowed me to use an office and teleprinter in the *Post* building whenever I was visiting the city. I was disappointed when Mr Rath was subsequently replaced as Editor. In Bonn a few years later, as head of Reuter's editorial operation in Germany, I discovered that he and another old journalist colleague, Egypt's news agency boss Mohamed Abdel-Gawad, would both be visiting the German capital at the same time. I had the pleasure of arranging a meeting and then left them alone to talk. They apparently got on like a house on fire.

At the other end of Israel's political spectrum, the hard-line settler movement Gush Emunim, headed by Rabbi Moshe Levinger, was becoming more and more of a problem for Israel's own rulers, let alone the Palestinians, and he was seldom out of the news. Levinger led the push for Jewish settlement in the major West Bank town of Hebron shortly after the Six Day War, but his proclaimed doctrine was 'not just settlement but sovereignty'. He began by renting rooms temporarily from a former mayor of Hebron and then refused to leave. Later he moved with his large family of eleven into a former army base on the hill overlooking the town and there, with the Israeli Government's assent, the settlement of Kiryat Arbah was established. For many years after that Levinger would be a thorn in the Israeli Government's flesh, leading regular settler marches through Arab land and assaulting – in one case shooting dead –

Palestinians. He would be in and out of jail through the coming decades. When I attempted to interview settlers at Kiryat Arbah, I found the hilltop settlement was blocked by fences. Unhelpful comments shouted back across the barrier were all in American English.

There were regular – and later bloody – scenes in the centre of Hebron around the historic Caves of the Patriarchs. The site is sacred to Jews, but also venerated by Christians and Muslims. Frequent disputes were reported, and I went to have a look at the scene. Young Jews were working to clear an area of waste ground. Most of them looked to be of student age, but it was impossible to interview them. As I approached the centre of the disturbances, along with Shefi and an employee of the local administration, one of Levinger's men thrust a rifle towards my belly and told me to leave. Sometimes discretion is truly the better part of valour.

Mayor Fahd Kawasma called Levinger and his cohorts 'madmen', saying, 'These crazy people at Kiryat Arbah can apparently do anything they please. They now have a town of their own. I don't know what more they want. They tell people the remains of three or four Jewish houses are down there.' He asked angrily, 'What about millions of Arab houses in the Israeli towns of Haifa and Jaffa?'

I reported the incident exactly as it was. My caution may have proved wise.

Disputes continued over the next decades, reaching a bloody climax in 1994, when a Jew called Baruch Goldstein took a sub-machine gun into the enclosure and killed twenty-nine Muslims who'd been at prayer, before himself being beaten to death. Riots followed and the shootings were universally condemned. Finally, much later, as part of the Arab–Israeli peace process, restrictions were imposed at Hebron for both Jews and Muslims.

The pitch was being slightly queered, and the Israelis to some extent let off the hook, by a few Palestinians themselves, who sold their land to Israelis. I wrote in a story given prominence in London's *Evening Standard*:

> While confusion still reigns about Israel's official policy on settlement in occupied areas, Jewish organisations are buying Arab land at ever-inflationary prices – and some Arabs are secretly

selling them despite the threat of death. As tension mounts on the occupied West Bank of the Jordan, the land deals are attracting increasing Arab resentment.

Jewish buyers were travelling as far as South America to buy the land from Arab émigré owners, I was informed. Palestine Arab guerrillas had executed at least three such land vendors. 'They took them from their houses in the night and shot them,' my informant said.

Nevertheless Israel, I was reliably informed, intended to keep its string of settlements along the Jordan Valley and the Golan Heights, in order to deter future Arab attacks, and the settlements around East Jerusalem would remain. Describing the Palestine Liberation Organisation under Yasser Arafat as 'a gang of murderers', Prime Minister Rabin said it was a cornerstone of Israeli policy that there should 'no Arafat state between Israel and Jordan'. So whatever the famous but now dormant UN Resolution 242 proclaimed, one of its principal provisions – withdrawal – was already dead in the water.

Apart from social contacts, music, in this rather tense society, provided relief. I was delighted on entering my first flat in Tel Aviv, rented in advance by Wally and his wife Shula, to find a piano against the wall of the living room. It was old and a bit battered, but still a piano, and I lost no time in trying it out. Gershwin, I thought, might be a suitable choice in the circum- stances, and I played a few numbers accordingly. Unfortunately, the elderly couple who owned the flat, when I met them later, were obviously not jazz lovers – or maybe they were worried I'd further downgrade the out-of-tune instrument. At any rate I came back to the flat one day to find they'd been there in my absence and, seeing the keyboard open, locked it. Or perhaps the neighbours complained.

I found another, and much more agreeable, flat in one of the city's more pleasant outer suburbs – and hired a piano this time. On the classical side, expectedly, there were lots of concerts in Tel Aviv, but very little jazz. When it did come to town, I was delighted to drive up to the ancient coastal town of Caesarea. Far from the conflict, sitting in the old Roman amphitheatre on a warm and sunlit summer evening, I heard American tenor sax star Stan Getz, last seen in Copenhagen, weave his familiar magic.

Christmas in Bethlehem. I could hardly miss the opportunity. The green invitation card from the 'Franciscan Custodians of the Holy Land' was unsurprisingly counter-stamped on the back by the Military Governor of Bethlehem. To get into town, I had another permit from the 'Israeli Defence Forces Command, Judea and Samaria Area, Military Commander, Bethlehem district'. Obviously the Israelis were taking no chances. Getting into Bethlehem was like entering an armed fortress, and only limited numbers were admitted, with security checks along the road.

Outside the fourth-century Church of the Nativity, Manger Square was already packed with tourists shopping for souvenirs. They were mainly from Germany and Scandinavia, but you also heard voices from Italy, England and the American Midwest. Choirs from the United States, Canada, Switzerland and other places were singing hymns on 'Shepherds' Field', the somewhat touristically named area where the shepherds traditionally 'watched their flocks by night'. From ninety minutes before midnight, you had to use your elbows to get through the crowds besieging the small entry door to the church itself. The only place I could find inside was on a church kneeler behind a pillar, from where I gradually worked myself into a more useful position. It was much like a European church, with a large portrait of the Virgin and Child over the high altar.

The Patriarch of Jerusalem, the elderly Italian Monsignor Beltritti, in gold-embroidered white vestments, led a procession up the central aisle. There were chants of various kinds before Mass started, and carol singing afterwards. I didn't hear much of the latter, for by then I was phoning a colour story from a phone box on the Jerusalem road to Tel Aviv, for relay to London. Then I drove across the hills to the village of Nazareth, scene of Christ's upbringing, and filed another story from there. I think it's the only time Reuters had Christmas stories from both the key biblical towns on the same day.

At the office, the drive for better writing continued. I was encouraging our local staffers to produce extended political stories, 'Focus' pieces as we then called them, and general features

– 'Situationers' was the term we used. And the usual office drills needed sharpening up a bit. Accordingly, this was my New Year message for 1976, frivolously dedicated to Alexander Pope and, perhaps over-optimistically, pinned on the office notice board. It may give the flavour of the problems of the period.

> These things I hope this Bright New Year
> That six-line Intros disappear,
> That countless Focus themes be found
> And Situationers abound,
> That no non sequiturs disturb,
> Or singular noun with plural verb.
> Let army jargon and party cant
> Be clarified for the ignorant,
> And tales of Israel's mounting woes
> Be told in clear, crystalline prose.
> Let daymen not forget the need
> For (skedded) solid, prompt Nightlead.
> Let evening duties peaceful be
> With time for sandwiches and tea,
> But file the Daylead ere you're through
> Lest London call at ten to two.
> I fear I too become prolix,
> So wish you well in seventy-six.

Well, at least some of the guys appreciated the humour, but you can't please everyone. Zvi Zipper liked it.

You can't be writing about war or politics all the time. A few features were needed to leaven the file. I got good play in the American press with the Mystery of the Dying Pines along the twisting road from the coast to Jerusalem. It had been the embattled supply route during the 1948 Arab siege of the city and remnants of old armoured cars still stand by the roadside as a monument. Now the pines were turning a ghostly white. A New York scientist finally traced the problem not to the Arab enemies of Israel but a microscopic insect called the Matsucoccus.

I drove into the Negev Desert for a series of interviews with nomadic Bedouin sheikhs (another group the Israeli state had absorbed), interviewing them sitting on carpets in the sand or inside tents flapping in a desert wind. The Israeli authorities wanted the Bedouins to cease their wandering life and move into purpose-built blocks of flats. The latter, from what I saw of them, looked ugly and incongruous and, at that time at least, there were few takers for this supposedly better way of life. A recent estimate says over 70,000 Bedouin still prefer to live in their traditional makeshift encampments predating the existence of Israel, though they are denied basic services like water and electricity. Nevertheless a few of their young men still volunteer for the Israeli Army, though not required to do so.

In February 1975, flash floods in usually arid north Sinai wreaked death and destruction among the desert dwellers. Dry wadis suddenly turned into raging rivers, engulfing sleeping Bedouin in their desert encampments. Israeli helicopters plucked more than 500 of the nomadic tribesmen from their encampments as gushing waters turned huge areas of the northern desert into lakes. Bedouin leaders said more than 200 people had lost their lives, together with hundreds of camels and sheep. Telephone and power lines were torn down and only Israeli army vehicles with supplies managed to get through. Survivors told of individual bravery of soldiers who jumped down from the helicopters to save children and old people from being swept out to sea. One aged Bedouin said, 'I never thought I'd take my first airplane ride this way. I hope it's my last.' It was a heart-warming story of hands across the Great Divide.

From quite another world, planeloads of Americans arrived in the Gulf of Aqaba for a gathering of the United Jewish Appeal. Under a disengagement agreement between Israel and Egypt, Cairo had reopened the Suez Canal, allowing free passage of non-military cargoes into the Israeli port of Eilat. New York requested cover. I found myself in a queue of well-heeled contributors to the Zionist dream as they climbed the steep gangplank of a huge freighter which had symbolically sailed through the canal. In the heat, the large lady puffing and gasping in front of me seemed unlikely to reach the deck. Her husband gripped her firmly by the arm. 'Honey,' he intoned theatrically, 'remember you're doing this for Israel.' She did make it to the top. My cameraman colleague Martin Fletcher, a sophisticated Jewish Londoner, looked uncomfortable at some of the proceedings. So did some of the Israeli Army's top brass.

Another Jewish newspaper colleague, Mario Chimanovitch, from Brazil, had his own opinions too about aspects of the Jewish homeland and was outspoken in his despatches to *O Globo*. We once drove across the Green Line into occupied territory on some story or other and came by chance into a village where an army truck was parked by the roadside. We stopped and watched as Israeli soldiers battered down the door of one house, dragged a couple of young Palestinians out and virtually threw them into the back of the truck. The soldiers were clearly displeased that we'd happened to be around. No story in it, nothing that we'd ever hear about it officially anyway. The men were perhaps terrorist suspects and justifiably detained. But the scene was an ugly one, and I was unfortunately reminded of events in the Third Reich, surely not the aim…

Inevitably, in a society of such varied origins, there's a certain rough and ready feel. There are also very many highly literate and articulate people. Israel's chief government spokesman was David Friedman, an impressive ex-Viennese intellectual who'd served in the British Army during World War Two. I found him both fair and outspoken. Introduced to the social scene by Wally and his wife Shula, I would join many a Friday evening gathering at the Friedmans' home. Intense discussion seemed to be the order of the day. The exchanges sometimes got quite fiery, and David would throw up his hands. 'With friends like these,' he asked me jokingly, 'who needs enemies?'

I was delighted a year later, after Wally's untimely death, when David, about to retire from government service, agreed to become Reuter's business manager in Israel. I remained chief representative, but could concentrate on news. David, who knew just about everyone in Israel, proved an admirable successor to Wally on the business side. I was sorry but hardly surprised to hear on the grapevine that some quarters in Tel Aviv were not happy about my succeeding an Israeli as boss. The feeling apparently was that the Reuter office had been 'lost'. But after the Six Day War, Middle East reporting had entered a new era.

I'd had the unhappy task of addressing mourners at a packed memorial gathering. Wally had been a good friend and had taken Reuters through difficult times. A kindly man, he'd had the unenviable task years earlier (a job he tried to get out of) of being one of three reporters designated to witness the execution of Nazi war criminal Adolf Eichmann. He stood a few feet away as the Austrian, kidnapped from Latin America to stand trial in Israel, had the noose fastened around his neck and dropped into the void. Only three reporters attended the execution, representing Israel, Germany and the international press. They then had to describe Eichmann's last moments to a packed international news conference, a devastating experience for Wally.

Memories of the Holocaust were not hard to find in Israel. Two pictures which now hang on the wall of my house near Evesham were sold to me by an art dealer in Tel Aviv who unbuttoned his left sleeve to show me the notorious tattoo. David Friedman's wife, from a Polish family, refused ever to set foot in Germany, though he himself took governmental visits there in his stride. One just hopes that the Arabs are not cast as surrogate Nazis.

With Resolution 242 in danger of becoming a dead letter, moves were now afoot to give a fresh boost to peace efforts. Washington was the key player, and in 1969 managed to bring about a ceasefire along the Suez Canal, but failed to get the Israelis to withdraw from the Canal Zone. Subsequently the Israelis had been caught completely off guard on the Jewish feast of Yom Kippur in 1973 when the Egyptian armed forces, scorned for too long, it seemed, succeeded in a blaze of gunfire in crossing the Canal. Though later driven back, the Egyptians had scored a diplomatic, military and morale-boosting success. The two antagonists eventually signed a ceasefire pact in a tent erected at 'Kilometre 101' on the Cairo–Suez Road. It was the first major agreement between Israel and an Arab country since the 1949 armistice.

Enter US Secretary of State Henry Kissinger, who in several years of shuttle diplomacy between the two capitals had achieved a Separation of Forces agreement, under which Israel withdrew from captured territory west of the canal and pulled its forces several miles back into the Sinai Desert. Further intervention by Kissinger halted several weeks of artillery duels between the Israelis and Syrians on the Golan front. Mr K had become a familiar figure in both Cairo and Jerusalem. His flights back and forth, spawning a new phrase in the diplomatic vocabulary, attracted enormous media interest and a whole pack of American correspondents descended on Jerusalem for his visits. I was virtually on permanent duty in the King David, where the US delegation was quartered. With mobiles still something for the distant future, I phoned my pieces from the hotel room to Tel Aviv for relay to London. I also made twice-a-day calls to our radio studios in London with news updates.

The sombre-looking US diplomat, with his distinctive low and gravelly voice, had few things to tell at the main news conferences. But I got permission to attend the regular private briefings he gave to US journalists – on condition I stayed right at the back of the room and asked no questions. It was all off-the-record stuff, but helped to enliven the story. Whenever Mr K was expected back from Cairo, there'd be a press pack waiting in the King David lobby. On one occasion, though, he was upstaged – by Elizabeth Taylor, who'd suddenly flown into town. Standing at the back of a crowd of pressmen quizzing and filming the lovely lady, I watched Mr K come through the front entrance and cross over to the elevators unnoticed. He didn't seem best pleased.

On 4 September 1975, the second disengagement agreement which Kissinger engineered would be signed in Geneva. Israel pulled its forces several miles further back from the Suez Canal, the relinquished area becoming a buffer zone, and vacated the Abu Reis and Ras Sudar oilfields in the Gulf of Suez. Later still, Egyptian President Anwar Sadat would fly to Israel on a historic State Visit. The 'shuttle' had paid off and, at least for Israel and Egypt, times were changing. But as I flew back to Britain at the end of my assignment, the Arab–Israeli conflict hadn't changed as a whole, nor has it to this day. Many would say it only gets worse.

The news came from head office that I was to be the next editorial boss in Germany, still a divided country of course and our biggest editorial operation outside London. It was a big promotion, and I had no hesitation in accepting the challenge. The erudite David Friedman gave me a crash evening course to improve my limited knowledge of German, and thus my seven years in the Middle East were over.

I'd made many good friends in Israel, in and out of the office. I'd learned not to be miffed or depressed at feeling an outsider in a basically all-Jewish environment. The Israelis are as they are, and there's good and bad there, as everywhere else. Which, when I got back to London, did not prevent our star sports reporter Steve Parry, a Jewish colleague who'd been one of the Reuter team at the 1972 Olympics, staring at me with simulated bemusement. He'd emigrated years before to Israel, but fairly quickly came back to England. 'How did you manage to stick it for two years?' he asked. 'They're so rude!'

Two letters landed at head office, 'attention Editor'. One of them was from our West Bank stringer Shefi Gabai, who said he would be 'very sad' at my leaving. 'The way he chooses to handle the news is very sincere and faithful,' he wrote kindly. And the Mayor of Bethlehem called me 'objective and sincere in reporting West Bank news in general, and of Bethlehem City in particular'. I truly appreciated such messages. But I'd only been doing what Reuters is supposed to be about.

The old enmities continued and there would shortly be more warfare, a particularly nasty affair after the Israeli Army invaded Lebanon in a bid to halt shellfire and guerrilla incursions across its northern border. I was extremely sad to learn that one of Zvi Zipper's two sons, whom I'd met at that hospitable house in the orange grove, had been killed in the fighting. Answering my letter of condolence, Zvi expressed bitterness at losing a son 'in a war I never believed in'.

Far be it from a mere reporter to make long-term forecasts; but tensions in the area do not diminish. Arab and Christian Israelis, predicted to become a majority of the population within a few decades, have been called a demographic time bomb. Israel shows little sign of halting the construction of new homes in East Jerusalem and the West Bank. Its own Association for Civil Rights acknowledged not long ago that restrictions on the movement of Palestinians had now virtually split the West Bank into six separate parts. The high and ugly concrete barriers snaking over the West Bank hills, unhappily reminiscent of the Berlin Wall, may well prevent suicide raids on Israeli population centres, but hardly seem like a long-term solution. The Prime Minister has said the Israelis will continue to build in heavily Jewish areas which they are determined to keep in a final peace agreement. Any such agreement, alas, seems a long way off.

Chapter 16
WAR CRIMES TRIALS AND BAADER-MEINHOF KILLINGS SHOCK GERMANY

I was back in the country where the Reuter story started a century and a half earlier in the small town of Kassel.

As a young clerk in his uncle's bank, Israel Beer Josaphat, to give him his original name, met Professor Carl Friedrich Gauss, who was trying to transmit electric signals by wire. As telegraphy evolved, young Julius developed these techniques and founded Reuters News Agency in the town of Aachen, on the German–Belgian border. Here, until the gap in the cable network was bridged, those famous pigeons flew in with the latest financial news from Brussels. They're still the popular symbol.

Almost since the Second World War, our headquarters in Bonn had been a rambling old villa on the road to fashionable Bad Godesberg. I'd visited the place for a briefing from Gerry Long before flying on to my first post in Copenhagen. The operation had vastly expanded by the mid seventies. In addition to covering Germany for world clients, we were producing a German-language service for local subscribers. My main responsibility was to see we got a comprehensive service for the world wire from both sides of the still divided country.

I'd much enjoyed working at the Munich Olympics with my indefatigable German colleagues Werner van Zoggel, Kurt Langartner and Hans Bolender. They knew their job, just got on with it, and never let us down. On the journalistic side, there were a few problems, however. Anglo-Saxon readers – and many others – like a rather lighter style of writing, and not just in the tabloids. Reading the more heavyweight German papers too often means ploughing through convoluted sentence structures, waiting breathlessly for the verb at the end. That's the way the German language is. Despite these differences in journalistic cultures, head office had now decided, unwisely in my view, that stories within Germany could be adequately covered for our World Service by either English or German reporters. It was frankly a non-starter.

Down-to-earth Gerd Schröter, a seasoned reporter of the old school, and his somewhat younger colleagues Peter Blechschmidt, Ernst Schreyer and Albrecht Hintze, all wrote well for the national media. But news writing in English is just... different. This was apparent when, in line with the new philosophy, one of our German staff was sent to report a trial. It wasn't a top story, but we needed cover. The theory was that the English Desk could simply translate the German version for the world wire. It doesn't work. What arrived was a straight up-and-down report of the court formalities. No ages, no descriptive details, no atmosphere. And I would find in reading the German papers that three or four pages of windy prose could often be boiled down to a few paragraphs.

There were no direct quotes. People 'indicated' something, or 'suggested' it. But what did the man actually *say*? You were never told. Several hundred words of high-flown prose, with facts few on the ground, would be described rather grandly as a *Kommentar*. One of our German reporters preferred to be addressed academically as 'Doktor'. The atmosphere at the regular government news conference was a trifle clubby as established local journalists sat in the front row to be briefed by the then Chancellor, Helmut Schmidt – quite a down-to-earth man himself. '*Darf Ich nur fragen, Herr Kanzler...?*' Some of them were almost tugging at their forelocks. They put few awkward questions and naturally never asked about the 'private sphere'. Things may have changed today, but I wouldn't count on it.

The English Desk were a nice bunch. No problems of journalistic etiquette here. I was delighted to meet our Chief Reporter, George Vine, whose features back in his *News Chronicle* days I'd always admired and even tried to emulate. With the demise of that paper, he'd joined the Reuter team in Bonn. The others were a good mix of personalities. Scott Thornton, as Scottish as the name suggests, was a glutton for work. Various paths had brought them into journalism, the younger ones via university, the exception being a friendly and knowledgeable sports specialist, Stan Parker. He'd started work as a railway fireman, shovelling coal on the Scottish express, later finding his way to Germany and sports reporting. Steve Powell had modestly done things like climbing Mont Blanc and crossing the Sahara on a camel. At amusing end-of-day gatherings over office drinks, George (as spry as ever recently at his ninetieth birthday party back in Hastings) would regale us with his latest jokes, expertly – or as some thought atrociously – mimicking Irish, Scottish or other accents. It was a good atmosphere. In Munich, Roley Eggleston was still covering events in Bavaria, while in Berlin there was the excellent Annette von Bröcker, later to become head of the German operation. Across the Wall, erected since I first visited both sides of the political divide, events in East Berlin were expertly reported first by Mark Brayne, later to join the BBC, and Mark Wood, who'd become Reuter Editor-in-Chief in London.

Despite the problems, one had to accept that our German staffers, protected by formidable union agreements pushed through since World War Two, had a far better deal than the rest of us. Their unions had won a fantastic array of benefits and days off, awarded for every conceivable reason. As editorial chief, I had five weeks' holiday, which I thought was pretty good. My senior German colleagues had seven. Good luck to them. But at national level, this proliferation of holidays and benefits could lead to encounters with the *Betriebsrat*, a sort of works council. Compared with England, I thought the locals in Germany were on to a good thing. Yet if I dared to make a half-caustic comment about it to the *Betriebsrat*, I'd be told, '*Das ist unfair*, John.' Amusing to be lectured by a German on a concept so essentially British.

The Germany of the mid-seventies had a distinctly odd feel, its two halves locked immutably it seemed into conflicting political systems. At the Munich Olympics, we'd covered the two rival teams, noting the ideological zeal with which the East Germans pushed their athletes. Even now, a few years on, in West Germany, passions still ran high in some quarters about the relative merits or otherwise of the communist East. There was a sense of impermanence about the political scene. When I'd visited Berlin in the late fifties, there was no Wall. I'd simply taken a taxi from the East to the West. Now things were different. To visit our East Berlin office I had to pass, documents at the ready, through checkpoints that had now become familiar worldwide in a spate of spy films and novels. Political sentiments were divided even at our Bonn headquarters. At least two local staff were sympathetic to the East German political system, which they must clearly have thought – or hoped – would ultimately take over in the West as well.

For the time being anyway, the birthplace of Ludwig von Beethoven had reluctantly accepted the role of Federal German capital. Its new political role was emphasised by the massive and unlovely government buildings along the road to bucolic Bad Godesberg. Otherwise, the old university town retained much of its provincial charm. Luckily, Bonn had not suffered unduly from Allied bombing or artillery during the closing stages of World War Two. With its old churches and attractive university precincts, good restaurants and an abundance of cheerful wine cellars, it was a green, leafy and pleasant place to live. If it was good enough for Beethoven, it was good enough for me. Certainly less abrasive than Tel Aviv!

The River Rhine flowed alongside the eastern suburbs and the town seemed surrounded by *dorfs* (villages) – Duisdorf, Lengsdorf, Ockensdorf and Dottendorf. I found myself a nice pad in another of these. At Ippendorf, on the hill overlooking town, I rented the upper half of a roomy suburban villa owned by a charming lady called Frau Weiling and her student son Klaus. I bought myself a dark blue six-cylinder Ford Capri, which proved an excellent motorway cruiser, while using my trusty old Swedish pedal cycle at weekends to explore the attractive network of forest footpaths west of town. To this stable I later added a cute little 80cc Honda motorbike – which didn't impress serious bikers, but drew a few laughs whenever I used it for short-distance trips, as well as some envious glances from pre-teenagers.

It was a strange sequence, coming straight from a still relatively young Jewish state to the country which had almost engineered the destruction of the Jews. And not too far beneath the surface of this modern, well-organised and prosperous state, the horrors of the Third Reich still lay buried. The longest and last Nazi war crimes trial in nearby Düsseldorf had already dragged on spasmodically for nearly three years and was now limping into a fourth. For some reason, Reuters hadn't been paying too much attention to it, and even at this snail's pace, if we didn't report the proceedings soon, they'd be over. Assigning a German staffer to cover the trial was not necessarily the best option, but I took one of the colleagues along with me to help with translation. In the space of a few days, I'd have my fill of the horrors of the concentration camps.

To call these court proceedings 'odd' would be an under-statement. Surrealistic might be nearer the mark. Apart from the large cross hanging on the wall behind the judges, the general atmosphere in the wood-panelled courtroom was that of an English magistrates' court. But these were not cases of breaking and entering. Behind the judges was erected a plan of the Maidanek concentration camp. It consisted of 125 barrack blocks, seven gas chambers and a crematorium. Inside that camp, the defendants, eight balding or grey-haired men and five stocky matrons, were accused of monstrous crimes. I wrote in my first report:

> With their bankers' clothes and grandmotherly spectacles, they hardly look like people accused of mass murders. But survivors of a Nazi concentration camp say they helped hang, flog and terrorise the inmates.

One survivor, Mrs Leah Givner, had flown in from Tel Aviv. She came close to collapse when standing face to face after thirty-five years with the now stooped and grey-haired Hildegard Laechert, accused of involvement in 1,183 murders (such numbers lost all meaning after a time):

> The defendant was known to inmates as 'Bloody Brigitte'. We called her that because she only wanted to see blood. She often stood by while another guard we called 'the Hangman' carried out executions.

Another witness testified that when a young Jewish girl condemned to death spat in her face from the scaffold, Laechert kicked away the stool on which the girl stood. Asked how she recognised the defendant, Mrs Givner said, 'By her eyes and her nose. She is very fat now and rather ugly. At that time she was a very beautiful young woman who rode on a horse with a whip and boots with spurs, trying to ride down anyone who came in her way.' She added sombrely: 'I was in my late teens. The best years of my life were destroyed.'

Mrs Rivka Landau, from Tel Aviv, also formally identified Laechert, shouting, 'It's no good trying to hide, Brigitte! You can't get away.' But, I observed in my report, some people might wonder whether Mrs Landau was right. Delayed by countless defence manoeuvres, the Maidanek trial had already lasted three years. Critics were asking just when the verdicts would be delivered, and whether all the defendants would be punished. One West German newspaper said this 'farce and ritual' would make the founders of the German legal system turn in their graves.

With the whole court sometimes flying first class to Israel, Poland or New York to hear witnesses, the trial had already cost $5 million and was dragging on at $12,000 a day. In these Alice-in-Wonderland proceedings, the thirteen defendants commuted to court every day from rooming houses in town and shopped during the lunch breaks. During an adjournment – a witness was too overcome to continue – I joined defendants, camp survivors and lawyers to troop out along marbled corridors to a cafeteria downstairs. A group of Jewish witnesses sat at one table. A man that one of them had described as 'the Hangman of Maidanek' sat at the next table, a few yards away, casually sipping coffee. I couldn't help wondering how easy it would have been for one of them to knife or shoot him.

German schoolgirls sat in the public gallery, listening to these ghastly stories. Court officials told me, 'We're booked up for school visits until next April.' Teachers gave the children background history lessons during the breaks. But it was clearly difficult for the kids to connect these apparently harmless old folk with mass murder. 'She looks just like my granny,' said one schoolboy of an elderly woman in the dock.

Only one defendant, Mrs Hermine Ryan-Braunsteiner, a

German who'd married an American soldier after the war and emigrated to New York, had her passport impounded and had to report her movements to police. Meanwhile she'd taken a small apartment in Cologne. In court, she was dressed entirely in a babyish shade of pink. Survivors of the death camp said she'd had a dog called *Mensch* (Human), which she turned on prisoners – whom she called 'dogs'.

'This is Kobyla the Mare,' said Mrs Landau, standing as if mesmerised in front of the tall burly blonde. 'I can hardly believe I'm standing here and looking at this woman of whom I was so terrified! We called her the Mare because she kicked and jumped on people.'

A Polish former inmate identified Emil Launch, whom they'd known as the Angel of Death. He'd dragged a young woman by her hair into the camp crematorium, from which the witness heard a muffled shot. In a mass murder in November 1943, the court heard, thousands of Jews were driven naked into mass graves and shot to the sound of marching music. On another occasion, hundreds of children were taken to the crematorium in trailers pulled by prisoners.

As the trial ran into its third year, the Vienna-born Ryan-Braunsteiner was taken into custody after screaming 'Liar!' at an elderly Polish witness and attempting to strike her. But a higher court ruled that the angry outburst was due to 'excitement' and not an obstruction of justice. The former domestic servant, tracked down by Nazi hunter Simon Wiesenthal, spent Christmas and New Year under arrest. But, I wrote later, 'She is now back in her comfortable two-room apartment a few minutes' walk from the court.'

The trial would finally end after five and a half years. Ryan, 'The Mare', accused of murdering nearly 1,200 prisoners and complicity in the deaths of 750 others, was the only one given a life sentence. Stripped of her American citizenship, she died in 1999 at the age of seventy-nine. Laechert, jailed for twelve years, died in 1995 at the age of seventy-five. Others received terms ranging from three to twelve years. When the sentences were read out at the final hearing, the spectators' gallery rang out with cries of 'Scandal!' The defendants, it was reported (I'd left Germany by then) remained silent and apparently unperturbed.

Relatively few youngsters had been on those court visits. The ugly past would blow up again in the face of Germans in their millions the following year, when the history of the Nazi murder machine was recounted in a four-night television series which left many Germans reeling. I reported:

> The US-produced series *The Holocaust* had already been shown in a dozen countries, but in none of them can it have had the savage impact it has had here – the country where much of it happened. Record audiences estimated at up to 13 million were glued to their TV sets and the effect on the population was traumatic. German youth, who according to some critics are not taught enough about the Hitler period, have in many cases seen the enormity of Nazi crimes, albeit in fictionalised form – for the first time.

Chancellor Helmut Schmidt gave his seal of approval to the showing of *Holocaust*. 'Although some parts may be false', he said during a parliament debate, 'the film is correct and compels us to critical and moral reflection.'

The series was shown with almost religious solemnity, and each two-hour episode was followed by lengthy debate among historians, psychologists and survivors of the concentration camps, who tried to decide, How could it happen?

With 180,000 US forces still stationed in the country, it wasn't a good time for the once-mighty dollar. In the late seventies, the greenback was plummeting lower every day on the foreign exchanges. Taxi drivers in West Berlin, Munich and Frankfurt were setting their own rate of exchange as the news got steadily worse. I wrote:

> In an almost incredible reversal of fortunes in West Germany, the dollar has become bad news and US troops and civilians stationed here have become the poor relations. There are reports of senior US officers moving back to barracks from executive apartments, of American families rummaging among furniture that West German families have thrown out, and of plans by some companies to move their executives out of West Germany altogether.

The currency crisis would get even worse before it got better.

One became accustomed to this unnerving seesaw between Germany past and present. Three decades on, one couldn't imagine a more pleasant and peaceful place than Bonn. The melancholy autumnal charm of the leafy streets beside the Rhine, the simple pleasure of pedalling through the woods outside town, attending Sunday Mass at old churches ringing to the music of Bach and Beethoven, the cosy wine cellars in the marketplace where one could relax over a glass of fresh Rheinwein. It was indubitably a country of contradictions. And despite, or perhaps because of, the plight of the greenback, one of Bonn's most popular venues was the American Club, if you fancied hamburgers and a beer for a change. Stanley regularly played tennis there.

I unwisely agreed to turn out for football one Sunday afternoon with a team organised by Scott Thornton. I must have been mad. Playing with flat-heeled tennis shoes on a bone-hard pitch, my ankles took a battering. I hadn't run as much in years and had severely strained the ligaments, our local *Sportsartzt* informed me. For four days I shuffled about in bandaged feet and decided my football days were over. All I had to remember was a cross which Scott sent soaring in from the corner flag. I connected with a left foot volley which nearly went in, hitting the angle of the crossbar. It would be my last (near) achievement on the football field.

On the social side, there was an upswing in my fortunes. At an embassy cocktail party, I met a lovely young lady from the North with hair like spun gold. We would soon be skiing in France.

It was time to go in search of those famous birds. Back in 1850, in a narrow three-storey house at Pontstrasse 117, Aachen, Julius Reuter opened the small operation which became Reuters. Then, as now, economic news was of primary revenue-raising importance. Young Julius spotted that the seventy-eight-mile gap in the cable link from Brussels presented a business opportunity. Young Reuter decided carrier pigeons were the answer. They could cover the distance, messages clipped under their wings, in two hours. He and his wife and son would scan the horizon for the birds' arrival, then unfasten the message containers and distribute the news, beating the railway post by seven hours. The pigeon service only lasted two years, by which time the cable gap had been closed. But it was enough to assure him an honoured place in news history. And he had a simple way of giving all his clients an even break. He locked them in the office until he'd given everyone the latest market-moving news.

The original house in whose loft the famous pigeons landed still stands. It became a place of pilgrimage. By the time I visited Aachen it had gone through various hands and was now in the late seventies a popular student pub, appropriately called *Das Reuterhaus*. My first visit turned out to be more than a sentimental journey, for mine host, Gert Minderjahn, was a keen jazzman who'd assembled a regular group from nearby towns. Every couple of weeks thereafter I'd drive to Aachen and join the Sunday afternoon party.

It was strictly traditional jazz and primitive blues, modernists beware! The heroes were people like Big Bill Broonzy, Robert Johnson, Blind Blake and Muddy Waters. In a very relaxed atmosphere, a variety of home-grown solos and group numbers accompanied the beer drinking. I got to join in occasionally on a piano which had seen better days. We made a record, inevitably entitled 'Reuterhouse Blues'. I'm heard on one track, a hectic bit of four hands boogie with regular pianist Raphael Rieck, a local teacher. For the recording date, I played alongside clarinettist Thomas Eulenberg in a minor key blues of my own invention. It went down well enough on the day, but was deemed 'too modern' to be included in the LP. They meant that it might have come from the thirties... Nice people though, all of them, and I forgive them. Before I left Germany they presented me with a hand-produced illustrated scrapbook, commemorating a warm Anglo-German friendship.

And after a gap of 128 years, in a special ceremony which made news itself, we took the Reuter service (in German) back to Pontstrasse. My old colleague from the Middle East, Shahe Guebenlian, now Publicity Manager, flew in from London to see the printer switched on. Local press and radio were at hand. A real-life pigeon was present for the ceremony, kindly provided by the president of the local racing pigeon club, Peter Kuckelkorn. These days, he told us, a good bird could cost up to £1,000 sterling and the best of them could fly as far as 1,000 kilometres at up to 100 kph. And they rarely get lost, he added. Back in the 1850s, Julius Reuter clearly knew what he was doing.

Shortly afterwards, the civic fathers in Kassel decided to honour the town's most famous son. His current successor, Gerry Long, was invited over. They pulled out all the stops and there was big media coverage. Asked at a news conference what was the secret of being first with the news, Long succinctly replied, 'No secret. Just hard work.' Typically, he also had some polite but well-chosen words to say about the so-called 'New World Information Order'. This grandiose title referred to a half-baked concept with sinister undertones, which was being batted around at that time by some Third World politicians and others within the UN Educational, Scientific and Cultural Organisation (UNESCO). They said too much attention was given in the media to the developed world and too little to the rest. They complained that the four main news agencies controlled over 80% of the global news flow, and only reported natural disasters and military coups rather than the 'fundamental realities' – whatever those might be. Not a complaint which would have found much resonance at Reuters, whose correspondents over the decades (including myself) had slogged away in poor as well as rich countries.

The crackpot idea that some supreme world authority should monitor the world news system and share things out between the nations duly bit the dust. It was never clear who was supposed to pay for it all. I was reminded of the familiar bleat which comes up every so often in England: 'Why don't the papers print some good news?' Well, I think that normality, like goodness, doesn't need publicity, and is perhaps better left alone. And I didn't feel guilty about the slap-up lunch laid on by the town, featuring *hausgebeizster lachs, ochsenschwanzsuppe, kalbsbruckensteak* and such exotica as *kiwis flambiert mit Pernod und vanille-eis*. The menu even earned Gerry's approval – wines and all.

A much grander occasion was a visit to West Germany by Queen Elizabeth and the Duke of Edinburgh. They stayed at a moated manor house twenty-five miles from the capital. The much more famous Petersburg Castle, standing like a mediaeval fortress over the Rhine, would have been preferred, but wrangling between its owners and the government had delayed restoration work. As an old hand in the newspaper game, I was intrigued when the visitors chose to visit the town of Mainz, where they saw the printing press developed by Johannes Gutenberg, the inventor of movable metal type back in the fifteenth century. It was the forerunner of what they'd be using five centuries later at my, and every other, local paper. Their visit to Mainz provided a brief talking point when I was lucky enough to chat with the Queen on the royal yacht *Britannia* before they left Germany from Bremerhaven. Both ship and waterfront were ablaze with lights. I was one of two British journalists invited to attend the reception, the other the *Daily Telegraph*'s Bonn correspondent. When my turn came on the receiving line, I was quite impressed by Her Majesty's apparent familiarity with the news business. She asked practical questions about our operation in Germany and I found her pleasant and easy to talk to. I couldn't help recalling the small boy who'd stood by the roadside in industrial Lancashire forty years earlier, waving a Union Jack as the previous Queen's limousine swept by.

The Munich massacres hadn't ended Germany's terrorism problem. Home-grown fanatics had taken over where the Palestinians left off. Their declared goal: to bring down West Germany's (to their mind) ultra-materialistic society.

Student radicals, alienated from parents who'd supported the Nazis, tacitly or otherwise, were on the move. They didn't like the smug materialism, as they saw it, of the post-war Federal Republic. They knew ex-Nazis held positions at national and local level. Revolution was in the air among the young. Other European cities were witnessing violent protests too about American foreign policy in south-east Asia. In West Germany, the firebrands were not downtrodden peasants or residents of unlawfully occupied territories, but the sons and daughter of well-to-do families. Their philosophy, spawned mainly on university campuses, contained few specifics, but reflected a generalised discontent with smug materialism, as they saw it. Their aims, to combat racism and imperialism and further women's liberation, mirrored slogans doing the rounds at Western universities. Some expressed support for what they considered a superior political system in East Germany – which none of these fiery students, of course, had experienced first-hand. They couldn't properly be called leftist, though they supported a mixture of left-wing causes. Germany's own communist parties disowned them.

Co-founders of the movement were Andreas Baader, a high school dropout and perhaps the only non-intellectual among the group, and Ulrike Meinhof, philosophy graduate and daughter of an art historian. Baader had been involved in anti-state activities since the late sixties, when he was arrested for setting off firebombs in Frankfurt department stores. Meinhof met him through her articles in the magazine *Konkret* protesting against the Vietnam War, then quit journalism to start life as an urban guerrilla. Despite the catchy title bestowed by the mass media – the movement's own members called it the 'Red Army Faction' – Ulrike's involvement was relatively small. But she'd laid down some of its aims in a book *The Urban Guerrilla Concept*.

In the ugliest and most cynically planned of a spate of killings, twenty-six-year-old Susanne Albrecht, a lawyer's daughter described by the authorities as an anarchist, called as a friend of the family with a bunch of roses at the home of a leading banker, Jürgen Ponto. Then she and her friends tried to kidnap him and, when he resisted, shot him dead. A few months later, the president of the West German Employers' Association, Hans Martin Schleyer, a former SS officer under the Nazis, was abducted. Five masked assailants shot and killed his driver and three policemen. A letter arrived at the Federal Government office demanding the release of eleven detainees.

It was the involvement of so many young women that had Germans particularly troubled. The Conservative daily *Die Welt* said, 'Women are becoming more violent, murdering, robbing banks, planning bomb raid and kidnappings.' I reported:

> In the violent world of the urban guerrilla, German women have certainly established parity with their menfolk. Almost without exception they are intelligent, and members of well-to-do families.

Sociologists tried to make some sense of it all. Germany's 'Daily Telegraph', *Die Welt*, said it was intolerable that the state should be challenged by these 'gun-girls'. Conservative opposition spokesmen blamed what they called the 'mental morass' of the universities for the corruption of both men and women from solid home backgrounds. Even the novelist Heinrich Böll, customarily sympathetic to left-wing causes, and a critic of the new affluent West German society, lamented that 'three decades after Hitler's death, students are again being taught to glorify murder as a political weapon'. These killings were 'cold-blooded, premeditated murders'. The fifty-nine-year-old author admitted he had underestimated the threat from the Baader-Meinhof group. The other leading German novelist, Günter Grass, leapt into the fray, talking of a witch-hunt of writers and clerics who in the past had shown some sympathy for critics of West German society. The fierce intellectual debate would continue for months.

The series of attacks included the kidnapping of a Christian Democrat politician in West Berlin and an armed raid on the West German Embassy in Stockholm, in which two diplomats died. Public anger mounted as the self-appointed social reformers assassinated West Germany's chief prosecutor, Siegfried Buback, his driver and his bodyguard in the town of Karlsruhe. I wrote:

> The triple murder signified for some commentators here a new trend – that of violence for its own sake. In this latest action, no attempt was made to take anyone hostage in return for money, political concessions or the release of colleagues from jail.

In an arrogantly worded letter circulated to news organisations, the group said that Buback – described by Chancellor Helmut Schmidt as a staunch and dedicated enemy of terrorism – had been 'executed'.

Other group members, branded 'dreamworld revolutionaries' by the prosecutors, admitted setting off bomb blasts at US Army bases and police stations. The threat seemed to be growing. Chancellor Schmidt's government warned against public hysteria. But the public had clearly had enough. Opinion polls showed nearly half the nation was in favour of reviving the death penalty – a big upswing from previous years, when the German nation had been trying to live down the horrors of Nazi days.

Chancellor Helmut Schmidt set up a crisis committee, hoping to win time. The crisis escalated internationally as a Boeing 737 Lufthansa airliner bound for Frankfurt with eighty-two passengers and a crew of five was hijacked. The five-day marathon which followed would test Reuters' reporting resources. When the plane landed in Rome for refuelling, the hijackers repeated their demands, plus the release of Palestinian prisoners in Turkey and a ransom of $15 million. When Bonn refused, the hijackers forced the pilot to fly on successively to Larnaca, Dubai, Aden (where the plane's captain was shot dead and dumped on the runway) and finally Mogadishu, the Somalian capital.

Logistically, it was one of the most difficult stories we'd ever covered as the action switched from one country to another. Our correspondents in Beirut, Rome, Cyprus, Dubai, Bahrain, Cairo, Nairobi and Abdu Dhabi – as well as we ourselves in Germany – were all working round the clock. The marathon ended in the small hours of 19 October, when a crack German team set up in the aftermath of Munich flew secretly to Mogadishu, landed in darkness and disabled the hijackers with stun grenades before gunning them down and releasing all remaining hostages.

The boil had been lanced. Baader and one of his colleagues, obviously realising they'd been beaten, were later found dead in their cells with gunshot wounds to the head; another founder member of the group, Gudrun Ensslin, was found hanged. An official inquiry decided it was collective suicide, though this was disputed. Shortly afterwards, in an obviously vicious act of revenge, Schleyer's body was found in an abandoned car trunk in Germany. In a bombastic statement to the French newspaper *Libération*, his killers declared, 'The struggle has only begun.'

But they were wrong. Germany's biggest crisis since World War Two had ended with victory for the government. Minor attacks gradually petered out in the nineties, but, for the young terrorists, the questionable glory days were over. The Baader-Meinhof group would not be formally disbanded until 1998, but the ramifications of the story would linger on. Thirty years later, in the summer of 2009, Verena Becker, now fifty-seven, was arrested on suspicion of involvement in the murder of the chief federal prosecutor. DNA evidence was found on a letter in which the group claimed responsibility for Buback's killing. As for my front-page story at the height of the emergency, I quote a letter to the *Evening Standard* from our Chief News Editor at the time: 'We were glad to see Reuter's daylead on the Schleyer killing made the splash lead today. But didn't the story rate a credit for Reuters, if not a byline for Chadwick?' Well, you can't win 'em all. Working for Reuters was often an anonymous job.

In an increasingly edgy political atmosphere following the TV screening of the *Holocaust* film, the government quickly put down claims by former Chancellor Willy Brandt that neo-Nazism was growing in West Germany. Brandt claimed that Nazi ideas were being 'publicly flaunted' up and down the country and the government did nothing about it. He said reports from local Social Democrats indicated a growth in such gatherings, a claim hotly disputed by Chancellor Schmidt. The opposition Conservatives were also furious at the allegations, saying they only did damage to the country's image abroad.

The furore came in the aftermath of another political bombshell, the spectacular escape of former war criminal and SS colonel Herbert Kappler from Italy. The wartime Gestapo boss in Rome had been serving a life sentence for the 1944 Ardentine Caves massacre of 233 Italian hostages. His wife, Anneliese, managed to spirit him out of a military hospital in Rome by lowering him with ropes from the third floor. On their return to the village of Soltau, the youth wing of West Germany's extreme right-wing National Democratic Party marked the occasion by parading in black leather uniforms outside the Kapplers' home.

It was the last thing the government needed after the furore over the *Holocaust* film. I reported:

> With a two-hour film about Hitler doing big business throughout the country and the faces of Hitler and his associates staring from magazine covers at every news-stand, the casual visitor to West

Germany might well feel the populace has been overcome by a Nazi nostalgia wave.

But, I added:

This is hardly borne out by a close look. The treatment of Hitler and his friends is largely documentary and far from flattering. Nevertheless, some fear that the 'Hitler Wave' in the media, the exploits of a few extremists and the publicity over the Kappler escape are combining to give a false picture of the country abroad.

The biggest threat to the country, asserted opposition parliamentarian Willi Weiskirch, was from young left-wing extremists, not remnants of the Nazis. And I think the vast majority of Germans would undoubtedly have agreed. Kappler survived only six months before dying of cancer in his own bed – his wife's declared aim in carrying out her daring rescue operation. According to evidence given at the 1947 tribunal, troops under Kappler's command had herded the Italian prisoners together, to be massacred with machine guns, hand grenades and flame throwers. Kappler's wife said after his death, 'He was only obeying orders.' Where did I hear that before?

I was to see quite a bit of Gerry Long, for many years a Germanophile. At the end of World War Two he served with the British Army in Berlin, helping to set up the post-war German press. He was undeniably quite an eccentric. But, however blunt and at times uncommunicative Gerry could be, I never found him in the least intimidating. Perhaps northern Englishmen have thick skins and know how to put up with each other's foibles. When his secretary rang every few months to inform me he'd soon be visiting I knew what to expect.

To meet him at the airport (I'd learned since Copenhagen days!) there was a regular drill. A young man from the garage next door to the Reuterhaus brought out their most glittering black Mercedes and I sat beside him to the airport. There he'd don a respectful chauffeur's cap for the return journey. While coming back into town I sat in the back with Gerry. First stop was not the office or his hotel but the noted Maternus Restaurant in Bad

Godesberg, an establishment which had for years attracted many prominent parliamentarians and journalists within its oak-panelled walls, including ex-Chancellor Willy Brandt, long a carouser, and Bavaria's Conservative leader Franz-Josef Strauss. It had long been one of the MD's favourite eating places too and, as we seated ourselves in a private corner, proprietor Ria Alzen would greet him effusively as a long-time regular as she handed us the menus. Having chosen what to eat, it was the turn of the wine list.

Though I was theoretically hosting the occasion, I'd hand the list to Gerry, who always thanked me effusively for giving him the privilege.

After lunch – and they were usually lengthy – the next stop was quite often his dentist, which seemed to be the immediate purpose of his visit. 'There are no good dentists in England,' declared the Reuter boss. At some stage during his two-day stay, he'd put in a brief appearance at the editorial offices too. Later he got the fitness bug. He'd located a North German spa he liked the sound of, and there I'd book him for a three- or four-day stay. I was also asked by his London secretary to provide him with a bicycle for some road exercise. My own secretary, Nina Fohren, dug out a bike shop in the area, which promised to deliver the necessary machine. The proprietor, clearly wishing to do his best for the prestigious visitor, wanted to know the client's inside leg measurements, which necessitated one of my more offbeat calls to London. Gerry's secretary came back with the requisite information. Well, it made a change from writing stories, but I sometimes wondered whether this was really what I should be doing... Not for me to reason why.

I'd got to know and like Gerry back in Copenhagen days. And he'd given me full backing when deciding after Arye Wallenstein's death that a non-Israeli should now be given the Tel Aviv bureau (some Israeli quarters lamented at the time that they had 'lost' Reuters). I never had any problems getting on with him, though he was notoriously moody. That's when his moustache began to bristle.

Three or four times a year, I'd visit our office in East Berlin. Not a very engaging place at that time, once you'd got beyond the architectural glories from the past along the Unter den Linden. Now there was a rash of ugly rectangular post-war office blocks, and beyond those things further deteriorated. I'd met the young Mark Brayne in London before he began his assignment in East Germany, and immediately took to this tall and engaging young man. He and his German wife coped cheerfully with life in the combined Reuter office and flat. It faced a blank high wall in a dreary street which reminded me of the industrial Lancashire of my youth. We seldom kept correspondents there (who once included *Day of the Jackal* author Frederick Forsyth) for more than a year or two.

I admired Brayne and his successor, Mark Wood, both fluent German speakers, for the good-natured enthusiasm with which they tackled a difficult job. Working in a communist state, where foreigners' movements were closely watched, had its perils. From Bonn, on the other side of the Wall, I could do little more than offer psychological support. Over the years, both Marks just buckled down to the job, and I can't remember we were ever beaten on a story. Brayne and his wife were keen musicians and found that a rewarding outlet in this challenging environment was to join a highly regarded church choir. There wasn't much even the communists could do with Johann Sebastian Bach! Of art too, beyond the Wall, there was plenty, old and modern, and with Mark's help I acquired some attractive old prints showing Berlin the way it used to look before two world wars and a Russian takeover. A couple of them hang on the walls here in Worcestershire.

The Braynes also took me to a few good restaurants which had survived all the political changes. But restless undercurrents were apparent. Once, we'd dined at an attractive little place equalling anything on the Western side.

'Well,' I observed to Mark as we finished our dessert, with the waiter hovering close by, 'I'm afraid I have to get back to West Berlin.' (One wasn't allowed to stay in East Berlin overnight.)

The waiter, overhearing, observed with caustic wit, 'He's *sorry* he has to get back to West Berlin, he says! Listen, I've been trying to get there for years and I still haven't made it!'

It came as no surprise to me later when the BBC snapped up

Brayne as their man in Berlin. He proved an excellent reporter for the Corporation there and later in China, particularly in his 'Our Own Correspondent' pieces, delivered in one of the most pleasant voices on the BBC. My contacts with his successor, Mark Wood, were over a much shorter period, but there was no doubt either of his energy and enthusiasm, essential characteristics of a Reuter man. Then one day I got an unexpected phone call in Bonn to say he'd been invited to become our European Editor. Mark, then a relative junior, was uncertain how to react and very politely asked my opinion. Was this not a bit too early, he asked, and wasn't he too young for the job? While my immediate reaction was much the same as his own, some odd things were beginning to happen at Reuters, and the only advice I could give him was, 'Take it.' He did an excellent job in his new post and we remained good colleagues up to the time of my retirement.

Germany now had other worries, and these would be mirrored in other parts of Europe in the decades to come. I reported:

> A huge Turkish ghetto is developing in the shadow of the ugly Berlin Wall. In Cologne, an Islamic centre has revived popular fears about alien cultures, and in the cities of Frankfurt and Hamburg, political activists have been involved in violence.

A harbinger of things to come, it proved, and a government report in the late eighties disclosed that one West Berliner in ten was now a foreigner. The so-called 'guest workers' and their families numbered close to a quarter million in a city whose overall population was continuing to decline – as it would until the Wall came down. Every third child born in Berlin was a foreigner and urgent measures were taken to stem a wave of Pakistani families who'd suddenly started flooding in through Communist East Berlin – where the authorities were only too happy to pass another expensive headache to the West.

In an airlift costing millions of marks, the West Berlin authorities flew thousands of them home. City officials said, 'We have enough social and educational problems with the foreign workers already here.' In another comment to be echoed in several other European countries, including Britain, in the years to come, a conservative politician, calling for integration efforts, spoke sardonically of his countrymen's attitude to the guest workers crowded into shabby blocks of flats near the Berlin Wall.

'Everyone knows they are needed as a labour force – but heaven forbid that one should have them as neighbours. It is better that the servants should sleep in the servants' quarters.'

The cultural gap was widest in the case of the Muslim community. Twenty years before similar issues hit the headlines in England, I reported:

> Germans, affected by stories they read of Islamic fundamentalism in the Middle East, are reacting with alarm to reports of concepts of crime and punishment being taught to Turkish workers' children here.

Social Democrat politicians were protesting about an Islamic culture centre in Cologne, where Turkish children, they said, were learning 'fascist' doctrines in the Koran class.

And the Arabs were fighting their own internecine wars from the comfort of Western Europe. From Aachen, I wrote:

> The slim minaret at the Islamic centre here contrasts with the spires of the cathedral where Charlemagne was crowned. In a third-floor apartment in a quiet suburb of the university town, on the eve of the Muslim fast of Ramadan, I talked to the leader of Syria's Moslem Brotherhood. I knew from Cairo days that Nasser had dissolved the movement in 1954 and executed several of its leaders. Now it seemed to be alive and thriving, and from this quiet suburb in the heart of Europe, Isam Attar, a quiet-spoken, grey-bearded man in a sober lounge suit, was distributing leaflets calling on his countrymen to overthrow the government in Damascus. Of recent killings in the Syrian capital, he said, 'I can understand people, especially young people, resorting to violence when their efforts in a just cause are frustrated.'

His comments, read again today, are eerily similar to those made by Muslim leaders in England.

The old Reuter headquarters in Germany was now bursting at the seams. It was time to find a new home, which manager Iain Smith and I eventually decided should be in a considerably less charming but more practical post-war building just down the road, almost opposite government offices. Quite coincidentally it was at the corner of Reuterstrasse (no connection to the famous Julius), a main artery into town. It was clear, after the advent of the German-language service and the explosive growth of economic reporting, that we needed a new video-editing system. In typical English fashion, a so-called expert at head office – probably just a couple of chapters ahead of the rest of us in the relatively new computer world – came up with what he called a 'cheap and cheerful' solution, which we turned down. Instead, we invited to Bonn two young men making a big name for themselves in this growing industry. They stayed for a week, during which we showed them all our editorial needs and asked them to come up with a solution, with which we were much impressed. Shortly afterwards the new system was successfully installed. The young men were the founders of Finland's now world-renowned Nokia. So much for cheap-and-cheerful solutions – a twentieth-century British disease.

My son was now in his late teens, and his mother reported that he wasn't the most assiduous student in Sweden. We decided, much to his delight, to send him off to the American School at Leysin, Switzerland – which made it easier for me in Germany to keep contact. We had regular Sunday evening phone chats, and, whenever I could, I flew down there. He got on extremely well with pupils from many countries. As well as becoming completely fluent in English, either British or American according to the company, and quite useful in French and German, he developed a confident ease of manner which would greatly help his later career. Pupils were mainly from well-to-do parents from East and West, prominent Germans and Americans, and Middle East millionaires. I was almost certainly the least affluent dad among them.

When I first dropped him off at the school one dark Sunday evening, he looked so lost and lonely, standing on the school steps, that I wept on the drive back down the mountain. Luckily, one of the wheels froze up and locked solid, bringing me to my senses. Peter quickly settled in at Leysin and became a member of the three-man ski team which competed against teams from similar colleges in Switzerland and Austria. He continued to give his father advice on getting down the more precipitous slopes at Flaine, the French ski resort south of Geneva where I'd bought a small studio. When – perhaps rashly, in view of my limited experience – I tried to follow him down a steep black run ominously called *Le Diamant Noir*, which he'd descended with fluent ease, I failed to complete a very tight turn and sped thirty yards down the slope on my back, skis in the air; he was very solicitous.

Back on the news scene, my career suddenly seemed headed in the wrong direction. The first hint came when Gerry Long, arriving for one of his periodic visits, advised me as we were descending the airport escalator to 'watch out' for two editorial executives, in London, who he said were 'after' me. Was some jiggery-pokery going on? If so, he was the boss, and if he didn't like it he could surely quash it. But for whatever reasons, simply boredom, I imagine, he didn't. I was not consulted, simply instructed out of the blue to move to Tehran, hardly a step upwards after seven difficult years already spent in the Near East. I declined the post and with support from others in London became Chief Correspondent in Switzerland. My second in command took over in Bonn, where my faithful secretary, Nina Fohren, had often told me – and I'd scoffed – that 'he is not your friend'. Shortly thereafter, I was in my Ford Capri, once again Geneva-bound.

Well, the burghers of Bonn finally got their town back. Maybe they thought it would never happen. But almost a decade after leaving the country, I was flying back to Germany in mid-November 1989 to join the Reuter team covering the top political story of the decade – the end of the Wall. Our people in Berlin were reporting the near madness which followed the break-up. In their eagerness for a weekend in the West, East Germans were storming dozens of special trains and jamming roads in the north of the country. They were rolling into Bavaria in their ancient fume-belching East German Trabants along an autobahn built in Hitler's time, abandoned for half a century and now reopened to help with the flood. The Transport Ministry said the situation at some train stations was 'barely under control, with passengers left behind'. Frustrated families sat on railway lines in protest when the trains ran out of carriages to take them to see relatives and go shopping in the West. Stores around the country did a roaring trade as luxury-starved visitors spent their 100-mark West German 'welcome money'. Soon, three million people had crossed the once militarily controlled border up and down the country. West Berlin's biggest and plushest department store said the most popular items with visitors were tropical fruits, coffee and bananas. But at least one visitor to Lübeck in north Germany, astonished at the stacks of bananas laid on for the East Germans, snapped petulantly, 'What do you think we are – monkeys?'

Meanwhile I'd been asked to do some news features from Bonn, still the seat of government. Excitement? I reported:

> In the sleepy little West German capital, you'd never believe a political revolution has been happening in Berlin. While crowds surge around the crumbling Berlin Wall and millions from both sides of the divided city celebrate the end of twenty-eight years of East–West separation, it's been pretty much as normal in Bonn. Ferries criss-cross the Rhine, students cycle sedately to the University along streets scattered with autumn leaves, and in the market square housewives in plant pot hats have started their Christmas shopping. 'I expected to see dancing in the streets,' one puzzled American visitor told me. 'It's just as if nothing has happened at all.'

The Rhineside town of 291,000 people had never been more than a capital by accident. It was chosen in preference to Frankfurt, the country's bustling financial centre, on the casting vote of West German's first Chancellor, Konrad Adenauer. He lived just across the river, and the story I'd always heard was that Adenauer, a keen gardener, wasn't willing to leave his precious roses behind and move upstream to Frankfurt. After Bonn became the federal capital, its townspeople enjoyed big federal subsidies for theatre, operas and concerts. But such was the local pride that residents of outlying villages, finally amalgamated amid grumbling into Greater Bonn, still refused to be known as 'Bonners' and preserved their own accents. Good luck to them, I'd always thought.

It was hardly surprising, I reported to London, if townspeople now declined to get too excited about what was happening in Berlin. I wrote:

> If Germany is ever reunified and Berlin once again becomes the capital, there is little doubt that Bonn could happily return to being a sedate university town – which happens to be the birthplace of Beethoven.

And so it would be.

Chapter 17
IN THE COUNTRY OF WILLIAM TELL,
SOME WOMEN STILL DIDN'T HAVE THE VOTE

'If I'd told friends in California I was going to a Specialised Agency, they'd think I meant a massage parlour,' declared a newly arrived American Ambassador to Geneva.

Beautiful country, Switzerland. A bit odd, though, in some ways. A spic and span place with the world's highest standard of living. Lovely countryside. Skiing in winter. The trains never ran late. No one threw litter on the streets. But they still, it seemed, hadn't given all their women the vote. And, ironically, this last bastion of male domination was the place where back in the fourteenth century Switzerland's stroppy hero, William Tell, refused to doff his hat to an Austrian bailiff and had to shoot that famous apple off his small son's head.

In opposing the Habsburg Empire, the region of Uri has been called the cradle of Swiss democracy, and its men revolutionaries. Yet, in the early 1980s, I was obliged to report that the men of the village of Altdorf had once again turned down proposals to give their women the vote. One typical husband told the newspapers, 'The woman should look after the house and the children. She has no time left for politics.'

Swiss feminists regularly complained that schoolbooks still depicted women alternatively as stay-at-home mothers, shop assistants, secretaries or waitresses. They'd only recently got the vote at national level – about half a century after the United States. And as one Swiss feminist writer commented acidly, 'That was only because we were beginning to look silly in the eyes of the world – and the Swiss don't like that.' It would take still another decade for women in those crusty old villages to get a voice in local affairs.

Paradoxically, Switzerland was host to a myriad international organisations dealing with world problems and the rights of minorities. It was the European headquarters of the United Nations – of which organisation it was, however, not yet a member. It valued its status as a neutral nation and, at the time of writing, had still had the good sense to stay out of the European Union. There are quite enough bureaucrats already in Geneva.

Switzerland was full of those 'specialised agencies' that the American diplomat was referring to. A bewildering world of acronyms. UNICEF, GATT and UNCTAD. Not to mention WHO, ICRC, ILO and UEFA. And there were many more, operating from the cities of Geneva, Zurich and Berne. Their activities all had to be covered – and humanised. And outside these august bodies there were many other good news stories. Geneva itself was a synonym for world diplomacy and peace. This had all started after World War One, but in the eighties the peace drive was still limping along a bit.

Take the UN Disarmament Committee. The afternoon I dropped in, the atmosphere in the lofty debating chamber was relaxed, almost drowsy. Delegates from forty nations slumped over leather-topped tables, shifting papers, twisting a pencil, sipping a glass of water. A delegate from Sweden, one of the leading scourges of the big powers, was sombrely listing the danger of a science-fiction-style nuclear war in outer space. He urged the United States and the Soviet Union to act quickly to prevent it.

Behind brass rails in the visitors' gallery, four shaven-headed Buddhist monks in saffron robes and tennis shoes listened intently. They were from Japan, which had seen the only atomic bombs dropped on people so far. In this comfortable Swiss setting, warm sunshine slanting in through the high windows, the ultimate nightmare appeared remote. Neither global catastrophe nor treaties to prevent it seemed likely in the near future. The Committee had already been meeting for twenty years, but the big arms agreements were settled outside the Committee by the superpowers.

I tried to tell it like it was. The ambience was perhaps as important as the words. On the walls, huge murals depicted the struggle for freedom of the world's toiling masses and oppressed peoples. On the debating floor, the mood was more like that of a gentlemen's club. Whatever perfidies Western or Soviet delegates might accuse each other of, they never called each other less than 'Distinguished Delegate'.

Post-war disarmament talks had been going on under one name or another for thirty years in that conference chamber – far longer than any play on Broadway or in London's West End, one delegate observed sardonically. And they had developed a certain style of their own.

Between debates, ambassadors from East and West, Asia and Africa entertained each other regularly in elegant apartments and country villas around Geneva. The business talk at such cocktails tended to be about 'ad hoc committees', 'subsidiary bodies' and other arcane procedures. Ask how the Americans and Soviets were actually getting on with reducing medium-range nuclear missiles in Europe and you might be told: 'That's a bilateral matter – not really much to do with us.' And, anyway, the Soviet-American negotiations had been suspended for the moment, each side saying the other didn't want to get down to hard bargaining.

In the always polite setting of the Disarmament Committee, Argentina's Julio Carasales gently chided the newly elected Japanese Chairman of the Month for saying that to save time he would do without the ritual statements of congratulations. 'This is something traditional among diplomats,' Carasales protested. On the actual agenda, he admitted, 'We have been discussing the complete prohibition of nuclear weapon tests for years and we are further away than ever.' On 'negative assurances' (Disarmament Committee jargon for the guarantees given by nuclear weapon states not to use them against countries that don't have them), he restated the fairly obvious fact: 'The only real guarantee is the elimination of nuclear weapons themselves.' But, as many of its members privately agreed, the Committee stood little chance of achieving that.

Then someone put the cat among the pigeons. In understandable despair at all this, Sweden's Sigvard Eklund, director of the International Atomic Energy Agency (IAEA), startled the diplomats by suggesting the solution might be to deliberately set off a nuclear bomb.

'Maybe it is the only way to convince the world of the danger of atomic weapons,' he said. 'It would give the news media the world over an idea of the destructive power of the new nuclear weapons and create massive public reaction against nuclear weapon states.'

Eklund's bizarre suggestion had those drowsy delegates sitting up in their seats – but it was not ridiculed. The American Ambassador said the proposal couldn't be dismissed out of hand, but added prosaically that such a blast might conflict with the 1963 treaty banning nuclear tests in the atmosphere, outer space and underwater. Britain's Douglas Hurd, possibly hoping to set a few worried delegates' minds at rest, suggested soothingly that the Swedish delegate had simply made 'a vivid point rather than a practical proposition'.

Reporting such proceedings, I figured that a lightly sceptical tone was about as far as one could go within Reuter limits. A leading American newspaper got it right when it headlined my story: 'Geneva Delegates Adopt Leisurely Approach to Warding off Armageddon'.

As if to underline the apparent futility of it all, Britain's ninety-two-year-old Nobel Prizewinner Lord Noel-Baker arrived to open an exhibition marking the fiftieth anniversary of the first World Disarmament Conference in Geneva, in which he'd taken a leading role. The former British minister laid the blame on the big powers and accused his own country years ago of scuttling US President Herbert Hoover's proposals for a complete weapons ban. He recalled, 'Germany said "Yes" to Hoover, the Soviet Union said "Yes", Italy said "Yes". But the British Admiralty said battleships were more precious than rubies.'

He was given a great ovation. But the historical exhibits on show – yellowing letters of former statesmen and copies of long-forgotten peace plans – were like sad tombstones. One biting cartoon prominently displayed at the exhibition depicted an international civil servant clattering on with her typewritten report while shells were flying in both directions overhead. 'Quiet, please,' she was protesting, 'I can't get on with my work.' A British newspaper cartoon from 1934 showed a stranded airship labelled 'Disarmament'. The caption read, 'Despite all the hot air, the balloon refuses to rise.' And, as I now reported from the UN (Geneva branch) in the eighties, the balloon remained stranded.

A worldwide wave of enthusiasm greeted the League of Nations, precursor of the UN, on its foundation in Geneva in 1923. Crowds massed in the streets, church bells rang and a dedication service was held in the cathedral. The biggest collection ever of world statesmen assembled in Switzerland for the occasion. My next-door neighbour in the *New York Times* office, Victor Lusinchi, was one of a few who remembered the old League, set up by the victorious allies after World War One.

'It was a different world, more relaxed and leisurely,' Vic told me. 'Some of the diplomats would travel down to Geneva from Paris on an overnight train. Hotels along the lake would be packed with world statesmen. The international set of the period liked to be seen in Geneva during assembly sessions, mingling with diplomats and their ladies in the salons of Geneva's leading hotels. I remember seeing the French Foreign Minister, Pierre Laval [who would be executed as a Nazi collaborator in 1945], strolling over the Mont Blanc bridge, the Aga Khan eating at a nearby table in the Globe restaurant, and Anthony Eden [then Britain's Foreign Secretary] strolling into a press conference in tennis clothes, coming straight from the courts. It was easier to meet them in those days.'

Geneva seemed a natural place for the brave new venture. Neutral Switzerland had long been an asylum for political refugees, scholars and artists, including Richard Wagner. The German composer arrived in town after taking part in an 1848 uprising in Saxony. Even before the League, Geneva's international role had been established by the founding of the Red Cross movement in 1864. The International Labour Organisation was set up in 1901. After World War Two, a host of other bodies ranging from the World Council of Churches to the World Wildlife Fund had opened up offices there. So had 150 other international organisations. We at Reuters did our best to cover them all.

Shortly after I arrived as Chief Correspondent in Switzerland, Geneva celebrated the sixtieth birthday of the League, which effectively died when the Germans marched into Poland and the

Russians attacked Finland. Its tarnished reputation was accurately portrayed at that time in Geneva's satiric magazine *Pillori*. Cartoons portrayed Adolf Hitler as the villain of the piece, pulling out the vital membership card that made the whole fragile stack collapse. Italian dictator Benito Mussolini was shown crowning himself ruler of Ethiopia after the Italian invasion, while Emperor Haile Selassie crept sadly out of Geneva after seeking help in vain from the League. By the late thirties, the League was being depicted in the magazine as a collection of waxwork dummies called 'Geneva's Madame Tussaud's'.

Now, in another post-war world, there were high hopes for the new United Nations. The intentions were impeccable, but some of the machinery seemed decidedly flawed. Like its big brother in New York, the Geneva operation seemed to me, after a few months covering its multitudinous committees, like some great machine churning out endless reports which few people read, and fewer acted on. Innumerable meetings which seldom reached a conclusion. It was hard to breathe journalistic life into some of these activities, worthy as they might be.

I've never been a great lover of bureaucracies, local or multinational, and today's European Union is a sad example of the latter. The political conferences at the Palais des Nations droned away steadily day after day, year after year, usually getting nowhere. Other less-reported UN bodies and church-based organisations in and around Geneva seemed to me to be doing much more practical work in Africa and other parts of the developing world.

The statistics reaching Geneva were horrendous. Millions of children around the world, a UN body on slavery was told, were working as virtual slaves or living by their wits as thieves, beggars, street traders or prostitutes. A ten-year-old boy in the Dominican Republic had been captured and sold to a sugar mill for the going rate of five pesos (then around $3.50). In Brazil, a teenage prostitute told investigators, 'I can make in twenty minutes with a gringo what my parents make in a month – and it's easy work.'

A child thief in Bogota described how thieving was done a century later but still much as in Dickens's *Oliver Twist*. 'The best way to steal a watch is to stand by the traffic lights in the rush hour and look for some fool with his window down and his hands on the steering wheel. You wait until the lights are changing, then whip his watch and run.'

Child workers and beggars were on the increase, the investigators reported, ranging from street singers and fire-eaters in Mexico City to nine-year-olds working in shoe factories. Such matters seemed to me as important to cover as arms negotiations that got nowhere.

All these organisations, whose staff and visiting delegates brought a great deal of money into Switzerland, provided work for close on 200 journalists. There was also UNCTAD (the UN's Conference on Trade and Development) and the dreaded GATT (General Agreement on Trade and Tariffs), which dealt with world trade disputes. We were lucky whenever veteran Reuter journalist Ronnie Farquhar agreed to plough through some heavyweight GATT document and dredge a story out of it.

Reporting from the Palais was a comfortable if occasionally tedious job, from which some correspondents never wander. The bigger organisations like Reuters or the American agencies had their own offices, however cramped. Others, including the BBC, made do with a desk in the general Press Room. For good or bad, the real action took place not in the UN's hallowed halls, but inside the delegations of the two big powers, the United States and the Soviet Union. Whenever these two missions called a briefing, everybody jumped. The US Mission was up the hill, the Soviet Mission just across the road. There was intense competition between the wire services to be first with any words of wisdom from either of the combatants. The Americans were considerably more forthcoming, but the Russians kept such a tight wrap on their policies that the slightest hint of change would quickly be seized on.

Putting diplomatic utterances into intelligible English was like straightening out barbed wire. 'Dip-Speak', I used to call it. US President Ronald Reagan was once scheduled to make an announcement in Washington about nuclear weapons. As American disarmament delegates were meeting the Russians in Geneva that day, I asked if their news release would be similar to that issued in Washington. 'Well, John,' the press attaché said, 'I think you can expect that it will strongly parallel the President's characterisation of the situation.' Ouch!

It was a ten-minute walk back to the Palais from the Soviet mission. I used a Honda minibike to solve the problem. I'd spotted a UN side entrance directly across the road. I'd park the little bike there and, once the news was out, leap aboard and speed through a maze of paths inside the Palais compound back to the Reuter office. In the era before mobile phones, nobody could be quicker. There was one occasion, though, when it didn't work. Our Diplomatic Editor, (the late) Sidney Weiland, always so hyped up over world events that he was affectionately known as Sizzling Sid, was over from London for US–Soviet talks. After lengthy diplomatic wrangling, all we needed to wrap up the story was a 'Yes' or 'No' from the Russians. Sidney wrote the story in advance, with alternative intros. My role was just to give the go-ahead after the Soviet news conference. I arrived back at the Palais on the motorbike and ran down the corridor to the Reuter office. Alas, in his haste to get the story to London, Sidney pressed the wrong button and what should have been a five-minute beat turned into a dead heat with Associated Press. I haven't the foggiest idea what the story was about. I'm sure it seemed very important at the time.

World crises linger on for decades, sports news is more ephemeral, but there's a lot of that to cover too. Switzerland is home to several world sports bodies, including the International Olympic Committee, headquartered in the country's unlikely little capital, Berne. This, and the European Football Union (UEFA) in Zurich, were usually covered by our energetic and impressively named local correspondent, Ivar von Roulach. I'd half expected a tall, blonde-bearded German-Swiss aristocrat. Instead I was shaking hands with a small, smiling and very friendly man from Ceylon whose name stemmed from colonial days. He knew the sports scene backwards. Clients would hover over their teleprinters as the draw for the European Football Cup was announced. We'd have the news to subscribers within a minute.

Equally time-critical were the regular conferences of OPEC,

the organisation of oil-producing countries. The price of oil, and the quantity of it being pumped from the fields, were becoming top news – and of course remain so. Every few months, markets around the world were hanging on what the OPEC ministers would decide. The delegates regularly met at Geneva's Intercontinental Hotel. There, to save valuable seconds in transmitting the news, we'd persuaded the management to let us set up a Reuter teleprinter just off the main lobby.

For days during the conferences, the hotel was crammed with reporters waiting to besiege delegates as they left the meetings. I could never get too excited myself about the price of oil, but these were vital decisions for the market.

London required blanket cover. Even the vaguest of hints from oil ministers, as they emerged, on prices or quantities had to be put on the wire post-haste. The frenetic scene was perhaps the nearest one ever got to the days when Julius Reuter was hastily unclipping the financial news from Brussels in that pigeon loft in Aachen. The trouble was, London didn't just want volumes and prices when these were announced. At conferences sometimes lasting days, the local Reuter team would be reinforced by economic specialists from head office. Nick Moore, conscientious to the point of frenzy, and his indefatigable Scottish sidekick, Tom Thomson, were expected to provide regular reports and predictions. Pre-scheduled Dayleads and Nightleads sometimes had to be constructed from the flimsiest indications of what was happening behind those closed doors.

Chief player at these regular OPEC jamborees was Saudi Arabia's colourful oil minister Sheikh Yamani, whom we all regularly badgered for a good quote. Within seconds of the Sheikh coming out of a meeting, even with his customary 'No comment', we'd have it on the wire. Whether that was useful or not is a matter of debate. The Reuter team took turns at doing the twice-daily Leads. I remember phoning Yamani in his room from the Intercontinental lobby one news-thin day in search of scraps, to be told by the Sheikh, in great good humour, 'Well, I saw your Nightlead on the wire, Mr Chadwick, and much admired it. It's all wrong, of course, but the story's very well written.' Well, that was some consolation, I suppose.

To anyone more used to action or human interest, OPEC was a necessary bore. Once one of these conferences was over, it took many beers and a long conversation about Ken Colyer and his band to get Nick, a traditional jazz lover, into recovery mode, ready for the flight home.

Life in Geneva, dominated by the famous *jet d'eau* shooting skywards over Lake Leman, the Alps a dramatic backdrop, was generally pleasant. Save for when the hazy summer 'föhn' blanketed the town for days. I found myself a nice flat on the fifth floor of a modern apartment block just up the road from the Palais des Nations and, as in Bonn, I could walk, drive or take the minibike to work. On the roof was an open-air swimming pool, much used by residents during the day, but by the time I got there after work after taking the lift to the top the pool would be smooth as a millpond. It was a small pool, so it wasn't too hard, changing strokes every so often (I only ever knew the breast- and backstrokes) to complete my self-allotted fifty-two lengths, one for every week of the year. Standing at the side of the pool, you had a panoramic view of the Alps, snow glistening on the peaks. In winter, I'd drive across the border into France to enjoy skiing at Flaine, from the small studio flat I'd bought some years before.

I'd celebrated the move to Switzerland by exchanging my faithful Ford Capri, at the urging of my car-crazy son, for a silver-grey Mazda RX7 sports car, newly on the market. Though its exotic rotary engine was a bit heavy on fuel, it was definitely a car to enjoy. And to be seen in, especially when my lady friend joined me for skiing in winter, country excursions in summer. Once, in Italian-speaking Lugano, as we stopped at traffic lights, a young Italian by the roadside shouted, '*Bella donna, bella macchina!*' Nicely and accurately put, I thought. The Italians have taste in these matters. The Swiss, on the other hand, can be slightly more laconic. One weekend, despite advance warnings from my fair passenger, I ran out of petrol in the fuel-thirsty Mazda on a country road, miles from town in the German-speaking part of Switzerland. Then I spotted a farmhouse on a distant hillside.

Seizing an empty fuel can, I tramped down into the valley and up the other side, and threw myself on the mercies of the dour farmer who emerged, dogs barking. I asked him humbly and without too much optimism, if he, perchance, had any petrol to spare. I'd fully anticipated a No, and would have fully understood. But his matter-of-fact response was to ask, '*Normal*? *Oder Super?*' The Swiss are always well organised. We were soon on our way again.

In another gesture of defiance to modernity which hit the headlines, the Swiss voted overwhelmingly against proposals by a government-appointed panel of lawyers, doctors and theologians to lower the age of consent to fourteen, bringing the country into line with neighbouring Austria, Italy and Germany. Only the small Socialist Party and the Young Liberals favoured change. A proposal to legalise incest between brothers and sisters over eighteen particularly enraged the Christian churches.

On the wider political scene, however, some younger Swiss were impatient for change. News reached us in the autumn of 1980 of rioting in the centre of Zurich, Switzerland's largest city and financial centre, and there I made my way. Street fighting had left the elegant city centre a shambles of broken glass and paving stones. The trouble started when the local authorities shut down an independent youth centre, which they'd allowed disaffected youth to set up after complaining their interests were being ignored. Switzerland's materialistic society, young people said, spent money on opera houses but not on popular culture. But following reports that the centre was harbouring drug addicts, foreign agitators and anarchists, the police closed it down in a dawn raid and arrested dozens of young people.

Running battles erupted around the railway station, Europe's largest, and the nearby Bahnhofstrasse, a centre of banking, business, expensive shops and elegant fashion houses. Police recovered explosives stolen from a construction site under one of the city's bridges. Though things calmed down, it was clear that neutral and prosperous Switzerland was not immune to the youth unrest sweeping Europe.

In Geneva, the UN was inundated by causes, large and small. In a tiny flat off the Rue de Neuchâtel, Geneva's best-known prostitute and several of her colleagues in the ancient profession invited reporters to a news conference as they launched a world campaign for understanding. Merry, from Paris, Carole of Marseilles, Jocelyn and Carmen from Lyons and Griselda from Geneva had just presented their complaints up at the Palais to the UN Division on Human Rights, and for support from around the world.

'We are harassed in France by police and tax inspectors alike,' complained Carole, a slim blonde in her twenties. 'The French authorities are hypocrites. We don't mind having to pay taxes, but why then are we persecuted by society?'

The women sought UN action on two fronts – to prevent forced prostitution, which they called slavery, and to improve the rights of women in the profession around the world. Their leader, raven-haired Griselda Real, a shapely fifty-two-year-old with a flowing black dress and a gold star in her hair, twice took telephone calls as we sat around for the news conference.

'I'm occupied at the moment, you'll have to call back later,' she told her male callers, with a smile to reporters. 'They don't always want sex, you know,' she said. 'Most of my calls come from people who are lonely or have trouble with their wives or psychological problems. They want companionship.'

In the very articulate Miss Real's walk-up apartment, Chinese lanterns, oriental screens and pink carnations in the window boxes went side by side with books by French writers Jean-Paul Sartre and Jean Genet and American black activist Angela Davis. As a member of Switzerland's Writers' Union, she'd published a book on her job. 'We're a persecuted minority,' she said, 'and a suitable subject for UN action.'

The Human Rights official had given them 'a courteous and attentive hearing', they said. But I think it was one of those subjects that officials at the Palais filed away, but did little about.

Other unexpected petitioners turned up at the Palais. A three-man team of Aborigines arrived from the other side of the globe and asked the world body to help save one of their sacred places from the oil drillers. Their leader, Jim Hagan, told a sub-commission dealing with the rights of minorities that the site in Australia's Western Desert was the home of the spirit of the

'Great goanna lizard' and the very essence of their law and culture. I don't think this group were entirely successful either.

Climate change, one of today's big issues, was already a quarter-century ago high on the agenda of World Wildlife Fund campaigners, but few people wanted to know. The Duke of Edinburgh, addressing the organisation's twentieth birthday meeting in Switzerland in 1981, accurately predicted the next two decades would be a critical time. WWF officials were warning even then of desertification through deforestation, with one more animal, plant or insect lost every ten minutes. But their pleas fell on largely deaf ears. No one at that time, unfortunately, took global warming seriously.

There were other diversions from Palais politics. One sure winner was the World Inventors' Exhibition, which annually attracted hundreds of entrants, regarded alternatively as geniuses, cranks or crackpots. There were old men with white beards and the pointed hats you used to see in children's comics, their visiting cards saying simply 'Inventor'. The papers loved it. There was 'Magic Water' from China which would make a bald man's hair grow again; and a toothbrush which played music – for what reason was not explained. And despite all evidence to the contrary, Yugoslav inventor Ivan Bakjac believed that by flapping wings man could fly.

Against a backdrop of Leonardo da Vinci drawings and complex charts illustrating the flights of birds and bees, the former Air Force jet pilot showed me a small balsa-wood mock-up of his aircraft. All that was needed, he said, was muscle power – 'And it's not so tiring as you may think. Some people might be able to fly for ten minutes, younger and fitter people for two hours. I would take off roughly the same way as the hang-glider people, by running down a slope with a vertical drop at the end. But whereas they take off from mountains, I would only need a drop of a few metres. Think of the advantages!' said Ivan. I could only think of the possible disasters.

Want to improve your golf swing? A lanky Australian, Bob Hansen, had the answer in a large metal hoop to which the club was attached, being kept on the correct path along a track established by high-speed photographs. The Sydney-born

297

inventor told me, 'The idea came to me at three o'clock one morning. I'd shot a sixty-six while practising for a tournament, then scored a lousy eighty-six in the event itself. I went home profoundly depressed and threw my golf clubs away. Then I woke up in the middle of the night and thought to myself – It's all a matter of the correct swing.' I ventured to suggest that this was a not uncommon problem among golfers. But Bob was hoping for big orders.

Korean inventor Lee Seong Yoo, who turned up regularly at these events, showed me his self-extinguishing cigarette. He lit up, took a couple of quick puffs, then stubbed it out in an ashtray. He wrinkled his nose. 'Dirty,' he said. 'Bad smell. And if extinguished on ground, bad for nature.' He added, 'This better.' Lighting one of his own special cigarettes, he inhaled twice and then gently squeezed the filter. 'Now feel ash,' he invited. The ash, I confirmed, was stone cold. The cigarette, he said, contained not just tobacco but a small jet of liquid which, when squeezed, put the fire out.

'Mr Lee not engineer,' said one of his smiling colleagues. 'He just simple inventor.' I could only wonder if it was all worth the trouble.

And in the new age of the urban guerrilla, self-protection had become big business. After a worldwide wave of kidnappings and abductions, one firm at Geneva exhibited colour-coordinated bulletproof vests; not any old vests, but 'stylish fabrics in neutral tones of brown, blue or grey'. 'It reflects the times we live in,' said the organisers. 'Definitely a growth industry.'

The East–West political battle shifted into another gear with the first signs of change in eastern Europe and a more relaxed attitude in Moscow. Poland's charismatic Lech Walesa, leader of the free trade union, Solidarity, unexpectedly turned up for the ILO's annual conference in 1981. The man from the Gdansk shipyard had become a world figure, much to the chagrin of Poland's communist leaders. I asked him at a news conference what he thought of Britain's trade unions. He thought they were too 'trigger-happy'. On return from Geneva, Walesa was detained and his free trade union, Solidarity, suspended.

But Poland's Pope John Paul, arriving in Geneva later from Rome, managed adroitly in an hour-long address to use the term 'Solidarity' no fewer than fifty-one times without once mentioning his native country. Warsaw's official delegates accused the West of shedding crocodile tears over men who'd brought their country close to anarchy. Nevertheless, within a few years Walesa would be Poland's new boss.

At the other end of the world, the Falklands War broke out. I was personally never fully convinced of Britain's eternal claim to these remote South Atlantic islands, and the Reuter reports remained objective during the conflict. In the middle of it, our new boss, the outspoken Australian (are there are any other kind?) Glen Renfrew, arrived in Zurich for a board meeting. In the middle of a big lunch for Reuter staff, he was called to the phone. He returned with an apology to tell us that Prime Minister Margaret Thatcher had been expressing displeasure at what she apparently considered Reuters' lack of support for the British side. I was glad to hear he'd told her office politely where to go. But I was surprised by the degree of support which the undoubtedly impressive military expedition to the South Atlantic evoked among foreign newsmen at the Palais. When it was all over, one correspondent after another from the Soviet Bloc countries stopped me in the corridors to shake my hand and offer congratulations.

A little later the Iron Lady arrived in Switzerland herself to thank the International Red Cross for its work during the conflict. In a brief address, she observed that 'there have always been wars and there always will be wars'. But, she added, wars should be civilised. *A civilised war*? I almost dropped my notebook. I was guilty of censorship, probably for the first and only time, in not making that the lead. I told myself the unfortunate phrase was maybe just the verbal equivalent of a slip of the pen; or maybe I misheard her.

Inside those glass-walled office blocks in Geneva was many a good yarn. At the WMO, I met a pilot from Florida, Howard Ticknell, whose job was 'to go looking for lightning'. One of a multinational team doing a weather probe over the Alps, he didn't try to avoid storms, but aimed his four-engine Lockheed research plane directly at them. 'Lightning can be pretty spectacular from the cockpit,' he said. 'Sometimes you see a bolt coming straight at you and you grip your seat belt. Boy, it really hits!'

I could imagine. My story got worldwide play and was given a centre-page spread in the UNESCO (United Nations Educational, Scientific and Cultural Organisation) magazine. They wrote saying I'd made a dry subject readable.

I also got plaudits from the bosses at the European Nuclear Research Centre (CERN) after investigating what was going on at this mysterious place straddling the Swiss–French border. On the surface it was a sprawl of factory-like buildings along tree-lined roads with names like 'Einstein Avenue' and 'Niels Bohr Street'. But deep under the fields, like something in a James Bond movie, was a ring of tunnels. There, infinitesimal particles of matter were flashing round at the speed of light in experiments which I was told were gradually unlocking the secrets of the universe.

Leading world physicists sat silently in front of television screens monitoring the process. At regular intervals around the ring were thousands of magnets, which sent electrons (particles of matter with a negative charge) and positrons (particles with a positive charge) whirling around the circuit in opposite directions, their collisions monitored at control points. In what they described as a historic event, the scientists said they'd recently succeeded in colliding matter with antimatter for the first time.

The aim of the $400 million project, said CERN's director, German Professor Herwig Schopper, was 'to penetrate the microcosmos. We are in a sense repeating what probably happened at the beginning of the universe. Then there was a Big Bang. We are producing mini-Big Bangs.' There were plans for an even bigger Big Bang (now long since realised). But at that time, the project was not popular with all the farmers on top. But it was all quite invisible from the surface and harmed no one. 'A very good article,' CERN told me later in a thank you letter. Nice to know. But it didn't make me want to study particle physics.

Other underground projects were going on. I drove to the St Gotthard Pass for the opening of the world's longest road tunnel. Bored out of the rock by a multinational task force of over 300 miners from several countries at a cost of $420 million (and nineteen lives), the tunnel gave motorists travelling between central Europe and Italy an easier alternative to the old twisting route through the high pass. But the country's Trade Union Federation protested, saying, 'Riddled with holes, we're looking more and more like a gigantic Swiss cheese.'

The environmental impact, it turned out, would be the least of the worries. The St Gotthard tunnel – and France's Mont Blanc road tunnel – would be ravaged in later years by major fires in which many travellers died. Those Swiss doubters had perhaps the right to be sceptical.

Chapter 18
A CHINESE SCHOLAR IN A PAPER HAT AND MEN IN WHITE COATS

With another sort of passport, I might have become United Nations press spokesman in Geneva, the soon-to-retire incumbent told me. 'You could have taken over from me,' the New Zealander said when I told him I was being pulled out of Switzerland, which seemed to occasion him some surprise. But he regretted my British passport wouldn't allow it. The UN secretariat was now all about 'geographical representation'. Well, we all knew there were a fair number of layabouts at the Palais des Nations who did little but collect their salaries.

Meanwhile, my critics at head office wanted me out of Geneva. For whatever reason remained unclear. The German manager in Zurich wanted my assignment in Switzerland extended. But at head office there were other ideas and I was not offered any sort of promotion, just a job on the desk. Old friends like Gerry Ratzin, from New York days and now in Reuters' Staff Department, urged me to stick it out. Things would change. He was right, of course, on both counts. At the UN you retire at sixty, and I'd have lost a lot of my Reuter pension if I'd quit. For the moment – it would last a few years – I remained at the whim of those Gerry Long had warned me about in Bonn. People who'd never, to the best of my knowledge, covered a war, a world conference – or even a town council meeting.

I was perfectly content to be 'back on the desk', as people put it. News is news, and if you're fascinated by it, it doesn't really matter which stage of the production belt you're at. Editing other people's writing never seemed to me as boring as it apparently is to some. Isn't creative subediting exactly what Ezra Pound did for T S Eliot's *Waste Land*? 'April is the cruellest month, mixing memory with desire...' Eliot's most famous poem didn't start off originally with that memorable lead. The other chap just lopped off about fifty lines or so of the original and the result was absolutely right. Subbing is an honourable job.

It must already have become more and more obvious for some time to people in London, if not in overseas posts, that major change was in the air at 85 Fleet Street, and in the period that followed Gerry Long's visit to Bonn this began to happen. The often brusque Yorkshireman, whose eccentricities were destined only to increase, may have just become tired of the game. I remembered him telling me years earlier in Denmark how he nearly joined the *Daily Express*, when it tried to poach him from Reuters. 'Maybe I should have gone,' he'd grumbled moodily over a drink at a pub off Copenhagen's Town Hall Square. But a couple of years later, at thirty-nine, he beat three other front runners to be given the top job. Now it wouldn't be long before he quit Reuters and joined *The Times* as Managing Director – a move that wouldn't end well.

Maybe his curious failure to support my tenure in Bonn – while disclosing I was under fire from some of his underlings – reflected a growing disinterest in the firm. He himself had never made any complaints about my work. He had a low boredom threshold, I think, and didn't want to be bothered any more with office politics. Gerry was in essence a newsman. In the years since he took over as Reuter boss and injected some new thinking into the firm, detailed company developments had largely been spearheaded by business-minded high-fliers like Glenn Renfrew and Michael Nelson, who pushed the company into different but increasingly profitable areas which, when Reuters was floated in 1984, would make them multimillionaires. Gerry Long, who'd left the company by then, got nothing. A poor reward for a man who'd colourfully represented Reuters around the world.

There were upsides in the eighties to being back at base. Our indefatigable representatives in the Reuter Chapel (branch) of the National Union of Journalists had managed to get us all a four-day week. A four-day week? Yes, such things really did exist – for a while. The late Dick Wagstaff, another Reuter man (and jazz organ enthusiast) who'd come up the hard way into journalism, now handled desk schedules. With his help, and by volunteering for permanent evening work instead of day shifts, I managed to convert two four-day weeks into a consecutive eight-day fortnight. The other six days, I'd fly to Geneva, where my close friend was now working. She'd arrived there the very day I was hoisted back to London. In winter, there was the ski flat in the mountains at Flaine, just across the French border. In Sweden, there was my son to visit, and in England I renewed acquaintances with family and friends whom I'd rather neglected during the years overseas.

In Fleet Street, two old *Bury Times* colleagues were within easy reach. Roy Heron was now a senior editor at Britain's domestic news agency just a couple of floors below Reuters, while across the road in the Daily Express building Brian Hitchen was steamrollering his way through the redtops. Alan Toft, co-founder of the old Cotton City Jazzmen and now occasionally given to fronting a big band, Sinatra-style, had forged a new career with his own successful business publication and there were pleasantly boozy and jazz-orientated weekends at his home just down the line in Eastbourne. It seemed an excellent time for a full-scale reunion. Frank Thomas, who'd become *BT* Editor, and (the late) Barry Gill, now a press and TV motor racing guru, were also roped in for a long and boozy evening at the Wig and Pen Club, a few paces up Fleet Street.

On a now fairly cosmopolitan World Desk, strengthened in recent years by an influx of Brits poached from our American rival Associated Press, I was among friends and respected colleagues. Troubleshooters Ron Thomson and Pat Massey and desk man Ron Sly were among the 'new immigrants'. On evening shifts, free of the new daytime bureaucrats, Australian Dave Mathew, veteran Bruce Cobb and I would drink at various bars off Fleet Street. From Canada, the World Desk had acquired the hard-nosed Jack Hartzman, Dave Nicholson (another jazz fan and a regular visitor to Ronnie Scott's Club) and the eccentric but loveable Cy Fox. For the latter, unhappily, the new technology was becoming a nightmare. He'd have been happier to stay with typewriters. When the rigours of ever-evolving keyboard routines finally became too much, he broke down in tears and quit.

Cy was happier in literary circles, and was an expert on the work of artist/writer Wyndham Lewis. It was a delight, as he humorously ended a talk on the writer's Vorticist movement, to see him punch the air and shout the title of Lewis's revolutionary magazine – *BLAST!* – over the heads of the audience. His home in the London suburb of Sydenham, a district which he once (unfairly to some minds!) excoriated, was a showplace of Lewis memorabilia. It was this amiable Canadian who introduced me to the late Alan Ross, editor of the *London Magazine*. During a delightful lunch at Alan's favourite restaurant in Kensington, I was invited as a start to review a jazz book which had just landed on his desk. Thus began a fruitful period in which, during several years up to his death, I'd write a series of pieces on music, literature and travel. And since whatever writing skills I had no longer seemed to be quite so valued at Reuters, I began doing it profitably for other people too.

Old colleagues in Stockholm roped me in for assignments in the press relations field. I wrote the major part of a booklet for Volvo. I translated into colloquial English texts by Swedish business executives who needed something in a hurry for a corporate speech. It was all grist to the mill. Most enjoyably of all, though with no financial reward, I walked up Farringdon Road to *Jazz Journal* one day to meet its editors, Eddie and Janet Cook, and their colleague Mark Gilbert (the latter would take over as Editor after Janet's death and Eddie's retirement) and thereafter started reviewing jazz records, which I still do off and on. In that context, the money didn't matter. There were many jazz fans at Reuters too, experts in most musical styles, from Louis Armstrong to Ken Colyer, Benny Carter to Sonny Rollins.

Another delightful character who became a close friend during those years was Sweden's Press Counsellor, the learned Alvar Alsterdal, who seemed to know every language, ancient or modern, and wrote a sparkling occasional column for the Swedish newspaper *Arbetet*. From his rambling flat in the Marylebone Road, its shelves packed with volumes of all descriptions, he went forth to just about every literary or artistic occasion worth knowing about. With his rumpled hair and stooped gait, Alvar looked every inch the scholar, but was also a delightful host.

Son of a butcher in the Swedish province of Värmland, he joined the *Social Democrat* newspaper and roamed around Central and Eastern Europe in the years before the Wall came down. He much loved the London pub scene and the capital's literary and musical events, inviting me to a concert by the Gothenburg Symphony Orchestra to introduce me to the music of Estonia's Arvo Pärt. There was little of London's cultural life not reflected in his pieces for the Swedish press, and it was a sad day when he died prematurely at sixty-four. After attending his late-in-life wedding to a charming Swedish lady, I was also at the thanksgiving service at St Bride's, Fleet Street, the journalists' church.

Reuters itself wasn't short of colourful characters – often the best writers. Another was Jim Flannery, from New Zealand. He'd worked at our Washington office but we'd never met during my time in the States. 'Oh, he's a poet,' said someone who'd worked with him there, with a mixture of admiration and mystification. Now in London, Jim invited me for a drink at his top-floor bachelor den up Gray's Inn Road.

I arrived at a rather dilapidated tenement building and climbed rickety twisting stairs. As I got nearer the summit I figured with some disappointment that he must have anther visitor already. It sounded like a Chinese gentleman. I knocked and entered a sort of attic. There wasn't much light. I stumbled over a long wire and piles of books and Jim shifted some papers off a battered armchair so I could sit down. Then I realised the reason for the gloom. All of the available electric power was going into a tape recorder standing in the middle of the table. The mystery was solved. It was the voice of Flannery, practising Chinese. It was not that he wanted a posting to Peking: he'd just decided to learn the language.

Jim was one of the great Reuter eccentrics. When a *Sunday Times* reporter called at 85 Fleet Street one day, seeking a story about the modern new Reuters – the firm had now been floated – the photographer correctly decided, rather unfortunately for the company's cherished new 'cutting edge' image, that the most interesting subject on the editorial floor was Flannery, sitting at a computer with his trademark paper hat on his head, as if this was one big Christmas party. The paper hat was just something Jim did. But he was also one of the sharpest editors on World Desk.

As was Englishman Peter Stewart, a World War Two Lancaster crewman, who combined a caustic tongue with a warm heart and generously gave up a lot of time to help juniors who'd recently joined the fray. One of them was a young lady from our Bonn office, who took quite a fancy to Peter, treating him like a friendly uncle. She told him he really must visit Hamburg. 'I've seen it,' was Peter's laconic reply, 'from 20,000 feet.'

Dave Goddard, whose hobby was model trains, incredibly drove in from Devon every day and worked permanently, one week on, one week off, on the overnight shift, for the sake of his family. Luckily for others, he was among a few Reuter men with no particular interest in a foreign posting. 'Abroad?' he'd say. 'I've *been* abroad – and it's nasty!'

In the mid-eighties, a mainly genteel sort of civil war raged at 85 Fleet Street. Veteran journalists, most of whom had come into general news the hard way, sensed a gradual takeover by the money-men. I don't knock economic journalism. How could I? Facilitated by rapidly expanding technology, it was to be the money-spinner which saved the firm and our salaries – and ultimately our pensions. Promoted successively, after the departure of Gerry Long, by top managers like Nelson, Renfrew and Peter Job, this inevitable move at a critical time for the agency into new electronic products, aimed squarely at the business and financial world, would save our collective bacon. And, after all, wasn't this the way Reuters started with the man from Kassel? But the relatively rapid makeover, poorly handled by editorial middle management, didn't make for smooth sailing on the fourth (editorial) floor. And for this, the top bosses must take some of the blame. Most of their attention was focused on the financial world – which I imagine remains so.

Already in Geneva I'd been rung by colleagues in London with alarming stories. One of my oldest friends and Reuter stalwarts, the late John Organ, I was told, had emerged weeping in the corridor from a confrontation with a new executive. No one could have been more loyal and hard-working than the mercurial Organ, a fervent Roman Catholic who'd enthusiastically covered the Second Vatican Council as Chief Correspondent in his beloved Rome. There was no explanation for what had happened. I'd figured then that I might be among the next destined for the chop.

It was hardly surprising, amid the turmoil of the period, that a sort of underground news service, scathing about company idiocies, as they were seen by many editorial staff, began to appear on terminal screens. It was the brainchild of Dave Mathew. Like most of his colleagues, Big Dave, as he was affectionately known, didn't have any more time than other Aussies for parvenus, phonies or management claptrap. Every time some new edict appeared, officially or in leaked form, on staff relations or working methods, it would quickly go the rounds worldwide. For staffers opening their terminals at the start of a new shift, the latest edition of 'Whitecoats', as it was appropriately labelled, became required reading. More often than not, the entries devastatingly hit the spot. Around the in-house Reuter network, 'Whitecoats' acquired worldwide readership.

Slowly – too slowly in many people's opinion – top management became aware of how serious tensions were on the editorial floor. One warning signal may have been a piece which appeared in the satirical weekly *Private Eye*, amid regular columns like 'The Old Bores Corner' and the exploits of 'Lunchtime O'Booze'. *Private Eye* reported:

> One might think that everything was sweetness and light at Reuters' newly sandblasted headquarters at 85 Fleet Street. But a check among journalists would show that morale, involvement and inspiration are at their lowest level for years. The more profits Reuters make, the less they are willing to spend on their news product, it would seem. Ring up this once-proud news agency with a good story at midnight and all you would get would be a telephone answering device – the night telephonists have been scrapped. World Desk editors have to rely on their memories for facts and figures wanted after about the same hour. The library is being decimated. Management have said they are prepared to see some deterioration in the editorial product.

Reuter journalists, said the article, had not seen a penny so far from the company's massive profits of recent years, and union officials had been told at an acrimonious wage negotiation session, 'If you don't like Reuters, you can leave.' Which some people understandably did. The article, appearing in the magazine's 'Street of Shame' column, could hardly have pleased Reuters' top management. It was a shabby period for the old firm, best forgotten. Some of those heads would later roll, or be shifted sideways.

I'd returned to an England obsessed with 'property'. In earlier times you simply bought or rented a flat, or started a mortgage on a house. It was a private (and really rather dull) matter. Now everybody in London seemed to be talking about property. 'Know what our house is worth now? And the Bloggs, just down the street, just sold theirs for £50,000. Ours must be worth at least that.' And so on, and so on. It was becoming a bore, and would remain so for a couple of decades to come, in fact until the whole process, egged on by foolish bank managers and greedy estate agents, collapsed with a big thud in 2008. Over the years, the jargon had become painful to hear on the many TV programmes devoted to this basically boring topic. You didn't just 'move' any more. You 'relocated' – which makes the process sound far more astute and far-seeing, I suppose. But who cares – except you?

I found (or should I say in the new parlance 'discovered') a nice flat in Primrose Hill, providing fine views over London and walks around Regent's Park and Hampstead Heath. I don't remember talking about my new 'property' to anyone except visiting friends or relatives. Later I moved to Wimbledon – I like to be near parks and open country – and after retirement came here to Middle Littleton (or Little Middleton, as some of my old colleagues at first insisted on calling it).

Gerry Long had lost out on the big money after the Reuter flotation. But it would be, as *The Times* headlined it, 'A Small Matter of the Cheese Board', which effectively ended his career in big-time journalism. Ever a wine lover and gastronome – which I could vouch for after those long luncheons in Bad Godesberg –

he seemed to have become increasingly fixated on this aspect of high life. After one company-financed meal for local executives in Bonn back in the eighties, I remember him waxing ecstatic about a particular and highly expensive vintage (selected by himself from the wine list at about £35 a bottle, even in those days) and telling me, 'I should put down a few dozen of these if I were you, John.' I replied with some humour, 'What, on *my* salary?'

Now Managing Director of *The Times*, Gerry seemed to let things get a bit out of hand. One fateful day in February 1982, an article under the headline 'A Small Matter Of The Cheeseboard' appeared in *The Times* over almost half a page. It consisted of a lengthy verbatim series of letters between Gerry and Mr Albert Roux, the proprietor of London's Le Gavroche restaurant. For whatever reason (I always suspected connivance by rival editorial chiefs) the paper carried the month-long exchanges in full.

The former Reuter boss, long a lover of French culture, had a highly critical set of comments to make, interspersed with frequent passages, in French, about the quality of the celebrated restaurant's food. His main complaint was that the contents of the cheese board – which he found 'perfectly respectable, if unremarkable' – were however wrongly described as 'farmhouse cheeses'. There followed a long dissertation, expanded over some weeks, in which Long admitted that 'there are as many definitions of cheese as there are holes in an Emmentaler', and gave a brief lecture on the processes of cheese making. The news value of all this was not clear.

'My visit to Le Gavroche was my first,' wrote Gerry. 'I found the food interesting, but I did not like it.' This was typical Long, pompous on the face of it, but also a bit tongue-in-cheek and deliberately provocative. He had, he wrote,

> made the mistake of choosing turbot, perhaps my favourite fish, in a port-wine sauce. The sauce was heavy, and succeeded in combining sweetness and bitterness in a way that is more usual in Chinese than in French restaurants.

I had to laugh as I read all this. But the proprietor of the restaurant must have been incensed. In his replies, also published in *The Times*, he stoutly but courteously defended his cuisine, while the Michelin organisation in Paris even became involved in the dispute. It diplomatically promised 'to note carefully Mr Long's comments'. As an olive branch, the proprietor of the restaurant invited Gerry and his wife to lunch or dinner, an invitation which he rather brusquely declined, ending the exchange by saying (somewhat to my own surprise), 'I eat very rarely in restaurants, in this country even less than in France.'

Publication, for whatever motives, of these hilarious exchanges about high life dining was reported to have infuriated proprietor Rupert Murdoch, particularly as he was about to slash 600 union jobs. Gerry was removed from his post shortly thereafter, though he stayed on as vice-chairman of *The Times* until 1984, when he retired to France.

I was rather saddened by the episode. Long was not to many people's liking, but I'd always got on with him and found his occasional brusque mannerisms more diverting than anything else. Perhaps it helped that we came from broadly similar Northern English backgrounds – he the son of a Yorkshire postman, myself the son of a Lancashire builder – and both with Irish mothers. I'd found his visits entertaining – certainly different. How many top MDs would ask you to arrange a bicycle for them? I find frankly ludicrous statements such as that in the 1992 official *History of Reuters* (Donald Read), attributed anonymously to a Reuter executive of the period, that local managers were struck down with 'terror' when having to organise Long's 'almost royal overseas tours, down to the last restaurant'. These people must have had pretty thin skins. Idiosyncrasies, yes. But haven't we all? Personally I found his company more entertaining than exacting. He was extremely unlucky to lose out when big money starting flowing into the Reuter coffers.

Even if I'd possessed that particular talent, the life of a non-journalist Reuter executive would never have been my scene. In more indigent days, of course, one had to be both correspondent and manager – as I was in Cairo and Stockholm. Business news had for decades been seen as a sideline. Back in Copenhagen days, I'd looked at the occasional call I was asked to make on our 'Comtel' correspondent, a nice chap called Arne, as a duty rather than anything else. We were never asked in those days for financial news. Then the Econ juggernaut rolled in.

Gerry Long was really the last old-style reporter to get the top job at 85 Fleet Street. The late Doon Campbell, who'd landed on a beach in Normandy on D-Day in 1944 and covered the assassination of Indian leader Mahatma Gandhi, came close. But by the eighties and nineties, the big bosses were generally coming from other backgrounds. My own interest always lay in writing. In happier days on the World Desk, which I eventually headed following executive changes, I was always glad to write specials for the Features Desk, now run by my old Australian colleague from New York days, Alan Barker.

I realised it was just a century since Sherlock Holmes and the faithful Dr Watson first appeared (in print) in foggy London. Yet another film version of the Holmes series had started on television. I'd always been a big Holmes fan and reckoned this was the time for a centenary piece.

It was an old-fashioned walking stick engraved with the date 1884 – Holmes deduced rather incredibly that it must belong to a house doctor at Charing Cross hospital who owned a dog 'somewhat smaller than a mastiff' – which plunged the pair into their most famous case, the Hound of the Baskervilles. The story had fascinated me from boyhood, since when I'd collected all the tales, some in several versions and editions, together with audio and film productions, ludicrously updated and inaccurate as some of the latter are. Right now the usual summer flood of visitors from around the world had started around 221B Baker Street, seeking signs of a detective who many of them believed had actually lived – or was even still alive.

'Where's Sherlock Holmes buried then, Grandma?' I heard a small cockney boy ask as I stepped off the Tube to do my own investigation on the fringes of Regent's Park, where so many of Holmes's adventures began.

'Somewhere around here, I 'spect,' replied his grandmother, who'd have been alive at the time Holmes returned to London from his apparent death plunge, along with arch-criminal Dr Moriarty, into Switzerland's Reichenbach Falls.

But the old lady and her grandson must have been disappointed not to find the famous Baker Street lodgings. On the site where they would have been – had they ever existed – workmen were finishing a new office block for a building society. There, I was told, inquiries still arrived regularly from around the globe. The owners always sent a polite form letter back, regretting that Sherlock Holmes was no longer resident. It made a good story for Reuters, used worldwide.

Another popular piece, judging by clippings which arrived from around the world, was an atmospheric (I hope) feature I wrote about a visit to Chequers, where, I said in my intro, 'the ghost of Winston Churchill still lingers'. Poetic licence. And in selling a story, it's the first paragraph that counts.

Chapter 19
IN THE FORMER COMMUNIST BLOC,
CENSOR-FREE JOURNALISM IS BACK

It was worth eating at Budapest's Barokk restaurant just for the menu. Starters included things like 'ice-Cooled Spawm', which turned out to be caviar with lemon. To follow, there was a choice of 'Cow-Meat, Suddenly Roasted' (impetuous people, these Hungarian cooks!); 'Boor, Freshly Killed' (and no more than he deserved); 'Miscue of Joint' (well, you can't win 'em all); or, hardly something for the squeamish, 'Grilled Lifer'.

The food was excellent, but it would take a bit longer before they sorted out those menus. These were still early days after the end of the Wall, and Budapest's hundreds of restaurants were doing their best to please the foreigners now arriving in droves, spending harder currencies than their own. I could have done without the waiters' eighteenth century costumes – the name of the restaurant should have warned us – and they were just that bit too attentive in refilling your glass. But they were doing their best to please, and maybe still a bit uncertain as to what the new tourist flood really wanted.

I was one of a Reuters' team there to run a course for young Hungarian journalists, and we'd have settled for something simpler and more traditional. But another evening it was a Hungarian guest, not we, who scoffed as a gipsy band played the kind of music many of us *did* want to hear. I liked these fiddlers, with their eccentric bowing and fingering techniques. The bassist, a real Balkan figure with flashing eyes and drooping moustache, pushed the group along with a verve which would have done credit to a jazz musician. A nearby party of Scandinavian diners asked, inevitably, for the famous 'Lark', the fiddler's showpiece, and the lead violinist was ready to oblige. But our Hungarian hosts, eager we should not hear too much musical kitsch, quickly requested a traditional folk melody, on which the musicians improvised with equal facility. This was the country, after all, of Bartók and Kodály, whose music, with roots in the countryside, had easily survived decades of communist rule.

Western music was flourishing too, it seemed, in post-communist Budapest. Later that evening at the Merlin Club, a vast converted warehouse, every table was packed as a bop quartet played a breakneck version of 'Days of Wine and Roses', and across town the Benko Dixielanders were performing. Despite all the political shifts and changes, Hungary remained a nation of musicians. My companion, one of the young journalists to whom we were trying to show the ropes of agency journalism, told me that in her spare time she played the cembalo, her father the zither.

In the aftermath of the Berlin Wall's collapse, The Reuter Foundation, with company funds, had for some time been regularly inviting over to London groups of promising young journalists from the old East Bloc, only accustomed to working in a controlled society. An old colleague of mine from Middle East days, Steve Somerville, was in charge of the Reuter operation. Now we'd started running occasional courses in the East European capitals themselves. Still a bit surprised by the reporting freedoms we in the West enjoyed, these journalists, not all of them young, were eager for change. They proved quick learners. Our veteran diplomatic correspondent, Sidney Weiland, Training Editor George Short (both sadly deceased) and I, as a former head of the World Desk, were in Budapest to run the course. The rest of the team arrived by plane or minibus from London; I drove there from a skiing week on the Austrian slopes. It was destined to be my last such venture. A troublesome hip – due for replacement, said the doctors – was increasingly hampering my movements on the white stuff, especially the quick turns needed on steeper runs. For a few decades, I'd thoroughly enjoyed my winter breaks in France and Austria – even in shivering Norway – but enough was enough.

I was glad Reuters was spending some of its new-earned money this way and, just retired from active service, I'd been roped in as one of the lecturers. I was impressed by the skills some of these journalists from capitals like Warsaw, Budapest, Sofia and Belgrade – not always in the first flush of youth – would quickly develop. The first thing that had to change was not so much writing as attitude. For years, under the heavy hand of communist rule, they'd been subservient to the political bosses. They had to be. Back in Cairo years earlier, I'd met many East Bloc correspondents and became especially good friends with couples from Poland and Yugoslavia. Egypt had been almost a client state of Moscow and its satellites, its security service set up by experts from the GDR. So the East Bloc correspondents knew what the bosses back home wanted, and this was to restate fossilised old positions, attack Israel and support the Arabs, whatever the merits of the issue. Washington and the so-called imperialist powers were always the assumed bogeymen, Moscow and its allies the Arabs' friends.

Many of these East Europeans spoke frankly about their difficulties and wished things were otherwise. On the other hand, we all knew that the Tass man in Cairo, who lived in a house opposite my flat, was a KGB colonel. One could hardly blame the correspondents from the satellite nations. They didn't have much choice. Post-Berlin Wall, one visiting editor from Poland for the first of our London courses said the saddest thing about recent years had been, as he put it, 'having to publish *some* things we knew to be incorrect – in order to get at least half of it in print'.

At tuition sessions, we didn't trumpet the merits of the British press, which we agreed contained a lot that was trivial and crude, acres of newsprint wasted on describing, accurately or not, the private lives of the rich and famous. It wasn't just East European papers that selected what and what not to print. I'd seen my stories from Nazi War Crimes trials in Germany splashed worldwide – but never saw a German reporter at the hearings. In blander Nordic societies, there was a tendency after decades of Social Democrat rule to assume everything in their political gardens was lovely. And Britain remained in many ways highly secretive as far as the monarchy, the law and the army were concerned. Once our students knew where we stood on news values, we all got along fine. Everybody in the news business could recall with some embarrassment how, one Sunday morning in 1956, as Soviet tanks rolled into the centre of Budapest to quell a popular uprising, a leading Hungarian playwright famously appealed to the world over the radio: 'Help, help, help!' The help never arrived. Maybe helping now to bolster a changing press was one small way of making amends. The initiative was warmly welcomed, at any rate.

I told the class, not too sententiously I hope (quoting from my first lecture):

> After years of restrictions, there may be difficulties in developing a good working relationship with government. There are bound to be suspicions, a certain nervousness perhaps on your side, a certain protectiveness on the part of government. Trust has to be built up on both sides and this may take time. A minister you've just met isn't going to open up his heart at the first interview. First of all they want to see how you write. There may be times when you have to stand up to officials, if you feel under threat. Once they know you can't be manipulated, it's interesting – at least in a democratic country – how often they back off.

I hoped we were getting it right. It was heartening back in London afterwards, anyway, to get floods of messages saying how much our students benefited from the course. The seminar was the first of its kind for journalists from central and Eastern Europe and, coinciding with the opening of Reuters' new Budapest office, received much local publicity.

Some of the young people helped by the Reuter Foundation went on to do great things in the media and arts. An excellent example is Barbara Stanislawczyk, of Warsaw. When I first chatted to her at our welcome cocktail party in a Fleet Street pub, I could tell she was something special. Back home, she developed strongly not just as a newspaper journalist but as a book writer. Her magnum opus was an absorbing study of the way, during World War Two, that some people in Poland, a country that had been notoriously anti-Semitic, helped Jews by hiding them away, much against the run of things. A pity it hasn't been translated for English-speaking readers, though I did my best to interest publishers. It provoked strong reactions in Poland, both for and against. She wrote to me caustically:

I am sure my book would be much more successful if I had written that Poles are anti-Semitic. The leftist papers have kept silent up to now. And you know that for any book, silence is the worst thing. Worse than criticism.

Another of these brilliant young women from Eastern Europe, helped by Reuter Foundation funds, was Sofia Yastrubenetskaya, a pianist from Moscow. I turned local impresario for a time to get her a concert engagement at Worcester's Huntingdon Hall, which was followed by another in Tewkesbury. Sofi charmed enthusiastic audiences with her Schumann, Chopin, Debussy and Rachmaninov. I was happy to edit and expand her programme notes and get some publicity for her in the regional press. She stayed on in England, her studies at the Royal Academy of Music subsidised by the Foundation, and later married Freddie Kempf (another outstanding young pianist from the Royal Academy who's won a high reputation in Britain and elsewhere). Reuters undoubtedly played a useful role at that time of major change in backing such bright young people from the former communist world, years before any of these countries became part of the European Union.

The Budapest course concluded, I wanted to take a longer look along the East–West corridor after the demise of the Wall and report it. So, instead of heading straight back to London, I took the road north towards the border of Czechoslovakia (as it then was). How much had changed on the ground? Names like Budapest, Prague and Dresden all conjured up past glories as well as the post-war East–West spy scene. I wanted to see these countries before they become just another part of the New Europe.

My first contact with officialdom on arriving in Hungary from Vienna had not been encouraging. An aftertaste of totalitarianism lingered at the crossing point. The young policeman was polite enough, quickly stamping my passport and waving me through. Changing money, however, I was back in the shabby, resentful world of the East Bloc. The woman behind the sticky-fingered glass was sour and silent as she slammed my forints down. (I would find the same dingy scene at the Hungary/Czechoslovak border.) The lady would almost surely have been there in communist times.

Such people don't change. But Hungarians' old entrepreneurial spirit seemed alive and kicking. Shortly after I'd crossed the border from Austria on the way to Budapest, roadside stalls were heaped with fresh vegetables, fruit, wine, cane chairs and carvings. And, judging by the number of cars with Austrian, German and Swiss number plates, doing pretty well already. I bought two bottles of red wine and, with the spring weather turning hot, a rakish straw hat which I've kept to this day. Decrepit little Yugos, Trabants and Skodas crawled along the inside lane, moving politely aside to let the big Mercedes and BMWs from Germany and Switzerland through. A convoy of trucks from Scotland laden with aid trundled towards Romania. Signs by the roadside, announcing the arrival of Swedish companies and courses in *Projektmanagement*, indicated the future.

Budapest's slightly tattered splendour quickly grew on me, something of a cross between Western Europe and Cairo. When I hesitantly expressed this analogy to a local man, he replied with dry Hungarian humour, 'Well, I guess we'd just like to be something in between.'

The buildings had a turn-of-century dignity which not even decades of neglect, and the garish posters plastered all over them at street level, could entirely efface. The yellow trams gave the city a look more akin to Munich or Helsinki. And at night the city was transformed, lights glittering along the walkways by the Danube, alive with open-air restaurants. It was heart-warming to see such magnificent buildings – Thomas Mann called Budapest the most elegant city in Europe – now being restored. The outside of St Stephen's Basilica, whose vast nave could accommodate 8,000 worshippers, was still mainly soot-blackened stone. But the scaffolding was up and one of the two towers had already been cleaned.

There were bad times in Budapest, of course, long before the communist interlude. Across the road from the new East-West Business Centre, where American, Swedish, British and German companies were moving in, stood the old Jewish synagogue, the largest in Europe. This Byzantine-style building had recently been restored, and a plaque bore the name of Israel's then President, Chaim Herzog, who'd been there to attend the inaugural ceremonies. But there were only a handful present for the Sabbath service the day I dropped in. Budapest's Jewish community was decimated under the Nazis (the narrow streets of the ghetto still bear the bullet marks), the survivors largely saved by the efforts of Swedish diplomat Raoul Wallenberg, who later disappeared into a Soviet prison camp. The Catholics had had their problems, too, but much earlier. Up on Castle Hill, across the water in Buda – once a separate town – the splendid Saint Matthias Church was converted into a mosque during the Turkish occupation. When I visited, music was all around as tourists flocked to the vantage point over the river. A fiddler and his accordionist son played traditional melodies on the ramparts of the Fishermen's Bastion, an architectural whimsy which looked like a Disney castle but had in fact been put up a century earlier for the city's thousandth anniversary.

For most Hungarians now, better times were tantalisingly still just around the corner. For the moment, even gifted intellectuals had to hustle. I was invited to lunch by a Hungarian journalist, one of those attending our course, and her husband, a Russian musician she'd met in Moscow. A taxi ride took me up lovely Andrassy Boulevard (formerly Stalin Avenue, later the Avenue of the People's Republic), lined with houses that looked like embassies, but were in fact the homes of former industrialists. We stopped at a dignified but run-down apartment block whose gloomy central stairwell was like a scene from that cold war movie *The Third Man*. Inside the apartment, though, the rooms were spacious and high-ceilinged. But the elegance was illusory. My host had conducted orchestras in Moscow and Israel, but couldn't yet find work in Budapest. In some ways, it was easier in Budapest to be a café musician. And, as well as her full-time job, his wife was working part-time for a foreign news agency.

In the sprucing-up business, the Czech capital Prague, next stop on my journey, was several stages ahead, the architectural jewel of Eastern Europe. My first glimpse of the still united country, the southern suburbs of Bratislava, capital of Slovakia, a few miles north of the Hungarian border, hadn't suggested it. Here, in roadside settlements which visitors seldom saw, were acres of appalling building block workers' flats, another dreary legacy of the communist dream. The walls were stained, washing strung from the balconies, the ground between the buildings bare and barren. An old man, hand in hand with a small boy, walked over the wasteland, symbols one hoped of the past and the future. I hoped life would be better for the youngster.

Prague had clearly escaped the worst ravages of World War Two. The heart of the city was a treasure house of Renaissance, baroque and Gothic buildings, mainly closed to traffic, making it a pedestrians' joy. I had to negotiate a maze of one-way streets and no entry signs to reach my hotel by car, and then left it in the underground garage for the rest of my stay. The city had seen good times and bad over the centuries. One memorial plaque commemorated the country's liberation from the Nazis in 1945, another the spot where twenty-seven leaders of a 1621 uprising against the Habsburgs were put to death. To one side was the famous astronomical clock of 1410. As it struck the hour, figures of the twelve apostles moved slowly across the face of the brick tower. A couple of blocks away was the splendidly refurbished neoclassical theatre where Mozart's opera *Don Giovanni* had its premiere. Later that evening the voice of a tenor singing '*Panis Angelicus*' soared among the sumptuous frescoes of the nearby church of Saint Nicholas.

In Letna Park, across the River Vltava – immortalised in Smetana's music – children played the unsophisticated games they used to play in the West. A small boy launched an elastic-driven model airplane just like the ones I'd built as a schoolboy, and two small girls played pony, swapping the reins every so often. A pair of swans glided over the smooth waters and in a quiet corner, a couple of teenagers kissed enthusiastically in the evening sunshine. There used to be a huge statue of Josif Stalin thereabouts but, mercifully, the Czechs had long since found an excuse to knock it down. Stalin didn't last long.

Prague Castle had stood for over 1,000 years, the heart of ancient Bohemia, and in 1918 became the home of Czechoslovakia's first president, Thomas Masaryk. Today any tourist could stroll through the ornate open gates, symbolically guarded by young soldiers standing stiffly on either side. Around the cobbled square were no fewer than five palaces. The tramp of boots sounded as I was photographing one of them, the Renaissance Archbishops' Residence. I managed to step aside before a platoon of red-coated soldiers strode past me down the hill for the changing of the guard. This area perhaps held the biggest single concentration of art and history in Europe – the lofty vaulted St Vitus Cathedral; the Golden Lane of sixteenth-century shops built into the castle walls (Franz Kafka stayed here); the church of Saint Nicholas, whose organist was Wolfgang Amadeus Mozart.

The fourteenth-century Charles Bridge, attractively poised on sixteen stone pillars, seemed unfortunately packed almost to the verge of collapse by student hordes, there to celebrate a revolution in which they'd fortunately not had to participate. Well-dressed Nordics basked in the comfortable afterglow of revolution, while young Czechs who'd lived through the hard times earned a few dollars by sketching the visitors. Pale-faced English waifs in long dresses were having their hair twisted by friends into long plaits. Guitarists with headbands played folk songs, their admirers squatting on the pavement and blocking the way for others. An earnest voice sang a familiarly trite sort of message, 'If you come to Czechoslovakia, you'll meet some very gentle people.'

Well, it wasn't gentle people who'd turfed out the communists, just ordinary citizens who'd had enough. I could imagine the locals feeling slightly irked by these johnny-come-latelys. Prague was becoming a hippy haven. I felt more comfortable amid the baroque splendour of the church of St Francis of Assisi at the end of the bridge, where a priest in traditional vestments was saying Mass, attended by old-fashioned altar boys. No guitars here. As we filed out, an organist was playing good old Johann Sebastian Bach.

I wondered how many of these young sightseers found their way to Lidice, about fifteen miles north-west of town, scene of one of the nastiest Nazi atrocities. Heading north on a grey and cold morning, I was the only visitor. Around a flagged courtyard ran a colonnade with a sculpted frieze of uniformed Nazis with whips, forcing women and children into a concentration camp. Here, on 19 June 1942, the Nazis shot all 192 townsmen in reprisal for the assassination of the hated Gauleiter, Richard Heydrich, then razed the village. I pushed open the door of the museum. A group of women attendants gave me a cursory glance but went on gossiping. They didn't seem interested in taking any money, so I walked on into the gallery. It was a sobering collection. There were faded photographs of the men who were shot, and their old work permits, some of them taken from their breast pockets pierced by bullets.

In a rather drab cinema, they were still running the communist version of events. The Nazis, said the commentary, had finally been destroyed by the 'Anti-Faschistiche Allianz'. Heroic Soviet soldiers were shown marching into Prague. And, interpolated with pictures of the grim events in Lidice, were shots from Vietnam depicting American bombing raids. Somehow, everything had been jumbled together into one big fascist plot. I noticed the film had been made in 1987, a few years before the demise of the Eastern Bloc. The unfriendly women at reception were presumably more of the old guard, still at work. I thought the new Czech authorities should do something about this place. And better signposting for visitors to Lidice on the main road would help.

Still heading north, it was an easy enough drive from Prague across the Erzegebirge hills, whose small pointed crests silhouetted against a hazy evening sky gave them a fairy-tale look, like illustrations for a book by the brothers Grimm. The autobahn petered out a few miles north of Prague, and from then on became just a glorified country road. Women in traditional headdresses stooped over the fields, as if nothing had changed in centuries. Except the route was crammed with trucks from many countries – another doubtful benefit of the new order. At the border with East Germany, an army of girl prostitutes lifting their skirts in front of truck drivers had become a public scandal.

Once over the crest, in Germany, the landscape changed as if by magic, and the road, neatly tarmacked and well edged, curved downwards in long loops to the plain, a stream tumbling merrily alongside. A battered Czech tourist bus belched diesel fumes in front of me as a long queue of traffic moved slowly into Dresden. Capital of Saxony and a magnet for Italian artists and craftsmen in the eighteenth century, it had once been called the Florence of Germany. But it was not as lucky as Prague, for, with World War Two nearly over, many of its fine buildings were destroyed in Anglo-American bomb raids regarded by many as a war crime. Nearly 40,000 people died in the firestorm which engulfed a city packed with refugees. The results of the bombing were still clear to see, almost half a century later. There was a bare, open look about the city centre. It needed more trees, more quiet corners – another thirty years, in fact; though now, since reunification, rebuilding was gathering pace.

The soot-blackened Royal Palace beside the charming old Augustusbrücke spanning the wide-flowing Elbe was being restored. And, at least in the suburbs, dignified old burghers' houses still stood, a monument to quieter and more prosperous times. In the pleasant suburb of Loschwitz stood the only one of eighteen bridges over the Elbe to outlive the war. It survived Nazi explosive charges because two citizens cut the wires laid by the retreating SS troops. A group of more modern buildings was described to me as the former headquarters of the feared communist Stasi secret police, whose records were now being closely scrutinised.

As I crossed back into what had for years been called simply 'The West', there was a heartening reminder of what reunification meant. Approaching a pretty town of red-brick and timber houses east of Frankfurt, I looked for signs of the old divide. I couldn't see any border posts: no wall, no fence. Then, to my right, I became aware of the wide brown swathe of newly ploughed land snaking over the hills. Soon the old Iron Curtain would be nothing more than the middle of a cornfield.

Chapter 20
POLAR BEARS AND AN ANGRY WALRUS IN
FRANZ-JOSEF LAND

The end of the Cold War had created a rare reporting opportunity. Covering the Cod War off Iceland had been my first foreign assignment for Reuters. A journey to the North Polar region would produce my farewell feature for the old firm.

Franz-Josef Land hadn't been open to visitors for half a century. The nearest solid land to the North Pole, it was discovered by Norwegian seal hunters in 1865. A few years later, an Austro-Hungarian expedition led by Julius von Payer and Karl Weyprecht landed and named the group of 191 islands after their Emperor of the time. The islands were taken over by the Soviet Union in 1926 but, unusually, the Russians left the name alone while letting the rest of the world know who was boss in the area.

The straggling archipelago is Russia's northernmost territory. At a nearby group of islands, Novaya Zemlya, Soviet scientists had conducted controversial nuclear tests, and for four decades the whole area was strictly off limits to foreigners. Now an expedition trip to the area was being advertised by an upmarket tour group under the intriguing title, 'Journey to a Forbidden Land'. I was among the first to apply.

Charts of the area, obtained at a specialist bookshop off the Strand, still carried the cold war warning that aircraft infringing territorial limits might be fired on without warning. But in the political and business free-for-all that followed the end of the Soviet Union, the Russians were using every opportunity to make some hard currency. A firm with American, British and Swedish links had seized the moment. I figured the door would not remain open for very long – and I was right. Getting in on this exotic trip made an excellent feature story for Reuters, widely published.

After flying north from Stockholm, where I'd been visiting my son at university, I found the elderly 3,400-tonne Yugoslav-built *Klavdiya Yelanskaya* tied up against a wharf in the north Norwegian port of Tromsø. Looking quite tiny against the mountainous backdrop flanking the fjord, she seemed rather a fragile vessel to be taking us into polar regions, but I knew we'd be linking up with a nuclear-powered icebreaker later.

It could have been the line-up for an Agatha Christie tale. Aboard were professional scientists planning to forage for rare plants and explore signs of global warming – one of them absent-minded enough to miss the ship after one stop. There were middle-aged retirees who were clearly on the trip because they could afford it. A couple of seasoned expeditioners wore anoraks plastered with stickers and crests showing they'd been to most out of the way spots around the world, and didn't mind you knowing. There were mature, no-nonsense sort of women with ample bosoms, big hips and stout walking boots, who'd probably have walked the Pennine Way before breakfast. A scientist was in search of 'pingos' in the permafrost, and a young artist had flown from his home in Spain to capture scenes from a hitherto unpainted landscape. Also aboard was a retired Canon of Southwark Cathedral, while a long-bearded and rather eccentric Swiss gentleman made known at an early stage his intention to bathe naked in the closest spot we got to the Pole – and did.

The lecturers were led by a distinguished old soldier, Major-General Sir Roy Redgrave, who'd had charge of the military in Cyprus during the fifties emergency, when the guerrilla movement EOKA was trying to end British rule. His American colleague, Joe Hobbs, had done many adventurous things, like living for years with the Bedouin in Sinai.

Mikhail, one of the crewmen who'd brought our ship round the North Cape from Russia, told me he was born in Vilnius, but now lived in Murmansk. Maybe he'd thought it wise to move out of Lithuania, I speculated. People in the newly free Baltic States were making no secret of their dislike of the former colonisers. Catering was in charge of Austrian chefs, who appropriately for our first luncheon aboard produced a delicious 'Fish Ragout North Cape Style'.

Among the Russian supporting cast, the first person to be seen, standing at the end of a welcome line as we came up the gangplank, was a lovely young interpreter. Viktoria (Vika for short), daughter of the ship's purser, would be admired by all, wooed by many, won by none. Unsurprisingly, she had a boyfriend back in Murmansk. The men found her adorable, the women said she looked 'sulky'. *Ochin krasivaya devushka*, I reflected in my rudimentary (and phonetically transcribed) Russian. Later we'd meet a brilliant group of Russian musicians, whose late-night performances became a high spot on the diary. A cosmopolitan bunch. But there were no murders, though there were one or two hairy incidents among the ice floes.

Right now, I was more interested in what sort of a vessel we were on. I asked the seaman, Mikhail, 'Is this a good ship?'

He made a disconcerting so-so sign with his right hand. 'Sometimes, when is storm, is like this,' he said, making rocking motions with the hand. Well, I'd rather expected that.

Meanwhile, I managed to exchange my share of a pre-booked double cabin, the cheapest available, for a single one at no extra charge. A few occasional extracts from my diary – luckily I could plug in my portable keyboard in the cabin – may give the flavour of the trip:

3 July: Amazing where some of these people have been. A fellow northerner, David Taylor from Yorkshire, has been to Antarctica aboard a Russian icebreaker, which he boarded at Cape Town. It ran into a violent storm the second day out, and was listing 45 degrees at times, he tells me. It took eight days to get to the ice and twelve days to get back to Australia afterwards, a month of punishment which cost him £7,000. There's another Yorkshireman on board, Arthur Wolstenholme, who seems to know east Greenland, of all places, like the back of his hand. He's been several times to Angmassalik, spent time with the Inuit, and even learned how to handle a ten-dog sledge on the ice cap. 'They told me the words for left, right and start, but they didn't tell me the word for stop,' he said. 'Would you believe, it turned out to be *Woah* – the same as we'd say to a horse!' I couldn't compete. And these guys weren't even journalists. Obviously, the travel world has more to offer these days than Florida or the Mediterranean – if you can afford it. Dinner tonight included giant prawns, strawberries and quite a good white wine.

4 July: First stop on the agenda was Bear Island, a rugged slab of rock midway between Norway's North Cape, the setting, I remember, for one of Alastair McLean's adventure novels. Discovered by Dutch explorer Wilhelm Barents in 1596, it was named after the polar bears he found there. I was out on the fore-deck when the island suddenly loomed ahead of us, half-veiled by low cloud. We were scheduled to step ashore this inhospitable piece of land, if at all possible. Donning life jackets, we piled into the big rubber dinghies which would be our main means of conveyance from ship to shore during the days ahead, and sailed along the island's west coast, seeking a likely spot to step ashore. But conditions were too rough for a landfall, and with ice encroaching, hopes of visiting an old, now-abandoned Norwegian meteorological station had to be abandoned. Our first port of call will now have to be Spitzbergen, 130 miles to the north-west, tomorrow. Close on midnight – the time of day doesn't seem to matter in these northern summers – I went upstairs to find Russian musicians performing Western pop in the lounge. They presumably assumed this was what was required, but when everyone but a couple of us had left started playing some quite fantastic Russian music. The wonderful balalaika player, Victor Bednyak, was considered, they told me with great exactitude, 'the second best on that instrument in Russia'. I didn't feel it necessary to ask who was Number One. After a mixture of romantic ballads and high-speed traditional numbers, the few still present applauded warmly, but by now almost everyone had left for their cabins.

5 July: This tour is full of surprises. The first is the sudden change of weather, from lowering grey skies to almost Mediterranean sunshine. I was up on deck in an open-neck shirt this afternoon, being photographed by one of our Yorkshiremen. Then nothing less than an ecumenical church service was sud-denly announced, and duly conducted, by our fellow-passenger, the former Canon of Southwark Cathedral. It must surely have been the northernmost church service in the world today. (I later learned there are plans by the Russian Orthodox Church to build the world's northernmost church in Franz-Josef Land. It will be named after St Nicholas.) I initiated a campaign – taken up by the tour organisers – to have the Russian musicians properly advertised to play their own kind of music, not Western pap. They're all excellent performers, with two electronic keyboards,

bass and balalaika. There was an enthusiastic turnout in the lounge this evening. Baritone Alexander Danilovsky, elegant in a dinner jacket, sang soulful songs of love, requited or otherwise, and is already a favourite among the ladies. Real Russian stuff, as I'd thought, is what these educated people want to hear. Strange that the organisers didn't see it.

6 July: In brilliant sunshine we docked at the Russian port of Barentsburg, on the west coast of Spitzbergen. The buildings, a drab mixture of timber and concrete, looked anything but attractive as we came alongside the wharf, but the setting is undeniably impressive, the still waters of the fjord half-enclosed by the dazzling white peaks of the mountains. The settlement is as dreary ashore as it looked from the rail of the ship. It's basically a mining community, a far Russian outpost. The Norwegians, living up the coast, apparently call it a blot on the landscape. The Russians stick it out there for the sake of its coal – and to have a base in the region not too far from the Americans in Greenland. Coal has been mined here since the late nineteenth century, but today only the Norwegians and Russians remain. The Russian settlement is largely self-supporting, said the town's tourism manager, Evgeny Busni, escorting us round a farm I'd hardly expected to see this far north. The cowshed smelled like any other cowshed, said a lady who told me she farmed in Cheshire. As for the pig farm, said Evgeny in his typical Russo-English phraseology, 'You can visit if you like. But myself, you see, I am not too fond of the special aroma in there – which I call Chanel Number 5.' There's also a big greenhouse where they grow everything from tomatoes to asters. 'In the four dark months, going inside there is real Heaven,' said the poetic Evgeny.

In a small square alongside the ship, residents had spread out their wares on tables – badges, old army caps, fur hats, babushka dolls – and were ready to exchange any hard currency you cared to name. I settled for a beautifully illustrated book about Spitzbergen, the text of which was in Russian, which doesn't really matter. They were all desperate for foreign banknotes, and I gave a twenty Norwegian kroner note to a delightful small boy who let me film him at the door of his house. As I walked on, a heavyweight Russian lady, presumably his mother or grandmother, appeared on the doorstep, called out, 'Thank You. Please Wait,' and sent him chasing after me with a small souvenir badge. The kids, in their bright woollen caps, are delightful. A crocodile of them was winding its way up the hill to school and a teacher gladly allowed me to film. As they passed, the kids smilingly cried out 'Hallo' and 'Goodbye'. Well, our visit is that short. Longyearbyen, further up the coast, is as bright and modern in the Nordic style as Barentsburg was drab. We bounced ashore, crowded on two rubber dinghies. I filmed from a kneeling position at the prow as we bumped along amid showers of spray. The weather is gorgeous, wide blue sky, warm sunshine. Can this really be so close to the North Pole? Everything is spic and span in the town centre of Longyearbyen, home to about 2,500 Norwegians. After passing a pub/motel, you find yourself in a supermarket which sells just about everything you can get at home. A monument honours the Norwegians who'd died under German occupation of the archipelago in World War Two. Steaming north now along a sheltered strait, we're heading towards the town of Ny Ålesund, which we'll visit tomorrow. I seem to have been absorbed into the Russian circle. I sit with them, drink with them, the boys even let me sit in on keyboard for a couple of numbers last night, though none of them speaks English – I converse with the keyboard player in German – and Vika frequently has to translate. All on the ship are thrown constantly into each other's company. It's a pleasant little cocoon, as if the rest of the world didn't exist. The sun, the glittering ice, the mountains, the wide vistas and sense of endless space, the long days when the sun never sets are all quite intoxicating.

7 July: It's been a long day. Ny Ålesund is a Norwegian research centre (global warming) and by nine o'clock, anchored in the bay, we were skimming ashore in the Zodiacs, the water smooth as silk. Here is preserved the restored engine of what was the world's northernmost railway until it closed just a few years ago. I sent postcards back to Lancashire from the world's northernmost post office. This is an impressive mini-town, but I don't know if I'd be all that keen on spending the winter in total darkness, as some of them do, with little chance of getting out of the place. There's no shortage of researchers willing to do it, though. By the waterfront, Arctic terns circle, screech and dive on intruders coming too close – it's the nesting season – and one of my fellow passengers got a wound on his balding pate. I escaped with showers of birdlime on the hood of my jacket. I interviewed a couple of nice young Danes who'd just sailed in from the Faroe Islands. They were impressed that I'd been there – and more

especially that I spoke some Danish. Good job they and their boat called here today. I learned at table this evening that one of our number, Barry Matthews, a geologist attached to Liverpool University, literally missed the boat when we left. We were under way down the fjord when an urgent radio message from the Danes was received on the bridge, saying there was an Englishman still on shore. A Zodiac was despatched back to the jetty. Without the Danes, there could have been a problem. Will the laggard ever admit the episode to his friends? I wonder. He joked about it to us. 'I might have been there all winter,' he said.

In late afternoon, we arrived in the very photogenic Magdalenafjord. Everything was shrouded in fog as we stepped ashore. I hardly recognised Alexander, dressed in military kit with a rifle slung over his shoulder. He's the sharpshooter, just in case of trouble with polar bears. There was a barbecue on the beach, lots of beer – and Russian vodka. When, after an hour, the silvery sea mist suddenly lifted, I realised we were in a fjord of breathtaking beauty, tall mountains and snow-white glaciers all around us. Now, across the bay, could be seen a much bigger Russian liner, disgorging dozens of tourists. Back on board, the magic of the day seemed to inspire what's already become a nightly performance of Russian music, the real stuff. Earlier, Alexander had invited Vika and myself to his cabin for a drink and to see his paintings. As well as a musician and sharpshooter, he's an accomplished artist and wants to sell some pictures to passengers. I said I'd gladly handle the publicity. I can't seem to escape the world of print.

8 July: I sat this evening with the boys of the band, who were joined later by Lerissa, a bouncy blonde who normally serves behind the bar but has been doing some singing the last few months. The Russians are planning to put on a variety show for us towards the end of the voyage and are regularly rehearsing in their off-duty hours. I was touched when, in gratitude for my promotion of him and the boys, Alexander publicly dedicated one of his vocals to me tonight. There's a lot of soul about these Russians. The advance material for his exhibition is another great success. I wrote introductory notes from what he told me – translated by Vika – and in the radio room, got printouts made. Alexander did a quick watercolour sketch at the top of each leaflet and one was pushed under every cabin door. I'm pleased to have helped, and Alexander is my friend for life, he says. His collection

will be on show in the Sports Room. On the debit side, the ship has been encountering some pretty steep swells, inducing a corkscrewing motion, and several people skipped lunch, I heard. I managed a light one and an equally light dinner, but stuck to soup, salad and sweet.

10 July: In a showpiece of expert manoeuvring by the two skippers off Franz-Josef Land, which I captured on film, we tied up today alongside the massive icebreaker *Tamyr*. Built at Finland's Va'rtsila Shipyard, with a crew of 110, it dwarfs our tiny vessel and carries its own helicopter. Using reporter's privilege, I got to sit next to the pilot, an ex-Soviet Air Force man called Vladimir, and got good film as we zoomed up from the rear deck, circled the ship and sped off across a mixture of ice floes and open water to Hooker's Island, perhaps the most famous of the group. Close on a century ago, it was a major base for polar expeditions and was visited by Germany's *Graf Zeppelin* airship in 1931. The island housed a meteorological station from 1929 to 1963 and staff there were marooned from 1941 to 1945 during World War Two. A graveyard touchingly remains. From the air, the broken drift ice looked rather like a huge jigsaw puzzle not quite fitting together. The landscape is bleak. One of our number inevitably complained it was nothing like Antarctica (where, of course, she'd been). But nobody thought it would be.

The long abandoned research station, surrounded by a straggle of old timber huts along the shore, looks rather like a deserted mining village in an American Western, walls and roofs falling apart, the weather drifting in through broken windows and doors. But it was, somewhat alarmingly, recommended to us as the refuge to aim for if any marauding Polar bears should disturb the scene. The whole terrain is brightened by some gorgeous and completely unexpected golden flowers, which I was told were Arctic poppies, and lots of tiny but colourful saxifrages and mosses in vivid reds and bright blues. There's a fragile, tentative beauty in the very short summer of this desolate place. Down by the shore, our Swiss friend was preparing to carry out his threat to swim at 80 degrees latitude and perhaps become the first man to bathe naked so close to the North Pole. I seemed to be the only one around with a camera, and took a series of shots, plus one with his own camera at his request, as he stripped to the skin on the beach, crawled across a ladder which he'd liberated from one of the shacks and slung across some small ice floes. He finally flung himself in, splashing six strokes across the water, startling some terns, and came swiftly back again, before hauling himself up on to the ice and nonchalantly towelling himself down with no particular urgency. He must be one of the few people, if there are any others, who've swum voluntarily in Franz-Josef Land! There's no accounting for tastes.

Back on the icebreaker, we were shown round by Chief Engineer Boris Girsh. The ship is as massive as an apartment bloc, the interior spic and span. There's a dining hall, gymnasium and hospital and, amidships, a large raked lecture hall. Most impressive – and not a little alarming – was to peer through thick protective windows at the nuclear power plant.

'Go ahead, take pictures,' Boris told us as we looked down into the huge eerily lit chamber where the twin reactors are housed – at one time these would have been state secrets. 'Don't worry,' said Boris. 'In any case of leakage we would shut down the reactors. There would be a flashing red light on the screen.' Fortunately for us and the Polar region, it never happened. A portrait of the former top Soviet official who launched the icebreaker still hangs on the wall. Boris shrugged. 'Which of us chooses our parents?' he quipped.

Naturally, for my story, I wanted to know about the economics of using huge and expensive vessels like this to plough a passage through the ice for frivolous groups of travellers and a few scientists. Who did such ships normally break through the pack ice for? 'For people like ourselves, of course!' cried a pompous know-all from the Home Counties. The chief engineer laughed politely but firmly at this asinine notion and confirmed that the icebreakers were mainly used to assist merchant vessels, as I'd imagined. Though reluctant to talk about financial aspects of the operation, Boris told me privately that running the ship cost nearly 2 million roubles a day. I learned later that the cruise firm had chartered ships from the Murmansk Shipping Company for six voyages, so maybe the figures nearly added up. Amid the political turmoil in Moscow, the Russians maybe think it's better to have the vessels used, and their crews to have work, than have them laid up in harbour. I'm sure these Russian naval ratings are being paid peanuts.

11 July: Another active day of helicopter and dinghy rides, first to Cape Flora, its steep mountain slopes shrouded by cloud towards the summit. The air was dense with the raucous cry of nesting

birds. Geologist Barry Matthews quickly got busy with spade and plastic bags. He's trying to gain facts about global warming and underground explosions, he told me. The 'pingos' he's looking for are conical hills of earth-covered ice, usually an indication of permafrost, which sometimes explode in summer, releasing high-pressure natural gas. It's all a mystery to me. His friend Robert, the artist, sat perched on a huge rock, sketching the scene. It's quite soggy underfoot, apparently because of the summer-thawing permafrost. 'This permafrost's a damn nuisance,' said Sir Eric gruffly, sounding very English. At one point I sank well below boot level, briefly evoking memories of the Great Grimpen Mire. Good to hear that the hard stuff seldom begins more than a foot down.

This afternoon we had a helicopter trip to Bell Island, an equally bleak but beautiful place. An Englishman called Smith sailed there twice a century ago. His boat sank on the second voyage, but he survived after building a timber house which still stands. I was photographed, as were a few others, holding a huge whalebone, part of the natural debris on the beach. 'It looks much longer when it's upright,' I observed, perhaps incautiously. Ian, the dry Scot taking the snapshot, replied with the old music hall retort featuring actresses and bishops.

A trip round the fjord in one of the motorised dinghies was swiftly terminated after a scary encounter with a male walrus. Reacting angrily as we circled the waters where he – and presumably the females – were swimming, he suddenly changed course and started power-swimming after us, his huge head jerking up in the air with each massive stroke. I had time to film the action. There was an ugly moment when he reared even higher out of the water, exhibiting two long pointed tusks – a scene luckily preserved on my film. I thought he was going to fling himself into the boat or take a bite at it. The Russian boatman told the young man at the stern to rev up fast. He needed no encouragement.

But the polar regions are all about those white cuddly looking bears, and we still hadn't seen any. On the tenth and last day of the trip, our luck changed. The captain of the icebreaker sent the helicopter up in a final attempt and a mile away a male, a female and two cubs were spotted ambling across the ice. As the helicopter swooped lower, its blades whirling noisily above them, the bear family, their yellowish coats highlighted against a broken mass of ice floes, changed tack and scurried away from the racket. The helicopter pilot, with some deft manoeuvring, nudged them back towards the ship and finally right across our bows. Cameras whirred as the animals padded past, the mother sometimes sheltering the cubs under her body, occasionally growling displeasure. The scene was fortunately bathed in bright sunshine. Standing in the bows just below the bridge I got two excellent film sequences, the mother and cubs up front, the male following behind. I've watched it many times since. But you can't please everyone. The irate Swiss gentleman called it a scandal to flush the animals out for the sake of tourists. He was in a small minority. The official lecturers, experienced explorers, said no damage would have been done to animals accustomed to natural challenges. One of them admitted that the helicopter went a bit close. 'We might do it a bit differently on another occasion,' he said, 'but let's keep things in perspective. Nobody's shooting polar bears any more.'

But there may not be any more such occasions. The voyages from Norway were discontinued, and it's not easy to get to Franz-Josef Land any more. You can travel to Murmansk by luxury train and then sail directly on the big icebreaker, with landings promised, and the same sort of helicopter trips we had in 1993. The price is not for the faint-hearted ($22,690 to 33,390). I hope at least they see some polar bears.

Sailing back south there was a mournful farewell blast from the bass hooter of the massive icebreaker as it forged past to disappear into the gloom. Spirits lifted the following day as we sailed in blazing sunshine past the northern shores of Russia and Finland. Off-duty crew members lay lazily on the decks, soaking up the warmth. The sight of a first fishing boat was a sign we were back off Europe's mainland. Then we were below the cliffs of the North Cape, the observatory perched on top. Years earlier I'd gazed from there over the waters to the north, not dreaming I'd ever get there. Flashes of sunlight reflected from car windscreens on the mainland. The following day we'd be back in Tromsø. From there the ship would make a second such voyage – the last of its kind. I'd got a good story, well used around the world. Curious to see it in Kuwait's English-language daily when I visited there a couple of months later.

On the last night aboard, our crew put on their last and biggest show. More than usually sentimental ballads from Aleksander, and a spirited performance by the band, by now glowing from the warm response they'd received. They brought the house (or the ship) down with a breakneck performance of Khachaturian's 'Sabre Dance'. And balalaika player Viktor dedicated a solo to me in recognition of my logistic support.

The Russians had all become friends. Did I ever see them again? I once saw Viktoria, her parents and fiancé, a nice young chap called Alex, when I broke off from a package tour to St Petersburg to fly up to Murmansk. I'd hoped to share a few memories with the whole gang. At the purser's family flat there was much talk and many drinks. But the boys from the band were now scattered around the country and we never made contact. Down at the quayside, before flying back to England, I saw the Klavdiya Yelanskaya being loaded with some rather dull-looking commercial cargo for a regular trip to settlements along Russia's north coast. It didn't seem fair on the old ship. I wish I'd never looked.

Chapter 21
I WASN'T GOING TO SIT BY THE WINDOW, WATCHING THE WORLD GO BY

Shortly after the seismic changes in the European political scene, Reuter bosses decided they could lose a few old-timers. And I'd figured, anyway, that my assignment to Bonn during the Big Change would probably have been the last foreign story I helped to cover for the old firm. Some people welcome the chance to retire, some don't. What matters, naturally, is the money. I gathered they'd make it worth your while to go and, since I had other irons in the fire, I went to see the Staff Manager. (I hate the phrase 'Human Resources', which didn't come in until later.) What difference, I asked, would going three years early make to my pension? I was told it would mean getting 62% of final salary, as against the maximum 65% I'd partly paid for with my own contributions over the decades. So I said, in effect, 'I'll sign.'

In the final years at Number 85, I'd become World Desk Editor, which meant I was responsible for the daily news file going to subscribers worldwide. Not as exciting as reporting the news – nothing is – but it was a prestige post and I think I knew as well as anyone at 85 Fleet Street the ins and outs of news agency reporting. It was no trouble compiling the News Schedule we put out to subscribers, after deciding what was most newsworthy, and in what order. I also had to produce annual reports on desk staff. I hope I was always fair. No one ever appealed, anyway, as they had a right to. Now it was perhaps time to call it a day.

And so one evening, at a congenial pub in Fleet Street, I was suddenly having one of those farewell parties you'd thought only happened to other people. What's more important, attended only by people you wanted to see, not those you didn't. Some of the latter, anyway, had now been moved sideways to posts better suited to their particular talents. It was heartening to get a flood of goodwill messages from abroad, particularly places where I'd worked and lived, from Karachi to Cairo, Geneva, Oslo, Stockholm, Bonn and New York, as well as from London staffers.

It was a good party, and one of the nicest presents, which hangs on the wall of my study here, was a very accurate cartoon drawing of myself as World Desk Editor looking rather harassed as our three graphics experts, Lance (who drew the cartoon), Kieron and Chee-Kin hover around me with their misspelt offerings and the clock on the wall ticked relentlessly towards the vital hour of 4 p.m., when the sked went out to subscribers around the world. This wouldn't be my worry any more.

I didn't wait for retirement to creep up on me. I'd no intention of sitting by that front window. So on the very first day of what promised, if I were fortunate, to be a delightful long holiday, I was sitting in the sun on a bench near the old Market Hall in the village of Chipping Campden, tying up the laces of my new walking boots for an assault on the Cotswold Way. My distant goal was the similarly named village of Chipping Sodbury, 100 miles south. I knew from my Old English studies that the name has nothing to do with chipping wood, or French fries, but stems from the old English word for a market town. And the Swedes, I now knew, had virtually the same word, pronounced somewhat similarly, as in Nyköping, Norrköping and all the other Kopings around Stockholm.

I'd planned it well in advance. Anorak and walking boots (a sprained ankle incurred during a twelve-mile walk in trainers had taught me to do things properly). My haversack was crammed with changes of shirt and underwear, mini-camera, binoculars, notebook and pen. Later I would add a plastic bottle, to fill with water every morning. I should have included sticking plasters, too. It would be the first time I'd walked so far.

I'd had to get out of London. Even Wimbledon Village, where I'd been living for two or three years, had become steadily less attractive as time went on. I had one of six flats in a former vicarage beside St Mary's Church – the one whose spire you see on television during the tennis fortnight. But the place lost some of its charm after the occupant of one basement flat died and her grandson moved in, ominously describing himself to me as a 'stoodent'. He thereafter invited in a motley collection of layabouts who littered the garden, blocked the drive with an old truck and played rock music at unsocial hours. The new English urban horror had arrived.

The gang was finally ousted, but not because of our complaints. A large posse of police officers arrived one Saturday morning, surrounded the house in two groups and escorted the residents of the basement flat to jail, to be convicted later of drug-running.

Wimbledon was supposed to be a prime residential area. But, for me, London – like many English cities – was rapidly losing whatever charms it ever had. I wasn't the only sufferer from the new plague. One of my colleagues and his wife, living in Canterbury, bought a flat for their student son, but immediately a gang of squatters broke in. This being England, they were not ousted by cops, of course. His solicitor advised him to pay for a gang of heavies, which he did.

When my plumber/handyman/friend Gil Hardy heard of our own trials and tribulations at Steeple Court, he offered to arrange a similar operation to rid us too of the plague. 'Any time you say, John, I'll bring the lads in,' he said. But I had to demur. In any case, I was only one of six flat-owners in the building. It was with satisfaction and relief, therefore, that I watched from my bedroom window and saw the 'stoodent' strong-armed through the garden, together with his hysterically screaming girlfriend and other assorted pals to the waiting police cars. Even better to read later in the local paper that the law had taken its course at Wimbledon Magistrates' Court. But of course my experience mirrored that of countless others whose lives were being made miserable, apparently without redress, by our pusillanimous local and national politicians in England's new 'politically correct' society. It was the drugs that did for the squatters, not our complaints. And as I no longer had to tramp down every morning to Wimbledon Tube Station and back up the hill every evening, it was out to the country for me.

Before making any big decisions, I wanted to have a look around. The Cotswolds were on my shortlist, as were East Anglia and the southern counties close to the Channel. I drove round a lot of small roads and villages along with my son, as keen as myself that I should find a congenial spot to relax after the days in Fleet Street and 'Abroad'. It was thumbs down to Kent (a crowded traffic corridor to the Channel, I thought), Sussex (too snobby and expensive), and East Anglia (as Noel Coward said – very flat). I didn't want mountains, but I wanted some hills, as in Northern England. But I'd decided that going back to old haunts in the north would be a mistake. I liked the people in that region, but not the weather. The Middle East had softened me.

So in my brand new leather hiking boots (not a good idea, I discovered later, I should have worn them in a bit first), I strode off down the main street of Chipping Campden, past the mediaeval market building which the Yanks had tried but failed to buy and move to America after World War Two, and a picturesque thatched cottage looking too good to be true, where the Graham Greenes once lived. It was a stiffish climb for a beginner. But once at the top, rambling along a much flatter meadow fronting a quiet country road, I knew this was the place to be. No cars, no fumes, no stoodents, only sheep. And a wonderful view of the surrounding hills. In all the years overseas, interesting as they'd been, I'd obviously been missing something.

The foreigners, it seemed, knew better. I'd meet the first of them after descending to Broadway (the original one) from the commanding stone tower at the top. It was built in 1799 by the Earl of Coventry because his wife fancied the view. Now mere commoners can see for a hundred miles in all directions on a clear day. Down in the town, my first bed-and-breakfast host turned out to be a charming Italian, who'd very sensibly been living there for years. Within minutes of my checking in, dusty and just a bit hot, Luigi had sent a pint of beer upstairs to my room – 'You looked like you needed it.' And his restaurant below was superb. He served me delicious *Fegato Veneziano* just the way I like it ('On a bed of onions,' he announced poetically) and a half-bottle of Frascati. That, plus a bed under the eaves, was my first taste of freedom. Within minutes of leaving Broadway's main street next morning, I was walking along hedgerows ablaze with dog roses, through fields golden with dandelions. The holiday world of lookalike airports and hotels seemed like a bad dream. Before long, the roads I was occasionally obliged to cross would seem an unpardonable intrusion, the automobile the enemy.

The Cotswold Way is a challenge, like Britain's many other long-distance walks. Not as tough as the West Highland Way, which had been traversed by my old Reuter chum, Ronnie Farquhar, inspiring me to do this one. A squad of British soldiers I chatted with south of Cheltenham in a field full of red poppies were doing the complete trek from Bath at a rate of twenty-five miles a day. More leisurely walkers do eight to twelve miles a day, stopping for sightseeing over the space of two weeks. Six American ladies staying at one of the bed and breakfast stops that punctuate the route were travelling in the grand style, having their luggage sent on by car from one village to the next.

The first person I met on a farm track high in the hills was a New York banker, and by all the evidence a successful one. He'd been coming here on extended summer breaks for years and thought the area enchanting. So much so that he'd bought a cottage in the next village. 'You'll like Stanton,' he said, which proved an understatement. As I walked on, meadowlarks warbled, sheep bleated, as if by order. It was the sort of landscape hinted at in the music of Vaughan Williams, Frederick Delius, George Butterworth. But where were the English people? The next walkers I met were a couple of Australians. As I slithered down the muddy track towards the village, Warren and Lynn, from Canberra, were toiling upwards. It was a very hot July, and Warren was stripped to the waist. We were all ready for a rest and a chat. The walker's world is a small one, I'd find. I wasn't surprised when Lynn turned out to be the sister-in-law of an old Reuter colleague of mine in Brussels.

Stanton was exactly the picture postcard place the American and the Australians had promised. Honey-coloured stone cottages lined the single main street, mullioned windows and steeply pitched stone roofs recalled the world of a Miss Marple or Mary Poppins. There was an old stone cross and sundial and a church dating back to the Norman Conquest. Other historical references abounded. Here the young Methodist campaigner John Wesley preached before departing for America in 1735.

But I was beginning to wonder where all the British walkers

were. Then, leaving Stanton by a stile near Chestnut Farm I met a merry couple from Banbury and, this being a very hot day, the talk turned naturally to refreshment.

'Not too many pubs round 'ere,' the man warned. 'But if you do find one, try Old 'Ookey.'

'Old Hookey?'

'Old 'Ookey. Now that's a real beer. Wouldn't do to be drivin' a car after a couple of pints o' that.' He chortled and they made off towards another pub they'd heard of over the hill.

Back on my own track, I never did find Old Hookey, nor any pub at all. Several cornfields later, I settled for a cup of cold, clear water. A workman painting a cottage kindly climbed down his ladder to get it. It tasted at least as good as Old Hookey.

You become part of a club, the walkers' club. Staying at the half-timbered White Horse Inn in the village of Winchcombe that evening, I was excited by the knowledge that I'd been treading a path once walked by pilgrims and mediaeval traders. In the bar were walkers from several continents. English couples in their seventies, seasoned hikers by the look of them, tucked into steak and kidney pie. A plumpish Italian sat gloomily with his wife in a window recess. They'd just arrived and been put out by what they'd heard about the steepness of the hills. 'They still wants to walk to Broadway tomorrow,' murmured the landlord as he pulled me a pint. 'I don't think they're going to make it.'

Well, there's undeniably a stiff climb every morning, since the villages where you stay are usually in the valleys. The following day I reached the highest point of the Way, near the Stone Age burial site of Belas Knap. Further along was Sleeve Common, a vast area of gently undulating grassland, full of the sound of larks. A stable boy from one of the nearby racing stables thundered past on a thoroughbred. The Irish, great racing lovers, take over every pub and hotel room in the area during the annual Cheltenham Gold Cup.

The following day I had great views of Gloucestershire and in the distance Wales before plunging into some rather gloomy beechwoods. I emerged thankfully at a place called Cooper's Hill, more than ready for my next stopover. Luckily, a lady called Rosemary Hellerman was busy in the garden of her cottage.

There was a dog too, and a cat – several cats. Mrs Hellerman seemed to be surrounded by flowers and animals. 'You'll be needing a cup of tea,' she said.

Also some minor medical attention. She provided me with a sticking plaster for one of my toes. Interpreting my wandering gaze, she said, 'Yes, it's more like an overgrown shed than a house.' But her guest book said she'd had 1,200 visitors for tea and scones or bed and breakfast during the past year. Mrs Hellerman was one of the Cotswold Way's unpaid wardens. She was also into local church activities. 'But we're losing members,' she said. 'Some of them won't have those guitars!' Hooray for them, I thought.

In the village of Painswick next day, needing more foot repairs, I bought new socks in a shop on the main thoroughfare, laid down in the year 1253 but still called New Street. Shaded by a line of yew trees beside the parish church, boots off and feet airing in full view of the populace, I ate my sandwich lunch. That night I stayed at a converted Methodist chapel on a hillside near the city of Stroud. Rain pelted on the slate roof during the night but it was sunny again as I joined a pair of teachers from Bolton ploughing further south along muddy green lanes. At Wotton-under-edge (the locals say ' 'Oot'n', I was told), my companions, seasoned walkers, pushed on. I soaked in a bath in a cosy room over a tea shop.

The proprietress kindly rang ahead and arranged a room with her friend Mrs Shipp, of Chipping Sodbury – my final destination. En route there, I called at a small village church in Little Sodbury, whose genial rector, the Rev. Keith Ensor, pointed out the church's chief treasure, an old oak pulpit at which once preached the famous churchman William Tyndale who, according to the plaque, 'heard the call to translate the Bible into English in 1523 and was martyred in 1534'. At that time, the original church was torn down. But Mr Ensor found the old baptismal font, now being used as a bird bath. The pulpit had disappeared, but with a tenacity worthy of Holmes and Watson he'd tracked it to a loft above the stables of a house sixty miles away.

Later, my overnight host, Mr Shipp, showed me the wild

flower meadow where, he said, a one-man circus used to come years ago. 'He had two horses and other small animals, including a tame rat which performed tricks. But the animal rights people got on to him and he had to close down.' Yet on an ancient common by an abandoned farm, the authorities had not stepped in to evict a straggle of decrepit trucks and cars.

'Squatters,' he said. 'They make my blood boil.'

'Not just yours,' I said. I was becoming familiar with the new priorities of English civil servants and the political classes.

Well, I'd made it, and lost a few pounds into the bargain. Some of the rarest pleasures hadn't been in the guidebooks. Like the tinkling brook near a village called Lower Kilcott where I slaked my thirst, washed boots encrusted with mud from a particularly sticky 'green lane', and then just let the water tickle my toes. I'd have paid a lot for that. Or when, after a long trek over the hills near Winchcombe, I lay prostrate on a bench in an orchard where I'd just quaffed a much needed bottle of cider. I gazed gratefully up at the sun-dappled leaves of the apple trees that made such bliss possible.

Returning by train, I gazed up with a certain pride at the long string of green hills I'd just walked. My account of the 100-mile hike was snapped up by the *Washington Post*, whose editors, when I sent them a first two-page treatment, asked, 'Why so short?' It was easy to treble the wordage and they used it over several pages. And with a new intro featuring the Aussies I'd met en route, I sold the story to *The Australian* newspaper too.

More importantly, the week-long walk decided where I wanted to live. It wouldn't be long before I exchanged Wimbledon for the Worcestershire village of Middle Littleton. Or Little Middleton, as some old Reuter chums insisted on saying before they got used to the name. My brother-in-law calls it 'Much Binding in the Whatsit'.

Visitors seem to like it. The house, an early barn conversion, directly adjoins a thirteenth-century tithe barn, two of whose buttresses are anchored in the guest bedroom, especially impressing American visitors. People arrive from around the globe to see the tithe barn, a National Trust site, and we often chat, exchanging places we've been.

In summer, only the bleating of sheep or the whinnying of horses in the next field disturb the peace and quiet. Or the occasional peal of bells from nearby St Nicholas' Church, where each November a dwindling band of ex-servicemen gather to honour the dead of all the wars. It's all a long way from the Middle East or Manhattan.

Chapter 22
'IF YOU HAS TO ASK WHAT IT IS,
YOU AIN'T GOT IT' – LOUIS ON SWING

The last obit I ever wrote for Reuters (news organisations always have them ready in advance), was on Ella Fitzgerald. Of her memorable interpretations of songs by George Gershwin, Cole Porter, Irving Berlin and the rest, I wrote that 'she sang the love songs of a whole generation', which was true enough. I'd retired by the time Ella died a few years later after a wretched time in medical care. I hope the Desk still used my Intro.

Occasions for jazz stories at Reuters were limited. In my early days with the agency, subbing on the Central Desk, as it was then called, I once rescued a story that had come in from New York about the English pop singer Tommy Steele. The Desk boss of the time didn't think it good enough for the Reuterwire. I rescued it from the spike, however, sharpened it up a bit and sent it to the *Melody Maker* newspaper. It seemed a pity to waste a good story. They made it a page lead and paid me a nice little sum. In post-Reuter days, I thought Louis Armstrong's centenary demanded something special too, and *London Magazine* Editor Alan Ross agreed.

Actually, I found, Satchmo hadn't been born, like Yankee Doodle Dandy, on the Fourth of July 1900, as he patriotically proclaimed. He'd simply changed the date by a couple of years. It made a good piece anyway, providing an opportunity to sum up what had been happening to jazz over the years – and indeed much of my own lifetime.

Jelly Roll Morton, pianist, pool shark, occasional pimp and self-proclaimed 'Inventor of Jazz', instantly recognisable by the diamond in one of his front teeth, once told jazz scholar Alan Lomax, recording the great man's piano version of 'Mamie's

Blues' over half a century ago, 'This is the first blues I no doubt ever heard in my life.'

Well, the Morton band's infectious 'Doctor Jazz', led off by Jelly Roll's high-pitched joyous shout, which still thrills after all the years, was the first jazz record I no doubt ever bought in my life. And decades later, the music of the Red Hot Peppers, which I always visualise as a vibrant clash of red, black and gold, remains a delight. His 'Deep Creek', one of the most melancholy tracks in the jazz repertoire, is a three-minute masterpiece unlike anything else in jazz before or since. And if the Morton was the first ten-inch LP I ever got, played on a simple turntable bought at the same time, the Armstrong Hot Fives closely followed. Louis put jazz on the world map. The man who was born in a log cabin in the slums of New Orleans and lived to be honoured by presidents perfectly personified the Jazz Century.

The years around 1900 were a sort of milestone in the history of jazz. In earlier decades, musicians like Louis Gottschalk, remembered for brilliant pieces like 'Banjo', and later Scott Joplin, with his stiffly syncopated rags (theme music, seventy years later in the film hit *The Sting*) seemed to have been intuitively feeling their way towards a more recognisable American kind of music. In 1899 another black pianist, Eubie Blake, who lived to be over a hundred, wrote the distinctly jazz-inflected 'Sounds of Africa' (later to be retitled the 'Charleston Rag'). Then the floodgates opened.

Yet, in a new millennium, we still don't seem to have decided exactly what jazz is – and maybe we never will. From the early years, even the name presented problems. The *New York Sun* said in a 1917 article that the new phenomenon had been variously called Jas, Jass, Jazz, Jacz and Jascz. I think posterity got it right. I see that fairly recent Chambers and Oxford dictionaries still talk lazily about 'syncopation' and 'ragtime', which smack of the twenties and thirties and don't tell us much about what's happened since.

The *Encyclopaedia Britannica* (15th edition, 1979), more perceptively, says of jazz:

> The performer is usually his own composer, in contrast to more conventional musical forms in which the artist is fundamentally an executant expressing the finds of the creative mind.

Louis, of course, used to brush off the problem. Of swing, that engaging and still highly popular product of the thirties and forties, he famously told one of those earnest American interviewers: 'If you has to ask what it is, you ain't got it.' Boogie-woogie, he added, was 'pretty much the same as the blues, only more rhythmatical'.

Duke Ellington, probably the greatest jazz composer, waved the matter aside, saying, ' "Jazz" is only a word and has no real meaning.' Personally, I always liked the definition by a later piano genius, Bill Evans, who said, 'Jazz is not a What, it's a How.' An approach to music, rather than the music itself. Which saves us from the perennial infighting of jazz addicts.

In mid-century England, jazz clubs, like billiard halls, were still seen by many as a bit dodgy, despite the fact that most 'trad(itional)' fans, as most of them were, always sat respectfully in their hairy tweed jackets and corduroys, drank their beer quietly, didn't disturb the musicians with unnecessary chit-chat and applauded at all the right times. The atmosphere in those old black-and-white recordings of London jazz concerts, compered by the equally solemn Steve Race, was almost that of a church service. (And not a church service of the hilarious kind depicted in that movie masterpiece *The Blues Brothers*.)

A far cry too from some of those live sessions recorded in New York night clubs which I occasionally get to review, on which one can hardly hear the music for the talking. Back in the fifties, a time when I was trying to play trad jazz myself, there was a near riot when Britain's aristocratic bandleader Humphrey Lyttelton first smuggled a saxophone into the traditional front line of trumpet (or cornet), clarinet and trombone. Trad fans called the interloper 'a dirty bopper'. And well into the twenty-first century, the same folk who tapped their feet in the Fifties to 'Muskrat Ramble' and 'Clarinet Marmalade' still regard all that as the only real jazz. The annual festival at nearby Upton-on-Severn, which I sometimes attend, might almost at times be an old folks' outing. Long may they last!

Rearguard actions are still being fought in some quarters against the doctrinal errors, as they are seen, of swing. I see in the latest issue of a jazz magazine regularly sent me by a thriving trad jazz circle in Bude, Cornwall, that some reactionaries were a bit uncertain in their reactions to a recent concert by a swing group. Swing? Isn't that a bit commercial? One can almost imagine the shudders. (I should add that the leader of the visiting group himself was a clarinettist in his seventies!)

Time has made them a slightly endangered species. I'd see them at lunchtime in my Reuter days, flipping through the racks of second-hand LPs or even 78s (of which they must already have had hundreds if not thousands) hunting for treasures in soon-to-disappear specialist shops around London's Charing Cross Road. And they turn up as faithful as ever, heavier, greyer or bald, in pubs, clubs, church halls and holiday camps around the country to listen to jazzmen who are maybe just as old. They don't shout and scream like rock fans or wave flags and sing 'Rule Britannia' like upmarket people on the last night of the Proms, and once the show is over they file out of church halls in orderly fashion and make their way home. Admirable folk, the Brits.

My jazz penfriend Bill Gallagher in California spends a lot of his free time holed up in his den, playing, taping or ordering jazz records, reviewing them for the local magazine, writing discographies and sending other members of the fraternity in America or abroad copies of re-releases or just-discovered works by the jazz greats. The private passion in his free time of a German banker I used to know in my Bonn days was playing and composing jazz on an electronic keyboard. He once sent me a coded birthday greeting consisting of a series of jazz chord symbols like A7 and Gmin6, from which he expected me to recreate his latest rather avant-garde blues theme to my own taste.

I'm just as crazy myself. When I returned to England and wanted to complete my collection of *Jazz Journals*, the bible founded in 1948, I visited a Lancastrian I'd heard of in search of the missing years (he kindly had them photocopied for me). His otherwise unassuming semi-detached house near Rochdale was a treasure house of jazz facts and figures. Occasionally he writes to *Jazz Journal* to put some reader or writer right about jazz history – and he isn't the only one. I was once rash enough to state in an article about that jazz piano 'aristocrat' Sir Charles Thompson that he'd recorded a certain track on 16 December 1953. Not so, a reader swiftly corrected me in the following issue. It was on 14 December. Who could help loving people like this?

That itinerant quarter-century as a foreign correspondent didn't do my embryo piano playing much good, but jazz, that near-universal language, just seemed to follow me around. I've earlier mentioned my German and Egyptian jazz friends in Cairo. A fly-poster I might easily have missed on a lamp standard in Geneva once sent me driving dozens of miles to hear American trumpeter Yank Lawson. Covering a European Foreign Ministers' conference in the same city, I caught another American veteran trumpeter, Bill Coleman. From my flat in Rome on another occasion, I trekked over to fashionable Trastevere to hear that idol of my youth, pianist Earl Hines.

He immediately impressed by shrugging off the non-arrival of his bassist and drummer and performing solo for the first set, which was even better, playing those famous rolled octaves for all of four closing choruses of 'St Louis Blues'. In Frankfurt, Errol Garner, who never studied piano in his life, sat seraphically on a piano stool supplemented by telephone directories while improvising brilliantly on three German folk tunes they'd given him earlier in the day. Jazz is where you find it.

Over the early decades of the twentieth century, European classical composers had been displaying lots of brain, not so much heart, and little that really connected with the life of the masses. If dark clouds with silver linings do exist, they must surely include the slavery system which brought Africans to America and the Nazi persecutions which brought the Jews. These twin influxes would provide the red blood and muscle for this new kind of music. The songwriters of America's golden age of musicals had the same creative vigour as the southern bluesmen. The work of George Gershwin (another immigrants' son), Irving Berlin and the rest put those pallid early twentieth-century songs by people like England's Roger Quilter in the shade. The musicians from the Delta had made the flattened third and seventh 'acceptable' chords. Then jazz, film and Tin Pan Alley composers alike, familiar with the more sumptuous harmonies of Richard Wagner, Richard Strauss and Frederick Delius, would extend the range, but accessibly so. The now familiar 'blue notes' were supplemented in popular music by the softer sixth and variously voiced elevenths and thirteenths, among which people like jazz's young genius Charlie Parker would revel.

Yet jazz had been slow to gain acceptance in the country of its birth. Under the loaded headline 'Does Jazz Put The Sin In Syncopation?', a lady with the unlikely name of Mrs Marx E Obendorfer, national music chairman of the General Federation of Women's Clubs, wrote in 1921:

> Never in the history of our land have there been such immoral conditions among our young people and the blame is put on jazz and its evil influence.

In Germany, under the Nazis, jazz was banned, and in Sweden – which in recent decades has produced some of the finest jazz instrumentalists – a hysterical book published during World War Two, when the country was flirting with the Third Reich, called 'Negro music a conspiracy to destroy European culture'. In contrast, in stuffy old England, even London society hostesses of the twenties took to jazz rather readily. The distinguished American jazz writer John Hammond said once that jazz might have been 'a permanent casualty' had it not been for its acceptance in England, where three major record labels were pushing the new music at a time when no American newspapers, the black press included, bothered to write about it. On its home ground, jazz had to fight off predictable racial and class tensions.

Clarinettist Benny Goodman, the King of Swing, as he came to be labelled, was one of twelve children of penniless Russian immigrants in Chicago. Often portrayed as a self-centred cheapskate who short-changed his musicians, Goodman, damned by both sides of the musical divide, helped to start dismantling the colour bar by employing the elegant black pianist Teddy Wilson for his famous Trio and Quartet recordings of the late thirties. Wilson would become a major influence in jazz piano playing, his treatment of songs like 'Body and Soul' emulated to this day in a thousand cocktail bars.

Being a bandleader was not a job for the faint-hearted. George T Simon wrote in a 1967 survey of the scene:

351

Their survival depended on how they dealt with managers, booking agents, ballroom, nightclub and hotel operators, head waiters, busboys, press, publicity men, publishers, radio stations and above all the ever-present public.

Blues and ballad-singer Billie Holiday's sad life epitomised the black artiste's struggle for survival – snatching a few hours' sleep on buses between one venue and the next, not always being made welcome on arrival, being paid a pittance – but still trying to send a few bucks home to Mom.

A world, one thinks, that the necessarily peripatetic young Wolfgang Amadeus Mozart, dependent on favours from the Archbishop of Salzburg and his like, would have recognised.

While classicists tend to get bogged down in rules or revolutions measured in decades or even centuries, nothing ever stands still for long in jazz. No sooner has one style coalesced than someone brings in something new. The stiff beat of the New Orleans Rhythm Kings of the twenties gave way to the swing of the thirties and the big band era. Then ever restless jazzmen, particularly black musicians such as Charlie Parker, moved on to something new – 'something whitey can't play'. I confess I couldn't stand (or rather *under*stand) Parker's whirlwind bop phrases when I first heard them, but it's amazing how quickly all becomes familiar. In ten or fifteen years, Parker's approach had been absorbed into the Mainstream (a term coined by British jazz critic, Stanley Dance).

There've been a few blind alleys since. So-called Free Jazz, rejecting set chord sequences and bar lines, fascinated some people for a number of years, notably the Germans, but how many kids even know the term today? With a new century well under way, a typical piano style might still contain the best of swing and bop, spiced perhaps with a few of Bill Evans harmonies or Herbie Hancock's gospel touches, while paying homage to the twelve-bar blues in all its variants, and well-known 'standards' by the American songsmiths.

Between jazz and the classical music world, the ice has been slow to melt. Only towards the end of the twentieth century did classical singers in Britain deign to start singing Gershwin and Jerome Kern. American artistes such as Leonard Bernstein and that brilliant keyboard master of all genres, André Previn, never had such problems, seeing the great musicals as the modern equivalent (at least) of European light opera of the eighteenth and nineteenth centuries and feeling no shame in composing for jazz clubs or concert halls alike, opera houses or Hollywood.

The cross-fertilisation process doesn't always come off. The great Yehudi Menuhin tried jazz violin duets with jazz master Stephane Grappelli, but his solos remain pretty decorations of the theme, whereas the Frenchman played more daringly and interestingly 'through the chords'. Better not dwell on opera diva Kiri Te Kanawa's attempts to sing the blues along with Previn in a well-meaning experiment perhaps doomed from the start. Backed by Previn's intuitively professional accompaniment, she contributes to the album a ravishing performance of Kurt Weill's 'straight' song 'It Never Was You', but her efforts to achieve swing and a jazz inflection are embarrassing to hear. To use Louis Armstrong's phrase again, she 'ain't got it'.

Some classical singers such as Sylvia McNair and Dawn Upshaw have more of the common touch required. Welsh baritone Bryn Terfel, whose own repertoire draws on everything from Schubert's '*Erlkönig*' to 'Some Enchanted Evening', predicted on BBC a decade ago that opera houses in Britain would eventually be staging musicals by Rodgers and Hammerstein. We're still waiting.

It's a pity Louis wasn't around to celebrate the end of the first jazz century. He'd surely have had something amusing to say. That veteran piano player Eubie Blake almost made it into the new century himself, saying in Sam Goldwyn fashion on his 100th birthday, 'If I'd known I was going to live this long, I'd have taken better care of myself.'

Chapter 23
DOWN THE SEWERS, FIFTY YEARS ON, IN THE FOOTSTEPS OF HARRY LIME

The Metro station at Friedensbrucke was close to one of those noisy inner-suburb road junctions that could as easily be in Birmingham, Dusseldorf or Copenhagen. Cars revved impatiently at the traffic lights, warning old ladies against trying to cross. The station building itself retained the fin de siècle charm of a more leisurely era, and the Viennese authorities had wisely left its off-white peeling stucco alone. The young waiter at the pavement café, serving coffee and *apfelküche* as I waited for the rest of the group, spoke better English than most of his age in England and wanted to talk about Manchester United. He'd never heard of Graham Greene or *The Third Man*.

It was already half a century (fictionally speaking) since a sleek, totally cynical but altogether charming drug racketeer played by Orson Welles had come to a sticky end in the sewers of war-battered Vienna. As with Sherlock Homes, new generations evidently find fiction just as compelling as facts. We were a mixed gaggle of Americans, Germans, Britons, Japanese and Scandinavians, and, like his friend Holly Martins, we were in search of Harry Lime. Anniversaries, I'd learned at Reuters, are always a good time to get in on the act.

Our leader, an Austrian historian, led us down a flight of stone steps to the riverbank and suddenly we were in a different world. A cavern yawned before us, the largest entrance to the Austrian capital's 6,000-kilometre network of sewers. The noise of traffic faded away as we moved along the underside of the highway. Then we were in the tunnels, where quietly rippling water, flickering shadows and a glimpse of light around the bends vividly recalled the atmosphere of the Carol Reed classic, still regarded by many as the all-time masterpiece of black-and-white film photography.

But our guide, though unashamedly a *Third Man* fanatic, was Germanic enough to insist on separating fact from fiction. 'You get the impression in the film that Harry Lime was pursued through these tunnels by a whole group of people. In fact there were only four policemen.'

She smiled indulgently. 'There was a lot of cheating in *The Third Man*,' she explained. Cheating? Well, I suppose magicians are cheats in a way. With Harry Lime's first appearance, Reed certainly transformed cinema clichés – a man huddled in a doorway, the sound of echoing footsteps down a dark street – into one of the great entrances of screen history.

Schreyvogelgasse remains a quiet backwater, though government buildings and the roar of traffic are not far away. The L-shaped cul-de-sac is almost hidden by a fringe of tall trees from the Ring and its clip-clopping horse-drawn tourist cabs. A plaque on the wall reminds you that Beethoven lived here from 1804 to 1815, composing among other things his Fourth Piano Concerto (always my favourite) and the 'Leonora' overtures.

Grass was growing between the sloping cobbles. Number 12 bore a bookseller's sign, Number 16 advertised Stempel und Schilder. The Schubertstuberl offered Viennese pastries and draught beer. Number 8 was a private house in rather worn white-and-yellow baroque. In its darkened doorway, a Western writer in the film, called Holly Martins, spotted the shiny shoes of an otherwise blacked-out figure. A cat was playing with the shoelaces. A light suddenly flashed on from an uncurtained window across the street, illuminating Welles's pale features and half-mocking smile.

Our guide nodded approvingly. 'It was a beautiful scene, shot at night when the cobblestones were wet. But, in reality, when you turn on the lights across the street nothing happens down here. And you can't train a cat to play with shoelaces. They put ketchup on the shoes, which belonged to the Viennese location manager. He'd had them custom made in London, paid a fortune for them, and he was furious when the cat relieved itself on the fine leather.'

Suddenly, in the film, Harry is just a shadow running off along the wall, to vanish in the adjoining square. There, Trevor

Howard's British Army officer, at first sceptical, spots the now famous advertisement kiosk with a spiral staircase leading down into the sewers. The zither of Anton Karas flares on the soundtrack, taking us into a new stage of the film.

'But there was no kiosk in this square,' said our guide. 'They used the one in the Karl platz.' And as for that shadow: 'We don't really know whether it was Orson Welles's shadow anyway. It could have been the stand-in.'

Stand-in? 'Yes. Orson Welles was not very happy about working in the sewers. What bothered him was the smell. He was also afraid for his voice. So in all the sequences where you see him running, it was a stand-in. It was a Viennese butcher, a large man with the same build.' She sighed, pointing to new scaffolding erected against the wall. 'Normally I am happy to see a building in Vienna restored. But in this case it will mean you no longer see the wall as it was when that famous shadow moved along it.'

No Lime, only a Viennese butcher! Soon, no wall either. All was illusion, it seemed. Seen in retrospect, it seemed a miracle that *The Third Man*, in the form we know it, ever got made at all.

After the success of Carol Reed's superb *Fallen Idol*, adapted from Greene's short story 'The Basement Room', the author was asked for a new script set in Vienna, a city with which he was familiar. It would have been called *Night In Vienna* if producer David Selznick had had his way. 'Who the hell', he asked, 'will go to see a film called *The Third Man*?' (Graham Greene: *Ways of Escape*).

The shattered Austrian capital and its four-power occupied status, Alexander Korda decided, would make a perfect venue for a film, but he might never have filmed there if he hadn't also wanted to spend his company's frozen Austrian cash reserves. When Greene, ever adept at probing 'the dangerous edge of things', arrived in Vienna in the spring of 1948, he was given three news stories by journalist/intelligence man Peter Smolka, the London *Times* man in Vienna – about the sewers, the divided city and the black market in newly discovered penicillin.

Michael Shelden, in his 1994 biography of the writer, records, 'After his long evening with Smolka, Greene took away these stories and three months later they emerged in different form in the first draft of *The Third Man*.'

Understandably, perhaps, Greene did not mention the fact (though our guide did) that he had been a close friend of British traitor Kim Philby, thought by many to have served as the basis for Harry Lime. Philby had been in Vienna back in 1934, helping left-wing fighters in the street battles of that time to hide in the sewers and smuggle them out of the country.

While Greene frequently professed unhappiness at being constantly associated with 'seediness', the shadier side of politics was undeniably grist to his mill and his views on crime and morality often seem frivolous (some would say downright perverse). This was the man after all who once delivered a lecture entitled 'The Virtue of Disloyalty', cultivated friendships with dictators like Cuba's Fidel Castro and would in 1963 write a flattering introduction to Philby's autobiography.

Questions lingered for years as to the authorship of the film script. The flamboyant Welles used to boast he had written much of it himself. This was of course nonsense, and Greene gave the answer to it in his annotated script of the film, sold at a Sotheby's auction in 1996. This carried a note by Greene emphasising the lines (the only ones) contributed by Orson Welles. The essence of Welles's contribution was Lime's famous remarks, after taking his old friend for a ride on Vienna's giant old Ferris wheel, about evil and the Swiss. And in truth his sarcastic quip – that the sum result of 500 years of democracy and peace in Switzerland was the cuckoo clock – always seemed to me facile and flashy, even for a Harry Lime.

Seen today, Selznick's suggested title for the film, smacking more of Lehar than Lime, seems ludicrous. Reed, more of a diplomat perhaps than the writer, fobbed off the producer effectively at the time by saying, 'Graham and I will think about it.' One shivers too when reflecting that Selznick and Korda originally wanted Noel Coward to play the drug racketeer and, when that fell through, suggested the young Robert Mitchum.

As it turned out, everything gelled perfectly. The initial casting insanities having been knocked on the head, Reed assembled a perfect team. As with Lime, the role of Holly Martins survived the transition from Greene's original story to American nationality. The Italian actress Valli was a perfect choice as Lime's

357

discarded girlfriend, a study in coolness and almost pathological fidelity (but this is Greene after all).

It cost $100,000 to get Orson Welles, the star of *Citizen Kane*, pretty good pay minute for minute, for a few brief appearances. Most people chiefly remember the shock entrance (not a word spoken) and the final sequence, where Welles (or his stand-in) fled along the sewers before ending up in a barred-off cul-de-sac and giving Holly the unspoken nod of assent to finish him off with a pistol shot. And of course the conversation with his reluctant pursuer about good and evil at the top of the Ferris wheel, from which humanity looked like so many small dots. If you were offered £1,000 for every dot that stopped, Lime challenges Martins, 'How many of them could you afford not to eliminate?'

Carol Reed also wanted sewer rats in the cast, and these he could have had for free. 'There were,' said our guide, 'an estimated two million of them swarming round the Vienna sewers, where workers wore boots of specially toughened calves' leather – they just gnaw through rubber ones.' But the rats weren't playing, at any price. 'They ran off as soon as the arc lights came on. So they got tame rats from the university – but as soon as these saw the lights, they started begging for food' As for that locked manhole cover, by the way, through which the trapped racketeer graphically thrusts his fingers in a last desperate bid for freedom, this was another bit of "cheating". 'Those gratings weigh 600 pounds. There is no way he could have lifted it to get out. And in any case, that scene wasn't shot in Vienna.'

I was beginning to wonder whether this tour was such a good idea after all.

The writer was the first to give credit to Reed's inspired choice of ending. If Lime's entry is classic, the finale, in which the dead racketeer's cool-as-ice girlfriend takes a long walk into the camera from the graveside, passing Martins without so much as a sideways glance, is equally masterful. (Did it inspire David Lean's similarly drawn-out scene of camel and rider approaching across the desert in *Lawrence of Arabia*, I wonder?)

Oddly, perhaps, to us today, Greene saw the story as no more than one of his 'entertainments', a 'fairy tale based on a grim truth', and too light for an unhappy ending. But he acknowledged later that Reed 'was proved triumphantly right'. To us, having observed the girl's almost irritating blind loyalty to Lime, the ending seems the only one possible.

Greene also lauded Reed's discovery of Anton Karas, who was to give the exotic zither unexpected world status. The director brought the café musician back to London, despite his protests that he wasn't a composer, and sat him down for six weeks watching rushes of the film while creating the now-famous theme. Deliberately repetitive, almost obsessive, the 'Third Man Theme' seems to me vital to key developments, eerie at all the right places and surely the perfect backup for 'that ending'. Reed also cannily uses the German language, in both Hochdeutsch and local variants and often untranslated, almost like background music to emphasise the foreignness of what had been enemy territory only a short while earlier. And the then 'grande dame' of the Vienna theatre is memorable in her first film as a whining landlady concerned amid the ruins just to run *'ein anständiges Haus'*. You could well imagine her nodding approval of Hitlerian *Ordnung* a few years earlier.

In the late nineties, when I took the tourist walk, there'd been parallels aplenty to the Harry Lime scene. He operated in a half-devastated city, with anarchy not far removed and criminals sprouting like weeds among the ruins. Now in the shifting borders of Central Europe, things had still not settled down after the cataclysmic shock of the breakdown of the Soviet empire. Drugs originating in Romania were being sniffed out near the cliffs of Dover, and any taxi driver in Budapest or Sofia would tell you that the new mafia (which often, they said, meant the old communists) were running the show. Geopolitical border shifts were producing new trades. Along what had been the East–West divide, a lucrative black market was thriving. Harry Lime would have made millions.

Chapter 24
ABOARD THE CALIFORNIA ZEPHYR, *I TAKE A SENTIMENTAL JOURNEY*

Seen from the driving cab, the rails stretched far ahead towards the Sierra Nevada. An old pickup truck waited at a level crossing. Our engineer blew the whistle – two shorts, one long – a haunting sound familiar from Hollywood.

A man in a Stetson waved from the truck as we swept imperiously by. Nobody was going to argue with the two big F40 locomotives pulling a string of coaches half a mile long. It was just as I'd imagined. I'd needed no second invitation to climb the vertical ladder to the cab and chat with the engineers. I wanted a story. I'd read that the money men in Washington wanted to close this cross-America rail line that was part of the nation's history. I reckoned it had to be now or never. So, bound for the San Francisco Jazz Festival, I took the train from New York. And, for a jazz lover of course, it had to be from Pennsylvania Station – though just a bit later than 'a quarter to four'.

In Glenn Miller's never-never land, homesick New Yorkers always took the night flier to places like Dreamsville and Kalamazoo. I wanted reality to be something like that. I'd been encouraged the night before, eating a burger in a restaurant off Times Square, to see a mounted policeman gallop his horse down Broadway between lines of honking cars. I'd thought that was just something policemen like McCloud did on television. Obviously, anything could happen here.

It was under the big clock at Penn Station that Judy Garland and Robert Walker met in that wartime black-and-white film classic *The Clock*. The clock was now gone, but on the electronic noticeboard the scheduled train names – the *Lakeshore Special*, the *Pioneer* and the *Desert Wind* – carried the same old magic. Boarding time was a bit later than for Glenn Miller's

'Chattanooga Choo Choo', and there wasn't a shoeshine boy in sight. But the long, gleaming corrugated aluminium monster of a train waiting in the bowels of the station was something I'd only seen on the big screen. And the jovial cabin attendant who hoisted my luggage aboard might have walked straight out of one of those corny old musicals where the trumpet-playing bellboy turns out to be Louis Armstrong. We rumbled off through subterranean Manhattan and lights glimmered along the New Jersey shore as we headed north up the Hudson River.

'Dinner in the diner, nothing could be finer': white linen tablecloths, smart-uniformed waiters. And, of course, as I scanned the menu, I was keeping an eye open for that sophisticated blonde secretary who, if Hitchcock's *North By Northwest* was anything to go by, should be taking a seat opposite me at any moment. She didn't show up. Well, there were 3,000 miles to go. The wheels clickety-clacked, the whistle sounded mournfully at intervals as we headed north and glided in darkness into the New York State capital, Albany. Alas, no tinkling white piano in the bar, and no signs yet of intrigue or romance. On such a night as this, in that other Hitchcock thriller *Strangers on a Train*, an oddball named Bruno had unveiled a bizarre double murder plot. Tonight I was amid groups of train buffs, the cognoscenti of rail travel, who like me feared the demise of journeys such as this. The bar shut at midnight and, regretting my decision to travel economy class overnight, I tried with limited success to curl up in one of the airline-type reclining seats. At 6.30 a.m. I was first in the queue in the dining car for scrambled eggs, hash browns and lashings of coffee.

'Chicago, Chicago, that wonderful town…' We rumbled along the southern shore of Lake Michigan. Freighters were moored in the creeks and miles of steel mills rolled past as we headed for the soaring twin spires of the Sears Tower. I still had memories of those hard-faced gangsters played by George Raft, Jimmy Cagney and Edward G Robinson, all spats, cigars, pinstriped suits and tommy guns. Today, Al Capone barely got a mention from our guide to the city. But our black driver knew all about Armstrong and Jelly Roll Morton, who'd recorded those three-minute jazz classics here in the late twenties. At Union Station, film buffs

361

rhapsodised about the lofty marbled passenger hall whose four-sided clock featured in many a Hollywood thriller. Wasn't it here, somebody asked, that Harrison Ford took part in that shoot-out in… what's the name of that film? The one where the baby's pram rolls slowly down the steps, almost like a scene from Eisenstein? 'That was *The Untouchables*,' someone else said, and it wasn't Harrison Ford, it was Kevin Costner, playing gangbuster Elliott Ness.

All aboard again, and as the *California Zephyr* sped across America's vast central plain, the incessant rhythm of Meade Lux Lewis's 'Honky Tonk Train Blues' was running through my brain. Cornfields, woods and timbered farms with a Scandinavian look flashed past as we headed for Omaha, a famed Missouri River crossing for the nineteenth-century west-bound pioneers. Then the season changed overnight, and in the mile-high city of Denver a herd of buffalo grazed obligingly in the snow near Buffalo Bill's grave, sparking a rush for camcorders. Then the *California Zephyr* climbed up the eastern slopes of the Great Divide into the Rockies, and in the top-floor observation lounge I finally got to sit in one of those swivelling seats I'd long fancied. You could sometimes see the back of the train – two coupled locos and fifteen passenger coaches – as we snaked around the single twisting track.

We emerged from the six-mile-long Moffat Tunnel into winter. In late October, the first ski runs were already open and at Fraser, the highest point of our journey at 3,000 feet, children were throwing snowballs. Then we were in Glenwood Springs, meeting place of the Colorado and Roaring Fork rivers, where notorious gunslinger Doc Holliday is buried. After an overnight delay at Salt Lake City, we were two hours behind schedule, and I politely asked why.

'Well, can you think of any place where the trains run on time?' our cabin attendant from Memphis replied crossly. I suggested Switzerland. 'Must be a wonderful country, that Switzerland,' he said scornfully. And who wanted to rush, anyway, as we spiralled through tunnels from one high fir-clad valley to another on the wildest and most spectacular part of the route?

A rewind button seemed to take us back to summer as the long string of silver coaches snaked down the Colorado River, and I swear I saw the stony shallows where John Wayne led that cattle herd across. The declining sun lit up red-stone canyons with crags like castle battlements. I half expected Clint Eastwood to come riding round the next outcrop. At the town of Promontory, Utah, the last link of this marvellous railroad had been completed and, just eighteen months after that, the first of those film-inspiring train robberies took place and a Wells Fargo consignment of gold disappeared.

Then there was a twenty-minute halt to change engineers, I seized the chance, walked along the platform and stood ogling the giant General Electric diesel locomotive with its red, white and blue horizontal stripes.

'Want to come up?' asked one of the engineers, and there was only one answer to that.

Up in the high cab, I filmed and took notes as we rumbled off towards the High Sierra, another name evoking movie memories, Humphrey Bogart this time, in the film of that name. In San Francisco I'd get to ride in a bucking, bell-jangling streetcar with a sign saying 'Humphrey Bogart Filmed Here'. And at the Jazz Festival I was taken backstage by San Francisco jazz writer Bill Gallagher to chat with two more of my old idols, veteran bluesmen Ralph Sutton and Jay McShann, whom the record companies once marketed as 'The Last of the Whorehouse Piano Players'. They've since both departed.

And maybe the *California Zephyr* wouldn't last long, I thought. Back in Europe, soon after, I read the bald wire-service story: 'Amtrak will close two US routes – the *Pioneer* service from Denver to Seattle, and the *Desert Wind* from Salt Lake City to Los Angeles.' Just like that. The *California Zephyr*, I guessed, could be next for the chop.

Maybe I'd just got in under the wire. A pity that mystery blonde never showed up, though. But, if old Hitchcock movies were anything to go by, she would not have been the first lady to vanish on a train.

Chapter 25
A BELATED RETURN TO ENG. LIT. –
THE SOMBRE WORLD OF OLIVER ONIONS

Between Ondaatje and Orwell, there was nothing on the shelves at Harrods or Waterstone's. Oliver Onions? How do you spell it? Like the vegetable? Sorry, sir, it seems to be out of print.

Well, fame's a transitory thing, I suppose. I'd been a fan of Oliver Onions from way back. Among those of my generation in the decade immediately after the Second World War, he was considered one of Britain's finest novelists. 'An inspired writer, a poet of prose', said John Betjeman in the fifties, and that was the time I got to know his work. His blend of history, danger, romance and social observation appealed to a reporter, I suppose. And Onions always had a good feel for the press of the era and its sins.

But getting hold of a book of his at the end of the century meant a long search in the basements of Charing Cross Road. Among younger bookstore assistants, the name evoked only a snigger. But with time and energy to spare after Reuters, I pursued the trail. Drifting around the world, I'd long mislaid my original copy of perhaps his best known novel, *The Story of Ragged Robyn* (1912). A search through magazine ads and my own contacts with literary gents enabled me to put a story together.

A couple of his novels could be had on request at my local Wimbledon Public Library and they were among his best: *Poor Man's Tapestry* (1946) and *Arras Of Youth* (1949), from his War of the Roses trilogy, and the oddly titled *Widdershins* (1911), a collection of ghost stories which at their best rival those of M R James. *London Magazine*'s late esteemed editor Alan Ross encouraged my quest for the near-forgotten writer and printed the results.

Like that other man from Bradford, Frederick Delius, Oliver Onions was admittedly never everyone's cup of tea. Stylistically, both were outside the mainstream, making no concessions to listener or reader. Delius has been better served by posterity, though. At least *The First Cuckoo In Spring* gets a regular airing on Radio Three. The name Onions raises a quizzical look, if not a smile. *The Story Of Ragged Robyn*, considered by many his masterpiece, is a disturbing tale set in the late seventeenth century, whose bleak setting and blend of poetry and menace recall the early films of Ingmar Bergman.

As a journalist, one of the things that first interested me about Onions was his depiction in his early work of the popular press and its idiocies. An art student born of humble parents in 1873, he drew on his early years with the Harmsworth Press for his novel *Little Devil Doubt*. Written as far back as 1909, it showed a sure satiric touch as well as a feel for characters, looking backwards to Dickens and forward to J B. Priestley. Here, in light-hearted ironic terms, is our hero sketching his first live model:

> All unconscious was the magnificent Miss Flo Sayers of the liberties that Georgie took with her behind her back. She did not know that in his mind he stripped her of her long blue pinafore, of her garments one and all, of her abundant fair flesh itself, penetrated into her most secret articulations, numbered her bones, from the atlas beneath her fair sprouting nape to the malleoli of her shapely ankles. She did not know that the knickerbockered boy behind her had chaste and studious desires to thumb her elbow and wrist whenever a dimply surface-form seemed to contradict the inflexible Miss Sayers of bone beneath. And Georgie wondered whether, had she known it, she would not have turned on her stool, chilled him with one look of her blue eyes, and said: 'Unhand Me, Sir.'

The book made mincemeat of the turn-of-the-century popular press, anticipating Evelyn Waugh by a few decades. To this day, there's a familiar look about the author's principal target, the tabloid world of *Billion*, *Sunny Sundays* and *Nonsuch*, with their three-hour Fleet Street lunches, 'What's Wrong?' picture competitions, 20,000 Nonsuch Nightie Prizes and the handsome Miss Carruthers, a flower-shop girl from the sticks who's become an editorial executive. Sex is paramount. 'If love makes the world go round,' wrote Onions, '*Nonsuch* gave it a weekly jog.'

Internationally, the slogan of the dailies was 'War At Any Price'. To mark the Boer War, he wrote, the figure of 'Black Sambo' had given way to 'Chris the Kaffir'. And there was of course the British Empire. 'Here's a story about Egypt,' the editor complains to an artist, 'and not so much as a Sphinx or a Pyramid. We mustn't play tricks on our readers like this.' And, of course, politics. 'These Labour men are a menace to Society.' Art? 'The public doesn't care a brass farthing for High Art.' Newspaper tycoon Jack Huddlestone discovers he's paying some of his journalists £5 a week. 'It's too much,' he says. 'There must be hundreds of youngsters in the provinces who'd give their ears for a start on a London paper.' It all sounds familiar. No wonder Onions appealed to a *Bolton Evening News* reporter, just arrived in Fleet Street.

But I felt other affinities with the world of Oliver Onions. From my late teens I'd been addicted to ghost stories, mysteries and the uncanny, and this author rated high. His *Beckoning Fair One* (1911), a ghostly tale in the Victorian tradition, is justly included in the anthologies. Tension is created subtly, from the first glimpse of a 'To Let' board outside a neglected house in Holborn (a favourite Onions location). Inside, Oleron, our hero, encounters some strange sights and sounds. An invisible hair-brush emits 'a sort of soft sweeping rustle'. With the trained artist's exact photographic eye and an ear for music, the author describes how the new tenant became conscious of the dripping of a tap. 'It had a tinkling gamut of four or five notes, on which it rang irregular changes. In his mind, Oleron could see the gathering of each drop, its little tremble on the lip of the tap and the tiny percussion of its fall.' Later, he sees 'the little glances of light from the bevels and facets of the objects about the mirror and the candle. But he could see more. There was one gleam that had motion. It was fainter than the rest, and it moved up and down through the air, and each of its downward movements was accompanied by a silky and crackling rustle.'

As with M R James, the final horror is suggested rather than described:

> The police inspector, kicking aside the dead flowers, noticed that a shuffling track that was not of his making had been swept to a cupboard in the corner. In the upper part of the door of the cupboard was a square panel that looked as if it slid on runners. The door itself was closed. The inspector advanced, put his hand to the little knob, and slid the hatch along its groove. Then he took an involuntary step back again. 'Ah!' said the Inspector.

(These days, I suppose, we might rather say 'Aaargh!')

The world's darker corners and the inevitability of violence would become an Onions speciality. His view of the First World War and its depression-blighted aftermath was a mordant one. In his novel *Cut Flowers* (1927), his out-of-funds sculptor asked himself bitterly: 'What was there to be glum about? The war memorials had hardly begun to spread over the land. There was not a large town but would want a dozen of them, not a village church but would set up its humble tablet of names.' The second world conflict would completely remove any remaining illusions about human behaviour.

It became clear that with his wide knowledge of arcane detail, previous centuries provided the best outlet for Onions's particular vision. In his historical fiction, he seems to be simply opening windows to the past, which is presented as a tapestry. The camera zooms in to a few figures locked into the frieze. They are summoned to life, the story begins and ends, then 'the worn web begins to fray, the warp to slacken like an unstrung harp'. He makes no value judgements, simply recording. Life, as he sees it, is brutally simple and unfair, punctuated by moments of delight.

The opening scene of *Ragged Robyn* is reminiscent of *Great Expectations*. For the Romney marshes, read the Lincolnshire fens. For Pip read thirteen-year-old Robyn, for Magwitch the self-styled and sinister Prince of Withernsea. There's the same sudden seizure in a lonely place, warnings of retribution. But there the resemblance ends. Magwitch becomes a beloved father substitute and benefactor. The Prince of Withernsea's threat comes to ugly fruition years later in a mock courtroom in the desecrated chancel of a ruined East Coast church. For Dickens's hero, the end is merely tragic; for Ragged Robyn, a nightmare.

Onions establishes the mood in just a few pages, as a youngster trudges home along a Lincolnshire dyke at sunset:

> Against the afterglow on the landward side a strange shape suddenly appeared. Still distant, it was lifted above the earth to twice the ordinary height of a man, and it advanced stiffly and staggeringly, yet with unusual speed for all its clumsy gait. It was a fenman on his stilts, with his twelve-foot pole to steady him, and bobbing and dancing halfway up in the sky like that, he had a gallows-like look, as if some malefactor from York Castle, swinging in his rusty hoops and shackles, had cut himself down for an evening stroll.

The romanticism of our hero's long journey north, gliding with great twenty-feet strides of his skates across an ice-covered fenland; the meticulously exact description of his apprenticeship as a stonemason in ancient abbeys and houses ('with the change to smaller tools, it was as if the stone itself had begun imperceptibly to move'); the understated, tantalising eroticism of his doomed love affair with a girl above his station, and the bleakness of his end, are masterfully handled. In the sombre ending, Robyn is hauled in a sham royal coach to a kangaroo court in a ruined chapel, where bottles of smuggled spirits and drinking cups have turned the altar into an inn table. His judge is the grotesque 'Queen of Withernsea', a cackling dwarf hideously decked in silver-embroidered green velvet, her hand cluttered with bejewelled rings. His jurors (precursors of Hitler's thugs?) were 'the refuse of the wars, the deserters from this powerful man's retinue or that, the rabble who knew no duty but to save their own skins, and what mercy could he hope for here?'

In *Poor Man's Tapestry* (1946) too, inevitably we are ultimately back again in a courtroom setting, where a reptilian Sir William with his 'fat, flat, implacable face' dispenses law by caprice. Our hero, Willie Middelmiss, who like any low-born figure in Onions's seventeenth-century world has survived by his wits, watches as a progression of ragged wretches are brought in for judgement. No Hollywood trappings here, and no one knew better than Onions how to convey the smell of fear.

Willie has won advancement in this castle on the Welsh borders, but has no illusions:

He watched My Lord with his cap of state and the glint of chain under his robe, that parted a few inches whenever the dipping finger approved the whipping. The man's mind was as hideous as his hands were crabbed and cramped, and he was making the sentence a pair of ears now, or a branding, or the thumb-cord, or a hand struck off. At the back there was a silence, not of protest, but a breathlessness, a dreadful thrill of waiting, a shuddering as each man rejoiced that the savagery was not for himself. Now Willie began to wish he was elsewhere.

But it is already too late. A defendant turns informer to save his own skin and suddenly the privileged spectator is himself under arrest. 'Willie's two attendants stood waiting till it was his pleasure to move, for in his mulberry velvet he was still to be treated with distinction.' But, fine robes or not, he will soon join the Italian prisoner in the cellars who no longer has a tongue to proclaim his innocence. Onions's message is basically a sombre one. But he deserves new readers.

Chapter 26
PALM TREES, MINARETS AND A BLUE SEA –
I'M BACK IN THE MIDDLE EAST

I'd retired, sort of. But I was doing lots of writing still, and, a couple of years after the first Gulf War, I responded to an invitation from Reuters head office to give some assistance to the Kuwait News Agency (KUNA), one of our old customers. Its editorial operation had for years been dominated by Palestinians – who've been called the intellectual mercenaries of the Middle East. After the country's liberation from Iraqi forces, these were all thrown out. Now the Kuwaitis had to staff the agency themselves, and not everything was going perfectly.

Vestiges of the Iraqi invasion were everywhere. There'd been mindless destruction, a lot of which had already been repaired. But many wrecked buildings remained. A burnt-out liner once used as a luxury hotel still stood at the waterfront. There was a field full of wrecked tanks, some bearing the chalked or painted slogan 'Saddam Shit'.

I'd already felt, heard and smelt the Arab world at London Airport. Tobacco smoke hung thick and grey in a very crowded departure lounge and the weary voice of an airport official came over the loudspeakers: 'May I remind you this is a no-smoking area?' Well, you could have fooled me.

In Kuwait city, everyone was friendly and helpful in traditional Arab style, taking me back to Cairo days. But the standard of writing was low, the organisation of stories and lead writing practically non-existent, though these were all well-educated people, often quite fluent in English. Some had attended American journalism schools. God knows what the people there had been teaching them. Some of these guys and girls were little more than beginners. Typing and spelling were uncertain. There were no proper archives. The first day I visited the News Desk, there was an important oil story going on in Geneva. We couldn't even find the name of the current Venezuelan oil minister – and that country, like Kuwait, was one of OPEC's main members.

But my hosts laid on a splendid lunch. Traditional robes were worn by the KUNA bosses, a musician played a tabla in the background, and there were lashings of good healthy food – salads, grilled prawns, koufta, tajina and foul, with that lovely pitta bread. Lively and friendly conversation, and I felt I'd already made a mark. They seemed to appreciate a straightforward view of their problems. To my pleasure, I was seated next to old Cairo colleague Bahgat Badie, there on a twelve-month contract to inject some day-to-day professionalism into the file. He was quite critical of the news operation. The Kuwaitis imported experts for everything, from bankers and businessmen at the top to humble workers from Asia to do the dirty work. Bahgat and I were the journalist mercenaries.

Another old friend and colleague from London, Australian Bill McLean, now Reuter correspondent in Kuwait, took me to dinner at one of the big hotels. In the lobby were several American journalists, there for a visit by ex-President George Bush. He was being given royal treatment as the saviour of Kuwait, and there was some flamboyant reporting in the newspapers. 'The wombs of Kuwaiti women could not produce such a hero,' said one slightly over-the-top editorial. Incredibly, Bahgat's story on the event for KUNA was absent-mindedly not even included on the agency's news schedule. There was clearly much to do. We decided to run three fortnight-long training courses for KUNA editorial staff at Reuter's Middle East headquarters in Nicosia.

Shortly thereafter, I was en route to Cyprus. The taxi driver to Heathrow was a corpulent, good-natured Londoner. During the twenty-five-mile journey, windscreen wipers swishing rapidly in what I hoped would be the last bad weather I'd see for a while, he told me a traveller's tale which might have come straight from Somerset Maugham. 'I got married without knowing about it,' he said mysteriously, and seemed to sense my ears had pricked up. The story had obviously been told before.

'All my friends but me were married,' he said, 'and someone

suggested I should take a trip to Thailand. Well, you're never alone there. They just don't let you be. If you go into a bar, in half a minute there's a couple of girls sitting at the counter chatting with you. This one started talking about marriage. I said, "Just come on holiday to England first and see if you like it, then you yourself will be making the decision." '

The lady came to London and liked it, and obviously my driver was now very happily married. 'She spoils me something terrible. My shirt and tie are laid out every morning when I get out of the bath. That's the way they are. Well, I was watching TV one night and they were showing this Buddhist ceremony in Thailand. They said it was a wedding. Then I suddenly remembered a similar ceremony I'd attended about eighteen months earlier but never understood what was going on. I told my wife about this and she said, "Yes, we were married that day. In the Buddhist way." She said it would have been regarded as dishonourable for her to come to England with me otherwise. Well, it turned out OK. I always tell my friends about it.' And I too always appreciate a good tale.

The Brits crowding the departure lounge were not so diverting. Travelling tourist class to Cyprus, I seemed to be the only passenger not dressed in baggy shorts, T-shirt and trainers in anticipation of Eastern Mediterranean sunshine. With the plane delayed, the hordes were celebrating in advance, pint in hand, sometimes in both, conversing at decibel level, kids squalling in the background. Not the most relaxing place to be. I hoped, perhaps snobbishly, that they'd all be heading for beer and chips with everything, on the island's South Coast. Which is pretty much what happened.

I parted company from the mob at the other end and thankfully took a taxi to my hotel in Nicosia. Rain again all the way. The windscreen wiper could hardly deal with it in the twenty-five miles from Larnaca to the Hilton. My driver was a refugee from Famagusta, thrown out after the 1974 Turkish invasion. He was working thirteen days a fortnight from 6 p.m. to six in the morning and earned ten Cyprus pounds a day (about £13) – hardly a fortune. He offered to take me round the island if I wanted to make any long trips later.

In brilliant warm sunshine the following day, I was truly back in the Eastern Mediterranean. It was like a mixture of Israel and the Arab world. The light, colours and general ambience reminded me of Jerusalem, but without any of its fine stone buildings. The square apartment and office blocks had more in common with Tel Aviv. I rang the doorbell at the Reuter headquarters and inside, large as life, was Dave Goddard, my old West Country colleague from the World Desk, now News Editor, Middle East. And this was the man who said he'd never go abroad again. Maybe Cyprus, because of all the British troops training there, didn't count as abroad. Also around were Australian Angus McSwan, American Jim Anderson and Polish-born Andrew Tarnowski, another music lover. I hadn't seen any of them for years. Manager Graham Stewart, another Aussie, who'd got me the job with the Kuwaitis, had obviously hand-picked a congenial bunch for his satellite Reuter HQ. He showed me the rooms he'd earmarked for my lectures to the three successive groups who'd be flying up from Kuwait, led by a trio of ladies. A few notes from my diary:

I'm installed this evening in a vast sprawling apartment with three bedrooms and as many bathrooms, though not all the plumbing is functioning and the washing machine doesn't work. There'd be room enough for a grand piano, but the simple upright I asked for in advance hasn't arrived. The problem is it has to be carried up six flights. The lift isn't big enough. They've talked of using a hoist to haul it through the window. I protested this was hardly necessary, and asked them to drop my request.

The ladies have arrived from Kuwait. So has the piano in my flat, an instrument of uncertain origin, reputedly Russian, in fair condition and in tune, though a trifle heavy compared with my own back home. But I can live with it. I hope my neighbours aren't allergic to scales, for my teacher Simone Dinnerstein has prescribed several of these to study. I'd never realised there were so many different kinds! I use the soft pedal to avoid giving offence. The Kuwait ladies and all the Reuterians were invited this evening for drinks at the Hilton. The visitors expectedly all declined alcohol, though Kholoud, a lively half-Lebanese lady, told me sotto voce she had in fact drunk it many times. Dina, the only one who wears a headscarf and looks the most demure of them all, is quite a girl, however. She's seen a lot of the world, travelling with her diplomat father, and has an astonishing story to tell of how, when he was shot and wounded during the Iraqi invasion, she drove him across the desert into Saudi Arabia, talking her way past all obstacles and road blocks until she had him safely under medical treatment.

Tonight the Tamowskis threw a party. They have a piano, and I accompanied a young Frenchwoman with a good jazz voice on a couple of numbers including, naturally in view of her origins, 'Autumn Leaves'. Nick Phythian, another old mate, is a guitarist and sings in the choir at Nicosia's Anglican Cathedral. They're quite a musical bunch here.

The students greatly improve. All three ladies made a good job of an exercise I set – to put a particularly stodgy and boring piece on the European Union by one of those heavyweight correspondents of the *Herald Tribune* into clear and attractive English. They got the idea straight away and made a good job of it, taking about twenty minutes. To bed early after reading a bit of an interesting book Simone lent me on the history of English. Lots of references, I notice, to Otto Jespersen, the Danish scholar whose book, *The Growth and Structure of The English Language*, prescribed for us sixth-formers at Thornleigh College, sparked off my interest in the subject. It's never waned since.

I ended up eating at the Hilton tonight after trying several restaurants, all fully booked. 'It's the end of the month,' said my taxi driver. 'Everybody gets their money and spends it. That's the way it is in Cyprus.'

I set a political 'curtain-raiser' exercise. The pretended subject was the resumption of Middle East peace talks, and again they made a surprisingly good stab at it. 'Why don't you come to Kuwait and be a permanent consultant with us?' the ladies charmingly ask.

Our first trip across the border to the Turkish side of the island, for which I borrowed an office car. You have to give full details of all passports in the party. I described myself as a company executive and the girls as office workers. Had we said we were journalists, we'd have been at the crossing point yet. I hoped the point was not lost on these budding writers. A drive through the mountains took us first to Hilarion Castle, first made known to me decades earlier in Lawrence Durrell's engaging memoir *Bitter Lemons*. I can see the attraction. Good views from the balcony down to the harbour at Kyrenia. When I asked at the bar for whisky, our cheerful bartender poured out a stiff shot as if it were beer. It would have been equal to seven or eight English measures. I got him to desist and settled for a double. He proudly showed the girls the corpse of a small snake he'd caught and put in a bottle standing on a shelf behind the bar. I tried not to look at it as I drank.

Kyrenia harbour is as pretty as it's described in the guidebooks. Most of the waterside tables seemed to be occupied by elderly Brits or Germans. To my delight, Kholoud, unprompted, buttonholed a UN soldier from Canberra, one of a twenty-strong Aussie contingent on the island, and got all the material needed for a story. I took a picture of the pair. Afterwards, we took the road up to the Bel Pais monastery – even closer to Durrell's one-time home in the fifties – and back over the mountains in good time for the 5.30 closure of the border. A good feature-making trip, and they're learning. Kholoud said she'd like to take me back with her to Kuwait. I must be doing something right... I spoke to KUNA on the phone and suggested that the features the girls had written should be put promptly on the wire. The women seem to be making the running in so many places.

The ladies are off to Paphos for the weekend, so I had my first sightseeing tour. I was interested to see the border area of the divided city, a subject I'll get my students to write about later. It's the first country in two halves I've seen since Germany. A few decades ago, one could move freely between the predominantly Greek and Turkish areas. Then came Enosis, the campaign for union with Greece, followed by an often brutal campaign by the guerrilla movement EOKA to end British rule, then finally a Turkish invasion and subsequent partition of the island.

Border areas are never pretty, and as I reached a scruffy square bisected by barriers a UN sentry perched on top of a building warned me not to use my camera. A bit stupid, really. I'm sure everything there is to know has been photographed and recorded a million times over by now. I took photos inside the Holy Cross Church instead and entered the old town behind the ancient Venetian ramparts. Outside a rather decrepit-looking cinema were some pretty explicit pictures of naked women. The shopping area had a tatty charm almost reminiscent of Cairo's souk. Buying myself a straw hat as the sun got stronger, I found myself at another roadblock.

A line of concrete flowerpots ablaze with geraniums marked the end of the street for motorists, but beyond was a café, where I sat and enjoyed a Coke. Metal-topped tables, plastic seats, Carlsberg sunshades over the tables – they must get them free – where three elderly men were playing checkers. The wall of the café is in fact the end of the Greek Cypriot sector, painted with the UN's blue-and-white stripes. You can't get closer than that. A few yards behind the barrier, another bored-looking UN guard sat perched up in his little tower, warning off photographers. Using the zoom, I simply filmed from the end of the street. The sun blazed, the heat became oppressive. The guard shouted down to a waiter, who a few minutes later handed him up a sandwich. Business goes on across many a political divide. I walked through narrow streets past cabinetmakers, tinsmiths and small shops. The sound of a muezzin drifted over the demarcation line from a mosque over in the Turkish sector. A fat black cat emerged from a ruined building on the Turkish side, holding a dead mouse in its mouth, and made off to eat it in another dilapidated building on the Greek side.

In the tiny St John's Cathedral, a lecturer held forth in German at great length to a bunch of tourists. The church is impressive, every inch of wall or ceiling full of frescoes or paintings, there's a gilded bishop's throne and glittering glass chandeliers hang from the ceiling like bunches of overripe grapes. At the Omeriyah Mosque, an attendant sat somnolently outside in the shade. I shed my shoes and walked into the coolness of the vast barnlike interior. As I was coming out again, he asked me whether I'd like to go 'upstairs', as he put it. 'Lift!' he shouted, pointing inside. I saw no lift, but in the semi-darkness the beginning of a flight of steps. He'd been saying 'Left'. He assumed I'd want to see the minaret, and so I did. I climbed exactly fifty steps to a central platform, from which I had good views over the roofs of the city, but then saw there was another flight of fifty, emerging on to a high balcony from which the views were magnificent, looking over the Green Line to the distant hills of the Turkish-occupied land. A loudspeaker beside me suddenly blasted into life as the muezzin called the faithful to prayer: 'Allah, Akhbar!' I saw tourists looking up startled to where I stood in my straw hat and sunglasses and hoped they didn't think I was responsible for the din. Three hours of tramping the pavements on a very hot day finally took its toll, and by the time I'd left the old city and slogged up the mile-long street to the flat I was ready for a snooze. Andrew Tamowski picked me up later for a Beethoven concert and lecture. The talk, unfortunately, was in Greek. Well, it's their country.

Enjoying a weekend off, I'm ensconced in a nice flatlet in the village of Kakopetria (how nicely the name trips off the tongue!). The Troodos Hills are a 45-mile drive from Nicosia, and I'd come in a Japanese four-wheel-drive car kindly lent by Nick Phythian. Leaving the capital, there's a wasteland of half-finished houses, telegraph poles lining the road, wires drooping all over the place – like a mixture of Israel in its early days and those depressing American small towns. At last, the roofs of Nicosia became just something in the rear mirror, and I was driving between fields of golden ripening corn, the roadsides ablaze with flowers, the hills hazy in the distance. Signs periodically told you: 'Don't forget, the Turks have occupied your land.' The occasional watchtower was another reminder of the unnatural border that had straddled the island.

I feared the worst when I stepped out of the car in the hill village of Kakopetria. But the hundreds of coach trippers were just departing. A Lancashire voice with a well-remembered accent shouted to a recalcitrant member of the party, 'We'll leave yer be'ind if yer don't 'urry oop!'

Groups of French and German tourists sat with a much more superior air on the balconies of small restaurants further along the street. It was clear that was the end of town to make for, not the kebab and chicken restaurants in the centre. As my guide book put it: 'You can do yourself a service by not sitting there amid the petrol fumes.'

At the hotel restaurant, John Aristides the owner emerged from the kitchen and gave me a nice seat by the window. I wanted to hear the story of the exotic building which had immediately engaged my eye. He'd worked thirteen years in the catering business, from Chelsea to Hampstead, then decided to return home, and had this remarkable place built. It's a strange mix of old mill, converted warehouse and mediaeval castle, staircases curving round the outer walls. Like something from a Hollywood epic. He apparently sketched it out himself and an architect did the rest. And what was the reaction in his own village? As I half expected: 'They didn't really like it. They're jealous of anyone who makes a success of something.'

Our talk over a bottle of white wine turned to walking, my main reason for coming up here. He said, 'Yes, there are some good walks.' But he added, 'You'll have to be a bit careful about the snakes, of course.'

'Snakes?' I echoed weakly. There'd been nothing in the guidebook about that. Yes, said John, there were three types, two of them poisonous.

'Adders?' I suggested. 'Zigzag patterns?'

'I don't know whether it's zigzag or what. It has a head like this.' He arranged his fingers into a sort of hostile V-shape. I looked at the asparagus heads on my plate. How big? He measured out the length with his hands. About eighteen inches. There was also a bigger, more dangerous one, he said, spreading his hands a yard apart. 'That one's a sort of beige colour.' And then there was the non-dangerous one: 'black, very thick'. He compared it with his upper arm. 'And very strong.' It didn't seem any less repulsive than the others. 'But don't worry,' he said, 'Snakes are very peaceful things. They only harm you if you frighten them. Just be careful you don't step on them. Or disturb them down at the waterholes when they're looking for birds…'

How'd he managed to keep the snakes out of this fine new building?

'I have three cats. They keep them away. Cats are very quick, you know, quicker than a snake. Dogs get bitten by snakes, but not cats. Their claws move too fast.' He illustrated the feline action with a fine snapping gesture. I looked with respect at the ginger tomcat sitting sedately on a chair. Maybe I should take him along with me. 'The snakes live in the old houses here, where they can get at the birds' eggs,' said John.

I resolved never to stay in an old house in Cyprus. Thank God the Maryland Lodge, where I was staying overnight, was just a few years old. As for that much anticipated walk, I now had visions of picking my way gingerly across a hillside swarming with adders and black non-poisonous reptiles as thick as my arm. But he assured me there was only one case every three years of somebody being bitten. He recommended I take a stick. A cleft stick? I felt like asking, but didn't. Where would I buy such a stick?

'Oh, just pick up a branch from the ground. But don't forget to tuck your trousers into your stockings. And keep your eyes open.'

378

I returned chastened to my room. Should I call the whole thing off?

Well, the following evening I could report that there were no snakes on the Troodos Mountains, not that I saw anyway. I'd driven seventeen winding kilometres from Kakopetria to the top through countryside that got greener all the time. The tangy smell of pines drifted through the open window of the Mitsubishi and the road was mercifully bare of the advertising signs you see further downhill. I must have seen more Pepsi ads in Cyprus than in my life elsewhere.

Troodos itself was little more than a collection of cafés offering chips with everything. I branched off along a side track towards the summit of Mount Olympus, where a small clearing marked the start of the circular Artemis trail. A serious-looking pair of German hikers had already arrived, and there were no socks tucked into their pants. Maybe they hadn't run into someone like John. But they had big rucksacks and were stylishly dressed for hiking. Did they look disapprovingly at my casual appearance, wearing the same lightweight trousers I'd worn for the Cotswold Way walk, feet in sneakers, camera dangling from one hand, the guidebook held in the other?

Well, I was glad not to be wearing hard-soled boots, fine for grassy terrain but not for this bone dry earth. There were sections when it was like walking through a quarry. I was glad when the Germans ahead of me branched off along another path. I followed the line of yellow arrows in solitary silence through glades of springy turf carpeted with pine needles.

Needless to add, I was watching the ground every inch of the way, but in a walk of about ten miles no snakes were to be seen and I began to wonder what all the fuss was about.

Back at the restaurant, there was a lively Saturday evening scene, except at the next table, where a bearded and professorial-looking American with rimless glasses sat with his dowdy wife and four children. I realised from the continuous low drone that he was reading aloud from what sounded like *The Lord of the Rings*. The family sat dumbly around the table in various attitudes of boredom and embarrassment, particularly the teenagers. Had Pater decided dinner must always be accompanied by some useful reading? *Asshole!* – as my old Canadian colleague Jack Hartzman would have said.

But then John emerged from the kitchen and we ended the

evening over a carafe or two of red wine. He told me more about his involvement in developing the village. There'd been quite a tussle with the authorities here and in Nicosia. I wasn't surprised to hear it was he who pushed through the refurbishment of the delightful old houses along the village street, which might otherwise have fallen into decay. Now their value had soared from a few hundred to as much as 100,000 pounds, as they were snapped up by rich Nicosians as weekend retreats away from the dust and the heat.

The women have departed for Kuwait and the first of the two male groups are here, appalled by the weather. They were thinking of this trip as a holiday and didn't expect thunder and lightning to be crashing over the roofs of Nicosia. I had them write a news feature. Abdel-Kerim wrote on challenges facing the Arab League, Anwar on Middle East peace talk prospects. Adnan surprisingly chose as a theme boxing and the campaign to end the sport. He seemed to know all about it. Steve Babbage, the jazz-loving friend of the Reuter boys, took me to hear a French jazz trio this evening, but it wasn't exactly my kind of jazz. Too much modal stuff. We left at the interval and drove to the English Club, unsurprisingly called 'The Elizabethan'. It's a slice of Essex suburbia, snooker table, large picture of a Spitfire on the wall, mock Elizabethan beamed ceiling and lots of laughter. The regulars are a pleasant bunch.

The Kuwaiti boys were good company as I took them round the Old City, where they made notes without being prodded. They knew they'd have to write about it later. At the UN checkpoint, I waited to see if any of them would try to get the sentry to talk, but as I half expected it was I who had to do it. *Talk to people*, I keep telling them, and Adnan was soon asking people as many questions as I myself. He also climbed the hundred steps of the Omeriyah Mosque with me. The two others stayed below, sitting in the shade. They all seem delighted to be getting so much attention. At head office, apparently, no one ever bothers. That's why I'm here – but I won't be around for ever. Bidding them farewell at the Romantika restaurant later, I found two of them already at the bar, drinking Scotch. They like a drink (or many) when away from home, and were having a last fling.

The last trio from Kuwait, due today, were nowhere to be seen at the Hilton. They'd never checked in. They'd managed to get arrested within hours of arrival by plain-clothes police, who brought them to the Reuter office for proof of identity. They'd apparently been hanging around outside the building, and the police, thinking their dress rather flamboyant (plus one of them had a beard!), roped them in. All was cleared up and they don't seem unduly offended. By the end of the day, they'd produced commendable pieces, the best one by Munir on the state of the Washington Middle East peace talks. Masoud, the baby of the trio, wrote a rather messy piece on problems still facing Kuwaitis two years after the war, but got some interesting facts in. The main thing is I'm getting them to think, and stretching their knowledge of English.

A couple of days later I've driven them to Famagusta, at the eastern end of the island. The narrow twisting main street seemed more Arab than anything else to me, and the Kuwaitis agreed. No guidebooks or postcards, nothing to tell the story of the fine old mosques, one of them a converted tenth-century abbey. Tourists expect more these days. The boys preferred Kyrenia and the Hilarion Castle, both looking at their best on a cloudless day. I had them write it all up in feature form. Their use of verbs is still a bit wonky, and adjectival endings don't always match the nouns – after all, English is not their first language. But with KUNA determined to produce an English-language service in addition to the Arabic one, they have to do it better. That's why I'm here. Mike Roddy and his wife hosted a party tonight (there hardly seems an evening without one of them somewhere). Mike, quite an accomplished classical pianist, sight-read some difficult Gershwin études, one of them in six flats. I feel duly chastened.

Before leaving Cyprus, I wanted to explore the Akamas peninsula at the far west corner of the island. I took the southern coast road, crawling behind trucks and buses as far as Paphos, which I decided was not my kind of town. The road further north got ever more secondary, petering out into a rough sandy track, curving and twisting through a desolate landscape of low scrub and rocks, a turquoise sea occasionally glimpsed below. I hoped this would eventually bring me through the mountains to the much-touted Baths of Aphrodite. But, after thirty miles or so, progress suddenly ended in the unlikely shape of two British marines sitting in a tent near a roadblock. That was as far as I could go, they said. Firing practice was about to begin. Even if it hadn't been, they wouldn't recommend the road through the mountains, even for a four-wheel-drive vehicle. I told them the track so far had been no worse than some roads I'd encountered in Iceland the year before. But I turned around anyway, and twenty miles back, found a road leading to the town of Petia, where there was a spanking new highway over the mountains.

Disappointingly, the Baths of Aphrodite turned out to be little more than a shady grotto with a mountain spring. I took snapshots for a friendly group of Italians and they did the same for me. Leaving the car for the time being, I trudged up a steep Nature Trail, all the time hearing the crump of explosives as the Army lads continued their fun and games on the other side of the hills. There were no coiled snakes on the hot stones, only lizards, scampering for cover as I approached. The top offered fabulous views across the mountains and, way below, a line of small bays along the north-west coast of the island. In this heat, I'd had enough by the time I got back to the car. The Drousha Heights Hotel provided a bed for the night, and next day the road took me to dilapidated Greek villages being spruced up under a government renewal scheme and the mediaeval church at Ayia Ekaterina.

Then, finally, my first sight of snakes. But safely in captivity, not in the wild. A roadside exhibition in a large tent, said the Austrian proprietor, had attracted 13,000 visitors the previous summer. For fifty cents you could see a variety of the creatures, including the blunt-headed viper I'd been warned about by John Aristides. Not everyone seemed to share my qualms. A large German lady didn't have any problem when allowed to pick up and stroke one of the long (but harmless) grass snakes on view. 'Ich habe kein Angst,' she told me. No accounting for tastes. Another grass snake lay sleepily coiled in one corner of a glass-topped cage, at the other end of which sat a small palpitating frog. Was the tiny creature about to become the snake's lunch? The proprietor must have noticed my revulsion. He shrugged and said, 'It is the nature. What shall I do?' Well, I thought, you could put them in separate cages for a start. I didn't linger longer.

Back in Kuwait a couple of months later on the last stage of my special assignment, I was whisked into town at 80 mph from the airport in the kind of eight-cylinder Japanese saloons they seem to go for. I brought with me a children's book for the young daughter of Editor-in-Chief Mohammed al-Ajeeri, a poor return for his lavish hospitality the last time in Kuwait, but I knew it would be appreciated. She was a charming child. A few diary notes may give the mixed flavour of this extraordinary society.

I groaned inwardly when I heard KUNA is considering setting up several big regional offices – my high-up informant talked of Cairo, Paris and London. To what end? I asked. The correspondents already there are not always up to the job. I think the bosses have been inspired by Reuters' regional bureaux, which, I pointed out, had specific operational functions, injecting stories directly on to the world wire. However, these rumoured ambitious plans are not as advanced as I feared. English Desk Editor Amal said they were simply talking about expanding in Cairo and Beirut, 'to see how it goes'. Depends whom you talk to here. And we were always told at Reuters to get all sides of a story.

I'd wondered why stories from KUNA's man in Rome seldom appeared on the wire. According to him, on a visit to head office, he files a lot of stories, but because they know little about Italy on the Desk, they don't bother to translate them. Whom to believe, here in the Arab world? There are plans for a reorganised structure here at head office, with all manner of fancy titles. I said, speaking as an outsider, that I'd be more concerned with the function of such jobs than the titles!

Bahgat, here again from Cairo, tells me his daughter has married some enormously rich Egyptian merchant. The wedding party out near the Pyramids cost about £60,000, with lavish entertainment, and a bottle of single-malt whisky stood in front of every plate.

A young Syrian I sat beside at a complimentary dinner laid on by the hotel's public relations department gave me another slant on some of the things that happened during the Iraqi invasion, when some of his family managed to bribe their way out to Jordan. His pregnant sister was asked by an Iraqi officer to body-search on their behalf two women trying to cross the border. She had no option but to do so, and was terrified when she found the women had wads of money strapped to their bodies. The dilemma: if she told the Iraqis what she'd found, the women might be shot. If she didn't and they found she'd lied, the same thing could happen to her. Pregnant and with a small son, she felt obliged to spill the beans. What happened to the other women, I asked. 'She doesn't know. She saw them being led away by the Iraqis.' Some people in this world have real problems.

One of the Editors kindly took me shopping this evening and bought me a radio/tape recorder (I'd made the mistake of mentioning my own was broken), but I dissuaded him from purchasing a huge and expensive one in favour of a smaller model. Meanwhile, a young musician from Goa, whose brother is on the KUNA payroll, having heard of my interest in jazz, kindly brought one of his own electronic keyboards round to the hotel, so I have music whenever I want to play (fairly softly, not to annoy the neighbours).

When only three young men from the Desk reported for the morning seminar, I went straight to the bosses and told them there wasn't much point in continuing like this. The culprits, however charming they have been to me, have been read the Riot Act. On the other hand, there's full and enthusiastic attendance by members of the so-called Research Unit (in other words Features Department), which I'm trying to get integrated into the Editorial proper. For some reason these guys are treated as second-class citizens by Desk members, who refer to them scathingly as the 'Poets' Corner'. Yet these are highly educated and politically aware men. One of them countered dismissively, 'The reporters wouldn't even know the way to our office.' I wonder why this enmity. I like the Poets and will do all I can to develop the service.

Living the high life, Kuwaiti-style. One of the big shots invited me to dinner at his home. We drove out there in a huge eight-cylinder Buick with enormous bumpers almost as big as they used to be in the sixties. The tank holds ninety-five litres, he says, which take it no more than 370 kilometres. Good thing petrol's cheap here. His other cars are American, Japanese and German respectively. There's a large carport in front of his three-storey house in a southern suburb. We sat in the capacious lounge and drank whisky and water while we listened to his latest CDs – Count Basie, Duke Ellington and Glenn Miller. The lavish lifestyle here is incredible. He's off to south-east Asia on holiday shortly, and I gather a lady companion is lined up for the occasion.

'You should stay with us all the time,' said English Desk editor Amal when I showed her an extra task I'd taken on, putting one of their Public Relations Department letters into rather more elegant English. I can't abide sloppy language.

One of the Editors kindly took me along to the annual car show. First stop was a small cafeteria run by Filipinos, where he ordered two plastic beakers of fresh orange juice, into which, as we sat in the car, he poured miniature bottles of vodka. Then we stopped en route at a car centre, where he took another look at a six-cylinder Mercedes 300 SL, which he's planning to buy his wife – as her *second* car.

This is no town for walking. You're taking your life in your hands when you cross the main roads. There are token pedestrian crossings, but they're mainly ignored. It's a car society. When I mentioned in the office that I'd like to take a walk occasionally, but the immediate area wasn't too attractive, one of the ladies asked, 'Why don't you walk in Salmiya?' (a rather posh suburb).

'How would I get there?' I asked.

'Take a taxi,' she said. I miss English parks.

'Did you hear the one about the Saudi King asking the people to pray for rain?' asked Bahgat. The high-ups had already seen on TV that rain clouds were heading for the Gulf. But when the rain arrived, simple people said, 'What a great man and prophet is the King – God is surely on his side!' Laughs among the Kuwaitis.

At dinner in one of the better hotels, a senior KUNA executive and I watched the antics of a trio of young Kuwaitis at the next table. One of them had lined up two Filipino girls, who were tucking into hearty meals, after which the young men strode out of the restaurant, the girls following in their wake. 'They'll take the girls to one of their flats and give them ten dinars each,' said my host. 'It's a common sight.' How about AIDS in all this? I wondered.

A complete breakdown of the system this morning. I went along to the wire room to see how things were going. Asked if anybody on the News Desk had been round to discuss the problem, the wire room boss said with a laugh, 'I don't think they would know where we are.'

I've signed off after having my detailed forty-page report printed, bound and handed to the Editor-in-Chief. I included a sort of league table of KUNA's overseas bureaux, recommending the weaker brethren should be replaced and recalled to head office. Their Cairo office is easily the worst offender, taking until mid-afternoon recently to report multiple shootings at a city centre hotel, a big story which Reuters had on the wire twelve hours earlier. I called for major changes in the set-up at head office, with more contact between desks and sharper news presentation. The problems were all fairly obvious and I didn't pull any punches. I was glad to praise the work of some of the younger staff, including a young woman I got transferred to the more interesting reporting unit after she'd decided to quit the company. It was the girl who'd interviewed the Aussie peace-keeper in Cyprus. The first feature she wrote back home, only lightly subbed by me, won excellent play in Kuwait's English-language daily. It can be done.

Bahgat, shown my report in advance, read it through in pretended bewilderment, shook his head, chuckled and said, 'You are wasting your time, my dear. *Wasting your time!* Nothing will ever change in this part of the world.' There spoke a man from the Middle East. We shall see. I've done what I'm paid for. The rest is up to the client.

But before leaving Kuwait, I wanted to take a closer look at the literary scene and the role of women in the national culture. First, as recommended by some of the reporters at KUNA, I went to talk to Fatma Al-Abdallah, a prominent government lawyer. Her office was in the parliament building, an elegant mix of Islamic and Scandinavian modern. The pace of work in the building didn't seem excessive. The busiest group seemed to be the uniformed guards, who shook their heads and waved a warning finger at my camera. In the cathedral-like atrium, groups of men in pristine-white jellabiyas sat like statues, fingering their worry beads, silently, it seemed, passing the time away.

Fatma's office was as long as a cricket pitch, the furniture leathery and luxurious. Through the panoramic picture window, the view was of the blue Gulf, where sons of the rich raced powerboats across the water. A servant glided in with tiny cups of Arab coffee, a male clerk appeared respectfully with documents to be signed. Fatma was helping to frame the country's laws, but didn't have the vote yet. One of the incongruities of Islam.

She was one of a new wave of women writers whose imagination had been fired by the first Gulf War and was happy to talk about the literary scene. In one of her latest poems, translated from the Arabic for me, Kuwait put the question to the Iraqi invaders:

> You, who were an old friend,
> Is this your reward for kindness?
> You, my neighbour,
> Is this your gratitude?
> To set fire to my wells?
> To seize my sons?
> To violate my virgins?

The references were real enough. On an August morning five years earlier, Kuwaiti women had carried banners protesting against the invasion. They were fired on, two of them killed. Hundreds of women were raped and tortured in the months that followed. A mother saw her son shot through the head on the doorstep. Hundreds of men were still missing. 'I couldn't write during that period,' Fatma told me. 'Once the Iraqis went, I started to write again.'

At the Islamic Heritage Museum, I asked owner/director Sheikha Hassa-al-Sabah, a member of the royal family, what seemed to make Kuwait women more focused and pragmatic than the men. She said, 'This characteristic of Kuwaiti women is an old thing. This was always a trading country of merchants. When the men were away on long trips, it was always the women who kept the show running. Not just the family, but the business.'

I heard similar sentiments from Thuraya Al-Baqsami, writer, painter and book illustrator whose vibrantly coloured works with oriental themes had been exhibited in Paris and London. She said with a smile, 'Women would only have to go on strike for three days and nothing would work.' Passionate about politics, she added, 'It's clear we want political rights. Some people are trying to pull women back in the name of Islam, to make them stay at home. They don't discuss our problems, such things as divorce laws. They waste hours talking about whether women should use make-up or drive cars. But I have the feeling there is hope – though they have given us so many promises in the past.'

The boys in KUNA's undervalued Features Unit pointed me towards the Kuwait Writers' Club, a quarter of whose members were women. The club gathered each Wednesday evening. Fronted by lawns, the white building looked a bit like an old-fashioned English tennis club. Globular lamps cast a cosy glow over the terrace as the warm dusk of the Gulf descended. In the football stadium just across the square, I was told, the Iraqi invaders had imprisoned and tortured their victims.

Conversation at the gathering was cosmopolitan, frequently poetic in the Arab way. Admired writers tended to be traditional, often documentary – Dickens, Tolstoy, Moravia, Dostoevsky. A science fiction specialist, Taiba al-Ibrahim, paid homage to H G Wells. Arabic's roots are in the Koran – 'We can pick up any literary work that has appeared over the centuries and understand it,' someone said – but there were now apparently moves towards a simpler style.

Laila Mohammed Salah said she wrote at night, in longhand, of religion, sex, politics. Some of her titles (*Rendezvous in the Rose Garden*, *The Season of Flowers*) smacked of Mills and Boon, but windy Arab hyperbole was firmly slapped down in the closing paragraph of her *Window of a New Day*.

> Next day, on the phone, he tried to apologise again. He said, 'You are my last refuge, whom I hurry to when I get the feeling of being lost. In your bosom I own the whole world. I forget my problems. Please understand me.' She hung up in his face. He didn't deserve even words.

Strong stuff in this area!

Someone mentioned Hemingway's *Old Man And The Sea*. 'Don't forget, Kuwait is country which arose from the sea,' I was told. And the sea was the image which the outspoken Laila al-Othman, perhaps the most successful of Kuwait's women writers at home and abroad, interestingly employed in her short story, 'The Demon'. The ocean, with its natural gifts of pearls and fish, is seen as the natural benefactor of the Kuwaitis. Then it declines into being just a means of transporting new oil riches. A sleeping man on the beach represents the Kuwaiti people, who have forsaken the life of their ancestors. Finally, suddenly, the sea is no longer blue.

The author used similar symbols in her story 'Zahra'. A young woman suddenly arrives in a neighbourhood. 'No one knew who she was, why and how she came…' The mysterious stranger is followed by a flood of relatives who gradually buy up all the village property and dispossess the original inhabitants. The political message in al-Othman's story was clear, however simplistic the theme might seem to an outsider. For 'Zahra', read 'Jewish Settlers'.

It's nice to know, a decade or more later, that Kuwait has finally elected its first women parliamentarians. In May 2009, four out of fifteen female candidates, all US-educated academics, who include campaigners for women's rights and a World Bank consultant, were voted on the fifty-seat parliament. 'It's a major leap forward,' said one of them, Professor Aseel al-Awadhi.

Chapter 27
'WELL, IT'S BETTER THAN WORKING, ISN'T IT?'

Inevitably, one of the Fleet Street wags would come out with that well-worn phrase as we gathered in mid-evening, the dust of the day washed off, in some hotel lounge in Cairo or Khartoum. Or, after a less strenuous political conference, in Geneva or Bonn. In Helsinki, the gathering place was usually the famous Marski Bar on the main street, where you could also take a sauna upstairs if you fancied it. In those days, we were rather like a bunch of schoolboys. It was only in later years that women began to take a bigger part in the show. To be a correspondent's wife could sometimes be difficult.

We liked to think, I suppose, that the job separated us from the herd. So it had been since early days at the *Bury Times*, when before the monthly Town Council meeting the gang gathered convivially over a mixed grill to decide who covered which committee, reassembling over drinks afterwards to double-check our shorthand notes. At home or abroad, there was the privileged feel of watching the show without being part of it (except when someone ventured too near the action in a place like the Middle East).

The story was what you made of it. While interviewing or assembling background material, you were already subconsciously thinking how to phrase the intro. It was easy to overstep the mark in those far-back Lancashire days, more over presentation than facts. If you pushed the story too far, there was the chance of being pursued by an irate householder. 'You'll get a Solicitor's Letter about this' – the magic formula then of aggrieved members of society. The Solicitor's Letter seldom arrived on the Editor's desk, but the threat of it kept you on your toes.

The media in this country know what's legally permissible. The tabloids do stretch the rules, most papers don't, but mistakes happen. At Reuters, the rules were clear. I liked the idea of an impartial press and that's why I joined the firm. It was nice to find, going through the clippings on return from my first big story, the Cod War, that papers as politically distinct as *The Times* and the communist *Daily Worker* had used the same piece, exactly as I'd written it. It's possible to be both bright and accurate.

Britain's newspapers, whether national or local, face major problems today, some of them self-induced. And it's not only in this country. Everywhere, new communications are inexorably turning people away from the printed page to the computer screen. The subsequent loss of advertising revenue has hugely affected company earnings – and staff jobs. I'd never have guessed, when working in the old *New York Times* 43rd Street offices, that this now 150-year-old paper – as much an institution as a newspaper – could ever hit the buffers. But, according to recent reports, it could happen unless new money is injected, along with radical marketing changes.

In Britain, the smell of newsprint which lured me into the editorial room of the local paper has long since evaporated. Younger journalists wouldn't even know what I'm talking about. And while TV 'stars' – whose exact qualities are sometimes hard for the occasional viewer to define – are paid monstrous sums of money, journalists lower down the ladder are squeezed.

Britain's *Journalist* magazine reports a big drift from the trade into better-paid PR jobs – and who can blame those involved? Writers who used to report for the local paper – usually unbiased, protective of personal privacy and quick to spot a scandal or a scam – now often decide to work for the Town Council instead. Can Public Relations people be relied on to report local affairs objectively – or aggressively if need be? They have their livelihoods to think about.

Back at the *Bury Times* half a century ago, virtually the entire reporting staff joined in covering the monthly Council meeting. The result was comprehensive cover of local affairs. Today, with many town authorities providing their own (inevitably one-sided) cover of such meetings, local papers might send just one or two reporters – or none – and rely on the Council's PR machine instead. It's easier, I suppose, on the wage bill. But it's the sort of local reporting I remember from Nasser's Egypt!

Guardian editor Alan Rusbridger has predicted that the crisis in the industry could lead to newspapers going out of business (in fact it's started to happen). He told BBC Radio, 'We have to face up to the prospect that major cities will be left without any kind of verifiable news. That hasn't happened for two or three hundred years.'

By the early autumn of 2009, the Guardian News and Media group itself, financially stretched after losing nearly ninety million pounds in a year, raised its prices. For the first time, *Guardian* readers had to stump up a pound for the famous daily and the group's owners, not ruling out redundancies, predicted other papers would soon be following suit. The future of Britain's newspaper industry – and those of other countries – was looking uncomfortably dark at both national and local level.

But perhaps things will change. This year's crisis over the expense scams of sanctimonious British politicians – with drastic reforms only made likely through the intervention of the *Daily Telegraph* in one of the news stories of the decade – will remind people how important newspapers are. How could this mind-boggling and graphic exposé of parliamentary cheating ever have been conveyed online? The answer's obvious.

The red blobs on the map have all but disappeared. Despite the big talk of some politicians, we're not a major country any more. We no longer make cars, trucks, ships or trains. The Germans, French and Italians do. The latest transatlantic liner was built in France. Closer at hand, Royal Worcester down the road from here is up for sale. The Asians do the job cheaper. Spaniards, Americans, Chinese, Indians and Russians own airports, shops, banks and football clubs. Even the Icelanders... until that bubble burst. We just let it happen. We're halfway to bankruptcy, but still have some of the old pretensions, fighting two wars in foreign places which really have little to do with us. I could never say that at Reuters of course, but I don't have to be impartial any more.

Coming back to England after thirty years abroad was a culture shock. Along with an obsession with property there seemed a very laid-back attitude to life. Whereas we as students used to work – we had to – during the holidays, they now had 'gap years', travelling the world at their parents' expense. More fool the parents. This nonsense may bite the dust as the true value of money becomes apparent again.

No one wants Mr Gradgrind back, but educational standards seem to deteriorate. The penny began to drop when, after retirement in the nineties, I joined a Russian class at Evesham Technical College. Our excellent teacher, Doug Willis, referred in passing to subjects and objects, verbs and adjectives. He saw that one of our number, a perfectly nice young woman in her late twenties, looked perplexed. Was something the matter, he asked. 'Well, we never learned about things like that at school,' she said.

Standards of literacy are low; just read the letters to the local papers. Discipline is sometimes non-existent. I entered a GCSE music course in Stratford-on-Avon at a fairly late age, like another retiree in the group. We were aghast when the youngsters in the classroom just ignored the teacher whenever they felt like having a chat. It was left to us seniors to intervene. And that was before mobile phones!

It's often the kids from immigrant families who shine. Maybe it's the old Hertz-and-Avis syndrome – the second in line has to try harder. It's no surprise that some of the new immigrants – just as the Poles and Ukrainians who came to Lancashire after the Second World War and the Irish before them – often do so well. We now have a Lewis Hamilton as a motor racing champion. A Pakistani/Brit in my Lancashire home town is a new British boxing hope. There'll be others, I'm sure. English craftsmen, at least, are as good as they ever were, judging from jobs done in my house. But there's still an implied dividing line in England between academics and the so-called 'working classes'. I don't find it in the Nordic countries that I frequently visit.

Apart from getting a full-page spread with one of your stories, one of the best things in life must be playing in a band. As a teenager I enjoyed the school orchestra, but didn't much like the violin, not after I'd heard American boogie. In post-Reuter days, for the first time since the Cotton City Jazzmen and the German trad group in Aachen, there was suddenly a chance to play in a band again. At Stratford College, our teacher Will Allen asked if I'd like to join the swing group.

Over three or four years we played to diverse audiences in community halls, pubs, a wedding reception, an old people's home, shopping precincts and a restaurant near the Royal Shakespeare Theatre. The repertoire was swing and 'standards', and I'd play a Basie-style intro to some of our medium-tempo blues. We must have looked a curious group: two retirees, a couple of ladies in their late thirties, the rest teenagers. If we ever earned any money, we seniors put our share back in the pot for the youngsters. The main thing is we were playing live music and people actually danced to it! Inspired (or maybe just a bit drunk) at one village hop near Stratford, I copied the great Earl Hines by playing three whole choruses with a rolled right-hand octave. And the floor was heaving with dancing couples. I asked myself, Can anything be better than this?

Well, as the old Duke Ellington song put it, 'Things ain't what they used to be.' Or, as the late Peter Sellers's crusty aristocrat said in one of those hilarious old records, 'I fear that not everything has changed for the bettah.' Though I suppose people have been saying that pretty much since the year dot.

During that first foreign assignment to Copenhagen, it had become increasingly clear that Britain was on the slide. A lot of pretensions, but nothing much to back it up. And it wasn't just the Suez fiasco of two years earlier, when Anthony Eden and his associates were given a bloody nose.

There were small, everyday things. A man I met in Sweden had always, pre-war, been a fan of Jaguar cars. Now, twelve years after the Second World War, he'd switched to Mercedes. He'd found Jaguars unreliable, delivery dates uncertain. A chap in Copenhagen had always bought fishing tackle from England. He eventually just gave up waiting for an order to be despatched and switched to Sweden's Abu. I could only sympathise.

I'd seen enough in the brief time spent in London before being posted to think England had a pretty decrepit social system. Southerners, especially, seemed riveted into pre-war patterns.

The ruling classes wore bowlers. The workers still touched their caps to those they considered their betters. The upper classes spoke, well, differently.

Heard today on old film, the commentators at Ascot or other 'Royal' occasions, with their infantile commentaries delivered in high-pitched 'eksents', or the protagonists in that rather over-praised film *Brief Encounter*, are hard to listen to without laughing.

The great Ealing comedies of the fifties pinned it all down. Traditional manager/worker relationships were memorably captured in the film *I'm All Right Jack*, which shows what happens after the workers turn bolshie. Sellers's trade union organiser, while determined to continue the all-out strike, feels he has to ape the manners and vocabulary of the managerial class. 'Care to imbibe?' he pathetically asks, offering a drink to one of the bosses (Terry Thomas) who's called round at his home to negotiate. Perfectly done.

Newly returned from Copenhagen in the early sixties and, living for the moment in a pokey rented Belsize Park flat, I'd half a mind to buy a house in Kent. I went along to a sales exhibition to look at their range of plans and asked the price of the biggest and best-looking one. The woman behind the counter said, 'Oh, those are not for us, dear.' Well, speak for yourself, madam. Maybe my northern accent didn't suit. Or maybe because at thirty I wasn't supposed to be earning that sort of money. I cancelled the order anyway when Reuters gave me the New York job.

I found New Yorkers blunter, but with no such hang-ups. If you could afford it, you bought it – even if, as with my Volvo car, it took three years to pay it off. The Nordic countries too, I'd already found, had much easier relationships between the social classes, though some of their ideas were a bit advanced for my taste. Political correctness was alive and well in Scandinavia long before it migrated to England.

Yes, times have changed. They always do. To see just how much so, I took a look at an original copy of the venerable *Times* – the paper I might once have worked for – from the day I was born. It made fascinating reading, adverts and all.

Spread out on a table, the thirty-two-page *Times* (London

edition) of 10 July 1929 is all of three feet wide and two feet long (today's tabloid *Times* is barely a quarter of that size). I wonder how the bowler-hatted bankers and civil servants travelling in their first-class compartments up to London managed not to entangle each other when unfolding those crisply folded pages. Maybe they saved it to read in the office. They'd have needed a lot of time, which perhaps some of them had.

With its lengthy reports of Parliament, world problems and the lives of the gentry, I can well understand *The Times* being regular reading for that chap in Somerset Maugham's lovely tale, 'The Outstation'. One of those pillars of Empire, he had it sent out East in monthly bundles from London. Upriver, he spent his evenings reading it, but only one day at a time, in the correct order. When a junior colleague, in his own absence upriver, ripped open the package, disrupting the sacred sequence, he had to be killed off and the even pattern resumed.

On this particular Tenth of July, I couldn't quarrel with *The Times*'s choice of top story. It was, unsurprisingly one of disaster. A naval submarine, the *H-47*, with twenty-four sailors aboard, had gone down in the Irish Sea off the south-west coast of Wales after colliding with another sub. At a depth of nearly sixty fathoms, there was no hope of survivors.

Downpage, in my native Lancashire, a quarter million weavers were threatening strike action against a threat to cut their wages by twelve and a half per cent. Nationwide, there was a big increase in unemployment. Lady Astor told a National Brotherhood conference in London that two million children between two and five were living 'in very terrible conditions'. There was a report on Poor Relief in the London suburb of West Ham. At the other end of society, the Duke of Gloucester had called at Buckingham Palace after a four-month trip to Canada and Japan.

These were relatively early days for aviation, which would become one of my interests as a boy. Transcontinental flights were top news. A Pathfinder aircraft had landed in Spain after a non-stop journey from America, while Britain's *Southern Cross*, flown by Captain Kingsford Smith, had arrived in Rome en route to England from Australia. And, under the headline 'A Flying-

Ship', a new twelve-engined Dornier with room for one hundred passengers had been unveiled to journalists at Lake Constance. A foretaste of the Luftwaffe's air prowess to come?

There were reports of 'Balkan Tensions' and drug smuggling in San Francisco – well, aren't there always? Another hint of impending trouble came in a story from Rome. Under the uncritical headline 'Fascism and Sport', Signor Mussolini, it was reported, was urging Italians to give up their 'pot-bellied peaceful life' to deeds of vigour and valour.

Presaging things to come in the sporting field, it was reported that several Italian soccer teams, a relatively new sport there, could now beat professional English sides.

English cricket remained inviolate, though an Indian, the famous Nawab of Pataudi, had played 'a very sound innings of 106' in the annual Oxford–Cambridge match. 'He went for the bowling with the utmost vigour and versatility of stroke,' said the *Times* correspondent approvingly. The Nawab, scion of a princely line in India, went on to score 84 in the second innings to save the match against Cambridge, and later captained India. Incredibly, *The Times* devoted a column and a half to that single university match.

For the third Test Match against South Africa, which was to start shortly, we were still in the age of Gentlemen (the amateurs) and Players (professionals). In the England line-up printed in *The Times*, the Gents were allowed to have their initials before their names, the professionals not. The team included an astonishing number of big names still remembered: Herbert Sutcliffe of Yorkshire, Henry 'Patsy' Hendren of Middlesex, Wally Hammond of Gloucestershire, Maurice Leyland of Yorkshire, Frank Woolley of Kent and the Nottinghamshire fast bowler Harold Larwood. The latter's almost lethal 90 mph bowling would lead to a nasty 'Bodyline' row with Australia. Asked hypocritically by England's cricketing authorities to apologise to the Aussies, the former miner refused and later emigrated to that country.

Britain still very much mattered industrially, though the rot would shortly set in. At sea, its vessels topped the world shipping league at twenty million tons, almost double that of the United

States, five times that of Germany or Japan. There was a wide choice of British cars – ranging from the budget-price Austin 'Swallow' to more upmarket Rileys and Armstrong-Siddeleys, and, for industrial users, Morris and Leyland trucks. Though most of these marques survived the Second World War, they've all bitten the dust since.

Under the headline 'Talking Pictures', *The Times* reported that a Mr Alfred Hitchcock had recently completed his first film, *Blackmail* – which still gets an occasional airing.

Author H G Wells was scheduled to give a talk 'on the wireless' on World Peace. It was a topic much on most people's minds. Just ten years after the First World War, in the close knit grey columns of *The Times's* front page, the anniversaries of some of the casualties (officers all) – the Somme, Ypres and Flanders – were being remembered.

In the small ads, it was as if the Victorian age hadn't ended. The upper classes were looking for Lady Housekeepers, Parlourmaids, Scullerymaids and Betweenmaids. One of the latter, whatever they were, was being sought 'to help Cook and make herself generally useful in a house at Highgate', while The Honourable Mrs Fordham, of Steeple Morden, wanted 'two Gentlewomen to do the work of a small house in a country village 40 miles from London'.

Clearly, a world away from industrial Lancashire, where, on the first day of my life, it would hardly have interested my mother – who I don't think ever read *The Times* in her life – to read a brief report from the 'Irish Free State', as the country of her birth was then called, that *Treasure Island* and *Lorna Doone* had been translated into Irish.

It was time to revisit Ireland, which had seen big changes under the aegis of the European Union. But it had been nice to see the Irish giving the bullies of Brussels a bloody nose over the plan to anoint their artificial empire stretching from the Atlantic to the fringes of Russia with a written 'Constitution' – largely drawn up by the French. Defying their own perhaps too complacent rulers, Irish voters showed they didn't care for being told what to do. They threw in the towel later, alas. But over the centuries, all such unions, confederations and empires have finally bitten the dust. Doesn't anybody read the history books?

In the idyllic summers of yesteryear, we'd always travelled quite agreeably on ferries from south Wales to Rosslare, at Ireland's south-eastern tip, from where it was just a pleasant run via Waterford and Carrick-on-Suir to the land of the Ryans. This time I'd flown to Dublin from Birmingham and it was to a vastly changed place. I used to like airports, especially the little ones in the middle of countries like Turkey or Sudan. They were friendlier places. Now Dublin Airport was getting to be a mini-metropolis like the rest of them in Europe – Paris, Copenhagen, Frankfurt, Amsterdam, and of course London, the most unpleasant of all. Long echoing corridors, grinding escalators, mechanical walkways and shops selling mountains of goods that few people need and even fewer can now afford.

Delivering me at my hotel close to Dublin Airport, my taxi driver (always the traditional first source in a foreign country!) was scathing about the European Union and its effects on Irish life. As in Britain, now suffering the grim results of overspending, the easy money days were over. There were no real farmers left in Ireland, he complained, for with the subventions they received from Brussels it was more profitable to stop producing food than actually growing it. Well, it was good to hear a bit of healthy Euro-scepticism so soon after arrival – and it wouldn't be by any means the last.

The Dublin papers, like their London counterparts, were full of doom and gloom. 'What Next For Irish Banks?' was the front page headline of the *Irish Times*. Property funds were, as the business pages politely put it, 'losing their shine'. Complaints about money mismanagement, said the Financial Services Ombudsman, had increased by a third in the past year. A flashy new skyscraper planned for Dublin's docklands at a cost of 200 million euros had been put on hold. There was a banking crisis almost rivalling those across the Irish Sea and the Atlantic, and the State might have to step in to stop the rot, as in Britain. And this was all on one page!

At ground level, people complained about the cost of living, which had rocketed with the advent of the euro. I was unsurprised. I'd been hearing similar complaints for years in countries like Germany and Finland, but governments there didn't seem to listen to ordinary people either. No one seemed to like euros, but somehow they'd become the fashionable currency – and would soon become an overinflated one.

Among the relatives in Dublin and Clonmel in the following days, conversation centred on more pleasant family matters, and it was clear the old Irish charm had not evaporated. I'd now been joined by my son and grandson Michael, the latter much the same age as Peter during those idyllic summers of yesteryear. My young cousin Sile, whose wedding I'd attended years earlier, was now settled comfortably with Martin and the kids in a roomy new house close to the River Liffey.

For those with Clonmel memories, it was mainly life in the seventies we were interested in. The youngsters gathered around the family table were as fanatic about cars and motorbikes as my son had always been. We elders reminisced about life in Tipperary when there were fewer cars, cheaper petrol, no mobile phones or Playstations and not even a hint of the profligacy and financial problems lying ahead. In simpler days, our pleasures consisted of an afternoon trip to the Disneyesque Carey's Castle, half hidden in the woods outside Clonmel, or the picturesque Saint Patrick's Well, its central island reached across a line of stepping stones. Or a climbing expedition with a battalion of the youngsters through tall undergrowth buzzing with bees up to Bagwell's Folly, a hilltop ruin that's a legacy of the old English presence.

We stopped on the way south at a bleak and windswept Rock of Cashel, where my grandson climbed about the ancient walls. Clonmel was bigger and busier than of old but relatively unscathed. First priority was to lay flowers at my mother's grave. Nearby headstones bore the names of other family members I'd known. The rest are scattered, living or dead, around Ireland, England or America in a typical twentieth-century emigration pattern.

The main street, where my cousin Dick Bolger once had that friendly late-night encounter with the local policeman, was now a one-way affair with not a parking place in sight. Our favourite eating-out place in the seventies, the Clonmel Arms, was shuttered up, with no immediate prospects of reopening, I was told. But there was splendid alternative accommodation at the Minella Hotel on the other bank of the River Suir (whose name, pronounced the English way, quite belies its sparkling prettiness).

We glanced nostalgically, driving by, at Number 4 St Patrick's Terrace, always my first port of call in Ireland, then turned off the road to Ardfinnan to see the house I'd had built thirty years earlier. It was now shrouded by thick trees I'd planted as saplings. I didn't knock, or ring the bell. Better to leave some memories intact. Sufficient reminiscences were shared at nearby Cherrymount, home of the Bolgers' son Liam and family.

A pilgrimage then into the Knockmealdown Hills, where decades earlier my son and I had ridden our small motorbikes across country, camping by a mountain stream. Then we drove west, always my favourite part of Ireland. The countryside was as attractive as ever, though eyes still boggled at the glaring pinks, blues, violets and greens of houses along the road. At least some things in Ireland don't change.

The following day, my grandson was predictably enraptured by the beauty of Lake Killarney, viewed from the terrace of our hotel room as a glowing evening sun sank behind the western peaks. The lasting charm of Ireland has much to do with its ancient ruins, lakes and rivers, mountains and old tracks – its history. The smooth new motorway along which we swept back across the flat midland counties to Dublin was impressive and time-saving – but is that enough? I remembered that old man by the roadside in Cork a few years earlier, regretting the straight new roads and loss of old village landmarks: 'Sure, you'll get there in no time.' My sentiments exactly.

I'd chased my Irish past. What about England?

I drove north and, on a bleak day in spring, was gazing down from the Lancashire moorland village of Affetside, highest vantage point in the area, over a well-remembered landscape. This was where I'd learnt the trade.

I'd chosen a bad time of year to come, though. The moors

looked mournful enough for a *Hound of the Baskervilles* film. Occasional breaks in the clouds allowed the odd glimpse of a pale blue wintry sky. But it was the changeable weather I remembered.

There were historical as well as geographic reasons for choosing this spot. Affetside goes back to the days of the Romans. A stone cross by the roadside is a reminder that you're on Watling Street, a road reputedly once trodden by the legions between the fortresses of Mancunium (Manchester) and Ribchester.

A veil of sleet swept across the valley, partly shrouding the dark shape of Holcombe Hill, the biggest landmark in the area I once covered for the local paper. On its crest stands the square-built Peel Tower, a memorial to parliamentarian Robert Peel, twice England's Prime Minister and Bury's most famous son.

They were nice people at the farm. They'd done a fine job converting an old barn into a comfortable modern holiday flat, which seemed to be attracting a good number of visitors, though usually at better times of year. I'd covered a good many stories in these parts. In the distance, below the tower, lay the small town of Ramsbottom, my first reporting beat, where I headed now.

In those streets I'd learned the ropes of journalism, operating from that corner house in Buchanan Street, headquarters of the Weavers', Winders' and Warpers' Association. Its general secretary, Councillor Gilbert Holt, was long dead. The house, now sandblasted clean of industrial soot, was for sale. I wondered who'd lived there in the fifty years between. I almost thought that, if I knocked, a rosy-cheeked old trade unionist might open the door and say, 'Come in, lad, and get warm.'

I was being driven around by a lifelong friend, John Bolton, a founder member of Bury Jazz Club. One of our old venues had been the Grant Arms, which overlooks Ramsbottom's cobbled main square. Astonishingly, until a few months earlier, the many times reconstituted Cotton City Jazzmen had continued to perform there. Now, alas, with dwindling audiences, the band had finally called it a day.

Despite the rain, the town seemed to be prospering. The main street, down which I'd often walked to the railway station and the Ramsbottom Cricket Club ground, now boasted cafés and smart boutiques. In the side streets beyond, the mills and factories which once produced so many news stories were long gone.

It wasn't the best day for sightseeing. The square was slippery with sleet and there were few people about. The weather didn't change as we toured a string of moorland villages with names like Edenfield, Summerseat and Shuttleworth, where at one time I got to know every vicar, factory owner and policeman.

From the oddly named village of Jericho, twisting country lanes that hardly seemed to have changed over the years brought us out on to windswept moors and the familiar sanctuary of 'Owd Bett's', a pub named after a lady from long ago. I'd often called there in the old days on farming stories. It was a good place to phone for some colour when heavy snow made the moorland roads impassable. People like weather stories.

In his later years, during my visits home from abroad, my father loved to revisit these parts. As I drove around, he'd point out big country houses or now abandoned mills where he'd done building jobs back in the twenties. He'd stand in the pub's front lounge before the open fire, warming himself with a drop of whisky and hot water as he recalled the past.

Bury, the town around which these old villages cluster, looks very different today. The fine Parish Church still dominates the town centre but seems in danger of being elbowed aside by the commercial developments swirling around it. The old *Bury Times* office, a handsome red-brick building, is vanished. I imagine the reporters' room would now lie somewhere in the middle of Marks and Spencer's store.

As well as mills, Bury had always had a thriving market. There was a cosy atmosphere in the town centre on Saturday afternoons after a football match at Gigg Lane. Spectators walking home bought hot potatoes, baked in a moveable oven, wrapped in white paper bags and eaten with a dash of salt: Northern England's equivalent, perhaps, of those Scandinavian hot-dog stands. That simple trade had long since disappeared. So had the old town abattoirs nearby, now the site of a traffic 'Interchange', where people swap buses from the suburbs for the train to Manchester.

A colourful brochure advertised the delights of 'The World-famous Bury Market'. It seemed a pretty big claim. I couldn't remember anybody mentioning it in my trips abroad. But, I was told, crowds arrive in coaches from at least as far as the Welsh valleys and north-east England, totalling twelve million people a year. I should feel proud. (Also of my home town's football club, which instead of teetering on the brink of relegation at the end of every season, this year finished close to the top.)

Could this be the same place I knew as a boy? Where, too close for comfort to the old Parish Church, there was once an evil-smelling tannery which we'd walk a long way round to avoid? No trace of it now, or of the echoing foundry on the other side of town, which with its dripping crucibles of white-hot metal seemed like the entrance to Hell when I entered there on a news story. Or of the road incongruously called Paradise Street, once the reputed preserve of dubious rag traders and assorted miscreants who regularly turned up in the Magistrates' Court. All long gone. A new bypass straddles the area.

Almost miraculously amid the massive changes, Wash Lane remains. So does York Street, where we played soccer with that tennis ball. The Church of England's Bell School still stands across the road, its 'BOYS' and 'GIRLS' entrance signs, etched in stone, unchanged. The biggest mills have gone, but otherwise the area seems to have resisted the bulldozers. The hat factory where my mother and her Irish sisters were once employed on arrival in England now houses a new wave of immigrants from East Europe who run a car-cleaning business, and do it well, I'm told. The old builders' yard has gone and the cinema where Mother later worked as cashier is now just a memory on a gravelled parking lot.

Back in the hills, the farmer's son proudly showed me his pet rabbits and an adorable pair of lambs, tottering around in the straw beside their mother. They'd been born just hours ago, he told us. A reassuring event. Some things at least don't change.

At last, a real summer day. Viewed from the slow stopping train, the English countryside – perhaps because we seldom see it in such weather – looks idyllic. I'm glad to be returning home from Oxford, thronged to bursting with tourists and shoppers. An early evening sun slants in through the windows as the train rolls slowly through a landscape that probably hasn't changed overmuch in the last century. The village houses have golden stone walls and red-tiled roofs. The capricious river Evenlode, fringed with willows, curves and twists its way alongside or underneath the track, keeping passengers company for most of the way home. The stations where we halt, with names like Ashton-under-Wychwood and Moreton-in-Marsh, could only be in England. From long habit, I count the seconds – twenty-five on average – as we speed through the only tunnel along the route. Then we emerge in the Vale of Evesham, slowing down for Honeybourne, where I've left the car. Another lovely name for a village. Who wouldn't like to live in a place like that?

From its tiny station, not big enough for a waiting room, it's just a ten-minute drive to Middle Littleton up another straight road over a hill which Roman soldiers once trod. Back home, I'll sit out in the garden for a while, watching the apples ripen. In the autumn, they'll be thrown over the fence, to be gladly crunched by the horses in the field. If the air gets chillier later, maybe I'll light a fire in the lounge, where the logs are already laid, and have a session on keyboard up in the minstrels' gallery. For the past year, I've been neglecting the piano.

Meanwhile, over in Sweden, my fourteen-year-old granddaughter seems to have inherited the writing bug, winning high praise at school for a smoothly written detective tale that reads like a television script. The future seems to be in good hands.

Well, as my old Aussie colleague Dave Mathew used to say, 'That's it, basically.'

Acknowledgements

Certain passages in this book originally appeared in *The Australian*, the *Birmingham Post*, the *Bolton Evening News*, the *Bury Times*, the *Guardian*, the *International Herald Tribune*, *Jazz Journal*, the *London Evening Standard*, *London Magazine*, the *Los Angeles Times*, the *Manchester Evening News*, the *Scotsman*, the *Washington Post*, and many other newspapers worldwide – to all of which, my thanks.

1382218R0

Printed in Great Britain by
Amazon.co.uk, Ltd.,
Marston Gate.